CONTEMPORARY
THEORIES
OF RHETORIC

Under the Advisory Editorship of
J. JEFFERY AUER

CONTEMPORARY THEORIES OF RHETORIC: Selected Readings

RICHARD L. JOHANNESEN
Northern Illinois University

HARPER & ROW, Publishers
New York, Evanston, San Francisco, London

CONTEMPORARY THEORIES OF RHETORIC: Selected Readings

Standard Book Number: 06–043318–3
LIBRARY OF CONGRESS CATALOG CARD NUMBER: 77–168354

CONTENTS

PREFACE

In both Susan Langer's *Philosophy in a New Key* and in Thomas Kuhn's *The Structure of Scientific Revolutions,* one of the major themes is that major advances in man's knowledge about himself and his environment are generated by the asking of perceptive questions and by the viewing of phenomena from altered perspectives. This anthology is offered in the hope that it might stimulate questions and perspectives to aid students of rhetoric in advancing their understanding of the rhetorical process. To generate insights that move beyond (but do not entirely deny) the Greco-Roman rhetorical heritage is an aim of this anthology.

For aid in the maturation of the editor's own view of a philosophy and theory of rhetoric, he is particularly indebted to the writings of Otis M. Walter, Maurice Natanson, Wayne Brockriede, Robert Scott, Douglas Ehninger, Kenneth Burke, Richard M. Weaver, and Lawrence W. Rosenfield.

R. L. J.

DeKalb, Illinois
July 1971

CONTEMPORARY
THEORIES
OF RHETORIC

EDITOR'S
INTRODUCTION: SOME TRENDS
IN CONTEMPORARY
RHETORICAL THEORY

When contemplating basic source materials for an anthology on contemporary theories of rhetoric, one might naturally consider the question: Is there a contemporary theory of rhetoric? Certainly not in the sense of a single, unified, complete, generally accepted body of precepts.[1] There are, however, diverse theories and perspectives concerning the nature and role of rhetoric—concerning the use of verbal and nonverbal symbols by man and his institutions to influence human behavior. This anthology is a collection of both writings by modern rhetorical theorists and analyses of the efforts of such theorists. The editor's introduction and the items anthologized represent one survey of the pluralism and ferment that characterize contemporary rhetorical theorizing.

Two literary critics, two professors of English, and two professors of philosophy represent the vanguard of contemporary scholars theorizing about modern rhetoric: Kenneth Burke, Ivor A. Richards, Richard M. Weaver, Marshall McLuhan, Chaim Perelman, and Stephen Toulmin. And in the pages of such journals as the *Quarterly Journal of Speech, Speech Monographs, College English,* and *Philosophy and Rhetoric* professors in the fields of speech, English, and philosophy probe the essence and boundaries of contemporary rhetorical theory.[2]

While no complete textbook for a course in contemporary theories of rhetoric presently exists, seminal analyses such as Daniel Fogarty's *Roots for a New Rhetoric* and W. Ross Winterowd's *Rhetoric: A Synthesis* prove useful. As a part of their efforts, both men sketch their view of ideal content for a course in contemporary rhetorical

---

[1] W. Ross Winterowd, *Rhetoric: A Synthesis* (New York, 1968), 77–78; Edward P. J. Corbett, "A New Look at Old Rhetoric," in Robert Gorrell, ed., *Rhetoric: Theories for Application* (Champaign, Ill., 1967), 16; Carroll Arnold, "Rhetoric in America Since 1900," in Robert Oliver and Marvin Bauer, eds., *Re-Establishing the Speech Profession* (Speech Association of the Eastern States, 1959), 7; John H. Mackin, *Classical Rhetoric for Modern Discourse* (New York, 1969) 28–29.

[2] See, for example, the entire issues of *Philosophy and Rhetoric,* 3 (Spring 1970), *College Composition and Communication,* XX (December 1969), *Today's Speech,* 18 (Winter 1970), and *Quarterly Journal of Speech,* LVI (April 1970). The Spring 1970 issue of *Philosophy and Rhetoric* is of special interest because most of its articles contribute to an attempt to define the nature of rhetoric.

theory.[3] Rhetorical insights from Aristotle, Cicero, Kenneth Burke, I. A. Richards, and Richard M. Weaver are skillfully utilized by Winterowd in his college freshman rhetoric textbook, *Rhetoric and Writing* (Boston, 1965).

What are the requisites of any adequate contemporary theory of rhetoric? As will be clear from reading the essays on theory construction in the first part of this anthology, no single answer seems possible. Various theorists offer different opinions. Consider, for instance, the view of Daniel Fogarty, who sees rhetoric as the study of symbolic "ways of arriving at mutual understanding among people working toward patterns of cooperative action."[4] He suggests the following four requirements for a new rhetoric:[5]

> It will need to consider its own basic presuppositions as all disciplines must do in a time of crisis and challenge; it will need to broaden its aim until it no longer confines itself to teaching the art of formal persuasion but includes formation in every kind of symbol-using, from a political speech to a kitchen conversation; it will need to adjust itself to the recent studies in the psychology and sociology of communication; and, finally, it will need to make considerable provision for a new kind of speaker-listener situation—the area of group discussion.

It is possible to isolate a number of trends in contemporary theorizing about rhetoric. Such trends represent some of the basic issues with which rhetorical theorists are grappling. By stating the issues and subissues largely in question form, hopefully one will be stimulated to probe little-explored or controversial areas. And the questions underscore the fact that few universally accepted conclusions mark the present state of modern rhetorical theorizing.

Should we distinguish between a theory of rhetoric and a philosophy of rhetoric?[6] A theory of rhetoric states the basic facts, central laws, and fundamental components of the rhetorical process. The theory describes how rhetoric operates in human communication transactions.

A philosophy of rhetoric, or metarhetoric, examines the underlying presuppositions and assumptions—the philosophical grounds and

[3] Daniel Fogarty, *Roots for a New Rhetoric* (New York, 1959), 116–140; W. Ross Winterowd, *Rhetoric: A Synthesis*, 153–172.

[4] Fogarty, *Roots*, 4.

[5] Fogarty, *Roots*, 130.

[6] See, for example, Maurice Natanson, "The Limits of Rhetoric," *Quarterly Journal of Speech*, XLI (April 1955), 138–139; Otis Walter, "On Views of Rhetoric, Whether Conservative or Progressive," *Quarterly Journal of Speech*, XLIX (December 1963), 367–383. Fogarty, *Roots for a New Rhetoric*, 4, 13, 121–126; Karl Wallace, *Understanding Discourse: The Speech Act and Rhetorical Action* (Baton Rouge, 1970), 3–21. James J. Murphy suggests use of the term "metarhetoric" for the study and explication of rhetorical first principles. An analysis of three metarhetorical views is Murphy's "Plato, Augustine, and McLuhan on the Metarhetoric," delivered as a lecture, November 4, 1969, at Indiana State University, Terre Haute.

starting points—that undergird any particular theory of rhetoric. With respect to any specific theory of rhetoric, a philosophy of that theory would explore at least the following questions: (1) What is the nature of reality and of knowledge embodied in the theory? (2) What is the nature of meaning and language? (3) What is the nature of man and what are his uniquely human characteristics? Is man *the* rhetorical animal by virtue of his unique symbol-manipulation capacity? (4) What is the personal, cultural, and societal role of rhetoric? (5) What ethical system explicitly or implicitly relates to the theory? (6) What definition of rhetoric does the theory present? What is the essential nature of rhetoric?

What is the relationship between rhetoric and philosophy?[7] Philosophical assumptions and implications of rhetorical theories are being examined and the role of rhetoric in philosophical argumentation is being scrutinized.

Should we speak of rhetoric, singular, or of rhetorics, plural?[8] Can there ever be a total and comprehensive rhetorical theory or must we build diverse theories? Are theories of rhetoric inherently bound by the cultures and subcultures, the philosophical assumptions, and the ethical systems in which they are immersed?[9] Must we build a pluralistic rhetorical theory that looks beyond persuasive public address to additional rhetorical aims, contexts, and verbal and nonverbal channels?[10] Should rhetorical theory encompass informative

---

[7] Henry W. Johnstone, Jr., "The Relevance of Rhetoric to Philosophy and of Philosophy to Rhetoric," *Quarterly Journal of Speech*, LII (February 1966), 41–46; Maurice Natanson and Henry W. Johnstone, Jr., eds., *Philosophy, Rhetoric, and Argumentation* (University Park, Pa., 1965); Henry W. Johnstone, Jr., *Philosophy and Argument* (University Park, Pa., 1959); each issue of *Philosophy and Rhetoric*, published quarterly by the Pennsylvania State University Press.

[8] Douglas Ehninger, "On Rhetoric and Rhetorics," *Western Speech*, XXXI (Fall 1967), 242–249; Ehninger, "On Systems of Rhetoric," *Philosophy and Rhetoric*, 1 (Summer 1968), 131–144; Wayne Brockriede, "Toward a Contemporary Aristotelian Theory of Rhetoric," *Quarterly Journal of Speech*, LII (February 1966), 33–40; Wallace, *Understanding Discourse*, 13–14.

[9] Robert T. Oliver, *Culture and Communication* (Springfield, Ill., 1962), esp. Preface and chaps. 7–12; Otis Walter, "On Views of Rhetoric, Whether Conservative or Progressive," *Quarterly Journal of Speech*, XLIX (December 1963), 367–382; Jack H. Butler, "Russian Rhetoric: A Discipline Manipulated by Communism," *Quarterly Journal of Speech*, L (April 1964), 229–239; Theodore Balgooyen, "A Study of Conflicting Values: American Plains Indian Orators *vs.* the U.S. Commissioners of Indian Affairs," *Western Speech*, XXVI (Spring 1962), 76–82; Paul Friedman and Gerald Phillips, "Toward a Rhetoric for the Poverty Class," *Journal of Communication*, XVII (September 1967), 234–249.

[10] See, for example, Herbert W. Simons, "Toward a New Rhetoric," *Pennsylvania Speech Annual*, XXIV (September 1967), 7–20; Dean C. Barnlund, "Toward a Meaning Centered Philosophy of Communication," *Journal of Communication*, XII (December 1962), 197–211; James Kinneavy, "The Basic Aims of Discourse," *College Composition and Communication*, XX (December 1969), 297–313; Ivan Preston, "Communication: Is It Always Persuasion?" *Quarterly Journal of Speech*, LV (October 1969), 312–315; Paul Ried, "A Spectrum of Persuasive Design," *Speech Teacher*, XIII (March 1964), 87–95; Leland Griffin, "The Rhetoric of Historical Movements," *Quarterly Journal of Speech*, XXXVIII (April 1952), 184–

discourse and small-group discussion? Do times of societal upheaval and conflict demand several, perhaps antagonistic, theories of rhetoric? Is there a special rhetorical theory to illuminate the rhetoric of confrontation or the rhetoric of black power?[11]

What is the proper role of empirical research methods, such as laboratory experiment or field study, in constructing contemporary theories of rhetoric? To what degree should a viable theory of rhetoric meet the requirements for a sound behavioral science theory?[12] Can behavioral scientists and humanistic scholars both contribute significantly to the construction of rhetorical theories? One view suggests that the behavioral scientist in rhetoric should focus primarily on questions of present fact and future factual inference, while the humanist should explore questions of past historical fact and issues of ethics, value, aesthetics, and societal role.[13] The humanist may generate testable hypotheses for experimentation and assist in evaluating the social implications of empirical research findings; he may gain dependable knowledge about the rhetorical process from the behaviorist's empirical studies. Clearly the cooperation of humanistic scholars and behavioral scientists is vital for the construction of viable modern rhetorical theories.

How can we modernize the rhetorical canon of invention to make

---

188; Herbert W. Simons, "Requirements, Problems, and Strategies: A Theory of Persuasion in Social Movements," *Quarterly Journal of Speech,* LVI (February 1970), 1–11; Dean Barnlund, ed., *Interpersonal Communication: Survey and Studies* (Boston, 1968), 511–542.

[11] Edward P. J. Corbett, "The Rhetoric of the Open Hand and the Closed Fist," *College Composition and Communication,* XX (December 1969), 288–296; Franklyn S. Haiman, "The Rhetoric of 1968: A Farewell to Rational Discourse," in Wil Linkugel, R. R. Allen, and Richard L. Johannesen, eds., *Contemporary American Speeches,* 2nd ed. (Belmont, Cal., 1969), 153–167; Robert Scott and Donald Smith, "The Rhetoric of Confrontation," *Quarterly Journal of Speech,* LV (February 1969), 1–8; Herbert W. Simons, "Confrontation as a Pattern of Persuasion in University Settings," *Central States Speech Journal,* XX (Fall 1969), 163–170; Robert Scott and Wayne Brockriede, *The Rhetoric of Black Power* (New York, 1969); Arthur L. Smith, *Rhetoric of Black Revolution* (Boston, 1969); Haig Bosmajian, "Obscenity and Protest," *Today's Speech,* 18 (Winter 1970), 9–14

[12] Wayne N. Thompson, *Quantitative Research in Public Address and Communication* (New York, 1967), chaps. 1 and 7; Wayne Brockriede, "Toward a Contemporary Aristotelian Theory of Rhetoric," *Quarterly Journal of Speech,* LII (February 1966), 33–40; John W. Bowers, *Designing the Communication Experiment* (New York, 1970), 111–119; Bowers, "The Pre-Scientific Function of Rhetorical Criticism," in Thomas Nilsen, ed., *Essays on Rhetorical Criticism* (New York, 1968); Raymond G. Smith, "Rhetoric, Experimental Research, and Men of Good Will," *Southern Speech Journal,* 30 (Fall 1964), 8–14; Ernest Bormann, *Theory and Research in the Communicative Arts* (New York, 1966), chaps. 3–6; Abraham Kaplan, *The Conduct of Inquiry* (San Francisco, 1964), chaps. 3, 4, 8; Johan Galtung, *Theory and Method in Social Relations* (New York, 1967), 458–466; Philip Emmert and William D. Brooks, eds., *Methods of Research in Communication* (Boston, 1970); K. E. Wilkerson, "On Evaluating Theories of Rhetoric," *Philosophy and Rhetoric,* 3 (Spring 1970), 82–96.

[13] Gerald R. Miller, *Speech Communication: A Behavioral Approach* (Indianapolis, 1966), 25–30.

it meaningful today?[14] Should we update the classical *topoi* and the Greco-Roman approach to invention?[15] Or should additional approaches to invention be explored?[16]

What is the nature and significance of metaphor in the rhetorical process?[17] While some theorists view it simply as an important stylistic device, others see it as one of the central elements of rhetoric.

To what degree must a rhetorical theory be axiological?[18] What roles do societal values play in the rhetorical process?[19] A value may be defined as a concept of The Good or the desirable that functions

[14] Elbert W. Harrington, "A Modern Approach to Invention," *Quarterly Journal of Speech*, XLVIII (December 1962), 373–378; Harrington, *Rhetoric and the Scientific Method of Inquiry: A Study of Invention* (University of Colorado Studies, Series in Language and Literature, #1, 1948); Dudley Bailey, "A Plea for a Modern Set of Topoi," *College English*, 26 (November 1964), 111–117; Richard Larson, "Discovering Through Questioning: A Plea for Teaching Rhetorical Invention," *College Composition and Communication*, 30 (November 1968), 126–134; William Nelson, "Topoi: Evidence of Human Conceptual Behavior," *Philosophy and Rhetoric*, 2 (Winter 1969), 1–11; William Nelson, "Topoi: Functional in Human Recall," *Speech Monographs*, 37 (June 1970), 121–126; Richard Huseman, "Modern Approaches to the Aristotelian Concept of Invention," *Central States Speech Journal*, XV (February 1964), 21–26.

[15] Edward P. J. Corbett, *Classical Rhetoric for the Modern Student* (New York, 1965), 34–272; Richard M. Weaver, *Composition: A Course in Writing and Rhetoric* (New York, 1957), iii–iv, 90–148; John Wilson and Carroll Arnold, *Public Speaking as a Liberal Art*, 2nd ed. (Boston, 1968), chaps. 5–7; Patrick Marsh, *Persuasive Speaking* (New York, 1967), 107–112, 184–189; John H. Mackin, *Classical Rhetoric for Modern Discourse* (New York, 1969), 49–128; Richard E. Hughes and P. Albert Duhamel, *Principles of Rhetoric* (Englewood Cliffs, N.J., 1966), chaps. 5–8; William Brandt, *The Rhetoric of Argumentation* (Indianapolis, 1970).

[16] Keith St. Onge, *Creative Speech* (Belmont, Cal., 1964), chap. 17; Virgil L. Baker and Ralph T. Eubanks, *Speech in Personal and Public Affairs* (New York, 1965), chap. 7; James C. McCroskey, *An Introduction to Rhetorical Communication* (Englewood Cliffs, N.J., 1968), chap. 7; Otis Walter and Robert Scott, *Thinking and Speaking*, 2nd ed. (New York, 1968), chaps. 9–13; Otis Walter, "Toward an Analysis of Motivation," *Quarterly Journal of Speech*, XLI (October 1955), 271–278; Jane Blankenship, *Public Speaking: A Rhetorical Perspective* (Englewood Cliffs, N.J., 1966), chaps. 3 and 4; Wayne Minnick, *The Art of Persuasion*, 2nd ed. (Boston, 1968), 215–221.

[17] See, for example, I. A. Richards, *The Philosophy of Rhetoric* (New York, 1936), chaps. 5 and 6; Manuel Bilsky, "I. A. Richards' Theory of Metaphor," *Modern Philology*, 50 (1952), 130–137; Michael Osborn and Douglas Ehninger, "Metaphor in Public Address," *Speech Monographs*, XXIX (August 1962), 223–234; Michael Osborn, "The Evolution of the Theory of Metaphor in Rhetoric," *Western Speech*, XXXI (Spring 1967), 121–131; John Bowers and Michael Osborn, "Attitudinal Effects of Selected Types of Concluding Metaphors in Persuasive Speeches," *Speech Monographs*, XXXIII (June 1966), 147–155; Michael Osborn, "Archetypal Metaphor in Rhetoric: The Light-Dark Family," *Quarterly Journal of Speech*, LIII (April 1967), 115–126; Philip Wheelwright, *Metaphor and Reality* (Bloomington, Ind., 1962); Owen Thomas, *Metaphor and Related Subjects* (New York, 1969); Kenneth Burke, *Permanence and Change*, 2nd rev. ed. (Indianapolis, 1965), 89–124; Arthur Hastings, "Metaphor in Rhetoric," *Western Speech*, XXXIV (Summer 1970), 181–193.

[18] Ralph Eubanks and Virgil Baker, "Toward an Axiology of Rhetoric," *Quarterly Journal of Speech*, XLVII (April 1962), 157–168; Baker and Eubanks, *Speech in Personal and Public Affairs*, chap. 6.

[19] Richard M. Weaver, *The Ethics of Rhetoric* (Chicago, 1953), chaps. 1 and 9; for analyses of the role of value theory in rhetoric see the pertinent articles in two issues of *Western Speech*, XXVI (Spring 1962) and (Summer 1962).

either as a goal in motivating human behavior or as a standard for assessing means. In what ways do values provide the substance of rhetoric or premises for persuasion?[20] Must a theory of rhetoric or a philosophy of rhetoric provide criteria for judging the ethics of rhetorical practices?[21]

Does the emerging concept of communication as dialogue provide a supplement to, or a substitute for, the traditional view of rhetoric as persuasion?[22] Rhetoric as persuasion, some argue, has the persuader manipulate and exploit the audience to achieve his specific ends; the persuader utilizes audience feedback only to gain more control over them. Dialogue, in contrast, is seen as involving mutual understanding, suspension of judgment, respect for the other person, and a receptive attitude in the sender. In dialogue the communication attitude of the participants is one of equality, honesty, genuineness, concern, and nonexploitation. Consider the following questions when analyzing this trend. What is an adequate description of persuasion? Can dialogue function equally well in varied communication contexts such as two-person, small group, public address, and mass media?

The eight trends briefly noted above are by no means a complete index of the varied concerns of contemporary rhetorical theorizing. But they are sufficient to illustrate the ferment and diversity in the field. And the essays collected in this anthology, illustrating some of the trends and pointing to additional ones, are reflective of its vitality. Theorizing about rhetoric is not a declining or dead activity; indeed, such activity is alive and vigorous.

[20] Karl Wallace, "The Substance of Rhetoric: Good Reasons," *Quarterly Journal of Speech,* XLIX (October 1963), 239–249; Edward Steele and W. Charles Redding, "The American Value System: Premises for Persuasion," *Western Speech,* XXVI (Spring 1962), 83–91; Wayne Minnick, *The Art of Persuasion,* 2nd ed., 215–221.

[21] W. Ross Winterowd, *Rhetoric: A Synthesis,* 8–14; Thomas Nilsen, *Ethics of Speech Communication* (Indianapolis, 1966); Richard L. Johannesen, ed., *Ethics and Persuasion: Selected Readings* (New York, 1967); Johannesen, "Ethics and Persuasion: Some Perspectives," in Robert King, ed., *Marketing and the New Science of Planning* (Chicago, 1969), 541–546.

[22] Floyd W. Matson and Ashley Montagu, eds., *The Human Dialogue* (New York, 1967), 1–10, 113–176, 246–284; Reuel Howe, *The Miracle of Dialogue* (New York, 1963); Georges Gusdorf, *Speaking,* trans. Paul Brockelman (Evanston, 1965), 57, 84–85, 101–108; Paul Keller and Charles T. Brown, "An Interpersonal Ethic for Communication," *Journal of Communication,* 18 (March 1968), 73–81; Carl Rogers, *Client-Centered Therapy* (Boston, 1951), 19–64; Dean Barnlund, *Interpersonal Communication* (Boston, 1968), 636–640; Maurice Friedman, *Martin Buber: The Life of Dialogue* (New York, 1960), 57–97, 123–126, 176–183. Among the writings of Martin Buber relevant to the emerging concept of communication as dialogue are *Between Man and Man, I and Thou, Pointing the Way,* and *The Knowledge of Man.*

PART I ISSUES IN
THEORY CONSTRUCTION

1 A CONSERVATIVE VIEW OF A PROGRESSIVE RHETORIC

WAYNE N. THOMPSON

Thompson appeals for increased use of experimental research and the use of communication-theory insights in building contemporary rhetorical theory. In the years following 1963, when the article was published, growing bodies of experimental research have focused on such rhetorical concepts as ethos, organization of arguments, fear appeals, evidence, and the logic-emotion relationship. Interaction between traditional rhetorical theory and modern communication theory has increased.

Several points made by Thompson might be examined. He states that rhetorical theory focuses primarily on linguistic matters while communication theory encompasses all modes of communication. But note that the classical canon of delivery to some degree can be equated with the contemporary emphasis on nonverbal dimensions of communication. And Kenneth Burke's view of rhetoric is broad enough to include nonverbal modes. Second, since this article was published, emphasis on the concept of feedback has increased in explanations of the rhetorical transaction. Finally, Thompson sees effectiveness of persuasion as the keynote of rhetorical theory while accuracy of meaning is the keynote of communication theory. Consider whether accuracy can be viewed as one type of effectiveness.

Source: Quarterly Journal of Speech, XLIX (February 1963), 1–7. Reprinted with permission of the author and the publisher.

Classical rhetoric is a compendium of so much wisdom that any sound new rhetoric must be an extension or a modification of the old and not a rejection of it. Careful empirical observation and a thoughtfulness characterized primarily by common sense produced in ancient times an organized doctrine which generations of observer-analysts have continued to find sensible.

Now available, however, are tools and approaches which our predecessors lacked, and responsible scholarship dictates that we use these to test empirically derived precepts, to view anew philosophically conceived principles, and to seek out possible new boundaries for the province of rhetoric.

The purpose of this paper is to consider two of the potentially valuable sources of material for a revised rhetoric—the experimental study and communication theory.

I

Although almost all scholars in public address know that classical precepts may serve as hypotheses for experimentation, our profession in practice has largely neglected the potential values of investigations employing refined methods. An occasional research study, true enough, has found its way into a modern textbook, and one or two determined writers have made genuine attempts to mold rhetorical principles out of scientific findings. The impact of experimental studies, nevertheless, has been slight. Serene and undisturbed, both writers and lecturers continue to express classical doctrines, and the main stream of rhetoric is proceeding uninterrupted and unchanged.[1]

This situation should not continue. Traditionalism and inertia should not negate the findings which our improved methods of observation permit—provided, of course, that experimentation leads to modification or rejection rather than to verification.

But why have experimental findings had so little impact? Perhaps by identifying the reasons we can point the way to improvement. First, disorganization characterizes the experimental approach to rhetorical theory. With only a few exceptions, research workers have chosen hypotheses reflecting personal interests rather than ones contributing to a unified investigation in depth. As a consequence, few, if any, classical precepts have been examined with sufficient thoroughness to justify modification or rejection. Although individual experiments have suggested the appropriateness of certain revisions, experimentalists have failed to follow these leads either with replicative studies or with research bearing upon the problem but modifying or changing the variables.

Second, inadequacies in the theory of induction weaken the impact of experimentalism. How many replications are necessary before findings warrant generalizations? How many facets of a rhetorical precept must be studied before meaningful conclusions are possible? How

---

[1] This view coincides with that of I. A. Richards in *The Philosophy of Rhetoric* (New York, 1936) and other works. In 1936 Richards saw no improvement over the situation in Whately's time. "Whately . . . says quite truly that 'Rhetoric is not one of those branches of study in which we can trace with interest a progressive improvement from age to age.' " Richards, p. 6.

many species of the variables must be subjected to experimentation prior to generalizations? How much confidence can be ascribed to a generalization based upon a given set of studies? Absolute answers to such questions are impossible, for the theory of induction is unsatisfactory even in fields less complex than rhetoric. Logicians and philosophers from Aristotle through Francis Bacon and John Stuart Mill to Keynes have found the problems of induction too slippery to permit the formation of a satisfactory theory. "The problem of induction," Julius R. Weinberg, a Cornell philosopher, concluded in 1936, "still awaits a satisfactory solution,"[2] and fifteen years later Georg H. Von Wright, a Cambridge professor of philosophy, referred to induction as "a scandal" to the name of philosophy.[3]

Scholars in logic and philosophy, nevertheless, have developed approaches to the problem of inductive theory which may be helpful to experimental workers in rhetoric. Mill's method of concomitant variations, the eliminative induction of Francis Bacon, the axiomatic treatment of probability by Lord Keynes and Reichenbach, and the attempt of the logical positivists to determine the simplest law verifying a singular assertion are formulations worthy of consideration. All of these admittedly have theoretical imperfections (or at least are controversial), and hence a fully satisfactory inductive theory for experimental rhetoric is impossible at present, if not forever. Some progress, however, can be made. Weinberg cites *The Golden Bough* as an example of research reporting in which conclusions based upon induction are useful.[4]

Despite these possibilities, no one, so far as the writer knows, has attempted to enunciate the principles of an induction for experimentalism in public address. Consequently, criteria at present are totally lacking for judging generalizations based upon a series of experiments. Imperfect though it would be, the best possible theory of induction would tend to bring about some order in the presently chaotic field of experimental studies.

Third, inadequate measures for publishing and collating results have contributed to the ineffectiveness of experimentalism. Here, *Speech Monographs* may be helpful, but the cooperation of investigators and project directors will be required. Collecting experimental findings in one place, classifying results according to the rhetorical precepts to

[2] *An Examination of Logical Positivism* (London, 1936), p. 142.

[3] *A Treatise on Induction and Probability* (New York, 1951), p. 11. Still another scholar with grave doubts about the status of induction is Bertrand Russell: "The problem of induction by simple enumeration remains unsolved to this day . . . neither Bacon nor any of his successors have found a way out of it." *A History of Western Philosophy* (New York, 1945), p. 545. Also: "What is called induction appears to me to be either disguised deduction or a mere method of making plausible guesses." *Principles of Mathematics* (New York, 1938), p. 11.

[4] *Op. cit.* p. 127.

which they pertain, and relating new data to preceding investigations in time could prove very helpful.

Fourth, the inertia which affects those of us who write and who teach contributes to the ineffectiveness of experimentalism. The dead hand of classical rhetoric is upon the shoulders of too many; the tendency is strong for graduate professor to pass on to graduate student, generation after generation, the doctrine he learned when he himself was a student. Hence, as a professional group we keep on saying and writing the same things year after year even though experimental findings may render some of these statements suspect.

That the call of the greatly respected Charles H. Woolbert has gone largely unheeded for thirty-seven years is indicative of this professional complacency:

I stand for a search for the facts; the facts of how speaking is done; of what its various effects are under specified conditions; how these facts can be made into laws and principles; and how other people can best be taught to apply them. The facts we use are too often guesses; our methods are purely personal; we need to get together on some common acceptable basis. The only one I know of comes from scientifically conducted investigations and research.[5]

Altering this situation will not be easy. Nothing will suffice short of a new comprehensive volume, which succeeding scholars can use as the basis for their own teaching and writing. To succeed, such a book must possess at least these characteristics: (1) "completeness" so that the temptation to combine parts of it with parts of other works will be minimal, (2) nonextremism (rejecting all classical doctrine is a likely danger), and (3) authoritativeness. Whether a volume written by a respected scholar and favorably reviewed could overcome the easy, comfortable urge to maintain the status quo is doubtful; that a contribution of any other sort could succeed seems impossible.

These difficulties in bringing about modifications in classical doctrine are ironic, for Aristotle was a man who in biology and the other sciences utilized the best means of investigation available to him. H. Rackham, a twentieth-century scholar at Christ's College, Cambridge, calls Aristotle "the father of European sciences," and cites Darwin as writing, "Linnaeus and Cuvier have been my two gods . . . but they were children to old Aristotle."[6] Aristotle, if alive today, probably would be the leader in the movement to find new, accurate data for the re-evaluation of his rhetorical precepts:

Aristotle . . . laid the foundation of many sciences, and wherever simple observation was adequate . . . his achievements were complete and surprising. But for the greater realms of science he had no starting point and no appliances.

---

[5] "A Problem in Pragmatism," *The Quarterly Journal of Public Speaking,* II (July 1916), 264.

[6] *Aristotle's Ethics for English Readers* (Oxford, 1944), p. 7.

. . . Of his method it may be said . . . that no one was ever more keen than he to make "fact" the basis of every theory.[7]

The experimentalists, to summarize, are a potential source of material for a new rhetoric. Their findings can be useful, however, only when a series of investigations provide the basis for generalizations which warrant respect. Experimentation so far has had but limited impact, for (1) the depth of exploration of individual rhetorical precepts, because of insufficient planning and coordination, has been insufficient, (2) criteria for judging generalizations and for guiding the design of experiments, because of inadequacies in induction, are virtually nonexistent, and (3) results gained through investigations, because of decentralized publication, have remained uncollated. "Some critical questions in the field . . . have been the subject of many experiments, but questions still persist"[8] is an accurate but discouraging conclusion.

II

A second potential source of material for a new rhetoric is *communication theory,* which in this article is a generic term encompassing cybernetics, general systems, information theory, certain forms of semantics and linguistics, and all other studies which search for the facts and the principles which underlie communication. Despite the diversity of these fields and the distinct, independent characteristics which each possesses, the common elements are such that the term *communication theory,* in the opinion of the writer, is defensible as well as useful.

A general view of the "core" of the area for which the words *communication theory* stand serves to introduce this section. As contrasted with experimentation, which is a means of testing individual hypotheses derived from existing knowledge, communication theory is a potential source of new precepts.[9] An interdisciplinary attempt to attain a theoretical foundation for the phenomena of communication, it is close enough to classical rhetoric to be relevant and far enough removed to stimulate freshness and creativity.[10] Initially the new doctrines which it

[7] Alexander Grant, "Aristotle," *Encyclopedia Britannica: A Dictionary of Arts, Sciences, and General Literature,* 9th ed. (New York, 1878). II, 520.

[8] J. Jeffery Auer, *An Introduction to Research in Speech* (New York, 1959), p. 201.

[9] ". . . scientists find only what they are looking for. And they are looking for one thing and not another because their imagination works one way and not another." See Stefan Themerson, "The Circle of Art and Science," *Etc.,* XVI (Spring 1959), 322.

[10] Not much is known about creativity, but some writers believe that examining dissimilar objects or ideas is stimulating. "Experience has shown that the comparison of Indo-European languages among themselves has yielded only modest increments of knowledge: the greatest gain has been made when our languages have been compared with strikingly different tongues, for example with the many Indian dialects of North America, a program of study in which Sapir and Whorf have been leaders." See Garrett Hardin, "The Threat of Clarity," *Etc.,* XVII (Spring 1960), 273.

may provide will be hunches or insightful guesses of varying degrees of wisdom, but in time philosophical, empirical, and scientific methods will result in the separation of contributions which are sound from those which are mistaken or foolish.

Of the many specific reasons for believing and hoping that communication theory may be a useful contributor to a new rhetoric, the writer has selected six for discussion in this paper.

First, the climate of communication theory is essentially different from that of rhetoric; such a different atmosphere, as indicated above, is likely to produce new approaches, to stimulate creative thought, and to suggest new directions for critical examination.[11] The experimentalist who works from a classical background is limited by this venerable context in his choice of hypotheses and in the insights which he can derive from his findings; the investigator who works from a communication framework, although also limited by his context, does not have the *same* limitations as those of the traditionalist.

Special differences in climate between communication theory and rhetoric are numerous. The essential atmosphere in which the communicationist typically works is experimental and scientific. His place is the laboratory; his tests of significance are statistical; his subject matter may be cells or electronic impulses; his closest colleagues often are biologists, psychologists, electronic engineers, or mathematicians.

The atmosphere around the rhetorician, on the other hand, is non-experimental. The place of study is likely to be the library, the method is value judgment perhaps based upon observation, and his colleagues are other rhetoricians, historians, and professors of literature. Aristotle created the contents of the *Rhetoric* by studying human nature, observing speech events, and reflecting upon these data. Lacking investigative procedures, he was unable to isolate variables for detailed, systematic, controlled study. In the main, the Aristotelian method of creating and re-examining rhetoric has persevered until the present day. The usual practice of the modern rhetorician is to restate classical precepts with such modifications as his personal observations and judgments render attractive.

Exceptions to the preceding statements, of course, exist, but as a general proposition the climate of the communication theorist and that of the rhetorician differ essentially. Even the experimentalist in rhetoric works from a context unlike that of his counterpart in communication.

Second (and closely related to the first reason), the sources from which communication theory and rhetoric are derived differ radically; hence, the expectation that communication may produce some new

---

[11] Auer seems to recognize the importance of these new sources: "Experiments do not always result in establishing new methods, for they are so often based upon present theories or practices." *Op. cit.,* p. 202.

rhetorical concepts is supported further. Logic, ethics, politics, and philosophy are the antecedents of rhetoric, whereas engineering, electronics, mathematics, biology, sociology, and psychology are among the sources of communication theory. Thus, although both rhetoric and communication deal at least in part with speaking and writing, they do so from different viewpoints.

Third, communication theory can bring to rhetoric the stimulation and the breadth of basic science. Practicality, which has been a major characteristic of rhetoric from Aristotle's time to the present,[12] has its virtues, but the creation of concepts in unexplored facets is not among them. Communication theory, in contrast to rhetoric, is largely a basic science with such concerns as the transmission of bits of information.

Some workers in communication, of course, attempt to apply basic insights to practical situations, and some scholars in rhetoric seek knowledge for its own sake; but in general the former is a basic science, and the latter is an applied one.

Fourth, the multimedial orientation[13] of communication theory may lead to insights which rhetoric with its essentially linguistic-semantic approach has overlooked. The contrast again is not between black and white, for man from the earliest times has sensed the communicative power of gestures, glances, shrieks, grunts, and tones. The point is that rhetoricians have been so fully occupied with the verbal dimension that other aspects have been neglected. On the other hand, communication theory, oriented toward engineering and the natural and the behavioral sciences where words are not the carriers of information, brings to human relations a nonverbal outlook, which some day may supplement and broaden rhetorical studies.

Fifth, the emphasis of communication theory upon circularity and self-correction directs attention to features which have been neglected in speech. Whereas feedback and entropy are basic to communication

---

[12] "Rhetoric may be defined as the faculty of observing in any given case the available means of persuasion." Aristotle, *Rhetoric*, trans. W. Rhys Roberts, I.2.1355b25.

"[Rhetoric] is, instead, a practical skill serving as a direct link between the individual and his immediate social environment on the one hand and the larger political pattern of the state on the other." See Lester Thonssen and A. Craig Baird, *Speech Criticism* (New York, 1948), p. 71.

"Rhetoric is the art of achieving an adjustment, or of establishing a relationship, between the subject matter and the auditor." See Robert Oliver, "The Confucian Rhetorical Tradition in Korea During the Yi Dynasty (1392–1910)," *QJS*, XLV (December 1959), 363.

[13] Definitions of communication emphasize the multi-medium characteristic. For example, Jurgen Ruesch and Gregory Bateson in *Communication: The Social Matrix of Psychiatry* (New York, 1951), p. 6, refer to communication as "all those processes by which people influence one another." Joshua Whatmough, distinguished Harvard linguist, concurs when he defines communication as "Any means which links one mechanism or organism with another." See Whatmough's "Mass Media and Mass Neurosis," *Logos*, II (1959), 84.

theory, self-correction is not at the core of rhetoric. Not only does responsiveness to the existing audience receive but little space in most works, but also the treatments focus upon adaptation as a means of obtaining effectiveness and not as a way of maximizing clarity. Moreover, clearness itself is viewed differently. In traditional rhetoric it is a stylistic quality and perhaps an ethical responsibility, but its role is not central. It is only one stylistic quality for the rhetorical critic to consider among others, and style is only one of many characteristics for him to appraise. That a speech may be effective with something less than "total" clarity is possible. On the other hand, for the communicationist to react favorably to an unclear speech is unthinkable. Clarity is *the* criterion, not a criterion; it is itself the end, not a means. In the satisfactory act the message sent and the message received are identical.

Sixth, this emphasis upon accuracy of transmission directs the efforts of research workers in communication into areas which rhetoricians, whose primary interest is effectiveness, tend to neglect. A quarter of a century ago I. A. Richards wrote about this possibility of amplifying the "old" rhetoric when he urged that "Rhetoric . . . should be a study of misunderstanding and its remedies."[14]

Although the objective here is essentially that of the communicationist, the means are different. Whereas Richards would improve rhetoric by a microscopic study of its linguistic components, the research worker in communication approaches the problem of accuracy from many directions. In utilizing whichever and as many contexts as the given problem warrants, as Richards probably would agree, the investigator is following a course which promises to make significant extensions to present theory.

The point of this optimistic predicting is not that accuracy is more important than effectiveness; any such argument would be futile. Nor is the intention to belittle rhetoric and to praise communication theory. The writer is primarily a classical rhetorician, and he suspects that he will always be one. Unlike Richards who would replace classical doctrine with a new rhetoric growing out of a study of the nature of language,[15] the writer favors the building of a new rhetoric upon the old

[14] *Op. cit.*, p. 3. This sentence is the thesis for the first lecture in the series comprising this work. Marie Hochmuth Nichols regards this thought as the central one in Richards' "New Rhetoric," as presented in his writings generally: "The new rhetoric which arises is a rhetoric concerned, not with persuasion as a specific end, but with the meanings of statements in any type of discourse." See "I. A. Richards and the "New Rhetoric," *QJS*, XLIV (February 1958), p. 9.

[15] The study of rhetoric is worthwhile "as a philosophic discipline aiming at a mastery of the fundamental laws of the use of language, not just a set of dodges that will be found to work sometimes." See Richards, p. 7.

The following criticism of Whately is further evidence of the attitude of Richards toward rhetoric: "What we are given by Whately instead is a very ably arranged and discussed collection of prudential rules about the best sorts of things to say in various

by subjecting the precepts of classicism to experimental investigation and by adding any new doctrine which creativeness can devise and philosophic thought, empirical observation, or experimentation can verify to a reasonable degree. And all three of these methods must be used; for although a strict scientific approach is preferable, statistical studies with defined, isolated, and controlled variables have limitations which must be recognized.[16]

Probability is an inevitable dimension of much of rhetoric. The realistic objective is to seek certainty wherever (and if) possible and elsewhere to establish higher degrees of probability than now exist. The rationale of past centuries must continue: the best available advice to students is superior to no advice.

III

What the writer deplores, to conclude, is the tendency to pass rhetorical doctrine down from one generation of scholars to the next without critical examination. The wisdom of those who created classical rhetoric is one of the marvels of the intellectual history of the world, but to ignore the opportunities which contemporary movements and tools provide for securing new truths and for testing old ones is a folly which warrants the charge of scholarly irresponsibility.

Modern investigation has had only limited impact, but an awareness of the reasons for this neglect may lead to the corrections needed to bring experimental findings effectively into the main stream of rhetoric. Similarly, a realization of the potential contributions of communication theory may lead to creative thought upon rhetorical problems, produce insights worthy of examination both empirically and investigatively, and assist experimentalists in devising hypotheses and interpreting results. The new rhetoric, if it comes about, will be much like the old, but its modifications and extensions should be in the direction of improvement.

---

argumentative situations, the order in which to bring out your propositions and proofs and examples, at what point it will be most effective to disparage your opponent, how to recommend oneself to the audience, and like matters. As to all of which, it is fair to remark, no one ever learned about them from a treatise who did not know about them already." *Ibid.,* p. 7.

[16] See Auer, pp. 201–202.

2 ON VIEWS OF RHETORIC, WHETHER CONSERVATIVE OR PROGRESSIVE

OTIS M. WALTER

Walter advances a plea for pluralism in the study of rhetorical theory. He warns against equating classical rhetorical theory with Aristotle's theory of rhetoric. He urges reexamination of the varied "starting points" of classical and modern theories. We must more fully understand how each theorist defined the nature of rhetoric and what the prerequisites and presuppositions are that undergird each theory. In essence he claims a need for reexamining the philosophy of rhetoric that forms the foundation of a specific rhetorical theory.

In counterpoint to Wayne Thompson's view, Walter argues that we must be wary of pitfalls in extreme devotion to the experimental method (or communication-theory concepts) in building modern rhetorical theories. He warns that too often experimentalists explore only the trivial or easily verifiable questions; he contends that there are metaphysical, ethical, and aesthetic questions not amenable to experimentation. Too frequently, Walter observes, we uncritically borrow concepts and methodologies from other disciplines rather than formulating ones uniquely applicable to rhetorical study. We can become subservient to communication theory just as easily as we often have become subservient to Aristotelian rhetorical theory. Is Professor Walter unjustifiably harsh in his criticism of experimental research as a tool for rhetorical study?

Source: Quarterly Journal of Speech, XLIX (December 1963), 367–382. Reprinted with permission of the author and the publisher.

1

Professor Wayne N. Thompson recently presented in this journal a problem that faces rhetoric. "Serene and undisturbed," he asserted, "both writers and lecturers continue to express classical doctrines, and the main stream of rhetoric is proceeding uninterrupted and unchanged." To remove the "dead hand of classical rhetoric," Mr. Thompson proposed two solutions: that we make more use of the experimental method and that we accept the potential contribution of communication theory. Professor Thompson stated with clarity a view of rhetoric probably held by more people in our discipline than any other view, and made many suggestions with which one agrees. Even so, the formulation of the problem—that classical rhetoric is a "dead hand,"—is in error and, I insist, the two solutions are unlikely to create a burst of productivity in which we may take pride.[1]

One agrees that the problem of nonproductivity is real, for it is clearly visible at three points: first, contemporary rhetoric has failed to uncover new doctrines or to modify its old ones in the way that contemporary thought has burst old limits in such disciplines as mathematics, psychology, and the sciences. Secondly, as a corollary, rhetoric has either failed to attract the brightest minds or has failed to stimulate them to work with their full vigor. Thirdly, one hears that "lightning has already struck a number of speech empires. . . . [Some] speech departments . . . have disappeared."[2] The abolition of departments of speech is a symptom and should warn us that an unhealthy condition exists; one does not hear of the disappearance of departments such as physics and philosophy.

Part of the disease, as Dr. Thompson correctly diagnosed, is our view of classical rhetoric.[3] But whereas Thompson views classical rhetoric as a body of hypotheses about persuasion to be tested, confirmed, modified, or rejected, I believe that such a view of the tradition of rhetoric is not only unproductive but is part of the disease. The significance of classical rhetoric cannot be seen if it is viewed only as a source of grist for the mill of an experimenter. The significance of classical rhetoric lies in its different *starting points,* its myriad assumptions, its contrasting aims, and not always in its hypotheses about persuasion. Unless these starting points are noted by the scholar, much of the value of classical rhetoric eludes one. Moreover, I believe that recognition of these starting points can help release the stimulating power of classical rhetoric. When one views rhetoric from these foundations, one sees sharply the richness, diversity, and especially the unfinished quality of the house of rhetoric, the mansions of which seem to be unnoticed. Let us look at some of these.

Sometimes the starting point of a rhetorical system has been *metaphysical.* Protagoras furnishes perhaps the simplest illustration. He started with the notion that when one's intelligence had pushed as far as intelligence could, it ended by discovering a set of contradictions, each of which was true. The aim of speaking, to Protagoras, was to take

[1] "A Conservative View of a Progressive Rhetoric," *QJS,* XLIX (February 1963), 1–7, *passim.*

[2] Raymond G. Smith, "The Dignity of a Profession," *Central States Speech Journal,* XIV (May 1963), 83.

[3] Another part, and a most important one, which Thompson does not mention, and which is neglected by me for want of space, is the superficial teaching in some undergraduate speech courses.

an audience as far as intellect could: speaking must reveal the contradictions of a metaphysical universe—contradictions that could neither be refuted nor reconciled. But this metaphysical base for a system of rhetoric, like other starting points in the discipline, never culminated in a system of rhetoric.[4]

Presumably a whole series of techniques of rhetoric, relevant to this particular view, await the discoverer. How does one discover "two *logoi* in opposition"? How can one test them to be sure that they are the ultimate product of intelligence? How does one present them to an audience so that the audience recognizes them as ultimate products? Thus, once one notes Protagoras' starting point, the shadowy outline of a different (but not necessarily better) system of rhetoric begins to appear. Yet such a rhetoric has never been written.

Protagoras furnishes a kind of paradigm for understanding other systems of rhetoric, for they, too, often present a starting point which has never been followed by a system of organized principles of rhetoric. We have been misled in studying the history of rhetoric by the example of Aristotle's *Rhetoric* which contains both a starting point and a system. Aristotle's starting point is stated in his definition of rhetoric as the art of discovering the available means of persuasion; the system of persuasion following that starting point is relatively elaborate. Some other rhetoricians, however, have *only* a starting point and have never constructed a system of principles consistent with their beginning.

Plato, who may be the most misunderstood of all writers on rhetoric, also started with a metaphysical base for his theories about rhetoric. His metaphysical view, however, is different from that of Protagoras, and his aim was markedly different from the nonmetaphysical base of Aristotle.[5] One may be misled by a quick glance at Plato, for one may easily assume that his rhetorical theory is entirely contained in those

---

[4] Although moderns have called Protagoras the "father of debate," he could deny such parentage since the offspring bears little resemblance to his own creation. In modern debate, each opponent tries to refute the other, but in Protagoras' system, such refutation would be senseless, since both sides are right and neither *can* be refuted. Modern debate seeks a judgment of which side is logically stronger as presented, but such judgments would be senseless in Protagoras' system, for both sides should be equally appealing.

For an exposition of Protagoras' doctrines (and one quite different from the impression one gets by reading Plato's *Protagoras*) see Mario Untersteiner, *The Sophists*, trans. Kathleen Freeman (New York, 1954), ch. III.

[5] It is, however, incorrect to say that Aristotle was entirely nonmetaphysical in his rhetorical method, for although his starting point was not founded on a metaphysical base, he assumes the position of naïve realism: the doctrine that the world is about as it appears. But this metaphysical assumption is not the consuming interest of Aristotle. His most characteristic interest is with the process of persuasion, or, more exactly, with the methods of persuasion—a concern not nearly so universal among rhetoricians historically as most of us moderns have assumed.

passages in which he uses the word *rhetoric*. There is, however, no single quotation from Plato using that word which one may lift from context and designate as his view of rhetoric. Remarks in the *Phaedrus* which pertain directly to rhetoric seem to be supplementary remarks offering suggestions about rhetoric that, perhaps, could not be deduced easily from the rest of Plato's philosophy. For example, that a speech should have a head, a body, and a foot, or that rhetoric should explore the nature of the human soul cannot, at least with perfect clarity, be deduced from the core of Plato's philosophy. These supplementary remarks, however, do not contain the starting point or the essence of Plato's theory of rhetoric.

The foundation for Plato's theory of rhetoric—as well as that for his philosophy—was his metaphysical conception of the World of Ideas. As is well known, Plato believed that there were certain Ideas or Forms (such as the Idea of justice) which were everlasting, knowledge of which (once one had *true* knowledge) never gets out of date, and which can guide men and states to their salvation. Once one knew the Idea of justice, he could act justly, know when an injustice was committed, write laws that were just, and create a just society. But without the Idea, one would be condemned unknowingly to live corruptly surrounded by corruption. Thus, a knowledge of the Ideas was fundamental to the best life.

Knowledge of the Ideas was also fundamental to a theory of rhetoric. In the *Gorgias*, Plato takes Gorgias and Polus to task for being unable to define *rhetoric*. The failure to define indicated that these rhetoricians did not know the Idea, for definitions to Plato were statements of the nature of the Idea. It is clear, then, why Plato thought that Gorgias and Polus had no real knowledge of rhetoric. This ignorance, Plato suggests, is typical among rhetoricians, for they lack understanding of that which they claim to teach. But Plato was not condemning rhetoric; he was condemning only a *genre* of rhetoric practiced in Greece.[6] Nowhere does Plato condemn the Idea of rhetoric. In the *Phaedrus* he makes suggestions for rhetoric, and offers perhaps the noblest view of rhetoric in existence, a view few seem to have grasped.

Fundamental to Plato's suggestions for rhetoric is the significance of the Ideas. In the *Phaedrus,* Plato illustrates the centrality of the Ideas for rhetoric by three speeches on love. The first speech, written by Lysias, appears, but only at first glance, to be a good one. Socrates

[6] See Edwin Black, "Plato's View of Rhetoric," *QJS*, XLIV (December 1958), 361–374. Black demonstrates that Plato did not have, as is often thought, an inconsistent view of rhetoric, condemning it in the *Gorgias* and looking on it more sympathetically in the *Phaedrus*. Rather, Plato is berating speakers in the *Gorgias* for not being concerned with Ideas and in the *Phaedrus* shows what can happen when a speaker sees them. See also, Richard Weaver's imaginative interpretation in "The *Phaedrus* and the Nature of Rhetoric," in *The Ethics of Rhetoric* (New York, 1953), pp. 3–26.

avows that he can give a better one. Lysias, after all, never defined love and has, therefore, no knowledge of it other than awareness of the hopelessly imperfect earthly imitations of the Idea of love. How much better a speech could be given by one, such as Socrates, who understands the Idea and who lets the speech materials follow from this perception of the Idea! Socrates proceeds, and in the second speech, which he invents on the spot for Phaedrus, presents the definition first. This definition is the philosophical starting point of the speech and the criterion by which the speech materials are determined, for all the contents of the speech are based on this definition. How better could one illustrate the centrality of the Idea for rhetoric?

There *is* a better way, and Socrates, in the third speech, uses it. Shortly after completing the second speech, Socrates discovers that he had a mistaken conception of the Idea of love: love is not evil, but supremely good; it is not a corrupter, but that which inspires and creates. There follows the startlingly brilliant third speech which illustrates that rhetoric must be concerned with the eternal Ideas which can guide, inspire, and lead men to bursts of genius and creativity. Thus, to Plato, rhetoric was not to be the technique of merely discovering the available means of persuasion—although true rhetoric *would* persuade—but rather the *process of discovering and communicating ways of life revealed by a true and inspiring vision of the Ideas.* Each speech of the *Phaedrus* illustrates something of the centrality of the Ideas: the first shows how wrong, superficial, disorganized, and, perhaps, evil, speaking is when completely divorced from a knowledge of Ideas. The second shows that it is easy to be wrong about what the Idea really is, and the third speech shows how an inspired and clear vision of the Idea can produce a creative and powerfully poetic speech that reflects the transforming power of the Ideas. As opposed to the false rhetoric practiced in Athens, true rhetoric was not merely an artificer of persuasion, but was to treat the soul in the way that medicine would treat the body.[7] Indeed, rhetoric, when founded on the Ideas, could save mankind from destruction and transform men. This starting point makes Aristotle's look tepid indeed.

[7] That the aim of rhetoric was to treat the soul by a knowledge of Ideas is recognized by Werner Jaeger, *Paideia,* trans. Gilbert Highet (New York, 1944), III, 22, and is almost directly stated in the *Phaedrus.* Even in the *Gorgias,* Plato suggests that there is an Idea of rhetoric: "And will not the true rhetorician who is honest and who understands his art have his eye fixed upon these [the lawful, the temperate, and the just] . . . ? Will not his aim be to implant justice . . . and take away injustice, to implant temperance and take away intemperance, to implant every virtue and take away every vice?" Even this dialogue, which is critical of rhetoric as practiced, suggests that there is another rhetoric, an Ideal rhetoric. It is difficult to see why so many have missed this concept of an Ideal rhetoric and have seen the *Gorgias* as a work that condemns all rhetoric instead of only certain practices of rhetoric.

But like Protagoras, Plato did not work out an intricate system of rhetorical principles. Although throughout the *Dialogues* there are suggestions for working out a rhetorical system, the principles by which one discovers and applies the Ideas to speaking are scattered and somewhat incomplete. Certainly Plato's student, Aristotle, did not provide a method of applying the eternal archetypes to speaking, since he did not accept Plato's theory of Ideas.[8] One is at a loss to understand why some scholars believe that Aristotle's *Rhetoric* was the fulfillment of Plato's suggestions about rhetoric. The error may be attributed to mistaking for the essence of Plato's theory of rhetoric those passages in which he uses the word *rhetoric* and looking at these passages out of context. Instead, these passages are supplementary to the actual starting point, the latter of which is more clearly his consuming interest. Although this starting point has remained without a codified rhetorical system for 2,400 years, perhaps there are ideas which may not only guide men and states but that may save us and transform us. That rhetorical theory after Plato neglected such a starting point is testimony, not so much to the good sense of later rhetoricians, as to their dullness.

Isocrates and Cicero began, not with a metaphysical system, but with a *social* starting point. The starting point was the notion that the good citizen was an orator-statesman; their rhetorics were attempts to produce great citizens. Thus, much of the writing of Cicero and Isocrates attempted to bring students to admire the noble, to love wisdom or philosophy, to seek worthwhile subjects for speaking, and to speak in such ways that men would be a credit to mankind. Perhaps their aim could be expressed by the question: *can men be taught speaking in such a way as to produce ideal citizens?* The question is a good one— if it can be intelligently answered—but the systems of rhetoric produced by these men following that starting point are not fully worked out, and are too much influenced and even occasionally corrupted by the rulebooks current at the time. The significant part of their theory is their starting point, and not the rules that they furnished, which were incomplete and sometimes inconsistent with this aim. Instead of turning out so many books on rhetoric that give watered-down Aristotelian rules of persuasion, it might have been better if some textbook writers had asked: can the teaching of speech be directed toward the creation of superior citizens? The question is worth returning to in our age, but it is not a question to which naïve moralists or platitudinous patriots can make a worthwhile contribution.

Cartesian philosophy furnished an *epistemological* starting point for

[8] See Aristotle, *Metaphysica*, i. 9. His "refutation," however, is, in my opinion, more in the nature of a counterplan and does not destroy the utility of Plato's theory of Ideas.

rhetoric. Descartes' system of reasoning was based on two kinds of truth: intuited truths whose logical strength came from their clarity, and truths that could be deduced from the intuited ones.[9] This logical system was modified and included (albeit with some important anti-Cartesian elements) in the philosophy of John Locke, and developed into a system of evidence for rhetoric by George Campbell in his *The Philosophy of Rhetoric,* in 1776. Rhetoric, Campbell thought, could find a base in certain ideas that were known to be true if one merely gave attention to the meaning of these ideas. This conception was unlike the starting point of any other rhetorician. Beginning with Descartes, seventeenth-century philosophers searched for truths that could not be doubted and inferred new truths from these undoubted ones. Accordingly, a valid argument must meet specific requirements:

. . . to reach the highest status in philosophy, it must be founded upon a self-evident major premise, that is to say, upon a proposition that would be equivalent to axioms and postulates in mathematics, and that would convince any reasonable man of its truth if he merely gave his attention to the ideas making it up.[10]

Professor Lloyd Bitzer says, *"There are certain common-sense principles which are intuitively certain and which provide the underpinnings for a multitude of other truths.* This is the distinctive feature of George Campbell's analysis of evidence."[11]

Professor Wilbur Samuel Howell shows that this philosophy of reasoning was exemplified in the Declaration of Independence, which was, Howell says, "a perfect example of the method of science" as described by a logician named William Duncan.[12] Howell showed that Jefferson probably studied Duncan's logical formulations in college, and that Duncan's *Elements of Logick* was in Jefferson's library. The famous second sentence of the Declaration, which begins, "We hold these truths to be self-evident," ("self-evident" was Duncan's term for "intuited truths") is testimony to the possible Cartesianism of this great document.

[9] For an analysis of the utility for rhetoric of Descartes' system of reasoning, see my "Descartes on Reasoning," *Speech Monographs,* XVIII (March 1951), 47–53.

[10] Wilbur Samuel Howell, "The Declaration of Independence and Eighteenth-Century Logic," *William and Mary Quarterly,* XVIII (October 1961), 478.

[11] "A Re-Evaluation of Campbell's Doctrine of Evidence," *QJS,* XLVI (April 1960), 140. One should note that Campbell's rhetoric has other starting points. Locke and Hume furnish other materials for Campbell's system of reasoning, and faculty psychology provides additional rhetorical starting points. See Frank Thomas Benson, "A Comparative Analysis of George Campbell's *Philosophy of Rhetoric,*" (unpublished Ph.D. dissertation, University of Minnesota, 1962), and Lloyd Frank Bitzer, "The Lively Idea: A Study of Hume's Influence on George Campbell's *Philosophy of Rhetoric* (unpublished Ph.D. dissertation, State University of Iowa, 1962). Both of these dissertations are abstracted in *Speech Monographs,* XXX (August 1963), 194.

[12] Howell, p. 478.

This distinctive starting point has been dropped from contemporary rhetoric. Rather, as Howell observed, contemporary rhetoric finds its logical security in amplification—endless examples, authorities, statistics, and analogies. It might be wise, he suggests, to re-examine seventeenth-century logic, for unlike our modern notions of endlessly amplified supporting material, the older system permits at once logic and brevity. Our contemporary notions, on the other hand, suggest that there is a contradiction between certainty and brevity. "That such a contradiction seems inherent in the culture of twentieth-century America is a sign, not that wisdom has increased since Jefferson's day, but that superficiality and confusion have come upon us."[13] Something may be gained by looking again at this three-hundred-year-old Cartesian starting point.

Nor are the views of rhetoric exhausted. One could discuss Quintilian's *educational-ethical* starting point, Augustine's *theological* starting point, Blair's *esthetic* beginning, and Whately's *logical* point of view. Those who have written discerningly on rhetoric in more recent times have found other starting points. James Albert Winans wrote with the *psychology* of attention as his starting point. In his *Public Speaking,* he remarked:

Our primary study in this chapter [ch. 9] is how to win belief . . . ; and on investigation we find we are facing the familiar problem of securing exclusive attention. "The most compendious possible formula, perhaps," says James, "would be that *our belief and attention* are the same fact."[14]

His applications of the psychology of attention to persuasion, to the speaker's own preparation, and to delivery are well-known. Winans' system may possibly be the most thoroughly worked-out system of all the systems of rhetoric. But not all moderns have been exclusively concerned with persuasion. I. A. Richards started with the question, What kind of rhetoric will uncover and prevent misunderstandings?[15] Since many (but not all, as some have assumed) of man's woes and illnesses originate with or are aggravated by his misunderstandings, the question is a good one. One may doubt that Richards' system in answer to the question is in any way complete, yet still admire his starting point. To it, rhetoricians may return and one day provide a better system. Alfred North Whitehead, in *The Adventures of Ideas,* offers some intriguing notions on a theory that is, at least, quasi-rhetorical: this theory seems to be one devised to answer the question, Under what conditions do ideas become effective and when do they become

[13] *Ibid.,* p. 484.

[14] *Public Speaking* (New York, 1915, 1917), p. 245; see also p. 194.

[15] *The Philosophy of Rhetoric* (New York, 1936). See also, "I. A. Richards: Rhetorical and Critical Theory," in Marie Hochmuth Nichols, *Rhetoric and Criticism* (Baton Rouge, La., 1963), pp. 93–107.

civilizing influences?[16] My own concern has been largely with this kind of question.[17]

The great theories of rhetoric, because they provide new starting points, are *revolutionary*. The "little" theories of rhetoric, on the other hand, are not; instead of revolutionizing, they *tinker*. The lesser works add another sail near the top of the mast or at the rear of the ship, while the greater rhetorical systems give up sails entirely and work to install a nuclear engine. As a paradigm of lesser theories of rhetoric, one remembers the pride that the author of the *Ad Herennium* took in his distinguishing three separate occasions for the *insinuatio*, a kind of indirect approach by which, for instance, one could tell an audience that he would not discuss the weaknesses and frailties of his opponents, even as he is doing so anyway, as, for example, saying, "I will not tell you what a derelict my opponent is nor how he deserted his wife and children." The unknown author of this little theory took a pride that amounts almost to *hubris* in pointing out that he was the only one who had discovered and recorded this technique! He was, of course, only tinkering with rhetoric—tinkering as did the countless Medieval theorists with this or that figure of speech, this or that mode of arrangement, and tinkering as do most modern books on public speaking with this or that form of support, and with this or that way of recording notes on file cards. This kind of tinkering drove the late George Saintsbury to say that rhetoric was everlastingly twining new strands of color into the rope that lets down the bucket into the empty well! The greater rhetorical systems give no mind to the color of the rope, but with whether or not one should drill for water, or for oil, or mine for gold, or do something of even greater merit. We have missed this revolutionary quality of rhetoric because we have neither noted nor analysed the starting points of our greatest predecessors.

These starting points seem to be of two kinds: first, they may consist of definitions of rhetoric. What a man means by rhetoric has sometimes led to great and sometimes to petty systems of rhetoric. When one defines rhetoric as the art of ornamenting a composition, one can hardly reach the heights achieved by those who meant by rhetoric the art of giving strength to truth, or the means of preventing misunderstandings, or, even, the art of discovering the available means of persuasion. We must take care in selecting our meanings of rhetoric for these meanings may lead us either to decadence or to grandeur. The meaning that rhetoric had for the Greeks was part of the force that produced the concern of the great ancient philosophers with the sub-

---

[16] (New York, 1933 and 1955).

[17] See my "On the Teaching of Speech as a Force in Western Culture," *The Speech Teacher*, XI (January 1962), 1–9, and chs. VIII, IX, X, XI, and XII of *Thinking and Speaking* (New York, 1962).

ject. That meaning, however, cannot be uncovered by looking up "Rhetoric" in a classical dictionary; it can be sensed only in the context of the life of the ancient Greeks. Certainly it did not mean, as it often does today, advice on public speaking as presented to schoolboys or businessmen. Although it included public speaking, it was the study of the technique by which one made his way in society, the means by which one succeeded as a human being, the means by which entire nations and civilizations were led either to destruction or to glory. Such matters *would* intrigue philosophers. Even Aristotle saw rhetoric as an "off-shoot" of logic, ethics, and politics. But when the discipline of rhetoric came to mean the art of declaiming or the art of injecting figures of speech to "pretty-up" a composition, men of philosophic breadth were not much concerned with it. Thus starting points may be concerned with the meaning or definition of rhetoric. These definitions are sometimes explicit and sometimes implicit, but either way, one must look carefully at the meaning he assigns to the discipline, for that meaning will determine, partly, whether or not what one does is worth doing.

Secondly, starting points are sometimes logically necessary prerequisites, assumptions, or presuppositions on which the rhetorical system itself rests. Campbell, for example, took faculty psychology as one of his presuppositions and adapted it to rhetoric. Winans took the Jamesian psychology of attention and adapted it to rhetoric, defining rhetoric, or persuasion, as a process of inducing others to give fair, favorable, or undivided *attention* to propositions. His major assumption—for which there is not only much evidence but also some serious philosophical objections—provided a key to unlock a series of vaults whose contents were new to rhetoric. Thus systems of rhetoric may be based on two kinds of starting points: definitions and working hypotheses, both of which may help unlock whole systems.

We must uncover these starting points in order to see the revolutionary character of rhetoric, and to be able to judge the value of the many rhetorical systems that have been produced. We need intelligent critiques of these foundations. Yet we find no critique in rhetorical literature of the metaphysical starting point of Protagoras, no critique of Plato's metaphysics in so far as it is useful to rhetoric, nor any critique of the social starting points of Isocrates and Cicero, and, indeed, few critiques of *any* starting point.

Thinking about starting points can not only help one see and understand the old and to judge it, but such thinking can suggest ways in which rhetoric might grow beyond its present state, and overcome its present limits. Doubtless the supply of starting points has not been exhausted. A former colleague of mine once suggested that every rhetorical system implies an ethical system. Following this idea, every ethical system may imply a special rhetorical system. We have already seen that some metaphysical and one epistemological system implied rhetorical systems, and it is not inconceivable that *every* philosophical system has rhetorical implications—implications that are somewhat different from that of the well-known and, perhaps, overused (but still incomplete) Aristotelian system. What are the implications for rhetoric of the various doctrines of phenomenology, of the analytic school, or of existentialism?[18] What kinds of theories of rhetoric may be used to create sanity—or its opposite? What kinds of rhetorical theory are consistent with and lead to the creation of an open society? What kinds of rhetorical theory lead to maturity? What kinds lead to problem solving? To civilization? It may well be that the most needed kind of rhetoric today is a *religious* rhetoric, at least in one sense. The great religions, as conceived by their founders, each grasped two fundamental truths that have more relevance today than ever before and, that may serve as criteria to distinguish between "religion" and "superstition": (1) man is in desperate need of transformation; and (2) there are means to effect such a transformation. It is especially pertinent to ask: what are the rhetorical means of leading men to the transformation that may save us all from destruction and make us worth survival? The possible starting points for theories of rhetoric appear limitless. However, only one has been exploited.

Mr. Thompson and many other rhetoricians apparently would have rhetoric concern itself with the testing of Aristotelian and similar rules about persuasion. Yet it is this system of rules that constitutes the "dead hand," and that has blinded us—albeit by its relative completeness and occasional brilliance—to other possible systems. Such dedication to one theory of persuasion will stultify instead of cause us to grow. Everlastingly to test hypotheses about persuasion will not energize us but will often ennervate.

The necessity for developing interests other than persuasion can be seen best in a study of rhetorical criticism. The critical question derived from a rhetoric of persuasion is clearly, Did the speaker discover the available means of persuasion? Such a starting point for a rhetorical critique is sometimes an intelligent one. It is often, but not always, intelligent in the classroom where one is trying to teach students to speak persuasively. Less often is it an intelligent standpoint from which

[18] For a description of an existentialist approach to rhetoric, see Raymond E. Anderson. "Kierkegaard's Theory of Communication," *Speech Monographs*, XXX (March 1963), 1–14. The article is especially significant since Kierkegaard was aware of the limitations of Aristotle's *Rhetoric* as a document about discourse on ethical and religious matters. Also see the brief but incisive article by Myrvin F. Christopherson, "Speech and the 'New' Philosophies Revisited," *Central States Speech Journal*, XIV (February 1963), 5–11, on the significance of Kierkegaard, Nietzsche, Heidegger, and Sartre.

to view an historically significant speech, but sometimes it can be worthwhile. For example, the aim of Lincoln's First Inaugural address was to prevent a civil war; it is intriguing to ask, Did Lincoln use all the available means of persuasion to prevent the war? as Marie Hochmuth Nichols asked.[19] But often the question is quite fruitless. How well did Pericles (or was it really Aspasia, who may have "ghosted" the speech?) use the available means of persuasion in the "Funeral Oration" in relation to the fifth-century Greeks who were listening? is almost ridiculous. Discerning and sensible critics have been asking better questions of this speech for 2,500 years, such as, How well did Pericles characterize the open society? or, What, according to Pericles, is the value of a free society? or Was Ancient Greece the kind of society that Pericles described in the "Funeral Oration"? But these questions are not permitted, if one avows that rhetoric is and should be concerned only with persuasion. Looking at rhetoric through the glass of persuasion may often give a strangely distorted view of things, and often an unintelligent view. Is it, after all, very important whether or not a certain sermon on a hillside used the available means of persuading a handful of shepherds? Is it not more important to ask about the meaning of the ethical doctrine expressed or to ask what changes in human motivation the speaker urged? To take the Aristotelian view of the Sermon on the Mount is limiting and does not permit the most intelligent view. Yet, if rhetorical criticism is anything, it must permit one to take an intelligent view of a speech.[20] To ask, Did Adolph Hitler discover all the available means of persuading Germans to hate Jews? is certainly not the best way to view Hitler's anti-Semitic diatribes. And how would speech teachers view the Gettysburg address through the Aristotelian glasses? Critics have sometimes claimed that Lincoln did not write the speech for the audience to which it was given, but clearly addressed it to posterity. (Lincoln did not wait for the crowd to be quiet when he gave it, and never spoke loudly enough to be heard by more than one-tenth of the audience.) If one took the usual Aristotelian view of this speech, he would have to analyze how well the speech was adapted to posterity; but posterity (assuming that

[19] Wayland Maxfield Parrish and Marie Hochmuth [Nichols] *American Speeches* (New York, 1954), pp. 21–71.

[20] See Robert D. Clark, "Lessons from the Literary Critics," *Western Speech*, XXI (Spring 1957), 89, for a discerning discussion of this point. The entire issue is devoted to some interesting non-Aristotelian points of view. See esp. the articles by Thomas Nilsen, "Interpretive Function of the Critic," pp. 70–76; Joseph L. Blau, "Public Address as Intellectual Revelation," pp. 77–83; Marie Hochmuth [Nichols], "Burkeian Criticism," pp. 89–95; and W. Charles Redding, "Extrinsic and Intrinsic Criticism," pp. 96–103. See also, the attack upon neo-Aristotelian rhetorical criticism and the constructive suggestions in Edwin Benjamin Black, "Method in Rhetorical Criticism," (unpublished Ph.D. dissertation, Cornell University, 1962). Abstracted in *Speech Monographs*, XXX (August 1963), 195.

one will have the good fortune to be followed by posterity) has not yet come into being, so one does not know what its characteristics will be. Therefore, one cannot discuss the extent to which this speech uses the available means of persuasion. Using the Aristotelian point of view, one would be unable to say much of anything about the Gettysburg address!

The point is clear: the Aristotelian framework often provokes irrelevant questions. Clearly we need to end the slavish devotion to one system of rhetoric and enrich ourselves by searching for and working out other views of rhetoric. We must uncover the starting points, the assumptions, the presuppositions of ancient and modern rhetorics if we are to understand the nature of our predecessors and to glimpse the revolutionary quality of rhetoric and if, indeed, we are even to see rhetoric clearly. We must, secondly, criticize these starting points and the way the attendant systems follow or achieve them if we are to be able to judge the merit of rhetorical systems. When we locate old starting points, criticize them and discover new ones, rhetoricians may accurately be said to be thinking philosophically, for one acceptable definition of philosophy is that it is a "critique of presuppositions."

2

The experimental method, if it is addressed to confirming, rejecting, or modifying the rules of Aristotelian, or other rhetorics about persuasions cannot remove the "dead hand," since too much concern for these rules is itself the dead hand.

Nor can such a concern for the testing of rules of persuasion always attract the best minds. In a world in which half the population is starving and the other half can blow the rest into eternal oblivion, it makes little difference whether, for example, climax order or anticlimax order is sometimes somewhat more or sometimes somewhat less effective. In these times, an energetic mind might be revolted by such trivia. Yet a good mind might be intrigued with the study of starting points which imply whole systems of rhetoric, ethics, logic, philosophy, and the like. But experimentalism can only *test* and cannot itself *discover* such starting points, and hence cannot be the method by which to stop the present suffocation. The experimental method is a useful method—or better, a tool. But it is a mistake to reverse matters and make rhetoric the tool of the experimentalist. Such a mistake is a symptom of the scientism of our age, which, by the desertion of philosophical analysis, has become naïve.

Another limitation to the hope that experimentalism will stimulate rhetoric lies in the kind of experiments rhetoricians have been performing. Although a few experiments are somewhat interesting, most follow a method of investigating that is naïve. These experiments frequently select a single variable and test its effectiveness. Thus, we have a multitude of experiments testing the influence of emotionally-toned language, of various orders of arrangement, the use of support of various kinds, and the like. There seems to be little attempt, however, to use the experimental method to test the consequences or validity of a starting point. The experiments are isolated bits, testing insignificant hypotheses having little relation to each other. Even though one multiplied them a hundredfold, he would not have much that would captivate keenly intelligent minds; rather, he would be endlessly letting down the bucket into the empty well.

Pasteur had a different approach to experiments. Instead of merely looking for a chemical or process that would save the wine which the French government commissioned him to keep from turning sour, he performed experiments on the wine that not only saved it, and perhaps, the economy of France, but also directed his work so that it supported a starting point for medicine. Since his studies were tied to the idea that diseases—whether in wine or man—were caused by unseen organisms that originated from outside the body, his experiments did more than merely investigate the effect of a certain process on the souring of wine: they provided an indispensable key to the study of medicine. Just so, the experimental method will serve us best in rhetoric if we can use this excellent technique not just to test isolated variables, but to shed light on the truth or falsity of higher orders of ideas and systems. It seems that for the most productive use of the experimental method one must be concerned with the foundation of systems.

Mr. Thompson is concerned with Hume's objections to empiricism.[21] Yet, as he seems to sense, such objections may not be an overriding difficulty in the productive use of experiments. Karl Popper has suggested a promising answer to Hume. He believes that the experiment can do two things to which no important philosophic objection can be made: first, the experiment can assert particular statements about existence.[22] "There are white crows" is such an existence-statement, and it is true if, indeed, *one* such crow is found. (To state the proposition according to the usual rules of logic, the statement should take a form such as, "Some crows are white.") Or, to take a more rhetorical idea: sometimes *ethos* is influential among audiences when they are under severe stress. Such particular existence-statements can clearly be supported by empirical methods, and the method of the controlled

---

21 Thompson, p. 2.
22 *The Logic of Scientific Discovery* (New York, 1959), esp. pp. 69–70.

experiment is the most sophisticated of these methods. But, Popper insists, these methods may make a second contribution in that they can be used to refute universal propositions. "There are no white crows" cannot be confirmed experimentally, but, it can be *refuted* if one white crow is found. Consequently, the proposition, "*Ethos always influences audiences when they are under stress,*" can never be established experimentally, but it might be refuted if one finds one case where *ethos* failed to influence such an audience.

The empirical and experimental methods can contribute a modest fare of information by refuting universal propositions and supporting particular ones. The use of carefully controlled experiments does not change the situation, for the controlled experiment simply insures that only one variable is producing the results. The experiment is, epistemologically, *an example.* No example, however sophisticated, does more than confirm particular statements or refute universal ones. There is one exception. This exception is often useful in public address. Examples—and experiments—may support universal propositions when the entire universe of examples is examined. Thus, if one asserts, "All Pennsylvania mental hospitals use Freudian techniques of psychotherapy," and one examines *all* mental hospitals in Pennsylvania, he may, with justice, make a universal proposition and support it with examples. But in rhetorical theory, such statements can seldom be made. One cannot state a universal proposition about the operations of "all" cases of *ethos,* because one cannot examine *all* cases of *ethos* —either of those from the past or those in the future. Consequently, the usefulness of the experiment in rhetorical theory to support universal premises is nearly negligible.

Despite these limitations, there is much that intelligent empiricism, experimental or otherwise, can do. We need to know as much as we can, even though our premises will still be particular, about what kinds of ideas influence our generation and what ideas influenced our fathers but now have little or no power even though they are still emphasized. We need to know the kinds of ideas that are of predominant influence in the sub-groups and sub-cultures on our earth. Are there ideas that attract all men in all ages? What makes ideas wax and wane in potency? If it is true that there is "no force equal to the power of an idea whose time has come," how may we recognize that time? We need to know how ideas mix with each other and what the effect of combining two or three—or a hundred—will be on those in whom they are combined. We need to know how people can come to believe philosophically contradictory ideas, and what kinds of ideas appear to them to be contradictory. In short, we need a kind of *chemistry of ideas* if we are to delineate how ideas and symbols influence people. These matters are all empirical, and although our empirical methods cannot bring certainty, they can support particular premises and refute mistaken universal ones.

There are, of course, many important questions that are not experimental: metaphysical questions, ethical questions and esthetic questions have, often, no immediate possibility of being confirmed by empirical methods. Moreover, "the quantitative and the real are not identical."[23] Justice may exist, but it is not necessarily measurable, although one might make useful measures of attitudes about justice. When one announces that "anything that exists, exists in some quantity and is, therefore, measurable," he may be, as Professor Edwin Black has pointed out to me, only defining his concept—and an overly simple one—of existence. The existence of subjective conditions, as many existentialists and phenomenologists have observed, is not the same as the existence of a table.

Let us not, therefore, be too quick to condemn the "arm chair" philosopher; nor is it shameful for man to sit down when he thinks. The scholar, after all, is not Man using the calculator, or Man using footnotes. He is, as Emerson said, Man Thinking. Short of thinking, there is little possibility of productive experimental work. The productivity of our empirical and experimental work in rhetoric depends upon the discovery of a significant hypothesis, which is to say, often depends on thinking and upon the discovery of significant starting points.

3

Professor Thompson suggests that we might borrow from communication theory. Indeed all disciplines should borrow from any scholarly bank that has the cash. I would like to borrow from sociology and anthropology, for example, a knowledge of what ideas are persuasive in our sub-cultures and in cultures other than our own.[24] I would like to borrow from philosophy the methods philosophers use in analyzing valuable judgments and incorporate such methods of analysis into our own doctrines of argument. I believe that the methods philosophers use in refuting each other should be analyzed by rhetoricians, for it seems probable that the methods of philosophic refutation will be, likewise, rhetorical methods. I would like to borrow from historians a knowledge of what ideas have changed the course of history; a complete analysis of this sort should be, at once, a kind of philosophy of history and a system of persuasion. Borrowing, indeed, can enrich

[23] Anderson, p. 14.
[24] For some excellent suggestions of methods useful to develop an anthropological approach to rhetoric see Huber Ellingsworth, "Anthropology and Rhetoric: Toward a Culture-Related Methodology of Speech Criticism," *Southern Speech Journal*, XXVIII (Summer 1963), 307–312.

rhetoric. And if communication theory has insights on how language transmits and evokes, let us borrow them.

But much of our borrowing has been done in a worshipful spirit. Let me select one borrowed item because it is better known than most. We have borrowed the behaviorists' motivation theory. Such a theory states that: (1) the organism develops a need which is the starting point of behavior; (2) this need leads to a search for solutions; and (3) when a solution is found, a reduction of the need results, and the solution is "stamped in." Unfortunately for rhetoric—and psychology—there are some enlightening exceptions to the theory. Paul Young shows that behavior exists in the absence of need: rats run a maze to sip unneeded saccharin water.[25] If need is the starting point of behavior, why does motivation often stop before the need is met, as in the case of rats when milk is inserted into their mouths? Their behavior changes before the milk is absorbed and, hence, before the need is met. If need is the starting point of behavior, why does behavior exist *contrary* to need, as in the case of the diabetic who craves but does not need sugar, or the moth, that flies into, but hardly needs, the flame? Nor do all needs *energize* the organism—such as the need for sleep or the need for vitamins, which needs may debilitate rather than energize.

Borrowing a psychological theory resulted in the current approach to motivation in rhetoric which is typified by the listing of various motives. But as I once pointed out, these lists of motives omit a consideration of stereotypes, opinion, attitudes, and emotions. Especially, they fail to reveal the complex possibilities available to a speaker or analyst of persuasion when the goals of the audience are blocked, or the even more complex persuasive possibilities when the goals of the audience are subjected to a threat.[26] We thought we had adopted our doctrine of motivation from an authoritative source, and our admiration of the source blocked our own thinking, as often happens with borrowed thinking.

It is doubtful that we can borrow directly from much of psychology because the psychologist asks questions that are slightly different from those of the rhetorician. The psychologist asks, vis-a-vis motives: what are the sources of human behavior that account for its direction, intensity, and quality? The rhetorician could learn much from an intelligent answer to such a question, and he might gain in sophistication, but the Aristotelian rhetorician asks a different question from a dif-

[25] *Motivation and Emotion* (New York, 1961).
[26] "Toward an Analysis of Motivation," *QJS,* XLI (October 1955), 271–278. I would like to add that we must understand the hierarchy of motives in much the way that A. H. Maslow does in his *Motivation and Personality* (New York, 1954), esp. ch. VIII. All motives are not equally important, and Maslow locates those that are prepotent.

ferent starting point: how may one, using the concept of motivation, discover the possibilities that are open both for persuading others and for analyzing persuasion? These possibilities cannot be discovered by mere lists of motives, however accurate—and the diversity of such lists suggests that some of them must be inaccurate. One should be wary of studies in psychology that are not really studies of man but studies of man inadvertently conceived of as a white rat. Moreover those psychologists who are imbued with the Darwinian philosophy, great though its contribution was, may overemphasize *need*. Susanne Langer has pointed out that man does not learn language because of a perceived need, but because of sheer delight.[27] The brain does not turn the raw data of sense experience into symbols because it needs to; it simply does so, and we do not know why.[28] Man can hardly be said to need art for survival—and yet primitive tribes, with no known exception, produce things that are artistic. Man may have other functions that cannot be explained on the basis of naïvely considered need. "Need" has, sometimes, no explanatory value, and our use of it is often comparable to saying, "Morphine puts people to sleep because of its dormative propensity." Thus we argue that man creates art because he needs to and we offer as evidence of his need the fact that he creates art!

It must be wise to borrow, but we must do so intelligently and with a full knowledge of the starting point that moves us to borrow. Communication theory, at least at present, may be too meticulously quantitative to be of much value to rhetoric. Its fault is not chiefly that it is quantitative, but that only the *easy* problems are immediately quantitative. Rhetoric itself, and perhaps communication theory, are much like the inebriate who, instead of looking for his keys in the dark alley where he dropped them, preferred to search under the street lamp because the light was better there. To struggle intelligently with a difficult problem—and fail—may be of more value than to solve an easy one. We have asked—and answered—How do babies' screams change in pitch? but we have left to others the more difficult struggle involved in the question, How do we learn language? It may be well to borrow from communication theory, or from anywhere, but clearly, not all borrowing is of value. We must, ourselves, meet the responsibility of finding intensely worthwhile problems for research and of designing techniques to solve them, and not forever be looking to psychology or linguistics, or semantics, or group dynamics, or role playing, or any of the other disappointing comets that in the past fifty years have appeared in our discipline.

[27] *Philosophy in a New Key* (New York, 1942, 1951), ch. V.
[28] *Ibid.,* ch. II.

4

When we borrow, we should not overlook philosophy. Here is, perhaps, the richest source for rhetoric. Philosophy, first of all, furnishes *information* that is helpful to rhetoric. For example, many debate coaches could discourse intelligently on why we use a modified Aristotelian logic, but how many could tell why we do *not* use Hegel's logic?[29] Philosophy presents thoughtful discourses on the significance of reason, and on the roads to it (and there are many more than that of Aristotle), as well as on the limits of reason, for reason may often be only "a little light that chills." Here we find the background which helps us understand the great rhetoricians, *all* of whom were—probably by no means coincidentally—also philosophers.

But besides furnishing us with information, philosophy can also give *methods* that are valid in any field of endeavor. Just as a chemist can think philosophically about the problems of chemistry, so can a rhetorician think philosophically about problems of rhetoric. But what is philosophical thought? It is curious that there is perhaps an overplus of books explaining the method of scientific thought, but one can find few about the method of philosophical thought. Those that are written generally pertain to methods of special schools of philosophy, such as the method of the analytic school or of phenomenology. Perhaps there is a paucity of books on philosophical method because philosophical thought is not a unitary method, but has differed widely in diverse times and places. My own hunch gives me a strange certainty that such is not the case, but I cannot yet prove it; I feel that there *is* a basic method that may be called "philosophical" and that it has not been completely stated. Moreover, this philosophical method is, at the same time, rhetorical.[30] But whether or not this unproved insight is correct makes little difference at the moment, for there are many ways of thinking that with justice may be called philosophical. One way of finding these ways is to follow the direction indicated by any of the definitions of philosophy. If, for example, we define philosophy as the search for principles of highest generality, we would be using a variety of philosophical thought. To an extent, I think that the rhetorical critics that I mentioned previously (see, *supra, n. 20*) are trying to find valid ways of stating the aims of rhetorical criticism at the most general level. They are, by definition, thinking philosophically. But I think that this particular definition might impale use eventually on the spear of a hypersensitivity to quantitative problems, although I may be wrong.

[29] One reason is that his "logic" is not a method of evaluating inferences; it is a metaphysical system.

[30] Such an idea contrasts with that of Henry W. Johnstone, Jr., *Philosophy and Argument* (State College, Pa., 1959), and finds some support in Maurice Natanson's "Rhetoric and Philosophical Argumentation," *QJS*, XLVIII (February 1962), 24–30. See esp. pp. 28–30.

Philosophy has also been defined as the search for ground points: ideas which cannot be proved, but without which knowledge is not possible. Just as science cannot prove scientific method, just as Euclid could not prove his axioms, postulates and definitions, so may a discipline assume certain kinds of ideas and build upon them. Thus rhetoric might investigate the ideas in virtue of which experience, or persuasion, or doubt, or belief exist—those unprovable underpinnings in the dark shadows of our metaphysical and psychical world that *must* exist if experience, persuasion, and the like are to occur. Or, a phenomenologist might define philosophy as the search for presuppositionless sense, and we might attempt to see if a presuppositionless rhetoric is either possible or desirable. Each school can contribute something: the utilitarians can help investigate some of the consequences of our principles and acts; the analysts can help clarify our statements; and the intuitionist can sharpen our sensitivity to the persuasiveness of presentational forms. There are other definitions of philosophy. The one applied during most of this paper is that philosophy is the critique of presuppositions. This definition can help us see the importance of our assumptions or starting points and urge us to analyze these and to discover new starting points. At the moment, this kind of philosophical thinking may be the most urgent for rhetoric, but we must be sensitive to other ways of thought, which one day, if not now, may suit our needs better.

Even if philosophy has no contribution to make in furnishing information, and even if following out its every definition leads to no positive conclusions, still it can disabuse one of provinciality and naïveté. Philosophy may never have found the perfect ethical system, but it can argue with cogency why something we thought was the right way of life is not. Philosophy may never have found the perfect system to explain a work of art, but it can tell us that some of the primitive notions we have of esthetics are unsophisticated and wrong, and tell us why. Philosophy may not have found answers to the Great Questions, but it can tell us why the wrong answers are wrong. Philosophy, in short, is at its most brilliant in the negative. Those who have the strength to know that they have been wrong and that they will likely continue to be, will welcome the gentle tyranny of philosophy which will not tolerate long the false, the cheap, the fake.

Finally, where rhetoric goes depends on how we view it. Traditionally and correctly, rhetoric is not just an experimental discipline. It has been and should be a humanistic study.[31] Its concern is with the nature of and problems of man. Since mankind has desperate need of

---

[31] For explications of the humanistic basis of rhetoric see Ralph T. Eubanks and Virgil L. Baker, "Toward an Axiology of Rhetoric," *QJS*, XLVIII (April 1962), 157–168; also, Robert P. Newman, "Ethical Presuppositions of Argument," *The Gavel*, XLII (May 1960), 51–54, 58, 62, 63; also, Donald C. Bryant, "Whither the Humanities?" *QJS*, XLII (December 1956), 363–366.

a new rhetorical theory and practice that will lead to sanity, to creativity, to wisdom, to freedom and to fulfillment, let us use any method—scholarly or scientific—or any discipline that will both lead men to understand our present state and to go beyond it. If rhetoric can react to the challenges before it, it might attract, once more, the best minds and may, again, provide knowledge that will be sought eagerly.

3 TOWARD A CONTEMPORARY ARISTOTELIAN THEORY OF RHETORIC

WAYNE E. BROCKRIEDE

Brockriede urges development of a monistic rhetorical theory of sufficient generality to apply in any cultural, ethical, or philosophical context. In your estimation, how realistic is this goal? Explore whether different philosophical and ethical systems generate their own appropriate rhetorical techniques to achieve appropriate ends. Would the kind of monistic theory the author advocates be so general and abstract as to be useless in accurate description and prediction of rhetorical phenomena?

To what degree would you accept the three descriptive differences Brockriede sees between ancient and contemporary rhetorical practice? Is Aristotelian rhetorical theory as speech-centered and nonaudience-centered as he claims? Do Aristotelian concepts such as ethos, wealth, and power allow for examination of "complexities in status relationships"?

Brockriede urges a contemporary Aristotelian theory of rhetoric not in the sense of adopting Aristotelian rhetorical principles but in the sense of adopting Aristotle's method of empirical description of the rhetoric that surrounds us. Would you accept his view of the *Rhetoric* as descriptive rather than normative or prescriptive? (See Edwin Black, *Rhetorical Criticism,* 128–131.) Brockriede correctly argues that an empirically derived rhetorical theory serves as a fruitful framework to guide subsequent experimental research. (See Abraham Kaplan, *The Conduct of Inquiry,* 161, 297.)

Source: Quarterly Journal of Speech, LII (February 1966), 33–40. Reprinted with permission of the author and the publisher.

Otis M. Walter's recent provocative essay contains radical criticism of rhetoric and makes a revolutionary proposal. He criticizes the almost exclusive reliance upon the Aristotelian paradigm of "finding the available means of persuasion" and argues that "such dedication to one theory of persuasion will stultify instead of cause us to grow."[1] He

---

[1] Otis M. Walter, "On Views of Rhetoric, Whether Conservative or Progressive," *QJS,* XLIX (December 1963), 375.

proposes that we end the "slavish devotion" by building upon new philosophical starting points and by developing new rhetorics, for example, Protagorean, Platonic, Ciceronian, Cartesian, and existential.

Whereas Professor Walter urges philosophical pluralism, Robert T. Oliver suggests a kind of cultural pluralism. He recommends that we abandon a unitary rhetoric and develop divergent cultural rhetorics, for example, Confucian, Taoist, and Buddhist. Professor Oliver argues that "classical rhetoric doesn't work now because (1) freedom varies widely from one country to another; (2) in different cultures people think about different subject matter; and (3) different people think in different ways about similar subject matter."[2]

Before one accepts completely either type of pluralism or both, however, he must distinguish among several senses in which the term "rhetoric" sometimes functions. Maurice Nathanson identifies four primary meanings:

> Rhetoric in the narrower aspect involves rhetorical intention in the sense that a speaker or writer may devote his effort to persuade for some cause or object. . . . The teacher of rhetoric investigates the devices and modes of argument, the outline for which is to be found in Aristotle's *Rhetoric* or other classical rhetorics. Reflection of a critical order on the significance and nature of the technique of persuasion brings us to rhetoric understood as the general rationale of persuasion. This is what might be termed the "theory" of rhetoric in so far as the central principles of rhetoric are examined and ordered. . . . Finally, we come to the critique of the rationale of rhetoric which inquires into the underlying assumptions, the philosophical grounds of all the elements of rhetoric. It is here that a philosophy of rhetoric finds its placement.[3]

Along three of Professor Nathanson's dimensions of rhetoric from the points of view of the speaker, the teacher, and the philosopher, the advice of Professors Walter and Oliver is most useful. Speakers[4] and teachers of rhetoric might discard the Aristotelian purpose of "finding the available means of persuasion" in favor of inculcating ideal truth, expressing what can be expressed on a subject, finding self-identity, identifying with others, becoming good citizens, achieving charismatic leadership, winning friends and influencing people, or other objectives. Philosophers may want to present a "critique of the rationale of rhetoric" from grounds other than Aristotelian realism, and choose, for example, Platonic, Cartesian, Kantian, utilitarian, phenomenological, Confucian, Taoist, or Buddhist thought.

---

[2] Robert T. Oliver, "Culture and Communication: A Major Challenge in International Relations," *Vital Speeches*, XXIX (September 15, 1963), 723.

[3] Maurice Natanson, "The Limits of Rhetoric," *QJS*, XLI (April 1955), 139. For a similar set of distinctions among the functions of rhetoric, see Donald C. Bryant, "Rhetoric: Its Functions and Its Scope," *QJS*, XXXIX (December 1953), 408.

[4] Throughout this paper the term "speaker" should be understood to refer to writers, discussants, and other persons of rhetorical intent.

The study of rhetoric as a *theory* to explain how contemporary man interacts symbolically and purposively with other men, however, is a monistic matter. There is one art of rhetoric, one systematic body of principles of symbolic and purposive human interaction, and its students must conceive and formulate a theory sufficiently comprehensive to accommodate all known moral objectives, cultural environments, and philosophical starting points. Although I am not altogether unconcerned with rhetoric from the points of view of the speaker, teacher, and philosopher—all of which invite pluralistic approaches—the emphasis in this paper is upon a monistic theory of rhetoric.[5]

My purpose is to argue that although the Aristotelian theory itself should be modified or discarded, the Aristotelian approach to the theory may be applied profitably in the modification or replacement. More specifically, I shall try to defend four statements. First, the essence of the Aristotelian study of rhetoric is not the system of finding the available means of persuasion; rather, it is the empirical description of rhetorical situations and the philosophical construction of an appropriate system of principles. Second, a modern application of such an approach should not copy the descriptions and precepts Aristotle found useful for the Greek society of the fourth century B.C.; rather, it should describe empirically twentieth century situations. Third, a theory derived from the new description should be dynamic and comprehensive. Fourth, achieving a modern theory of rhetoric would yield advantages for the experimental researcher, the rhetorical critic, and the teacher.

1

In developing a theory of rhetoric, Aristotle observed oratory as it occurred in the assembly, the law courts, and the ceremonies of his day, and he perceived the paradigm of one person doing what he could to persuade many persons on a particular occasion. What followed in the *Rhetoric* was a description of the sources and types of proof which speakers use or invent, a characterization of emotional states and types of auditors, and a discussion of those matters of style and arrangement by means of which speakers present suasives to audiences. "The meaning that rhetoric had for the Greeks," writes Professor Walter in a remark particularly appropriate to Aristotle's conception, "can be sensed only in the context of the life of the ancient Greeks."[6]

Because Aristotle's *Rhetoric* was so appropriately related to the relatively simple Greek society of his day, it predictably is less suited as a

---

[5] In this paper the term "rhetoric," unless qualified, is used in its theoretical function.
[6] Walter, pp. 373–374.

theory to explain the more complex and very different rhetorical practices of today, several differences of which are discussed briefly later. Although in part its inadequacy for the present day may be due to the relatively unsophisticated investigative procedures Aristotle had to use,[7] the primary reason is that it is based upon phenomena, descriptions, and values which do not correspond to present rhetorical practices.[8]

But in Aristotle's theory of rhetoric, just as in Theodore Parker's view of Christianity, there is a permanent value as well as the transient. The permanent value of Aristotelian rhetoric, indeed the essence of Aristotelianism, is its method of empirical description and theoretical system.

2

That contemporary students of rhetoric have not applied this method is readily apparent. Implicit in many of our textbooks and journal articles is the prescription of precepts derived from ancient, not contemporary, practice. Moreover, although experimental researchers and rhetorical critics have sometimes contributed stimulating insights into contemporary rhetorical behavior, these insights generally have come in bits and pieces, and one is left to wonder how they fit together. As David K. Berlo has observed, "Regrettably, there is no hypothetical-deductive . . . theory of rhetoric."[9] Perhaps the closest attempt to formulate a contemporary theory is found in the writings of Kenneth Burke; but unfortunately not even his clearest expositor, Marie Hochmuth Nichols,[10] has been able to transform his acute perceptions into a system which seems adequately to account for the wide range of contemporary rhetorical acts. No one has had the necessary perception, imagination, and presumption to try to systematize principles derived from an observation and understanding of current rhetorical practice.

Admittedly, such a task is difficult. In applying his method to his own culture, Aristotle, with other classical rhetoricians, created what is justly regarded as "one of the marvels of the intellectual history of the world."[11] However, new obstacles are added to the difficulties Aristotle tried to resolve. The contemporary object of the description and theory

[7] See Wayne N. Thompson, "A Conservative View of a Progressive Rhetoric," *QJS,* XLIX (February 1963), 1, 5; and Bryant, p. 404.

[8] See Bryant, p. 404; and Irving J. Lee, "Some Conceptions of Emotional Appeal in Rhetorical Theory," *Speech Monographs,* VI (1939), 66–68.

[9] David K. Berlo, "Problems in Communication Research," *Central States Speech Journal,* VII (Fall 1955), 4.

[10] See, for example, Marie Hochmuth, "Kenneth Burke and the 'New Rhetoric,'" *QJS,* XXXVIII (April 1952) 133–144; and Marie Hochmuth Nichols, "Kenneth Burke: Rhetorical and Critical Theory" in her book *Rhetoric and Criticism* (Baton Rouge, 1963), pp. 79–92.

[11] Thompson, p. 7.

is far more complex than its ancient counterpart.[12] Furthermore, the allied disciplines of logic, ethics, politics, and psychology from which a theory of rhetoric gains its power have all experienced explosions of new knowledge and new methods since Aristotle's day. For these and other reasons, the modern Aristotelian expositor must feed into the system more data and account for more variables than did the Greek rhetorician.

I make no attempt here to develop a theory of contemporary rhetoric. I shall merely suggest (1) three descriptive observations which may be relevant to such a system and may illustrate what necessitates and what must be accommodated by a new description and a new theory and (2) two of the principal qualities which such a theoretical system should achieve.

First, although rhetorical events in Greece during the fourth century B.C. were limited almost exclusively to the public address setting of one man talking to one audience, today rhetorical acts do not even primarily occur in such a situation. Hence, the classical precepts which presuppose such a setting are not always relevant to present practice. Probably more frequent and more significantly the art of rhetoric today is manifested in the mass media world of newspapers, books, magazines, radio, and television. It is sometimes initiated by organized groups of speakers, including national states, and addressed to massive and multiple audiences. Furthermore, the art of rhetoric is revealed in written discourse as well as spoken.[13] Even when rhetorical behavior is oral, it is as likely to occur at a conference table as in an auditorium. Disputes at law are more likely to be settled out of court through a conference than in court at a trial. More legislative controversies are resolved in committee meetings than on the floor of Congress. Any viable system of contemporary rhetoric must accommodate what happens in the mass media, in written discourse, and in discussion.

Second, Greek culture focused considerable attention on the discourse itself. The audience responded aesthetically to the techniques embedded in the discourse as well as suasively to the decision called for by the orator. In such a climate Aristotle is perhaps justified in restricting the study of *ethos* to what the speaker does in the speech itself to recommend his credibility. Such a restriction is misleading today since audiences appear very much affected by the image of authoritativeness and reliability which speakers have developed prior to any given discourse. Other classical theorists of such a discourse-oriented rhetoric

[12] The variation in complexity is illustrated below in the discussion of three descriptive differences between ancient and contemporary practice.
[13] A good justification for including written discourse within the scope of rhetorical theory is found in Bryant, p. 407; and in Ch. Perelman and L. Olbrechts-Tyteca, "The New Rhetoric," *Philosophy Today*, I (March 1957), 7.

are perhaps justified in stressing the parts of a speech, in classifying the figures of speech, and in discoursing on niceties of an elegance no longer requisite.

Today, however, the emphasis appears to center more upon the interaction between speaker and audience. This emphasis is stated succinctly in the frequently-quoted assertion of Donald C. Bryant that the rhetorical function is the *"function of adjusting ideas to people and of people to ideas."*[14] Lloyd F. Bitzer offers a somewhat fuller statement of this view of the rhetorical act:

An orator or a dialectician can *plan* a rhetorical or dialectical argument while sitting at the desk in his study, but he cannot really *complete* it by himself, because some of the materials from which he builds arguments are absent. The missing materials . . . are the premises which the audience brings with it and supplies at the proper moment provided the orator is skillful. . . . The relationship of practitioner of rhetoric to audience . . . is . . . the successful building of arguments [which] depends on cooperative interaction between the practitioner and his hearers.[15]

Terms such as "interaction," "adjustment," "adaptation," "identification," and others characterize the idea that rhetorical practice is the process of relating speakers and audiences, rather than merely representing a finished product, an art object.[16] If contemporary practice is essentially interactive, the theorist, accordingly, might appropriately be concerned along a *personal* dimension with the images that speakers and audiences have of themselves and of one another, along an *ideational* dimension with the strategies for material and formal identification, and with the conditions under which the reciprocal images and attitudes of speakers and audiences may change.

Third, the relationship between rhetor and respondent is more complex now than it was 2300 years ago. Public address than occurred predominantly among men who were approximately equal in social class, in political and legal opportunities, and in education. The major public address occasions, deliberative and forensic, were restricted to citizens. In politics, the audience consisted of Athenian citizens, and any member of the audience was eligible to speak. The Athenian jurors were selected by lot from the citizen class to provide an audience of approximate peers for the litigants. Only epideictic speaking was available to

[14] Bryant, p. 413.

[15] Lloyd F. Bitzer, "Aristotle's Enthymeme Revisited," *QJS*, XLV (December 1959), 407.

[16] In "The New Rhetoric," Perelman and Olbrechts-Tyteca apply this conception of the rhetorical function to philosophical argument: "If an orator is going to fulfill his function he must adapt himself to his audience. Understandably, then, the discourse that is most effective with an incompetent audience is not necessarily the one that will beget conviction in a philosopher" (p. 8).

non-citizen orators.[17] Although doubtless the status of deliberative and forensic speakers differed to some extent from that of their audiences, rhetoric was essentially a form in which men spoke to their equals.

Today, the relationship of speakers and audiences is not so simple. Although men still discourse with men of approximately equal status,[18] two different kinds of relationship also exist. The high-status figure may talk to the lower-status listener: the dictator exhorts the masses and the boss chairs a staff meeting. In addition, the lower-status man may address the high-status audience: one significant example is the relationship between the presidential advisor and the president.[19] The practitioner of rhetoric may speak in situations involving all three kinds of relationships: a senator may speak to the president, to his congressional colleagues, and to the voters back home, sometimes to all three audiences in one rhetorical act.[20] Classical rhetoric provides no precepts of which I am aware to account for these complexities in status relationship.

The contemporary student who wants to develop an Aristotelian approach to rhetoric must notice these and other features of current rhetorical practice. He must revise the Aristotelian description of the kinds of occasions in which rhetorical events take place. He must concern himself with the interaction of speaker and audience as well as with the discourse itself. He must describe how speakers relate to their various audiences in status. Such observations, and others, when systematized in a meaningful way, may explain how ideas are adjusted to people, and people to ideas.

3

But what qualities must a systematic theory of rhetoric attain? First, in at least two senses, the theory should be dynamic. It should change as new methods for observing and testing contemporary rhetorical precepts are developed.[21] It should also be dynamic in the sense of

[17] See J. Richard Chase, "The Classical Conception of Epideictic," *QJS*, XLVII (October 1961), 293.

[18] The term "status" refers to any of several kinds of hierarchy.

[19] See Theodore Sorensen, *Decision-Making in the White House: The Olive Branch or the Arrows* (New York, 1963).

[20] The concept of status differential in rhetorical interaction is suggested in part from small group theory, about which a literature relevant to rhetoric is plentiful. In "The Nature of Modern Rhetoric," an unpublished speech presented at Wayne State University, June 6, 1963, Huber Ellingsworth has approached the question of hierarchy from the point of view of the "social-order rhetoricians." The analysis of status differential may also be assisted by the ideas developed in Ch. Perelman and L. Olbrechts-Tyteca, "Act and Person in Argument," *Ethics*, VI (July 1951), 251–269.

[21] Theory as perpetually generating better theory is discussed in Philipp Frank, *Philosophy of Science: The Link Between Science and Philosophy* (Englewood Cliffs, N. J., 1957), pp. 343–360.

being perceived as itself a process which reflects the continual changes in rhetorical activity. As Aristotle's rhetoric is no longer an appropriate theory to explain current practice, so the best possible theory for our time will no longer be appropriate in years hence. A rhetorical theory must not be regarded as a finished and immutable product, but as a flexible construct which can continually be adjusted to meet the dynamics of rhetorical practice.[22]

Second, in many senses, the contemporary rhetorical theory must be comprehensive. This idea is central to the preference expressed in this paper for a single theory which accounts for all rhetorical manifestations regardless of culture, philosophical starting points, occasions, contexts, or moral ends and methods of speakers, as opposed to a pluralistic approach to rhetorical theory.[23] A monistic rhetorical theory has value only if it accommodates the entire range of rhetorical experience. Thus, whereas Professor Oliver, in referring to the cultural dimension, argues that we should abandon "our traditional concept of a unitary or generic rhetoric" and develop "the ability to deal with a complex series of divergent rhetorics,"[24] I should prefer a unitary theory which explains the generic principles of divergent cultural practices in rhetoric. Whereas Professor Walter seeks the development of rhetorical theories from many philosophical starting points, I should prefer the formulation of a single theory as useful to the phenomenological and the Platonic world views as to the Aristotelian starting point. Not only should such a theory cover each class of rhetorical occasions, but it should also account for the many possible contexts which serve as dimensions within the occasions.[25]

Finally, any theory of rhetoric must be comprehensive enough to permit the practitioner and critic various moral points of view, for, as Professor Bryant points out, attempts to define rhetoric lead "almost

[22] See Edward D. Steele, "Social Values, the Enthymeme, and Speech Criticism," *Western Speech,* XXVI (Spring 1962), 70–75. Not only do we live in a world of changing values, but rhetorical practices are changing at an alarmingly increasing rate. To note this truism is not to contradict the assertion made earlier in this paper that the *theoretical* function in rhetoric is best approached monistically. At any given point in time one should be able to explain contemporary rhetorical practices within the framework of a single theory; changes in the practice, of course, will require appropriate changes in the theory.

[23] This preference is based on the belief that the principles of an art should be extended to the highest level of generalization of which they are capable, so that a theory achieves an optimum simplicity. Such principles, of course, may require special qualifications as they are applied to divergent cultures, philosophical starting points, and ethical codes; to apply the theory as broadly as possible should have the salutary effect of testing and refining it.

[24] Oliver, p. 722.

[25] An extremely interesting and relevant discussion of the role of the context in logical analysis is made in Rupert Crawshay-Williams, *Method and Criteria of Reasoning* (London, 1957).

at once into questions of morals and ethics."[26] Much of the moral concern involves how speakers relate to audiences. Implicit in any rhetorical theory must be the conception of "the possibility of an infinite variety of audiences—starting from anyone who deliberates in secret up to the concrete universality (that is, the whole of mankind).[27] A rhetorical theory must be relevant to the moral purpose of achieving self-discovery through indirect rhetorical methods,[28] to the objective of effecting "a cure of souls by giving impulse, chiefly through figuration, toward an ideal good,"[29] to the attempt to win audience assent only when that assent is freely given and for good reason,[30] as well as to the goal of persuasion at any cost with its assumption that an audience is an object to be manipulated. Not only should a rhetorical theory accommodate all moral ends of speakers, it should also permit a variety of views concerning the morality of certain rhetorical methods. Thus, for example, rhetorical theory should be broad enough to explain a rhetoric of "disguise" or "concealment," but it should also include within its scope an "open" rhetoric.[31]

4

Apart from a conviction that systematic knowledge is justification enough for systematizing knowledge, what are the values of a contemporary theory of rhetoric?

[26] Bryant, p. 403.

[27] Ch. Perelman, "How Do We Apply Reason to Value?" *Journal of Philosophy,* LII (December 22, 1955), 800. See also Perelman and Olbrechts-Tyteca, "Act and Person in Argument," pp. 251–252; and Maurice Natanson, "Rhetoric and Philosophical Argumentation," *QJS,* XLVIII (February 1962), 26.

[28] See Natanson, "Rhetoric and Philosophical Argumentation," p. 27; and Harry S. Broudy, "Kierkegaard on Indirect Communication," *Journal of Philosophy,* LVIII (April 27, 1961), 225–233.

[29] Richard Weaver, *The Ethics of Rhetoric* (Chicago, 1953), p. 18.

[30] In his "Can Philosophical Argument Be Valid?" *Bucknell Review,* XI (1963), 89–98, Henry W. Johnstone, Jr., makes a distinction between argument in philosophy in which the "only action correlative . . . is that which marks a genuine understanding of the position assented to" (p. 92) and in rhetoric in which a man sets out to win assent regardless of his audience's reasons for assenting. (This distinction is discussed also by Natanson in "Rhetoric and Philosophical Argumentation," p. 25.) My view is that a rhetorical function may presuppose either the intent Johnstone assigns to rhetoric or the intent he assigns to philosophy. Central to the rhetorical function is the notion of purposeful interaction between speaker and audience; the interaction can follow from a variety of moral purposes of speakers.

[31] Some writers assume that concealment is the essence of rhetoric. See, for example, Henry W. Johnstone, Jr., *Philosophy and Argument* (University Park, 1959), pp. 19, 46–47, 52–53; and Natanson, "Rhetoric and Philosophical Argumentation," p. 25. Although some rhetoricians may prefer to conceal their technique, others reveal it openly as a matter of choice or as a necessity. The debater, for example, either lays his rhetoric open for inspection willingly or (as part of the conventions of the debate process) his opponents reveal it to the audience for him. See Douglas Ehninger and Wayne Brockriede, *Decision by Debate* (New York, 1963), Chapter 2.

First, however tentative and unsatisfactory an initial formulation might be, an empirically-derived theory might guide experimental research. One occasionally hears or reads the complaint that Wayne N. Thompson recently made, "Few, if any, classical precepts have been examined with sufficient thoroughness to justify modification or rejection."[32] But why examine classical precepts based upon classical practices when presumably the objective of the experimenter is to make explanations and predictions about contemporary rhetoric? Why not directly observe current practices, derive contemporary precepts, and put these to the test?

One also occasionally hears or reads the complaint that experimental research is disorganized.[33] Perhaps one of the difficulties is that in the absence of a theoretical system the experimenter studies one unit at a time without understanding very well how what is being studied relates to relevant matters not being studied. Behavioral scientists[34] tell me that experiments impelled by a theoretical framework are more likely to be productive than those that are not so impelled, and that experiments, in turn, contain powerful methods which can refine the theory. Each needs the interaction of the other.

Second, a contemporary theory of rhetoric would also interact advantageously with the criticism of contemporary rhetoric. Albert J. Croft has argued persuasively that one of the functions of rhetorical criticism is "to modify contemporary rhetorical theory through the examination of the adaptive processes in speeches."[35] Such a function follows logically from the thesis of this paper that a theory should evolve from an observation of contemporary rhetorical practice. A good analysis of how speakers adapt ideas to audiences should provide descriptive data for the system-builder. But contemporary theory also aids contemporary criticism. Where is a critic to get his tools for analyzing the adaptive processes of a speaker unless he understands the theory of adaptive processes? How can he learn what is unique about a speaker unless he knows the norms? How appropriately can he assess a contemporary speaker by applying classical precepts derived from classical norms?

Finally, in what ways would a contemporary theory of rhetoric be valuable to the teacher? In the first place, presumably one would teach the theory. A theory might make "Fundamentals of Speech" courses more nearly what the term "fundamentals" implies. Instead of offering under its guise a course in public speaking or taking students on a tour

[32] Thompson, p. 2.
[33] See Berlo, pp. 4–5; Thompson, p. 2; and Walter, p. 377.
[34] Professors Roger E. Nebergall and Jack E. Douglas, University of Oklahoma.
[35] Albert J. Croft, "The Functions of Rhetorical Criticism." *QJS*, XLII (October 1956), 287.

through assorted speech activities, the teacher might describe a set of principles that are indeed the "fundamentals" of rhetoric in whatever situation they occur, whether public speaking, discussion, debate, or others. If, as I think, rhetoric and not orality is the essential common feature which unifies our discipline, then pedagogically as well as theoretically that commonality should be explored. An investigation of rhetoric as the synthesizer of our pedagogy might lead to radical revisions of curricula and teaching methods in ways I am not now prepared to outline.

To say that a single, contemporary theory of rhetoric is valuable for teachers, of course, is not to say that the goals and methods of teachers will or should become single or standard. Courses in rhetoric will and should reflect the moral values and philosophical starting points of the teacher, whether these be Protagorean, Platonic, Aristotelian, Ciceronian, Cartesian, Kantian, utilitarian, phenomenological, or whatever. But any of these ways of looking at rhetoric requires something to look at. Our discipline needs the description of current situations, within various cultures and across them, and the construction of a modern theory of the art broadly enough conceived to permit many philosophical starting points.

4 TOWARD A NEW RHETORIC

HERBERT W. SIMONS

The "new rhetoric" described by Simons is offered as a supplement rather than a substitute for the "old rhetoric," which emphasizes achievement of a speaker's persuasive intent in public address. Simons' new rhetoric focuses on two-way communication interaction between sender and receiver, on mutually satisfactory resolutions of differences, and on finding discursive means of managing social problems. In going beyond persuasive and informative public address, principles of the new rhetoric, he maintains, must encompass communication in such settings as small-group discussions, interviews, and labor-management negotiations.

Of particular interest are the five rhetorical goals of the new rhetoric: understanding, reconciliation, compromise, judgment of others, and de-escalation of conflict. Consider whether the goal of debating claims and submitting them to judgment by a third party can be viewed as also within the tradition of the old rhetoric. Special attention is merited for the goal of de-escalation of conflict. Especially today when the rhetoric of confrontation is both studied and practiced, this goal necessarily must be pursued with diligence and dispatch. And we need a theory of confrontation rhetoric with explanatory and predictive capability.

Professor Simons requested that the following note (circa 1970) be added: "The rising tide of domestic and international conflict has reinforced my conviction that the new rhetoric of conflict manage-ment is to be applauded. I am no longer convinced, however, that rhetoric must be normative. Hence, I would also applaud those rhetoricians with source orientations who aim at discovering principles with which communicators may maximize ther own interests."

Source: Pennsylvania Speech Annual, XXIV (September 1967), 7–20. Reprinted with permission of the author and the publisher.

To the extent that theory is sterile, its applications will inevitably be barren as well. There can be no criticism without standards, no fruitful analysis or understanding of human interaction without acceptable conceptual underpinnings. It is noteworthy, therefore, that a mounting array of published criticism has been levelled at both our classical and modern theories of rhetoric. Among the more responsible of these attacks has been Thompson's allusion to traditional rhetoric as a paralytic "dead hand,"[1] and Wallace's derision of contemporary rhetorical works for failing to deal with values, the "substance of utterance."[2] In an essay especially pertinent to this article, Walter admonished, not the older approaches, but their curent users, who have failed to "locate old starting points, criticize them and discover new ones."[3]

It is the burden of this paper that a significant new starting point for rhetoric has indeed been evolving over recent years, a beginning which, more precisely, is not one approach but an amalgam of many, all of which focus on the role of communication in the management of interpersonal relations within social systems. The still uncrystallized rhetoric derives from the relatively recent profusion of works on communication in speech and in the social sciences, particularly those addressed to study of the causes and reduction of social problems.

Not all of the present day concern with the communication process is new or necessarily rhetorical. As conceived here, to be new requires an axiological departure from that traditional body of neo-Aristotelian principles about discursive influence, first systematized by Aristotle[4] and later modernized and extended by his disciples to include (with less emphasis) informative speaking and written communications.[5] To constitute a rhetoric requires a collection of empirical data and explanatory constructs which can aid teachers and critics to render meaningful prescriptive and judgmental statements about intentional, popular discourse.[6] Rhetoric is intrinsically normative; it utilizes ob-

[1] Wayne Thompson, "A Conservative View of a Progressive Rhetoric," *QJS*, XLIX (February 1963), 1–7.

[2] Karl Wallace, "The Substance of Rhetoric: Good Reasons," *QJS*, XLIX (October 1963), 239–249.

[3] Otis Walter, "On Views of Rhetoric, Whether Conservative or Progressive," *QJS*, XLIX (December 1963), 367–382.

[4] Professor Walter rightly maintains (*Ibid.*, p. 368) that there are many classical rhetorics. Because none are so popular or so well developed as the neo-Aristotelian, however, the writer feels justified in referring to that system exclusively when speaking of the "old" or "classical" rhetoric.

[5] Some writers insist that neo-Aristotelian rhetoric is only concerned with oral speech; others exclude informative discourse from traditional rhetoric's scope. Professor Edwin Black includes written communication but minimizes the place of informative speaking, insisting that its treatment in modern textbooks "can be attributed to expedient or commercial considerations." See Edwin Black, *Rhetorical Criticism: A Study in Method* (New York. 1965), pp. 10–16. The dispute appears to be one of emphasis; neo-classical scholars have been largely but not entirely concerned with oral, suasory discourse.

[6] By "intentional, popular discourse" is meant the goal-directed language of the teacher, the salesman, the lawyer, the statesman, etc., as opposed to the language of poetry and drama (poetics) and the language of philosophical and scientific inquiry (dialectics).

servational research, not simply in order to describe what is, but as a basis for claims about what should have been or ought to be. In that he serves as a guide for practitioners and as an evaluator of speech practice, the rhetorician must have, as Marie Nichols suggests, "a set of values pertaining to the ends of society; the causes one may ethically advance."[7] Says Nichols, "there is a higher principle of rhetoric than technical effectiveness."[8]

By the above standards, telecommunication theory, cybernetics and descriptive linguistics, although new, are not rhetorical in that they neither focus on attempts at discursive influence nor contribute directly to normative judgment.[9] In contrast, most of the experimental research by the late Carl Hovland and his associates at Yale (together with its contemporary applications to advertising, public relations, psychological warfare, etc.),[10] while admittedly rhetorical, is not new in that it is an extension of the Aristotelian tradition; a continued search for the available means by which message-senders may secure their intended effects.[11]

A sizeable segment of the research and theory on communication in speech and the social sciences has been new and rhetorical. The persons referred to here as "representatives" or "advocates" of the "new" rhetoric have not defined themselves as such. Yet they warrant the labels by a shared humanistic approach to study of the speech process and by a common focus which diverges, in important ways, from present day rhetoric's neo-Aristotelian perspective. In spelling out the beginnings (and *only* the beginnings) of the "new" rhetoric the writer is reflecting his own synthesis or integration of these disparate elements around what appear to be their major points of convergence.

The first section of this paper describes the emergence of the "new" rhetoric and delimits its essential characteristics. The next section contrasts the normative orientations of the non-traditional system and its neo-Aristotelian counterpart. The "new" rhetoric is defined in the third section and the terms of that definition are examined. In the final section a list of rhetorical objectives is set forth. The term, "new" rhetoric, is used, not in an exclusive sense, as if to deny the place of other emerging rhetorics, but by way of contrast to the classical tradition.[12]

[7] Marie H. Nichols, *Rhetoric and Criticism* (Baton Rouge, 1963), p. 16.

[8] *Ibid.,* p. 16.

[9] See Colin Cherry, *On Human Communication* (New York, 1956), p. 9.

[10] See for example, Carl I. Hovland, Irving L. Janis and Harold H. Kelly, *Communications and Persuasion* (New Haven, 1953).

[11] Black, *op. cit.,* pp. 33–34. Professor Black excludes only the Yale research on persuasibility from this category.

[12] For an explication of other recently developed starting points, see Daniel Fogarty, S. J., *Roots For a New Rhetoric* (New York, 1959). Dean Fogarty's conception of the general semanticist's contribution to a comprehensive rhetoric is similar to my own.

I. OBJECTS OF STUDY

The new rhetoric owes its impetus to what has familiarly become referred to as the "communications boom," dating from the late forties, a period partially marked by two complementary trends: (1) Among those concerned with the causes and amelioration of man's problems, psycho-social concepts have been reformulated to reflect greater sensitivity to the influence of communication patterns on thought and action; and (2) Whereas earlier efforts among those previously interested in rhetorical discourse had focused on the *platform speaker,* the attention of some of them has shifted since the forties to the *communicator,* a "speaker-listener" who reciprocally interacts with others, usually in informal settings. A body of normative canons about how man may responsibly influence through talk (and listening) was fashioned out of a fusion of the above trends.

The first of these developments took on rhetorical significance when social scientists who had been constructing interdisciplinary theories of communication for purely descriptive and explanatory purposes began to apply communication perspectives in studying problems of interpersonal relations reflected in popular discourse.[13] They noted, for example, that impasses in negotiations between labor and management were often attributable to breakdowns in communication,[14] that errors in medical diagnoses were commonly the result of poorly worded questions,[15] that failure to listen to subordinates was a chief cause of poor policy-making among administrators.[16] Initial observations of this kind led to more widespread changes in focus and in language. Organizational theorists who had been preoccupied with improving technological efficiency and bureaucratic structure during the twenties and thirties turned their attentions to human relations problems [17] and found, furthermore, that many of the abstract concepts which they had used to characterize organizational structures and functions could profitably be translated into communication concepts whose referents were observable.[18] Psychiatrists such as Harry Stack Sullivan evinced greater interest in the interview process[19] while others

[13] Ralph F. Hefferline, "Communication Theory: I. Integrator of the Arts and Sciences," *QJS,* XLI (October 1955) 223–233.

[14] See, for example, William F. Whyte, *Pattern for Industrial Peace* (New York, 1951).

[15] See, for example, Robert L. Kahn and Charles F. Connell, *The Dynamics of Interviewing* (New York, 1957).

[16] Earl Planty and William Machaver, "Upward Communications: A Project in Executive Development Using the Syndicate Method," *Personnel,* XXVIII (January 1952), 304–318.

[17] See, for example, Burleigh Gardner and David G. Moore, *Human Relations in Industry,* 3rd. ed. (Homewood, Ill., 1955).

[18] See for example, John T. Dorsey, Jr., "A Communication Model for Administration," *Administrative Science Quarterly,* II (December 1957), 307–324.

[19] Harry Stack Sullivan, *The Psychiatric Interview,* (New York, 1954).

in that field, such as Ruesch and Bateson, began to treat communication as the "social matrix of psychiatry."[20]

One effect of the newly acquired communications orientation among applied social scientists was the development of training programs designed to modify interview, conference and day-to-day human relations behavior. Through such pedagogical techniques as role-playing, case study and "t-group" training, participants were sensitized to sources of social problems which are subject to human control. The National Training Laboratory noted for its focus on group problem-solving was founded at Bethel. At the University of Michigan "action researchers" created a Center for Group Dynamics. And out of the Harvard Business School came a "Training Within Industry" program with a heavily accented communications orientation which was said to have prepared almost a half million foremen during World War II. Practicums on group discussion and interviewing have since found their way into the academic classroom.

While applied social scientists were enlarging their interest in informal communication behavior and finding modern communication theory increasingly helpful in analyzing and ameliorating social problems, most classical rhetoricians persisted in focusing on formal public address. Historical-critical studies continue to deal, almost exclusively, with public speaking settings characterized by formality and one-way communication, a relationship between active speakers and passive listeners. Likewise, principles of classical rhetoric are designed for platform speakers with only tangential relevance to those who rarely speak formally but who nevertheless are constantly involved in informal reciprocal interactions. Despite the fact that "contemporary practice is essentially interactive,"[21] that many of our society's most pressing problems properly receive airings in conferences and corridors, classical rhetoric remains virtually inapplicable to two-way communication settings.

It was out of disenchantment with neo-Aristotelian rhetoric's parochial concern with platform speech that certain scholars in speech such as Wendell Johnson, Elwood Murray, Franklyn Haiman and Dean Barnlund joined forces with applied social scientists in fashioning a new rhetoric. They recognized that in two-way communication settings most classical principles of invention, arangement, delivery and style are of little value. A conferee's posture, articulation or vocal quality is generally less important, for example, than his sensitivity to sources of misunderstanding or his capacity to question, to pattern planned re-

[20] Jurgen Ruesch and Gregory Bateson, *Communication: The Social Matrix of Psychiatry* (New York, 1951).

[21] Wayne E. Brockriede, "Toward a Contemporary Aristotelian Theory of Rhetoric," *QJS*, LII (February 1966), 36.

marks flexibly, and to listen, evaluate and adjust responses almost simultaneously.

Dean Barnlund has ably articulated the dissatisfaction with classical rhetoric among non-traditionalists in the profession.

There is little in the traditional view of speech that is helpful in the analysis of conversation, interviewing, conflict negotiations, or in the diagnosis of the whole span of communicative disorders and breakdowns that are receiving so much attention currently. Upon so limited a view of communication it is unlikely that there can be developed theories of sufficient scope and stature as to command the respect of other disciplines or of the larger public that ultimately decides our role in the solution of man's problems. The field of speech seems to be fast approaching a "checkpoint" where one loses the freedom to choose between alternative flight plans, between a limited interest in speechmaking and a broad concern with the total communicative behavior of man.[22]

Many of those in the speech profession who opted for the broader view were admirably suited to advance the new rhetoric as theorists, researchers and teachers. Ralph Nichols' treatise on listening evoked widespread interest in the neglected process among educators and businessmen.[23] Wendell Johnson's famous model of the communication process gave structure to the field.[24] Influenced by Johnson and by Irving J. Lee's summer visit to Harvard, Carl Rogers and F. J. Roethlisberger were prompted to write their now classic definitions of success and failure at communication.[25] Discussion texts authored by persons in speech infused in the new rhetoric those aspects of the old which are especially applicable to interactive settings: principles of message clarity, uses of evidence, methods of reasoning and the like.[26]

From the joint efforts, then, of small group theorists, of clinical psychologists and psychiatrists, of industrial sociologists and political scientists and of persons in speech, a new perspective emerged and with it an accumulated body of research, an inter-disciplinary language of description, explanation and prescription, and a set of techniques

[22] Dean Barnlund, "Toward a Meaning Centered Philosophy of Communication," *Journal of Communication,* XII (December 1962), 202.

[23] Ralph Nichols and Leonard Stevens, *Are You Listening?* (New York, 1957).

[24] Wendell Johnson, *People in Quandaries,* (New York, 1946).

[25] Carl Rogers and Fritz Roethlisberger, "Barriers and Gateways to Communication," *Harvard Business Review,* XXX (July–August 1952), 46–52. Roethlisberger's characterization of the evaluated criteria associated with contrasting "schools of thought" closely resembles my own distinction between the new and the old rhetoric. "One school assumes that communication between A and B, for example, has broken down when B does not accept what A has to say as being fact, true or valid; and that the goal of communication is to get B to agree with A's opinions, ideas, facts or information. The position of the other school . . . assumes that communication has failed when B does not feel free to express his feelings to A because B fears they will not be accepted by A. Communication is facilitated when on the part of A or B or both there is a willingness to express and accept differences." (p. 50).

[26] See, for example, John W. Keltner, *Group Discussion Processes* (New York, 1957).

by which behavior could be modified through training. The shared concern with interactive rhetorical discourse, and the consequent reformulation of speech principles and redirection of teaching and research energies constitute distinguishing hallmarks of the new rhetoric. Still another defining feature of the new rhetoric that has been refered to is its objective of judiciously "managing" social problems, a normative goal orientation, which is contrasted with the normative framework of neo-Aristotelian rhetoric in the next section.

II. NORMATIVE ORIENTATION

The old rhetoric's primary focus is on the personal effectiveness of a speaker; the new centers on the social effectiveness of alternative patterns of managing social problems.

The cornerstone criterion of at least the main stream of traditional rhetorical theory and criticism is a peculiar blend of honor and expediency in which ethics has played step-sister to effectiveness, the favorite son. From Aristotle onward, the primary differentiator of success and failure at communication has been the test of intended effect. Whether applied to classroom speeches or to campaign orations, communication is deemed to have succeeded to the degree that the received message elicits the response intended by the sender of the message; it has broken down to the extent that the sender's purpose has not been achieved. It is this tenet, write Thonssen and Baird, which is "basic to all analyses of the theory and practice of rhetoric. . . . Men use speech not simply to hear themselves talk, but to achieve certain responses from hearers."[27]

The place of ethics in classical or neo-classical rhetorical systems has not been entirely clear. The "intended effect" yardstick certainly implies neither sanction nor censure of the ends or substance of communication. And, for some, effectiveness seems to be a stopping point. "Today's critic," Baskerville maintains, often sidesteps inquiry into the basic soundness of the speaker's position, offering the excuse that truth is relative, that everyone is entitled to his own position, and that the rhetorical critic's task is to describe and evaluate the orator's skill in his craft and not to become entangled in complex ethical considerations."[28] To be sure, rhetoricians have not wholly ignored ethical considerations in studying communication. Yet, for the most part, principles of ethics and effectiveness have been bifurcated, with ethical judgments tacked on to the central, amoral, pragmatic criterion of intended effect. Thus it is that a discussion of ethics constitutes but one chapter in each of

[27] Lester Thonssen and A. Craig Baird, *Speech Criticism* (New York, 1948), p. 5.
[28] Barnet Baskerville, "Emerson as a Critic of Oratory," *The Southern Speech Journal,* XVIII (March 1953), 161.

our major texts on persuasion.[29] The bulk of these texts deals with effectiveness. Says Oliver, "for students of persuasion, it is helpful to make a clear-cut distinction between what is effective and what is ethical. If we are to have a science of persuasion, it can be developed only as we keep our attention centered on the single question: what actually does achieve persuasion?"[30]

The alliance between the yardsticks of ethics and effectiveness has not been an easy one for the rhetorician, partly because he has accepted normative obligations while simultaneously maintaining what Berlo has called a "source orientation."[31] Such an orientation involves, not only a focus of study on the speaker, but an identification with his speech objectives.[32] The rhetorician has attempted to be both referee and coach, incompatible roles which require renderings of dispassionate moral judgments on the one hand and "amoral," technical advice on the other. One cannot seriously question the social desirability of a speaker's goals and at the same time identify with those same objectives. Nor can one fuse the criteria of ethics and effectiveness into a single critical evaluation while holding to a source orientation. Such a fusion can only be accomplished when the overriding concern of the critic is with social, rather than personal, consequences of communication.

Even if it should be assumed that a source orientation is appropriate in evaluations of platform speeches, it is nevertheless inappropriate in analyses of interactive relationships. Situations characterized by two-way communications are of two types: (1) those such as counseling interviews, problem-solving discussions and educational seminars, in which group participants share roughly similar goals and (2) those such as labor-management contract negotiations, diplomatic conferences and reprimand interviews in which there is conflict over values and/or scarcity. The first of these types poses no especially significant ethical problems since goals are shared. It makes little sense to adopt a source orientation in analyzing a cooperative group inquiry but neither does

[29] See Winston L. Brembeck and William S. Howell, *Persuasion* (Englewood Cliffs, New Jersey, 1952); Wayne C. Minnick, *The Art of Persuasion* (Boston, 1957); Robert Oliver, *The Psychology of Persuasive Speech,* 2nd ed. (New York, 1957).
[30] Oliver, *op. cit.,* p. 25.
[31] David Berlo, *The Process of Communication* (New York, 1960), p. 115.
[32] Lawrence W. Rosenfield, "Rhetorical Criticism and an Aristotelian Notion of Process," *SM,* XXXIII (March, 1966), 1–16. Rosenfield depicts neo-classical models as postulating an exploitative view of rhetoric. "Such models focus on the communicator as the focus of power; they tend to depict receivers of messages somewhat like inert lumps of clay waiting to be modeled to a predetermined shape by means of a wide range of brainwashing, hidden persuasion and manipulative techniques at the disposal of the communicator." (p. 15). Rosenfield rejects source of orientation on grounds that they are inconsistent with Aristotle's own animistic philosophy. My own concern is over the ethical implications of such an orientation.

it do much harm. It is with respect to the second type of setting that normative judgments and source orientations are incompatible. Analyses of exchanges by conflicting parties require from the rhetorician, a detached, yet essentially moralistic perspective, an angle and scope of view which enables him to consider the needs of all who participate in a communicative relationship, and those whom they affect. To conclude that a meeting among disputants has been successful when one of the participants has "won" the conference is obviously to ignore the needs and aspirations of the other conferees, let alone the supraordinate interests of the social system within which they clash. If he is to do more than enunciate principles of technical effectiveness, the critic is obliged to step back from the fray, to pose as referee rather than as coach or combination of referee and coach; in short, to look in at conflict relationships from the outside.

The emphasis of the new rhetoric is on problem-solving or problem-reduction rather than persuasion; on mutually satisfactory resolutions of differences rather than victory for one party. When a communications consultant advises managers on how they can secure worker loyalty through indoctrination programs he illustrates an application of the old rhetoric. When the consultant recommends communication attitudes and practices designed to fuse the needs of management and the needs of the workers he illustrates an application of the new rhetoric.

III. DEFINITION

The new rhetoric may now be defined as the search for available discursive means of managing social problems judiciously. Regarded as social problems are those circumstances in which two or more parties share a "felt need" which they attempt to meet cooperatively and those situations wherein two or more parties are in conflict. With respect to conflicts the new rhetorician seeks to discover which of two or more behavioral alternatives are preferable; i.e., which discursive patterns of conflict management get at causes rather than effects, produce long-run resolutions rather than short-run adjustments, yield reconciliations rather than compromises, etc.

The term "judicious" raises fewer problems than may at first be imagined. Many communication practices are intrinsically judicious or injudicious. No research is needed, for example, to determine whether it is helpful to treat inferences as facts or to confuse levels of abstraction. These principles of general semantics need only be applied to social settings. Other practices are admittedly of doubtful value but their merits may be testable through research. Although generalizations must ultimately be made contingent upon existing conditions, research does indicate, for example, that cooperative discussions of differences are usually more productive than competitive clashes,[33] that participative patterns of deliberation yield less attitudinal rigidity than representative patterns[34] and that judicious resolutions of heated controversies are more likely when combatants are required to restate the positions of their opponents.[35] These findings are derived in much the same way that the neo-classical rhetorician obtains his data on the effects of given speech patterns. The essential difference is that, whereas the traditionalist generally employs as his dependent variable some measure of intended effect such as attitude change or voting behavior, the new rhetorician utilizes a yardstick of social effectiveness such as group productivity.

There is considerable danger of course, in clouding the already dim objectivity of social analysts with value terms such as "socially effective" and "judicious." Normative terms must nevertheless have a place in rhetorical systems; moreover, their use in a rhetoric does not preclude the development of "pure" research as part of such a system. The heart of Boulding's major treatise on conflict management consists in mathematical decision theory models. Yet its avowed purpose is to reduce the chances of needless violence among men.[36] Experimental research in which the social consequences of alternative communication patterns are compared can also be objectified. It is likely that common agreement can be secured as to the social desirability of certain social consequences (human understanding, solutions which get at causes, etc.). Where disagreement might obtain, research conclusions may be treated as "if . . . then" propositions. If Y (a social consequence) is more socially desirable than X (an alternative social consequence), then A (a communication attitude or practice) is preferable to B (an alternative communication pattern). One need not accept the assertion that a given end is socially desirable to accept the truth of the "if . . . then" conclusion.

IV. TYPOLOGY OF GOALS

The new rhetoric is by no means a well integrated body of principles, research and pedagogy. It is at a stage, however, where a number of rhetorical goals, primarily applicable to interactive settings, may be

[33] See for example, Robert R. Blake and Jane S. Mouton, "Comprehension of Own and Outgroup Positions Under Intergroup Competition," *Journal of Conflict Resolution*, V (December 1961), 304–310.
[34] Herbert W. Simons, "Representative Versus Participative Patterns of Deliberation in Large Groups." *QJS*, LII (April 1966), 164–171.
[35] Irving J. Lee, "Procedure for Coercing Agreement," *Harvard Business Review*, XXXII (January 1954), 39–45.
[36] Kenneth Boulding, *Conflict and Defense* (New York, 1963), pp. vii–viii.

tentatively specified. Corresponding to man's own varying limits on communicative capacity, the objectives delineated here are varyingly limited, ranging from attempts to keep conflict within bounds to efforts at producing empathic understanding among participants in joint inquiries. The classification of goal alternatives is intended as a structure or typology for the new rhetoric, corresponding to general ends of speech listed in public speaking texts.

(1) By all odds the most dominant concern among new rhetoricians has been with promoting *understanding* between "speaker-listeners." Misunderstandings have been traced to a variety of communication attitudes and practices: to psychological by-passing and psychologically closed doors,[37] to linguistic ambiguity and culturally ingrained language habits,[38] to channel noise and the selection of inappropriate channels,[39] etc.

Apart from its intrinsic desirability, understanding is ancillary to the realization of other rhetorical goals. Where harmonious relationships obtain, understanding is often sufficient to produce goal achievement. Where serious conflict exists understanding does not generally end conflict but it renders the conflict explicable; hence, more subject to rational control.

(2) When conflict is more apparent than real, *reconciliation* of viewpoints becomes possible. It may be accomplished in one of two ways. One party may convert the other(s) to his way of thinking through traditional rhetorical techniques. Or, both parties may reorganize their perceptual fields but not their basic aims. Through two-way communication the parties may creatively discover new solutions which bridge dilemmas and circumvent impasses, thus effecting a harmonious integration of beliefs.

(3) Conflicts have too often been depicted as resulting solely from breakdowns in communication.[40] Martin J. Maloney has observed that magical properties are popularly ascribed to human speech.

The troubled parents, confronted with their nervous teen-age offspring feel sure that all of the problems with puberty would vanish if only they could achieve understanding. Even the happy hipster, fingering his copy of Alan Watts on Zen, will tell you that the trouble with squares is that they don't—and can't—communicate.[41]

[37] William V. Haney, *Communication Patterns and Incidents* (Homewood, Ill., 1960), pp. 41–72.
[38] Harry Weinberg, *Levels of Knowing and Existence* (New York, 1959).
[39] Wilbur Schramm, "How Communication Works," in Schramm (ed.), *Process and Effects of Mass Communication* (Urbana, 1954) 1–59.
[40] Stuart Chase, *Roads to Agreement* (New York, 1951).
[41] Martin J. Maloney, "The Critical Instrument in Communication Study," in Nebergall (ed.), *Dimensions of Rhetorical Scholarship* (Norman, Oklahoma, 1963), 2.

Some conflicts must be managed rather than resolved. Both real and apparent, they do not terminate with understanding and are not amenable to reconciliation. One means by which conflict may be managed is through the negotiation of *compromise*. Associated with compromise is the largely neglected rhetorical process of bargaining.

(4) If those in conflict are unable to reconcile their differences or negotiate a compromise, they may debate their respective claims and submit to a judgment by a third party or by a body of which they are a part. Court awards, Congressional votes, elections, arbitration board decisions, are examples of conflict management through the judgments of others, all mandated by clash over irreconcilable values and/or by the need for either-or decisions.

(5) When disputants are not willing or able or obliged to end conflict by the non-rhetorical devices of force or avoidance or by any of the rhetorical alternatives just discussed, conflict is maintained. Some conflicts are both desirable and inevitable; they are the drama and vitality of life. But unchecked conflicts often take on a destructive force of their own. Hostility begets more hostility until the effect of positive feedback becomes uncontrollably by either party. A fifth rhetorical function, then, and probably the least studied, must be *de-escalation* of conflict. Short of cathartic safety-valve devices or intervention by third parties, little is known about how to restore conflict equilibria.

SUMMARY AND CONCLUSIONS

This paper has outlined the beginnings of what has been referred to as a "new" rhetoric, an amalgam of efforts by applied social scientists and persons in speech who are bound together by a common focus and a normative orientation which contrasts sharply with the traditional neo-Aristotelian perspective.

The new rhetoric was defined as the search for available discursive means of managing social problems judiciously. Centering upon interactive popular discourse (interviews, conferences, etc.), those classified as "new rhetoricians" have accumulated an interdisciplinary body of theory, research and pedagogical techniques appropriate to their realization that success or failure at contract negotiations, diplomacy, psychotherapy, education, etc., is frequently a function of communication attitudes and practices. Research has been aimed at promoting goal realization among those communicators with shared objectives and at ameliorating differences among those in conflict. Five rhetorical approaches to reducing differences have been recognized: (1) mutual understanding, (2) reconciliation of beliefs, (3) compromise, (4) judgments by others (verdicts) and (5) de-escalation of conflict. The appropriateness of each alternative in any given situation hinges on the degree to which interacting parties differ initially.

By the standards recently advanced by Wayne Brockriede the new rhetoric is neither monistic nor complete. It is not a single compendium of principles "sufficiently comprehensive to accommodate all known moral objectives, cultural environments and philosophical starting points."[42] Primarily adapted to interactive settings, its applicability to formal public address is limited. It is a normative orientation, moreover, and is therefore incompatible with amoral rationales of popular discourse.

Whether the new rhetoric is compatible with the old can be answered equivocally. There is a conflict between the two perspectives over whether the teacher, researcher or theorist should hold to a source orientation. But the issue is not so crucial that the systems cannot peacefully co-exist or even engage in a mutually profitable trade of ideas. Research on sources of misunderstanding, associated with the new rhetoric, should be useful to the platform speaker in that clarity is prerequisite to persuasion. Traditional principles of persuasion should correspondingly be applicable to the "speaker-listener" as he attempts to manage conflict judiciously. Classically minded public speaking teachers might well borrow the techniques of sensitivity training devised by non-traditionalists. They, in turn, should emulate the historical-critical research of neo-Aristotelian scholars by evolving an analogous body of criticism devoted to historically significant interviews and conferences. The new rhetoric, as described, will not replace the old. Nevertheless, it should be an energizing influence in a field whose major work was referred to, somewhat sardonically, as the "solitary instance of a book which not only begins a science but completes it."[43]

---

[42] Brockriede, op. cit., p. 34.
[43] Welldon, quoted in Black, op. cit., vii.

5 IN LIEU OF A NEW RHETORIC

RICHARD OHMANN

Ohmann, a professor of English, isolates several commonalities that bind together disparate contemporary theories of rhetoric. In doing so, he contrasts these common threads with the stance of the old rhetoric. In lieu of a new rhetoric he describes some trends in contemporary theorizing. Note particularly Ohmann's view that the new rhetoric emphasizes cooperation, mutuality, and social harmony rather than manipulation to overcome resistance to a course of action. And Ohmann contends that the new rhetoric involves the pursuit of truth as well as the transmission of convictions.

Do you feel that the outlines of the new rhetoric as described by Ohmann, or by Thompson, Walter, Brockriede, or Simons, are primarily realistic or idealistic? Can the new rhetoric explained by Ohmann and Simons cope with contemporary rhetorical practices such as protest rhetoric of confrontation, "body rhetoric" of demonstrations, or "black power" rhetoric?

Source: College English, 26 (October 1964), 17–22. Reprinted with permission of the National Council of Teachers of English and Richard Ohmann.

The warriors of Homer regularly spoke "winged words," or so Lang, Leaf, and Myers translated the formula in the version of the *Iliad* that college freshmen used to read. The measured speech of a bard had even greater force: when Demodocus sang of the Trojan War in the court of Alcinous, he was "stirred by a god," and his tale made Odysseus weep. Anglo-Saxon heroes, under the influence, perhaps, of a sterner climate, tended to speak "stidum wordum"; for a more grandiloquent speaker the formula might be "word-hord onleac." Greek or Germanic, these heroes of oral epic wielded an awesome power when they spoke: among pre-literate peoples, apparently, skilled rhetoric approximated to magic; certainly it was an expression of charisma on a plane with heroic deeds. Plato seems to have preserved Homer's attitude toward rhetoric, though he tempered awe with distrust, and assigned the rhetorician powers of evil as great as his power to move the soul in pursuit of the Good.

The more analytic Aristotle domesticated rhetoric by enclosing it in a reassuring system of rules and procedures. And like ethics, metaphysics, and poetics, rhetoric maintained a formulation close to Aristotle's for a good long time. Most rhetorical treatises, down through those of George Campbell, Hugh Blair, and Archbishop Whately in the eighteenth and nineteenth centuries, took it as their main business to supply a portfolio of strategies and devices of argumentation and oratory, however imposing the rubrics under which these strategies were arrayed.

Great though the difference is between rhetoric as mysterious power and rhetoric as calculated procedure, these two conceptions share one feature which, for my present purposes, is the most important one: both take rhetoric to be concerned, fundamentally, with *persuasion.* The practical rhetorician—the orator—seeks to impel his audience from apathy to action or from old opinion to new, by appealing to will, emotion, and reason. The theoretical rhetorician—the rhetor— sets down methods of persuasion. And the novice—the student—learns the tricks, almost as he would learn a new language, proceeding from theory through imitation to practice.

Writers in the field have been saying for a hundred years that this notion of rhetoric shows marks of weariness, and that a new rhetoric is in the offing. Perhaps the expectation has sublimed itself into a belief; in any case, rhetoricians have lately taken to using the phrase "new rhetoric" as if it had a reference like that of the word "horse," rather than that of the word "hippogriff." I am not at all sure that the wings have done more than sprout.

But if the new rhetoric has yet to appear, there is no shortage of new ideas about rhetoric: even the briefest survey of definitions and positions uncovers a somewhat bewildering variety. I. A. Richards has it that rhetoric "should be a study of misunderstanding and its remedies," "a persistent, systematic, detailed inquiry into how words work."[1] Richards' definition branches two ways. His stress on inquiry and system is behind the definition offered by Daniel Fogarty in a book called *Roots for a New Rhetoric:* rhetoric is "the science of recognizing the range of the meanings and of the functions of words, and the art of using and interpreting them in accordance with this recognition."[2] The other side of Richards' definition, its therapeutic intent, is second cousin to the conception of rhetoric (or antirhetoric?) implied by the work of Korzybski and Hayakawa: the rhetorician, in their view, should work to quiet the insistent clamor of words, which, if left to themselves, tend to drown out experience and reality. Kenneth

---

[1] I. A. Richards, *The Philosophy of Rhetoric* (New York, 1936), pp. 3, 23.
[2] Daniel Fogarty, S. J., *Roots for a New Rhetoric* (New York, 1959), p. 130.

Burke takes a different line: according to him, "The key term for the 'new' rhetoric would be *'identification'*."[3] Rhetoric should build on the "consubstantiality" of men, their shared modes of feeling, thought, and action. Its goal is cooperation. Richard Weaver argues that rhetoric is the "intellectual love of the Good," and that it "seeks to perfect men by showing them better versions of themselves."[4] The newest book on the subject, *Rhetoric and Criticism*, by Marie Hochmuth Nichols, tells us that rhetoric is "the theory and the practice of the verbal mode of presenting judgment and choice, knowledge and feeling. . . . It works in the area of the contingent, where alternatives are possible."[5] And, to make an end, Northrop Frye calls rhetoric "the social aspect of the use of language."[6]

Clearly, the meaning of "rhetoric" is not clear. We have here one of those infinitely expandable and contractable notions—such as "democracy" and "virtue"—that can be suited to the exigencies of the moment. (I have not even mentioned hostile definitions—rhetoric is propaganda, or lying.) I do not propose to add a definition to the ample supply already available. Nor will the "new" rhetoric make its dramatic appearance by the end of this paper. Instead, I would like to suggest one way in which contemporary ideas of rhetoric, however disparate, resemble each other more than any of them resembles older ideas.

Whereas classical rhetoric, in practice if not always in theory, accepts persuasion as its domain, writers on rhetoric since the romantic period have increasingly strayed from this well-traveled province, or at least enlarged its boundaries. Persuasion is but one use of language, as Richards pointed out; modern theorists have wished to incorporate others: communication, contemplation, inquiry, self-expression, and so on. They have moved away from the simple and convenient picture of a wily speaker or writer attempting to sway a passive or refractory audience, and turned their attention to the whole spectrum of linguistic processes. As a corollary, they have looked less at specific tropes and tactics, and more at rhetorical *patterns,* whole works, and basic features of meaning.

Let me try to outline, schematically but in somewhat greater detail, the relationship of current theories to older ones. In the first place, traditional rhetoric, as I have noted, tends to conceive the task of eloquence in terms of overcoming resistance, to a course of action, an idea, a judgment. There is an intimate link between rhetoric and

[3] Kenneth Burke, "Rhetoric—Old and New," *The Journal of General Education,* 5 (April 1951), 203.
[4] Richard M. Weaver, *The Ethics of Rhetoric* (Chicago, 1953), p. 25.
[5] Marie Hochmuth Nichols, *Rhetoric and Criticism* (Baton Rouge, 1963), p. 7.
[6] Northrop Frye, *The Well-Tempered Critic* (Bloomington, Ind., 1963), p. 39.

action, rhetoric and decision. The speaker is, in some manner, to impose his will upon the audience. Modern rhetoric lowers the barrier between speaker or writer and audience. It shifts the emphasis toward cooperation, mutuality, social harmony. Its dynamic is one of joint movement toward an end that both writer and audience accept, not one of an insistent force acting upon a stubborn object. Theorists like Kenneth Burke conceive of the discourse as itself a form of action, not simply an inducement to action.

Second, classical rhetorical theory assumed that the speaker or writer knows in advance what is true and what is good; he tries to convey a truth, or enjoin a moral commitment, at which he has previously arrived. Modern rhetoricians tend to see truth and attitude as inseparable from the discourse. Truth is not a lump of matter, decorated and disguised, but finally delivered intact; rather it is a web of shifting complexities whose pattern emerges only in the process of writing, and is in fact modified *by* the writing (form is content). Thus in the newer view rhetoric becomes the *pursuit*—and not simply the transmission—of truth and right.

The third shift in our conception of rhetoric follows from the second. As rhetoric absorbs truth, it splits off from conscious stratagem. The writer does not begin in secure command of his message, and try to deck it out as beguilingly as possible; he sets his own ideas and feelings in order only as he writes. Thus canny persuasion actually threatens good rhetoric, for the writer who manipulates his audience is in danger of deceiving himself. If rhetoric is self-discovery, candor is not merely an incidental virtue in the writer, but a necessary condition of his labor.

Fourth, another corollary: as theorists from Pater and Symons on have stripped rhetoric of guile, they have naturally come to conceive the finished product as a revelation of the writer's mind and of his moral character. The style may always have been the man, but now the equation holds by fiat. In this point, rhetorical theory has accompanied post-romantic critical theory in general: the writer holds the mirror up, not only to nature or to the audience, but to himself. Rhetorical theory supplies a justification for the critical methods that trace the writer's psyche in his imagery, his tone, his syntax. As Northrop Frye puts it, "genuine speech is the expression of a genuine personality."[7]

"Because it takes pains to make itself intelligible," Frye continues, "it assumes that the hearer is a genuine personality too—in other words, wherever it is spoken it creates a community." Modern rhetorical theories make the same claim for writing that Frye makes for speech, and his notion of "community" leads to my fifth and final

[7] *The Well-Tempered Critic,* p. 41.

point. The community that a piece of genuine writing creates is one, not only of ideas and attitudes, but of fundamental modes of perception, thought, and feeling. That is, discourse works within and reflects a conceptual system, or what I shall call (for want of a term both brief and unpretentious) a world view. Experience, subtle shape-changer, is given form only by this or that set of conceptual habits, and each set of habits has its own patterns of linguistic expression, its own community.

It is easy to postulate a hierarchy of world views and corresponding communities. Most generally, there is the set of conceptual modes (seeking causes, categorizing) that belong to the community of all men, and are perhaps dictated by our biological makeup. Culture and language organize men into smaller communities. The speaker of an Indo-European language does not come at experience in the same way as a speaker of Chinese (so runs the Whorfian hypothesis, still disputed, but compelling). The world view of a language community divides into special world views that characterize smaller subgroups—speakers of a certain dialect, professional groups, people of a given educational background, writers for *Time* or for the *New York Review*—and each group has its characteristic idiom. Still more particular is the worldview of a single writer (or even of a single work), those ways of experiencing that reflect themselves in his unique employment of language, that leads him to begin his story with "Call me Ishmael" instead of "It is a truth universally acknowledged that a single man in possession of a good fortune, must be in want of a wife." Recent stylistic studies, more than rhetorical theories, work from the premise that rhetorical practice grows out of deep intellectual and moral habits.

This, roughly, is the core of views and assumptions about rhetoric that emerges from a good deal of recent work on the subject. Let me repeat a cautionary word: there is nothing approximating unanimity in current definitions. Certainly this or that rhetorician would quarrel with this or that point in my summary. But for the purposes of this paper my summary need not lay claim to comprehensiveness. It is enough that the assumptions I have listed are ones to which I myself adhere, and that they are shared in large part by many people who teach or write about rhetoric today.

Our primary subject is the college curriculum in English, not the bodies of theory behind it, and I want to spend the rest of the available space sketching out some ways in which the curriculum might respond to the rhetorical theory I have described. Though I shall recommend a few new approaches, my proposals do not imply wholesale abandonment of traditional emphases. Rather, I hope to suggest how the things many of us already teach under the heading of rhetoric or composition or communication might find a comfortable place within a framework that derives from modern rhetorical theory.

But before theory abducts us altogether, let it be admitted that the freshman course must confront one hard reality: some of our students (their numbers vary from place to place, but they exist everywhere) do not control the English language well enough to make rhetoric a genuine possibility for them. Rhetoric, pursued in the grotesque idiolect of an ill-trained freshman, is not a phenomenon for which the average instructor can generate much enthusiasm; and no amount of rhetorical theory can remove the necessity of reinforcing the student's grammar and his rapport with words and idioms. Several years ago a student of mine began her first freshman paper (an essay on language) like this: "Mankind perpetuates themselves by means of a fundamental cooperative act that bears the word-name of language." Now, there are, certainly, rhetorical maladies in this sentence, aside from the *double-entendre*. The "Mankind . . ." opening establishes a relationship of writer and audience that no freshman can hope to sustain, and the instructor might have something to say about the portentousness of the final clause. But most would think that the failure of grammatical agreement and the neologism, "word-name," are prior concerns. The red pencil is a perennial solution, to be sure, but I believe that the red pencil does more good if the student understands its rationale. The freshman course, then, might well begin with some direct study of language. I do not mean an abbreviated course in linguistics or a survey of English grammar, but an attempt to give the student some notion of what his language is and what limits there are to the torment he can impose upon it.

The student should have a brief but systematic introduction to the concept of linguistic structure, to the intricate regularity of patterns in English, to the operation of form classes, to immediate constituent analysis, and to the grammatical signals of meaning. It is in the context of such a discussion that the question of usage may most profitably be raised. The student should see that rules are not made up by grammarians, that a dialect is a set of conventions, always changing but with traditional provenance. He should be aware of the ways in which his own dialect differs from standard written English, and should realize that to master standard written English is to become capable of participating in a linguistic community of considerable importance in our culture. If he approaches the subject this way he will discover in grammar more than mystery and arbitrariness; he may even develop a respect for the extraordinary system he imperfectly controls, and a posture of courtesy toward it.

A treatment of semantics should follow the study of structure. It should include such familiar topics as denotation and connotation, ambiguity, abstraction, the effect of context on the meaning of a word, and the extension of meaning through metaphor. These subjects lead easily into that of synonomy and the consequences of choosing one word over another. And the course might move, finally, from lexical alternatives to syntactic alternatives—to the stylistic differences, for instance, among

1) Just how Parliament functions is a tricky but explorable question.
2) Just how does parliament function? This is a tricky question, but an explorable one.
3) The question "just how does parliament function?" is tricky but explorable.
4) It is a tricky question just how parliament functions. But it is an explorable question.

And so on. The machinery of transformational grammar will be useful here to those instructors who know something of it, but not essential. One way or another the student should be made aware of the abundance of syntactic patterns available to him. If this happens, he will find it easy to extricate himself from those impasses that occur when he has begun a sentence or a paragraph infelicitously; and he may for the first time get a sense of genuine stylistic choice.

With the treatment of stylistic variation the course will have slid imperceptibly into rhetoric: it will have moved from language to *uses* of the language, from *langue* to *parole*. If this focus is made explicit, the student will be prepared to consider intelligently the differences (partly structural, partly semantic) among the traditional types of written discourse: definition, description, classification, analysis, comparison, narration, and so on. He can also study modes of coherence and order as special uses of language, and then move naturally to the major types of proof. This section of the course is given over to distinctions.

But most of the rhetorical theory I have drawn on insists or implies that such distinctions are secondary, and that the central concerns of rhetoric are the same for description and comparison, narrative and argument, induction and deduction. If so, the heart of the freshman course should be an attempt to confront problems inherent in *all* expository writing. The drift of modern theory, as outlined above, suggests a four-part framework for the consideration of such problems.

1) The relationship between a piece of writing and its content. If content becomes tangible and complete only in the process of writing, the novice should study the ways in which rhetoric modulates meaning. The use of example, the process of generalization, the deployment of value-laden terms, the ethics of precision: these and other similar topics can conveniently be managed at this point in the course.
2) The relationship between a piece of writing and its author. How do his awareness and his attitudes evolve in the course of composition? How are

they reflected in his prose? If the student can come to see his choice of emphatic device, metaphor, tone, economy, and the like as self-defining and self-revealing, that understanding will go some way toward convincing him that rhetoric has consequences he should care about—that verbal form has an importance barely hinted at by the notion of correctness.

3) The relationship between a piece of writing and its audience. The student should also discover that verbal forms carry an appeal to the audience for assent to more than the ideas. The writer asks his reader to share, for the nonce or for good, an attitude, a habit of mind, a set of values, a concept of civility, a way of being human. To see rhetoric as a means of alliance, a search for what Burke calls "identification," is to come at problems of tone, emotional distance, diction, and the like in a mood of high seriousness.

4) World views. Through the three pedagogical steps just outlined, it will scarcely be possible to ignore world views, as modifying content, as implicated in the student's definition of himself, and as shared with an audience. I suggest—and this is my only radical departure from recent tradition—that the freshman course come finally to an explicit discussion of world views. That the world is not conceptually available to all men in the same way, that we organize experience differently, that writing, like all uses of language, reflects one or another mode of experiencing—these ideas are both important and, to a freshman, strange; and they seem to me to infuse the rhetorical theory that has lately been emerging, as well as much of the literary criticism. We can hardly expect to transmute freshmen (or ourselves) into skilled analytic philosophers, but I think we can sketch out to some purpose competing ways of conceptualizing action, mind, the past, cause, space, society, etc. (If this sounds absurdly ambitious, remember that it is no more than we attempt when, for instance, we try to analyze with students the "world" of a novel or a play.) Admittedly, a freshman is not likely to make dramatic advances in composition as a direct result of such a study: the benefits are more remote. The student who understands that world views differ, and that he himself employs one, has prepared himself for the informed encounter with experience that precedes good writing. He becomes a voting citizen of his world, rather than a bound vassal to an inherited ontology.

A required course must earn its slot in the curriculum by demonstrating its general educational worth, not merely its heuristic value within a particular discipline; I think that the course outlined here meets the broader test. But it is worth pointing out that students going on from such rhetorical training to do work in literature would take along some useful equipment. They would possess already a considerable critical vocabulary, the more valuable because evolved through application to their own writing. They would have some formal background in language, and hence a sensitivity to the medium of literature. They would be thoroughly instructed in the concept of the speaker's or narrator's "voice." And they would be prepared, through their work on world views, to apprehend the ordering of experience peculiar to a literary work, to an author, to a genre, or to an historical period. Theories of rhetoric have always been close to theories of literature, and in this matter our century is no exception.

Can a freshman course on this model cope with the inevitable and ordinary deficiencies in writing which our students bring with them each fall? I see no reason to think that the view of rhetoric here proposed is incompatible with the humbler virtues of good writing. If anything, the student who sees rhetoric as implicated with his own identity, with integrity, with community, and with an interpretation of experience should be especially ready to grant the importance of choosing words with care. The trouble with composition courses is less often in the substance of what is taught than in the intellectual framework provided for that substance, and in the motivation offered for mastering it. Though we are not likely to invest rhetoric with magic again, perhaps, by accepting the pedagogical implications of our convictions, we can at least justify to ourselves and our students the privileged place of rhetorical instruction, now as two thousand years ago, in education.

PART II KENNETH BURKE

6 A GRAMMAR OF MOTIVES AND A RHETORIC OF MOTIVES

KENNETH BURKE

Kenneth Burke defines man, in a tentative way, as "the symbol-using (symbol-making, symbol-misusing) animal, inventor of the negative (or moralized by the negative), separated from his natural condition by instruments of his own making, goaded by the spirit of hierarchy (or moved by the sense of order), and rotten with perfection." (See *Language as Symbolic Action*, 3–22.) An understanding of Burke's theory of rhetoric demands a thorough understanding of these key concepts. Other basic concepts in Burke's theory are: identification; consubstantiality; strategy; action versus motion; motive; rhetoric as courtship; the dramatistic process of guilt, mortification, victimage, catharsis, and redemption; and the pentad of act, scene, agent, agency, and purpose.

An examination of Burke's voluminous writings might lead one to define rhetoric as the conscious or unconscious use of verbal or nonverbal symbolic strategies to achieve identification between men. The function of rhetoric, urges Burke, is to induce cooperation and to transcend hierarchy and estrangement in achieving the Good Life.

Brief selections from Burke's writings cannot possibly summarize the essence of his view. The following excerpts can only point the way. The first selection presents Burke's explication of the Dramatistic Pentad. The second series of excerpts presents one of his analyses of the nature of identification, persuasion, and rhetoric. Note, too, that Burke attempts not to renounce the Aristotelian rhetorical heritage but to supplement it.

Source: "The Five Key Terms of Dramatism," from Kenneth Burke, *A Grammar of Motives* (Berkeley and Los Angeles: University of California Press, 1969), xv–xxiii. Excerpts from "The Range of Rhetoric," from Kenneth Burke, *A Rhetoric of Motives* (Berkeley and Los Angeles: University of California Press, 1969), pp. 20–23, 35–46. Reprinted by permission of The Regents of the University of California.

THE FIVE KEY TERMS OF DRAMATISM

What is involved, when we say what people are doing and why they are doing it? An answer to that question is the subject of this book.

The book is concerned with the basic forms of thought which, in accordance with the nature of the world as all men necessarily experience it, are exemplified in the attributing of motives. These forms of thought can be embodied profoundly or trivially, truthfully or falsely. They are equally present in systematically elaborated metaphysical structures, in legal judgments, in poetry and fiction, in political and scientific works, in news and in bits of gossip offered at random.

We shall use five terms as generating principle of our investigation. They are: Act, Scene, Agent, Agency, Purpose. In a rounded statement about motives, you must have some word that names the *act* (names what took place, in thought or deed), and another that names the *scene* (the background of the act, the situation in which it occurred); also, you must indicate what person or kind of person (*agent*) performed the act, what means or instruments he used (*agency*), and the *purpose*. Men may violently disagree about the purposes behind a given act, or about the character of the person who did it, or how he did it, or in what kind of situation he acted; or they may even insist upon totally different words to name the act itself. But be that as it may, any complete statement about motives will offer *some kind* of answers to these five questions: what was done (act), when or where it was done (scene), who did it (agent), how he did it (agency), and why (purpose).

If you ask why, with a whole world of terms to choose from, we select these rather than some others as basic, our book itself is offered as the answer. For, to explain our position, we shall show how it can be applied.

Act, Scene, Agent, Agency, Purpose. Although, over the centuries, men have shown great enterprise and inventiveness in pondering matters of human motivation, one can simplify the subject by this pentad of key terms, which are understandable almost at a glance. They need never to be abandoned, since all statements that assign motives can be shown to arise out of them and to terminate in them. By examining them quizzically, we can range far; yet the terms are always there for us to reclaim, in their everyday simplicity, their almost miraculous easiness, thus enabling us constantly to begin afresh. When they might become difficult, when we can hardly see them, through having stared at them too intensely, we can of a sudden relax, to look at them as we always have, lightly, glancingly. And having reassured ourselves, we can start out again, once more daring to let them look strange and difficult for a time.

In an exhibit of photographic murals (*Road to Victory*) at the Museum of Modern Art, there was an aerial photograph of two launches, proceeding side by side on a tranquil sea. Their wakes crossed and recrossed each other in almost an infinity of lines. Yet despite the intricateness of this tracery, the picture gave an impression of great simplicity, because one could quickly perceive the generating principle of its design. Such, ideally, is the case with our pentad of terms, used as generating principle. It should provide us with a kind of simplicity that can be developed into considerable complexity, and yet can be discovered beneath its elaborations.

We want to inquire into the purely internal relationships which the five terms bear to one another, considering their possibilities of transformation, their range of permutations and combinations—and then to see how these various resources figure in actual statements about human motives. Strictly speaking, we mean by a Grammar of motives a concern with the terms alone, without reference to the ways in which their potentialities have been or can be utilized in actual statements about motives. Speaking broadly we could designate as "philosophies" any statements in which these grammatical resources are specifically utilized. Random or unsystematic statements about motives could be considered as fragments of a philosophy.

One could think of the Grammatical resources as *principles,* and of the various philosophies as *casuistries* which apply these principles to temporal situations. For instance, we may examine the term Scene simply as a blanket term for the concept of background or setting *in general,* a name for *any* situation in which acts or agents are placed. In our usage, this concern would be "grammatical." And we move into matters of "philosophy" when we note that one thinker uses "God" as his term for the ultimate ground or scene of human action, another uses "nature," a third uses "environment," or "history," or "means of production," etc. And whereas a statement about the grammatical principles of motivation might lay claim to a universal validity, or complete certainty, the choice of any one philosophic idiom embodying these principles is much more open to question. Even before we know what act is to be discussed, we can say with confidence that a rounded discussion of its motives must contain a reference to *some kind* of background. But since each philosophic idiom will characterize this background differently, there will remain the question as to which characterization is "right" or "more nearly right."

It is even likely that, whereas one philosophic idiom offers the best calculus for one case, another case answers best to a totally different calculus. However, we should not think of "cases" in too restricted a sense. Although, from the standpoint of the grammatical principles inherent in the internal relationships prevailing among our five terms, any given philosophy is to be considered as a casuistry, even a cultural situation extending over centuries is a "case," and would probably require a much different philosophic idiom as its temporizing calculus of motives than would be required in the case of other cultural situations.

In our original plans for this project, we had no notion of writing a "Grammar" at all. We began with a theory of comedy, applied to a treatise on human relations. Feeling that competitive ambition is a drastically over-developed motive in the modern world, we thought this motive might be transcended if men devoted themselves not so much to "excoriating" it as to "appreciating" it. Accordingly, we began taking notes on the foibles and antics of what we tended to think of as "the Human Barnyard."

We sought to formulate the basic stratagems which people employ, in endless variations, and consciously or unconsciously, for the outwitting or cajoling of one another. Since all these devices had a "you and me" quality about them, being "addressed" to some person or to some advantage, we classed them broadly under the heading of a Rhetoric. There were other notes, concerned with modes of expression and appeal in the fine arts, and with purely psychological or psychoanalytic matters. These we classed under the heading of Symbolic.

We had made still further observations, which we at first strove uneasily to class under one or the other of these two heads, but which we were eventually able to distinguish as the makings of a Grammar. For we found in the course of writing that our project needed a grounding in formal considerations logically prior to both the rhetorical and the psychological. And as we proceeded with this introductory groundwork, it kept extending its claims until it had spun itself from an intended few hundred words into nearly 200,000, of which the present book is revision and abridgement.

Theological, metaphysical, and juridical doctrines offer the best illustration of the concerns we place under the heading of Grammar; the forms and methods of art best illustrate the concerns of Symbolic; and the ideal material to reveal the nature of Rhetoric comprises observations on parliamentary and diplomatic devices, editorial bias, sales methods and incidents of social sparring. However, the three fields overlap considerably. And we shall note, in passing, how the Rhetoric and the Symbolic hover about the edges of our central theme, the Grammar.

A perfectionist might seek to evolve terms free of ambiguity and inconsistency (as with the terministic ideals of symbolic logic and logical positivism). But we have a different purpose in view, one that probably retains traces of its "comic" origin. We take it for granted that, insofar as men cannot themselves create the universe, there must remain something essentially enigmatic about the problem of motives, and that this underlying enigma will manifest itself in inevitable ambiguities and inconsistencies among the terms for motives. Accordingly, what we want is *not terms that avoid ambiguity, but terms that clearly reveal the strategic spots at which ambiguities necessarily arise.*

Occasionally, you will encounter a writer who seems to get great exaltation out of proving, with an air of much relentlessness, that some philosophic term or other has been used to cover a variety of meanings, and who would smash and abolish this idol. As a general rule, when a term is singled out for such harsh treatment, if you look closer you will find that it happens to be associated with some cultural or political trend from which the writer would dissociate himself; hence there is a certain notable ambiguity in this very charge of ambiguity, since he presumably feels purged and strengthened by bringing to bear upon this particular term a kind of attack that could, with as much justice, be brought to bear upon any other term (or "title") in philosophy, including of course the alternative term, or "title," that the writer would swear by. Since no two things or acts or situations are exactly alike, you cannot apply the same term to both of them without thereby introducing a certain margin of ambiguity, an ambiguity as great as the difference between the two subjects that are given the identical title. And all the more may you expect to find ambiguity in terms so "titular" as to become the marks of a philosophic school, or even several philosophic schools. Hence, instead of considering it our task to "dispose of" any ambiguity by merely disclosing the fact that it is an ambiguity, we rather consider it our task to study and clarify the *resources* of ambiguity. For in the course of this work, we shall deal with many kinds of *transformation*—and it is in the areas of ambiguity that transformations take place; in fact, without such areas, transformation would be impossible. Distinctions, we might say, arise out of a great central moltenness, where all is merged. They have been thrown from a liquid center to the surface, where they have congealed. Let one of these crusted distinctions return to its source, and in this alchemic center it may be remade, again becoming molten liquid, and may enter into new combinations, whereat it may be again thrown forth as a new crust, a different distinction. So that A may become non-A. But not merely by a leap from one state to the other. Rather, we must take A back into the ground of its existence, the logical substance that is its causal ancestor, and on to a point where it is consubstantial with non-A; then we may return, this time emerging with non-A instead.

And so with our five terms: certain formal interrelationships prevail among these terms, by reason of their role as attributes of a common ground or substance. Their participation in a common ground makes for transformability. At every point where the field covered by any one of these terms overlaps upon the field covered by any other, there is an alchemic opportunity, whereby we can put one philosophy or doctrine of motivation into the alembic, make the appropriate passes, and take out another. From the central moltenness, where all the elements are fused into one togetherness, there are thrown forth, in separate crusts, such distinctions as those between freedom and necessity, activity and passiveness, coöperation and competition, cause and effect, mechanism and teleology.

Our term, "Agent," for instance, is a general heading that might, in a given case, require further subdivision, as an agent might have his act modified (hence partly motivated) by friends (co-agents) or enemies (counter-agents). Again, under "Agent" one could place any personal properties that are assigned a motivational value, such as "ideas," "the will," "fear," "malice," "intuition," "the creative imagination." A portrait painter may treat the body as a property of the agent (an expression of personality), whereas materialistic medicine would treat it as "scenic," a purely "objective material"; and from another point of view it could be classed as an agency, a means by which one gets reports of the world at large. Machines are obviously instruments (that is, Agencies); yet in their vast accumulation they constitute the industrial scene, with its own peculiar set of motivational properties. War may be treated as an Agency, insofar as it is a means to an end; as a collective Act, subdivisible into many individual acts; as a Purpose, in schemes proclaiming a cult of war. For the man inducted into the army, war is a Scene, a situation that motivates the nature of his training; and in mythologies war is an Agent, or perhaps better a superagent, in the figure of the war god. We may think of voting as an act, and of the voter as an agent; yet votes and voters both are hardly other than a politician's medium or agency; or from another point of view, they are a part of his scene. And insofar as a vote is cast without adequate knowledge of its consequences, one might even question whether it should be classed as an activity at all; one might rather call it passive, or perhaps sheer motion (what the behaviorists would call a Response to a Stimulus).

Or imagine that one were to manipulate the terms, for the imputing of motives, in such a case as this: The hero (agent) with the help of a friend (co-agent) outwits the villain (counter-agent) by using a file (agency) that enables him to break his bonds (act) in order to escape (purpose) from the room where he had been confined (scene). In selecting a casuistry here, we might locate the motive in the agent, as were we to credit his escape to some trait integral to his personality, such as "love of freedom." Or we might stress the motivational force of the scene, since nothing is surer to awaken thoughts of escape in a man than a condition of imprisonment. Or we might note the essential part played by the co-agent, in assisting our hero to escape—and, with such thoughts as our point of departure, we might conclude that the motivations of this act should be reduced to social origins.

Or if one were given to the brand of speculative enterprise exemplified by certain Christian heretics (for instance, those who worshipped Judas as a saint, on the grounds that his betrayal of Christ, in leading to the Crucifixion, so brought about the opportunity for mankind's redemption) one might locate the necessary motivational origin of the act in the *counter-agent*. For the hero would not have been prodded to escape if there had been no villain to imprison him. Inasmuch as the escape could be called a "good" act, we might find in such motivational reduction to the counter-agent a compensatory transformation whereby a bitter fountain may give forth sweet waters. In his *Anti-Dühring* Engels gives us a secular variant which no one could reasonably call outlandish or excessive:

It was slavery that first made possible the division of labour between agriculture and industry on a considerable scale, and along with this, the flower of the ancient world, Hellenism. Without slavery, no Greek state, no Greek art and science; without slavery, no Roman Empire. But without Hellenism and the Roman Empire as a basis, also no modern Europe.

We should never forget that our whole economic, political and intellectual development has as its presupposition a state of things in which slavery was as necessary as it was universally recognized. In this sense we are entitled to say: Without the slavery of antiquity, no modern socialism.

Pragmatists would probably have referred the motivation back to a source in *agency*. They would have noted that our hero escaped by using an *instrument,* the file by which he severed his bonds; then in this same line of thought, they would have observed that the hand holding the file was also an instrument; and by the same token the brain that guided the hand would be an instrument, and so likewise the educational system that taught the methods and shaped the values involved in the incident.

True, if you reduce the terms to any one of them, you will find them branching out again; for no one of them is enough. Thus, Mead called his pragamatism a philosophy of the *act.* And though Dewey stresses the value of "intelligence" as an instrument (agency, embodied in "scientific method"), the other key terms in his casuistry, "experience" and "nature," would be the equivalents of act and scene respectively. We must add, however, that Dewey is given to stressing the *overlap* of these two terms, rather than the respects in which they are distinct, as he proposes to "replace the traditional separation of nature and experience with the idea of continuity." (The quotation is from *Intelligence and the Modern World.*)

As we shall see later, it is by reason of the pliancy among our terms that philosophic systems can pull one way and another. The margins of overlap provide opportunities whereby a thinker can go without a leap from any one of the terms to any of its fellows. (We have also likened the terms to the fingers, which in their extremities are distinct from one another, but merge in the palm of the hand. If you would go from one finger to another without a leap, you need but trace the tendon down into the palm of the hand, and then trace a new course along another tendon.) Hence, no great dialectical enterprise is necessary if you would merge the terms, reducing them even to as few as one; and then, treating this as the "essential" term, the "causal ancestor" of the lot, you can proceed in the reverse direction across the margins of overlap, "deducing" the other terms from it as its logical descendants.

This is the method, explicitly and in the grand style, of metaphysics which brings its doctrines to a head in some over-all title, a word for being in general, or action in general, or motion in general, or development in general, or experience in general, etc., with all its other terms distributed about this titular term in positions leading up to it and away from it. There is also an implicit kind of metaphysics, that often goes by the name of No Metaphysics, and aims at reduction not to an over-all title but to some presumably underlying atomic constituent. Its vulgar variant is to be found in techniques of "unmasking," which would make for progress and emancipation by applying materialistic terms to immaterial subjects (the pattern here being, "X is nothing but Y," where X designates a higher value and Y a lower one, the higher value being thereby reduced to the lower one).

The titular word for our own method is "dramatism," since it invites one to consider the matter of motives in a perspective that, being developed from the analysis of drama, treats language and thought primarily as modes of action. The method is synoptic, though not in the historical sense. A purely historical survey would require no less than a universal history of human culture; for every judgment, exhortation, or admonition, every view of nature or supernatural reality, every intention or expectation involves assumptions about motive, or cause. Our work must be synoptic in a different sense: in the sense that it offers a system of placement, and should enable us, by the systematic manipulation of the terms, to "generate," or "anticipate" the various classes of motivational theory. And a treatment in these terms, we hope to show, reduces the subject synoptically while permitting us to appreciate its scope and complexity.

It is not our purpose to import dialectical and metaphysical concerns into a subject that might otherwise be free of them. On the contrary, we hope to make clear the ways in which dialectical and metaphysical issues *necessarily* figure in the subject of motivation. Our speculations, as we interpret them, should show that the subject of motivation is a philosophic one, not ultimately to be solved in terms of empirical science.

THE RANGE OF RHETORIC

Identification and "Consubstantiality"

A is not identical with his colleague, B. But insofar as their interests are joined, A is *identified* with B. Or he may *identify himself* with B even when their interests are not joined, if he assumes that they are, or is persuaded to believe so.

Here are ambiguities of substance. In being identified with B, A is "substantially one" with a person other than himself. Yet at the same time he remains unique, an individual locus of motives. Thus he is both joined and separate, at once a distinct substance and consubstantial with another.

While consubstantial with its parents, with the "firsts" from which it is derived, the offspring is nonetheless apart from them. In this sense, there is nothing abstruse in the statement that the offspring both is and is not one with its parentage. Similarly, two persons may be identified in terms of some principle they share in common, an "identification" that does not deny their distinctness.

To identify A with B is to make A "consubstantial" with B. Accordingly, since our *Grammar of Motives* was constructed about "substance" as key term, the related rhetoric selects its nearest equivalent in the areas of persuasion and dissuasion, communication and polemic. And our third volume, *Symbolic of Motives*, should be built about *identity* as titular or ancestral term, the "first" to which all other terms could be reduced and from which they could then be derived or generated, as from a common spirit. The thing's *identity* would here be its uniqueness as an entity in itself and by itself, a demarcated unit having its own particular structure.

However, "substance" is an abstruse philosophic term, beset by a long history of quandaries and puzzlements. It names so paradoxical a function in men's systematic terminologies, that thinkers finally tried to abolish it altogether—and in recent years they have often persuaded themselves that they really did abolish it from their terminologies of motives. They abolished the *term,* but it is doubtful whether they can ever abolish the *function* of that term, or even whether they should *want* to. A doctrine of *consubstantiality,* either explicit or implicit, may be necessary to any way of life. For substance, in the old philosophies, was an *act;* and a way of life is an *acting-together;* and in acting together, men have common sensations, concepts, images, ideas, attitudes that make them *consubstantial.*

The *Grammar* dealt with the universal paradoxes of substance. It considered resources of placement and definition common to all thought. The *Symbolic* should deal with unique individuals, each its own peculiarly constructed act, or form. These unique "constitutions" being capable of treatment in isolation, the *Symbolic* should consider them primarily in their capacity as singulars, each a separate universe of discourse (though there are also respects in which they are consubstantial with others of their kind, since they can be classed with other unique individuals as joint participants in common principles, possessors of the same or similar properties).

The *Rhetoric* deals with the possibilities of classification in its *partisan* aspects; it considers the ways in which individuals are at odds with one another, or become identified with groups more or less at odds with one another.

Why "at odds," you may ask, when the titular term is "identification"? Because, to begin with "identification" is, by the same token, though roundabout, to confront the implications of *division*. And so, in the end, men are brought to that most tragically ironic of all divisions, or conflicts, wherein millions of cooperative acts go into the preparation for one single destructive act. We refer to that ultimate *disease* of cooperation: *war*. (You will understand war much better if you think of it, not simply as strife come to a head, but rather as a disease, or perversion of communion. Modern war characteristically requires a myriad of constructive acts for each destructive one; before each culminating blast there must be a vast network of interlocking operations, directed communally.)

Identification is affirmed with earnestness precisely because there is division. Identification is compensatory to division. If men were not apart from one another, there would be no need for the rhetorician to proclaim their unity. If men were wholly and truly of one substance, absolute communication would be of man's very essence. It would not be an ideal, as it now is, partly embodied in material conditions and partly frustrated by these same conditions; rather, it would be as natural, spontaneous, and total as with those ideal prototypes of communication, the theologian's angels, or "messengers."

The *Grammar* was at peace insofar as it contemplated the paradoxes common to all men, the universal resources of verbal placement. The *Symbolic* should be at peace, in that the individual substances, or entities, or constituted acts are there considered in their uniqueness, hence outside the realm of conflict. For individual universes, as such, do not compete. Each merely *is*, being its own self-sufficient realm of discourse. And the *Symbolic* thus considers each thing as a set of interrelated terms all conspiring to round out their identity as participants in a common substance of meaning. An individual does in actuality compete with other individuals. But within the rules of Symbolic, the individual is treated merely as a self-subsistent unit proclaiming its peculiar nature. It is "at peace," in that its terms *cooperate* in modifying one another. But insofar as the individual is involved in conflict with other individuals or groups, the study of this same individual would fall under the head of *Rhetoric*. Or considered rhetorically, the victim of a neurotic conflict is torn by parliamentary wrangling; he is heckled like Hitler within. (Hitler is said to have confronted a constant wrangle in his private deliberations, after having imposed upon his people a flat choice between conformity and silence.) Rhetorically, the neurotic's every attempt to legislate for his own conduct is disorganized by rival factions within his own dissociated self. Yet, considered Symbolically, the same victim is technically "at peace," in the sense that his identity is like a unified, mutually adjusted set of terms. For even antagonistic terms, confronting each other as parry and thrust, can be said to "cooperate" in the building of an over-all form.

The *Rhetoric* must lead us through the Scramble, the Wrangle of the Market Place, the flurries and flare-ups of the Human Barnyard, the Give and Take, the wavering line of pressure and counterpressure, the Logomachy, the onus of ownership, the Wars of Nerves, the War. It too has its peaceful moments: at times its endless competition can add up to the transcending of itself. In ways of its own, it can move from the factional to the universal. But its ideal culminations are more often beset by strife as the condition of their organized expression, or material embodiment. Their very universality becomes transformed into a partisan weapon. For one need not scrutinize the concept of "identification" very sharply to see, implied in it at every turn, its ironic counterpart: division. Rhetoric is concerned with the state of Babel after the Fall. Its contribution to a "sociology of knowledge" must often carry us far into the lugubrious regions of malice and the lie. . . .

Ingenuous and Cunning Identifications

The thought of self-deception brings up another range of possibilities here. For there is a wide range of ways whereby the rhetorical motive, through the resources of identification, can operate without conscious direction by any particular agent. Classical rhetoric stresses the element of explicit design in rhetorical enterprise. But one can systematically extend the range of rhetoric, if one studies the persuasiveness of false or inadequate terms which may not be directly imposed upon us from without by some skillful speaker, but which we impose upon ourselves, in varying degrees of deliberateness and unawareness, through motives indeterminately self-protective and/or suicidal.

We shall consider these matters more fully later, when we study the rhetoric of *hierarchy* (or as it is less revealingly named, *bureaucracy*). And our later pages on Marx and Veblen would apply here. But for the present we might merely recall the psychologist's concept of "malingering," to designate the ways of neurotic persons who, though not actually ill, persuade themselves that they are, and so can claim the attentions and privileges of the ill (their feigned illness itself becoming, at one remove, genuine). Similarly, if a social or occupational class is not too exacting in the scrutiny of identifications that flatter its interests, its very philosophy of life is a profitable malingering (profitable at least until its inaccuracies catch up with it)—and as such, it is open to either attack or analysis, Rhetoric comprising both the *use* of persuasive resources (*rhetorica utens,* as with the philippics of Demosthenes) and the *study* of them (*rhetorica docens,* as with Aristotle's treatise on the "art" of Rhetoric).

This aspect of identification, whereby one can protect an interest merely by using terms not incisive enough to criticize it properly, often brings rhetoric to the edge of cunning. A misanthropic politician who dealt in mankind-loving imagery could still think of himself as rhetorically honest, if he meant to do well by his constituents yet thought that he could get their votes only by such display. Whatever the falsity in overplaying a role, there may be honesty in the assuming of that role itself; and the overplaying may be but a translation into a different medium of communication, a way of amplifying a statement so that it carries better to a large or distant audience. Hence, the persuasive identifications of Rhetoric, in being so directly designed for *use,* involve us in a special problem of *consciousness,* as exemplified in the Rhetorician's particular *purpose* for a given statement.

The thought gives a glimpse into rhetorical motives behind many characters in drama and fiction. Shakespeare's Iago and Molière's Tartuffe are demons of Rhetoric. Every word and act is addressed, being designed to build up false identifications in the minds of their victims. Similarly, there is a notable ingredient of Rhetoric in Stendhal's Julien Sorel, who combines "heightened consciousness" with "freedom" by a perversely frank decision to perfect his own kind of hypocrisy as a means of triumphing over the hypocrisy of others. All his actions thus become rhetorical, framed for their effect; his life is a spellbinding and spellbound address to an audience.

Did you ever do a friend an injury by accident, in all poetic simplicity? Then conceive of this same injury as done by sly design, and you are forthwith within the orbit of Rhetoric. If you, like the Stendhals and Gides, conceive a character by such sophistication, Rhetoric as the speaker's attempt to identify himself favorably with his audience then becomes so transformed that the work may seem to have been written under an esthetic of pure "expression," without regard for communicative appeal. Or it may appeal perversely, to warped motives within the audience. Or it may be but an internalizing of the rhetorical motive, as the very actions of such a representative figure take on a rhetorical cast. Hence, having woven a rhetorical motive so integrally into the very essence of his conception, the writer can seem to have ignored rhetorical considerations; yet, in the sheer effrontery of his protagonist there is embedded, however disguised or transformed, an *anguish* of communication (communication being, as we have said, a generalized form of love).

As regards the rhetorical ways of Stendhal's hero, moving in the perverse freedom of duplicity: After the disclosure of his cunning, Julien abandons his complex rhetorical morality of hypocrisy-to-outhypocritize-the-hypocrites, and regains a new, suicidally poetic level of simplicity. *"Jamais cette tête n'avait été aussi poétique qu'au moment où elle allait tomber."* The whole structure of the book could be explained as the account of a hero who, by the disclosure of his Rhetoric, was jolted into a tragically direct poetic. Within the terms of the novel, "hypocrisy" was the word for "rhetoric," such being the quality of the rhetoric that marked the public life of France under the reign of *Napoléon le Petit.*

Rhetoric of "Address" (to the Individual Soul)

By our arrangement, the individual in his uniqueness falls under the head of Symbolic. But one should not thereby assume that what is known as "individual psychology" wholly meets the same test. Particularly in the Freudian concern with the neuroses of individual patients, there is a strongly rhetorical ingredient. Indeed, what could be more profoundly rhetorical than Freud's notion of a dream that attains expression by stylistic subterfuges designed to evade the inhibitions of a moralistic censor? What is this but the exact analogue of the rhetorical devices of literature under political or theocratic censorship? The *ego* with its *id* confronts the *super-ego* much as an orator would confront a somewhat alien audience, whose susceptibilities he must flatter as a necessary step towards persuasion. The Freudian psyche is quite a parliament, with conflicting interests expressed in ways variously designed to take the claims of rival factions into account.

The best evidence of a strongly rhetorical ingredient in Freud's view of the psyche is in his analysis of *Wit and Its Relation to the Unconscious.* In particular, we think of Freud's concern with the role of an audience, or "third person," with whom the speaker establishes rapport, in their common enterprise directed against the butt of tendentious witticisms. Here is the purest rhetorical pattern: speaker and hearer as partners in partisan jokes made at the expense of another. If you "internalize" such a variety of motives, so that the same person can participate somewhat in all three positions, you get a complex individual of many voices. And though these may be treated, under the heading of Symbolic, as a concerto of principles mutually modifying one another, they may likewise be seen, from the standpoint of Rhetoric, as a parliamentary wrangle which the individual has put together somewhat as he puts together his fears and hopes, friendships and enmities, health and disease, or those tiny rebirths whereby, in being born to some new condition, he may be dying to a past condition, his development being dialectical, a series of terms in perpetual transformation.

Thus by a roundabout route we come upon another aspect of Rhetoric: its nature as *addressed,* since persuasion implies an audience. A man can be his own audience, insofar as he, even in his secret thoughts, cultivates certain ideas or images for the effect he hopes they may have upon him; he is here what Mead would call "an 'I' addressing its 'me' "; and in this respect he is being rhetorical quite as though he were using pleasant imagery to influence an outside audience rather than one within. In traditional Rhetoric, the relation to an external audience is stressed. Aristotle's *Art of Rhetoric,* for instance, deals with the appeal to audiences in this primary sense: It lists typical beliefs, so that the speaker may choose among them the ones with which he would favorably identify his cause or unfavorably identify the cause of an opponent; and it lists the traits of character with which the speaker should seek to identify himself, as a way of disposing an audience favorably towards him. But a modern "post-Christian" rhetoric must also concern itself with the thought that, under the heading of appeal to audiences, would also be included any ideas or images addressed to the individual self for moralistic or incantatory purposes. For you become your own audience, in some respects a very lax one, in some respects very exacting, when you become involved in psychologically stylistic subterfuges for presenting your own case to yourself in sympathetic terms (and even terms that seem harsh can often be found on closer scrutiny to be flattering, as with neurotics who visit sufferings upon themselves in the name of very high-powered motives which, whatever their discomfiture, feed pride).

Such considerations make us alert to the ingredient of rhetoric in all *socialization,* considered as a *moralizing* process. The individual person, striving to form himself in accordance with the communicative norms that match the cooperative ways of his society, is by the same token concerned with the rhetoric of identification. To act upon himself persuasively, he must variously resort to images and ideas that are formative. Education ("indoctrination") exerts such pressure upon him from without; he completes the process from within. If he does not somehow act to tell himself (as his own audience) what the various brands of rhetorician have told him, his persuasion is not complete. Only those voices from without are effective which can speak in the language of a voice within.

Among the Tanala of Madagascar, it is said, most of those tribesmen susceptible to *tromba* ("neurotic seizure indicated by an extreme desire to dance") were found to be among the least favored members of the tribe. Such seizures are said to be a device that makes the possessed person "the center of all the attention." And afterwards, the richest and most powerful members of the sufferer's family foot the bill, so that "the individual's ego is well satisfied and he can get along quite well until the next tromba seizure occurs." In sum, "like most hysterical seizures, tromba requires an audience."

The citations are from A. Kardiner, *The Individual and His Society* (New York: Columbia University Press). They would suggest that, when asking what all would fall within the scope of our topic, we could also include a "rhetoric of hysteria." For here too are expressions which are *addressed*—and we confront an ultimate irony, in glimpsing how even a catatonic lapse into sheer automatism, beyond the reach of all normally linguistic communication, is in its origins communicative, addressed, though it be a paralogical appeal-that-ends-all appeals.

Rhetoric and Primitive Magic

The Kardiner citations are taken from a paper by C. Kluckhohn on "Navaho Witchcraft," containing observations that would also bring witchcraft within the range of rhetoric. Indeed, where witchcraft is imputed as a motive behind the individual search for wealth, power, or vengeance, can we not view it as a primitive vocabulary of *individualism* emerging in a culture where *tribal* thinking had been uppermost, so that the individualist motive would be admitted and suspect? And any breach of identification with the tribal norms being sinister, do we not glimpse rhetorical motives behind the fact that Macbeth's private ambitions were figured in terms of witches?

At first glance we may seem to be straining the conception of rhetoric to the breaking point, when including even a treatise on primitive witchcraft within its range. But look again. Precisely at a time when the *term* "rhetoric" had fallen into greatest neglect and disrepute, writers in the "social sciences" were under many guises, making good contributions to the New Rhetoric. As usual with modern thought, the insights gained from *comparative culture* could throw light upon the classic approach to this subject; and again, as usual with modern thought, this light was interpreted in terms that concealed its true relation to earlier work. And though the present writer was strongly influenced by anthropological inquiries into primitive magic, he did not clearly discern the exact relation between the anthropologist's concern with magic and the literary critic's concern with communication until he had systematically worked on this *Rhetoric* for some years. Prior to this discovery, though he persisted in anthropological hankerings, he did so with a bad conscience; and he was half willing to agree with literary opponents who considered such concerns alien to the study of literature proper.

Now, in noting methodically how the anthropologist's account of magic can belong in a rhetoric, we are better equipped to see exactly wherein the two fields of inquiry diverge. Anthropology is a gain to literary criticism only if one knows how to "discount" it from the standpoint of rhetoric. And, ironically, anthropology can be a source of disturbance, not only to literary criticism in particular, but to the study of human relations in general, if one does not so discount it, but allows *its* terms to creep into one's thinking at points where issues *should* be studied explicitly in terms of rhetoric.

We saw both the respects in which the anthropologists' study of magic overlaps upon rhetoric and the respects in which they are distinct when we were working on a review of Ernst Cassirer's *Myth of the State*. The general proposition that exercised us can be stated as follows:

We must begin by confronting the typically scientist view of the relation between science and magic. Since so many apologists of modern science, following a dialectic of simple antithesis, have looked upon magic merely as an early form of bad science, one seems to be left only with a distinction between bad science and good science. Scientific knowledge is thus presented as a terminology that gives an accurate and critically tested description of reality; and magic is presented as antithetical to such science. Hence magic is treated as an early uncritical attempt to do what science does, but under conditions where judgment and perception were impaired by the naïvely anthropomorphic belief that the impersonal forces of nature were motivated by personal designs. One thus confronts a flat choice between a civilized vocabulary of scientific description and a savage vocabulary of magical incantation.

In this scheme, "rhetoric" has no systematic location. We recall noting the word but once in Cassirer's *Myth of the State,* and then it is used only in a random way; yet the book is really about nothing more nor less than a most characteristic concern of rhetoric: the manipulation of men's beliefs for political ends.

Now, the basic function of rhetoric, the use of words by human agents to form attitudes or to induce actions in other human agents, is certainly not "magical." If you are in trouble, and call for help, you are no practitioner of primitive magic. You are using the primary resource of human speech in a thoroughly realistic way. Nor, on the other hand, is your utterance "science," in the strict meaning of science today, as a "semantic" or "descriptive" terminology for charting the conditions of nature from an "impersonal" point of view, regardless of one's wishes or preferences. A call for help is quite "prejudiced"; it is the most arrant kind of "wishful thinking"; it is not merely descriptive, it is *hortatory*. It is not just trying to tell how things are, in strictly "scenic" terms; it is trying to *move people*. A call for help might, of course, include purely scientific statements, or preparations for action, as a person in need might give information about particular dangers to guard against or advantages to exploit in bringing help. But the call, in itself, as such, is not scientific; it is *rhetorical*. Whereas poetic language is a kind of symbolic action, for itself and in itself, and whereas scientific action is a preparation for action, rhetorical language is inducement to action (or to attitude, attitude being an incipient act).

If you have only a choice between magic and science, you simply have no bin in which to accurately place such a form of expression. Hence, since "the future" is not the sort of thing one can put under a microscope, or even test by a knowledge of *exactly equivalent conditions* in the past, when you turn to political exhortation, you are involved in decisions that necessarily lie beyond the strictly scientific vocabularies of description. And since the effective politician is a "spellbinder," it seems to follow by elimination that the hortatory use of speech for political ends can be called "magic," in the discredited sense of that term.

As a result, much analysis of political exhortation comes to look simply like a survival of primitive magic, whereas it should be handled in its own terms, as an aspect of what it really is: rhetoric. The approach to rhetoric in terms of "word magic" gets the whole subject turned backwards. Originally, the magical use of symbolism to affect natural processes by rituals and incantations was a mistaken transference of a proper linguistic function to an area for which it was not fit. The realistic use of addressed language to *induce action in people* became the magical use of addressed language to *induce motion in things* (things by nature alien to purely linguistic orders of motivation). If we then begin by treating this *erroneous* and *derived* magical use as *primary*, we are invited to treat a *proper* use of language (for instance, political persuasion) simply as a vestige of benightedly prescientific magic.

To be sure, the rhetorician has the tricks of his trade. But they are not mere "bad science"; they are an "art." And any overly scientist approach to them (treating them in terms of flat dialectical opposition to modern technology) must make our world look much more "neo-primitive" than is really the case. At the very least, we should note that primitive magic prevailed most strongly under social conditions where the rationalization of social effort in terms of money was negligible; but the rhetoric of modern politics would establish social identifications atop a way of life highly diversified by money, with the extreme division of labor and status which money served to rationalize.

Realistic Function of Rhetoric

Gaining courage as we proceed, we might even contend that we are not so much proposing to import anthropology into rhetoric as proposing that anthropologists recognize the factor of rhetoric in their own field. That is, if you look at recent studies of primitive magic from the standpoint of this discussion, you might rather want to distinguish between magic as "bad science" and magic as "primitive rhetoric." You then discover that anthropology does clearly recognize the rhetorical *function* in magic; and far from dismissing the rhetorical aspect of magic merely as bad science, anthropology recognizes in it a pragmatic device that greatly assisted the survival of cultures by promoting social cohesion. (Malinowski did much work along these lines, and the Kluckhohn essay makes similar observations about witchcraft.) But now that we have confronted the term "magic" with the term "rhetoric," we'd say that one comes closer to the true state of affairs if one treats the socializing aspects of magic as a "primitive rhetoric" that if one sees modern rhetoric simply as a "survival of primitive magic."

For rhetoric as such is not rooted in any past condition of human society. It is rooted in an essential function of language itself, a function that is wholly realistic, and is continually born anew; the use of language as a symbolic means of inducing cooperation in beings that by nature respond to symbols. Though rhetorical considerations may carry us far afield, leading us to violate the principle of autonomy separating the various disciplines, there is intrinsically rhetorical motive, situated in the persuasive use of language. And this persuasive use of language is not derived from "bad science," or "magic." On the contrary, "magic" was a faulty derivation from it, "word magic" being an attempt to produce linguistic responses in kinds of beings not accessible to the linguistic motive. However, once you introduce this emendation, you can see beyond the accidents of language. You can recognize how much of value has been contributed to the New Rhetoric by these investigators, though their observations are made in terms that never explicitly confront the rhetorical ingredient in their field of study. We can place in terms of rhetoric all those statements by anthropologists, ethnologists, individual and social psychologists, and the like, that bear upon the *persuasive* aspects of language, the function of language as *addressed*, as direct or roundabout appeal to real or ideal audiences, without or within.

Are we but haggling over a term? In one sense, yes. We are offering a rationale intended to show how far one might systematically extend the term "rhetoric." In this respect, we are haggling over a term; for we must persist in tracking down the *function* of that term. But to note the ingredient of rhetoric lurking in such anthropologist's terms as "magic" and "witchcraft" is not to ask that the anthropologist replace his words with ours. We are certainly not haggling over terms in that sense. The term "rhetoric" is no substitute for "magic," "witchcraft," "socialization," "communication," and so on. But the term rhetoric designates a *function* which is present in the areas variously covered by those other terms. And we are asking only that this *function* be recognized for what it is: a linguistic function by nature as *realistic* as a proverb, though it may be quite far from the kind of realism found in strictly "scientific realism." For it is essentially a realism of the *act:* moral, persuasive—and acts are not "true" and "false" in the sense that the propositions of "scientific realism" are. And however "false" the "propositions" of primitive magic may be, considered from the standpoint of scientific realism, it is different with the peculiarly rhetorical ingredient in magic, involving ways of identification that contribute variously to social cohesion (either for the advantage of the community as a whole, or for the advantage of special groups whose interests are a burden on the community, or for the advantage of special groups whose rights and duties are indeterminately both a benefit and a tax on the community, as with some business enterprise in our society).

The "pragmatic sanction" for this function of magic lies outside the realm of strictly true-or-false propositions; it falls in an area of deliberation that itself draws upon the resources of rhetoric; it is itself a subject matter belonging to an art that can "prove opposites."

To illustrate what we mean by "proving opposites" here: we read an article, let us say, obviously designed to dispose the reading public favorably towards the "aggressive and expanding" development of American commercial interests in Saudi Arabia. It speaks admiringly of tremendous changes which our policies of commerce and investment will introduce into a vestigially feudal culture, and of the great speed at which the rationale of finance and technology will accomplish these changes. When considering the obvious rhetorical intent of these "facts," we suddenly, in a perverse *non sequitur,* remember a passage in the Kluckhohn essay, involving what we would now venture to call "the rhetoric of witchcraft":

In a society like the Navaho which is competitive and capitalistic, on the one hand, and still familistic on the other, any ideology which has the effect of slowing down economic mobility is decidedly adaptive. One of the most basic strains in Navaho society arises out of the incompatibility between the demands of familism and the emulation of European patterns in the accumulating of capital.

And in conclusion we are told that the "survival of the society" is assisted by "any pattern, such as witchcraft, which tends to discourage the rapid accumulation of wealth" (witchcraft, as an "ideology," contributing to this end by identifying new wealth with malign witchery).

Now, when you begin talking about the optimum rate of speed at which cultural changes should take place, or the optimum proportion between tribal and individualistic motives that should prevail under a particular set of economic conditions, you are talking about something very important indeed, but you will find yourself deep in matters of rhetoric: for nothing is more rhetorical in nature than a deliberation as to what is too much or too little, too early or too late; in such controversies, rhetoricians are forever "proving opposites."

Where are we now? We have considered two main aspects of rhetoric: its use of *identification* and its nature as *addressed*. Since identification implies division, we found rhetoric involving us in matters of socialization and faction. Here was a wavering line between peace and conflict, since identification is got by property, which is ambivalently a motive of both morality and strife. And inasmuch as the ultimate of conflict is war or murder, we considered how such imagery can figure as a terminology of reidentification ("transformation" or "rebirth"). For in considering the wavering line between identification and division, we shall always be coming upon manifestations of the logomachy, avowed as in invective, unavowed as in stylistic subterfuges for presenting real divisions in terms that deny division.

We found that this wavering line between identification and division was forever bringing rhetoric against the possibility of malice and the lie; for if an identification favorable to the speaker or his cause is made to seem favorable to the audience, there enters the possibility of such "heightened consciousness" as goes with deliberate cunning. Thus, roundabout, we confronted the nature of rhetoric as *addressed* to audiences of the first, second, or third person. Socialization itself was, in the widest sense, found to be addressed. And by reason of such simultaneous identification-with and division-from as mark the choice of a scapegoat, we found that rhetoric involves us in problems related to witchcraft, magic, spellbinding, ethical promptings, and the like. And in the course of discussing these subjects, we found ourselves running into another term: persuasion. Rhetoric is the art of persuasion, or a study of the means of persuasion available for any given situation. We have thus, deviously, come to the point at which Aristotle begins his treatise on rhetoric.

So we shall change our purpose somewhat. Up to now, we have been trying to indicate what kinds of subject matter not traditionally labeled "rhetoric" should, in our opinion, also fall under this head. We would now consider varying views of rhetoric that have already prevailed; and we would try to "generate" them from the same basic terms of our discussion.

As for the relation between "identification" and "persuasion": we might well keep it in mind that a speaker persuades an audience by the use of stylistic identifications; his act of persuasion may be for the purpose of causing the audience to identify itself with the speaker's interests; and the speaker draws on identification of interests to establish rapport between himself and his audience. So, there is no chance of our keeping apart the meanings of persuasion, identification ("consubstantiality") and communication (the nature of rhetoric as "addressed"). But, in given instances, one or another of these elements may serve best for extending a line of analysis in some particular direction.

And finally: The use of symbols, by one symbol-using entity to induce action in another (persuasion properly addressed) is in essence not magical but *realistic*. However, the resources of identification whereby a sense of consubstantiality is symbolically established between beings of unequal status may extend far into the realm of the *idealistic*. And as we shall see later, when on the subject of order, out of this idealistic element there may arise a kind of magic or mystery that sets its mark upon all human relations.

7 KENNETH BURKE AND THE "NEW RHETORIC"

MARIE HOCHMUTH NICHOLS

Burke offers both a theory of rhetoric and a philosophy of rhetoric. He examines both the functioning of rhetorical techniques and the fundamental assumptions of his rhetorical view. As a philosopher of rhetoric, he expounds a metaphysical interpretation of "consubstantiality," attempts definition of the essence of rhetoric, probes the nature of language as "symbolic action," advocates a particular societal role for rhetoric, and presents a rhetorical view of man's basic nature as the "symbol-using animal."

Burke is open in identifying some of his sources of inspiration. Drawing upon the insights of I. A. Richards, he considers "attitude" as incipient action or as a substitute for action. (See *Grammar of Motives*, 235–236, 476.) And Burke notes the Aristotelian sources of his Dramatistic Pentad: act, scene, agent, agency, purpose. (See *Grammar*, 227–231; Aristotle, *Nichomachean Ethics*, Bk. III, Chap 1, 1111a.)

Since its publication in 1952 this essay by Nichols has remained a benchmark interpretation of Burke's rhetorical system. (See William H. Rueckert, ed., *Critical Responses to Kenneth Burke*, 286–287.) You may wish to compart Nichols' analysis with that of Daniel Fogarty. (See Fogarty, *Roots for a New Rhetoric*, Chap. 3.)

A basic guide to understanding Burke is William Rueckert, *Kenneth Burke and the Drama of Human Relations*. For an excellent explication of the potential "ratios" of the Pentadic terms see Hugh D. Duncan, *Communication and Social Order*, 431–438.

Source: *Quarterly Journal of Speech*, XXXVIII (April 1952), 133–144. Reprinted with permission of the author and the publisher.

"We do not flatter ourselves that any one book can contribute much to counteract the torrents of ill will into which so many of our contemporaries have so avidly and sanctimoniously plunged," observes Kenneth Burke in introducing his latest book, *A Rhetoric of Motives*, but "the more strident our journalists, politicians, and alas! even many of our churchmen become, the more convinced we are that books should be written for tolerance and contemplation."[1] Burke has offered all his writings to these ends.

Burke's first work, *Counter-Statement,* published in 1931, was hailed as a work of "revolutionary importance," presenting "in essence, a new view of rhetoric."[2] Since that time, he has written a succession of books either centrally or peripherally concerned with rhetoric: *Permanence and Change,* 1935; *Attitudes toward History,* 1937; *The Philosophy of Literary Form,* 1941; *A Grammar of Motives,* 1945; and his latest, *A Rhetoric of Motives,* 1950. An unfinished work entitled *A Symbolic of Motives* further indicates his concern with the problem of language.

Sometimes thought to be "one of the few truly speculative thinkers of our time,"[3] and "unquestionably the most brilliant and suggestive critic now writing in America,"[4] Burke deserves to be related to the great tradition of rhetoric.

Although we propose to examine particularly *A Rhetoric of Motives* we shall range freely over all his works in order to discover his principles. We propose to find first the point of departure and orientation from which he approaches rhetoric; next to examine his general concept of rhetoric; then to seek his method for the analysis of motivation; and finally, to discover his application of principles to specific literary works.

In 1931, in *Counter-Statement,* Burke noted, "The reader of modern prose is ever on guard against 'rhetoric,' yet the word, by lexicographer's definition, refers but to 'the use of language in such a way as to produce a desired impression upon the reader or hearer.' "[5] Hence, accepting the lexicographer's definition, he concluded that "effective literature could be nothing else but rhetoric."[6] In truth, "Eloquence is simply the end of art, and is thus its essence."[7]

As a literary critic, representing a minority view, Burke has persisted in his concern with rhetoric, believing that "rhetorical analysis throws light on literary texts and human relations generally."[8] Although Burke is primarily concerned with literature "as art,"[9] he gives no narrow

---

[1] Kenneth Burke, *A Rhetoric of Motives* (New York: Prentice-Hall, Inc., 1950), p. xv. Reprinted by permission.

[2] Isidor Schneider, "A New View of Rhetoric," *New York Herald Tribune Books,* VIII (December 13, 1931), 4.

[3] Malcolm Cowley, "Prolegomena to Kenneth Burke," *The New Republic,* CXXI (June 5, 1950), 18, 19.

[4] W. H. Auden, "A Grammar of Assent," *The New Republic,* CV (July 14, 1941), 59.

[5] *Counter-Statement* (New York, 1931), p. 265.

[6] *Ibid.,* p. 265.

[7] *Ibid.,* p. 53.

[8] *A Rhetoric of Motives,* pp. xiv, xv.

[9] *Counter-Statement,* p. 156.

interpretation to the conception of literature. He means simply works "designed for the express purpose of arousing emotions,"[10] going so far as to say, "But sometimes literature so designed fails to arouse emotions—and words said purely by way of explanation may have an unintended emotional effect of considerable magnitude."[11] Thus a discussion of "effectiveness" in literature "should be able to include unintended effects as well as intended ones."[12] "By literature we mean written or spoken words."[13]

As has been observed, the breadth of Burke's concepts results "in a similar embracing of trash of every description. . . . For purposes of analysis or illustration Burke draws as readily on a popular movie, a radio quiz program, a *Herald Tribune* news item about the National Association of Manufacturers, or a Carter Glass speech on gold as on Sophocles or Shakespeare. Those things are a kind of poetry too, full of symbolic and rhetorical ingredients, and if they are bad poetry, it is a bad poetry of vital significance in our lives."[14]

Sometimes calling himself a pragmatist, sometimes a sociological critic, Burke believes that literature is designed to "do something"[15] for the writer and the reader or hearer. "Art is a means of communication. As such it is certainly designed to elicit a 'response' of some sort."[16] The most relevant observations are to be made about literature when it is considered as the embodiment of an "act,"[17] or as "symbolic action."[18] Words must be thought of as "acts upon a scene,"[19] and a "symbolic act" is the "*dancing of an attitude*,"[20] or incipient action. Critical and imaginative works are "answers to questions posed by the situation in which they arose." Not merely "answers," they are "*strategic* answers," or "*stylized* answers."[21] Hence, a literary work is essentially a "*strategy for encompassing a situation*."[22] And, as Burke observes, another name for strategies might be "*attitudes*."[23] The United States Constitution, e.g., must be thought of as the "*answer*" or "*rejoinder*" to "assertions current in the situation in which it arose."[24]

Although Burke distinguishes between literature "for the express

[10] *Ibid.*
[11] *Ibid.*
[12] *Ibid.*
[13] *Ibid.*
[14] Stanley Edgar Hyman, *The Armed Vision* (New York, 1948), pp. 386, 387.
[15] *The Philosophy of Literary Form* (Louisiana, 1941), p. 89.
[16] *Ibid.*, pp. 235, 236.
[17] *Ibid.*, p. 89.
[18] *Ibid.*, p. 8.
[19] *Ibid.*, p. vii.
[20] *Ibid.*, p. 9.
[21] *Ibid.*, p. 1.
[22] *Ibid.*, p. 109.
[23] *Ibid.*, p. 297.
[24] *Ibid.*, p. 109.

purpose of arousing emotions" and "literature for use," the distinction is flexible enough to permit him to see even in such a poem as Milton's *Samson Agonistes*, "moralistic prophecy" and thus to class it as "also a kind of 'literature for use,' use at one remove. . . ."[25]

In further support of his comprehensive notion of art is his conception that since "pure art makes for acceptance," it tends to "become a social menace in so far as it assists us in tolerating the intolerable."[26] Therefore, "under conditions of competive capitalism there must necessarily be a large *corrective* or *propaganda* element in art."[27] Art must have a "hortatory function, an element of suasion or inducement of the educational variety; it must be partially *forensic*."[28]

Burke thus approaches the subject of rhetoric through a comprehensive view of art in general. And it is this indirect approach that enables him to present what he believes to be a "New Rhetoric."[29] In part, he has as his object only to "rediscover rhetorical elements that had become obscured when rhetoric as a term fell into disuse, and other specialized disciplines such as esthetics, anthropology, psychoanalysis, and sociology came to the fore (so that esthetics sought to outlaw rhetoric, while the other sciences . . . took over, each in its own terms, the rich rhetorical elements that esthetics would ban).[30]

II

Sometimes thought to be "intuitive" and "idiosyncratic" [31] in his general theories, Burke might be expected to be so in his theory of rhetoric. "Strongly influenced by anthropological inquiries,"[32] and finding Freud "suggestive almost to the point of bewilderment,"[33] Burke, essentially a classicist in his theory of rhetoric, has given the subject its most searching analysis in modern times.

According to Burke, "Rhetoric [comprises] both the *use* of persuasive resources (*rhetorica utens,* as with the philippics of Demosthenes) and the *study* of them (*rhetorica docens,* as with Aristotle's treatise on the 'art' of Rhetoric)."[34] The "basic function of rhetoric" is the "use of words by human agents to form attitudes or to induce actions in other human agents. . . ."[35] It is *"rooted in an essential function of language itself, a*

---

25 *A Rhetoric of Motives,* p. 5.
26 *The Philosophy of Literary Form,* p. 321.
27 *Ibid.*
28 *Ibid.*
29 *A Rhetoric of Motives,* p. 40.
30 *Ibid.,* pp. xiii, 40.
31 *The Philosophy of Literary Form,* p. 68.
32 *A Rhetoric of Motives,* p. 40.
33 *The Philosophy of Literary Form,* p. 258.
34 *A Rhetoric of Motives,* p. 36.
35 *Ibid.,* p. 41.

function that is wholly realistic, and is continually born anew; the use of language as a symbolic means of inducing cooperation in beings that by nature respond to symbols."[36] The basis of rhetoric lies in "generic divisiveness which, being common to all men, is a universal fact about them, prior to any divisiveness caused by social classes." "Out of this emerge the motives for linguistic persuasion. Then, *secondarily,* we get the motives peculiar to particular economic situations. In parturition begins the centrality of the nervous system. The different nervous systems, through language and the ways of production, erect various communities of interests and insights, social communities varying in nature and scope. And out of the division and the community arises the 'universal' rhetorical situation."[37]

Burke devotes 131 pages to a discussion of traditional principles of rhetoric, reviewing Aristotle, Cicero, Quintilian, St. Augustine, the Mediaevalists, and such more recent writers as De Quincey, De Gourmont, Bentham, Marx, Veblen, Freud, Mannheim, Mead, Richards, and others,[38] noting the "wide range of meanings already associated with rhetoric, in ancient texts. . . ."[39] Thus he comes upon the concept of rhetoric as "persuasion"; the nature of rhetoric as "addressed" to an audience for a particular purpose; rhetoric as the art of "proving opposites"; rhetoric as an "appeal to emotions and prejudices"; rhetoric as "agonistic"; as an art of gaining "advantage"; rhetoric as "demonstration"; rhetoric as the verbal "counterpart" of dialectic; rhetoric, in the Stoic usage, as opposed to dialectic; rhetoric in the Marxist sense of persuasion "grounded in dialectic." Whereas he finds that these meanings are "often not consistent with one another, or even flatly at odds,"[40] he believes that they can all be derived from "persuasion" as the "Edenic" term, from which they have all "Babylonically" split, while persuasion, in turn "involves communication by the signs of consubstantiality, the appeal of *identification.*"[41] As the "simplest case of persuasion," he notes that "You persuade a man only insofar as you can talk his language by speech, gesture, tonality, order, image, attitude, idea, *identifying* your ways with his."[42]

In using *identification* as his key term, Burke notes, "Traditionally, the key term for rhetoric is not 'identification,' but 'persuasion.' . . . Our treatment, in terms of identification, is decidedly not meant as a substitute for the sound traditional approach. Rather, . . . it is but an accessory to the standard lore."[43] He had noted that "when we come upon

---

[36] *Ibid.,* p. 43.
[37] *Ibid.,* p. 146.
[38] *Ibid.,* pp. 49–180.
[39] *Ibid.,* p. 61.
[40] *Ibid.,* pp. 61, 62.
[41] *Ibid.,* p. 62.
[42] *Ibid.,* p. 55.
[43] *Ibid.,* p. xiv.

such aspects of persuasion as are found in 'mystification,' courtship, and the 'magic' of class relationships, the reader will see why the classical notion of clear persuasive intent is not an accurate fit, for describing the ways in which the members of a group promote social cohesion by acting rhetorically upon themselves and one another."[44] Burke is completely aware that he is not introducing a totally new concept, observing that Aristotle had long ago commented, "It is not hard . . . to praise Athenians among Athenians,"[45] and that one persuades by "identifying" one's ways with those of his audience.[46] In an observation of W. C. Blum, Burke found additional support for his emphasis on *identification* as a key concept. "In identification lies the source of dedications and enslavements, in fact of cooperation."[47] As for the precise relationship between identification and persuasion as ends of rhetoric, Burke concludes, "we might well keep it in mind that a speaker persuades an audience by the use of stylistic identifications; his act of persuasion may be for the purpose of causing the audience to identify itself with the speaker's interests; and the speaker draws on identification of interests to establish rapport between himself and his audience. So, there is no chance of our keeping apart the meanings of persuasion, identification ("consubstantiality") and communication (the nature of rhetoric as 'addressed'). But, in given instances, one or another of these elements may serve best for extending a line of analysis in some particular direction."[48] "All told, persuasion ranges from the bluntest quest of advantage, as in sales promotion or propaganda, through courtship, social etiquette, education, and the sermon, to a 'pure' form that delights in the process of appeal for itself alone, without ulterior purpose. And identification ranges from the politician who, addressing an audience of farmers, says, 'I was a farm boy myself,' through the mysteries of social status, to the mystic's devout identification with the source of all being."[49] The difference between the "old" rhetoric and the "new" rhetoric may be summed up in this manner: whereas the key term for the "old" rhetoric was *persuasion* and its stress was upon deliberate design, the key term for the "new" rhetoric is *identification* and this may include partially "unconscious" factors in its appeal. Identification, at its simplest level, may be a deliberate device, or a means, as when a speaker identifies his interests with those of his audience. But *identification* can also be an "end," as "when people earnestly yearn to identify themselves with some group or other." They are thus not necessarily acted upon by a conscious exter-

44 *Ibid.*
45 *Ibid.*, p. 55.
46 *Ibid.*
47 *Ibid.*, p. xiv.
48 *Ibid.*, p. 46.
49 *Ibid.*, p. xiv.

nal agent, but may act upon themselves to this end. Identification "includes the realm of transcendence."[50]

Burke affirms the significance of *identification* as a key concept because men are at odds with one another, or because there is "division." "Identification is compensatory to division. If men were not apart from one another, there would be no need for the rhetorician to proclaim their unity. If men were wholly and truly of one substance, absolute communication would be of man's very essence."[51] "In pure identification there would be no strife. Likewise, there would be no strife in absolute separateness, since opponents can join battle only through a mediatory ground that makes their communication possible, thus providing the first condition necessary for their interchange of blows. But put identification and division ambiguously together . . . and you have the characteristic invitation to rhetoric. Here is a major reason why rhetoric, according to Aristotle, 'proves opposites.' "[52]

As a philosopher and metaphysician Burke is impelled to give a philosophic treatment to the concept of unity or identity by an analysis of the nature of *substance* in general. In this respect he makes his most basic contribution to a philosophy of rhetoric. "Metaphysically, a thing is identified by its *properties*,"[53] he observes. "To call a man a friend or brother is to proclaim him consubstantial with oneself, one's values or purposes. To call a man a bastard is to attack him by attacking his whole line, his 'authorship,' his 'principle' or 'motive' (as expressed in terms of the familial). An epithet assigns substance doubly, for in stating the character of the object it . . . contains an implicit program of action with regard to the object, thus serving as motive."[54]

According to Burke, language of all things "is most public, most collective, in its substance."[55] Aware that modern thinkers have been skeptical about the utility of a doctrine of substance,[56] he nevertheless recalls that "substance, in the old philosophies, was an *act;* and a way of life is an *acting-together;* and in acting together, men have common sensations, concepts, images, ideas, attitudes that make them *consubstantial*."[57] "A doctrine of *consubstantiality* . . . may be necessary

[50] Kenneth Burke, "Rhetoric—Old and New," *The Journal of General Education*, V (April 1951), 203.
[51] *A Rhetoric of Motives*, p. 22.
[52] *Ibid.*, p. 25.
[53] *Ibid.*, p. 23.
[54] *A Grammar of Motives* (New York, 1945), p. 57. For discussion of *substance* as a concept, see, *Ibid.*, pp. 21–58; Aristotle, *Categoriae*, tr. by E. M. Edghill, *The Works of Aristotle*, ed. by W. D. Ross, I, Ch. 5; Aristotle, *Metaphysics*, tr. by W. D. Ross, Book Δ, 8, 1017b, 10; Spinoza, *The Ethics*, in *The Chief Works of Benedict De Spinoza*, tr. by R. H. M. Elwes (London 1901), Rev. ed., II, 45 ff; John Locke, *An Essay Concerning Human Understanding* (London 1760), 15th ed., I, Bk. II, Chs. XXIII, XXIV.
[55] *The Philosophy of Literary Form*, p. 44
[56] *A Rhetoric of Motives*, p. 21.
[57] *Ibid.*

to any way of life."[58] Like Kant, Burke regards substance as a "necessary form of the mind." Instead of trying to exclude a doctrine of substance, he restores it to a central position and throws critical light upon it.

In so far as rhetoric is concerned, the "ambiguity of substance" affords a major resource. "What handier linguistic resource could a rhetorician want than an ambiguity whereby he can say 'The state of affairs is substantially such-and-such,' instead of having to say 'The state of affairs *is* and/or *is not* such-and-such"?[59]

The "commonplaces" or "topics" of Aristotle's *Rhetoric* are a "quick survey of opinion" of "things that people generally consider persuasive." As such, they are means of proclaiming *substantial* unity with an audience and are clearly instances of identification.[60] In truth, *identification* is "hardly other than a name for the function of sociality."[61] Likewise, the many tropes and figures, and rhetorical form in the large as treated by the ancients are to be considered as modes of identification.[62] They are the "signs" by which the speaker identifies himself with the reader or hearer. "In its simplest manifestation, style is ingratiation."[63] It is an attempt to "gain favor by the hypnotic or suggestive process of 'saying the right thing.' "[64] Burke discusses form in general as "the psychology of the *audience*,"[65] the "arousing and fulfillment of desires."[66] The exordium of a Greek oration is an instance of "conventional"[67] form, a form which is expected by the audience and therefore satisfies it. Other recognizable types of form are "syllogistic progression," "repetitive" form, and "minor or incidental" forms which include such devices as the metaphor, apostrophe, series, reversal, etc.[68] The proliferation and the variety of formal devices make a work eloquent.[69]

Reviewing *A Rhetoric of Motives,* Thomas W. Copeland observed, "It gradually appears that there is no form of action of men upon each other (or of individuals on themselves) which is really outside of rhetoric. But if so, we should certainly ask whether rhetoric *as a term* has any defining value."[70] The observation is probably not fair, for Burke does give rhetoric a defining value in terms of persuasion, identifica-

[58] *Ibid.*
[59] *A Grammar of Motives,* pp. 51, 52.
[60] *A Rhetoric of Motives,* pp. 56, 57.
[61] *Attitudes toward History* (New York, 1937), II. 144.
[62] *A Rhetoric of Motives,* p. 59.
[63] *Permanence and Change* (New York, 1935), p. 71.
[64] *Ibid.*
[65] *Counter-Statement,* pp. 38–57.
[66] *Ibid.,* p. 157.
[67] *Ibid.,* p. 159.
[68] *Ibid.,* pp. 157–161.
[69] *Ibid.,* pp. 209–211.
[70] Thomas W. Copeland, "Critics at Work," *The Yale Review,* XL (Autumn 1950), 167–169.

tion, and address or communication to an audience of some sort, despite his observation, "Wherever there is persuasion, there is rhetoric. And wherever there is 'meaning' there is 'persuasion.' "[71]

It is true that in his effort to show "how a rhetorical motive is often present where it is not usually recognized, or thought to belong,"[72] Burke either points out linkages which have not been commonly stressed, or widens the scope of rhetoric. A twentieth-century orientation in social-psychological theory thus enables him to note that we may with "more accuracy speak of persuasion 'to attitude,' rather than persuasion to out-and-out action." For persuasion "involves choice, will; it is directed to a man only insofar as he is *free*." In so far as men "*must* do something, rhetoric is unnecessary, its work being done by the nature of things, though often these necessities are not of natural origin, but come from necessities imposed by man-made conditions,"[73] such as dictatorships or near-dictatorships. His notion of persuasion to "attitude" does not alter his generally classical view of rhetoric, for as he points out, in "Cicero and Augustine there is a shift between the words 'move' *(movere)* and 'bend' *(flectere)* to name the ultimate function of rhetoric." And he merely finds that this shift "corresponds to a distinction between act and attitude (attitude being an incipient act, a leaning or inclination)."[74] His notion of persuasion to "attitude" enables him to point out a linkage with poetry: "Thus the notion of persuasion to *attitude* would permit the application of rhetorical terms to purely *poetic* structures; the study of lyrical devices might be classed under the head of rhetoric, when these devices are considered for their power to induce or communicate states of mind to readers, even though the kinds of assent evoked have no overt, practical outcome."[75]

In his reading of classical texts, he had noted a stress "upon *teaching* as an 'office' of rhetoric." Such an observation enables him to link the fields of rhetoric and semantics. He concludes that "once you treat instruction as an aim of rhetoric you introduce a principle that can widen the scope of rhetoric beyond persuasion. It is on the way to include also works on the theory and practice of exposition, description, *communication* in general. Thus, finally, out of this principle, you can derive contemporary 'semantics' as an aspect of rhetoric."[76]

As he persists in "tracking down" the function of the term *rhetoric*, Burke notes an ingredient of rhetoric "lurking in such anthropologist's terms as 'magic' and 'witchcraft,' "[77] and concludes that one "comes

[71] *A Rhetoric of Motives*, p. 172.
[72] *Ibid.*, p. xiii.
[73] *Ibid.*, p. 50.
[74] *Ibid.*
[75] *Ibid.*
[76] *Ibid.*, p. 77.
[77] *Ibid.*, p. 44.

closer to the true state of affairs if one treats the socializing aspects of magic as a 'primitive rhetoric' than if one sees modern rhetoric simply as a 'survival of primitive magic.' "[78] Whereas he does not believe that the term *rhetoric* is a "substitute" for such terms as *magic, witchcraft, socialization,* or *communication,* the term *rhetoric* "designates a function . . . present in the areas variously covered by those other terms."[79] Thus, one can place within the scope of rhetoric "all those statements by anthropologists, ethnologists, individual and social psychologists, and the like, that bear upon the *persuasive* aspects of language, the function of language as *addressed,* as direct or roundabout appeal to real or or ideal audiences, without or within."[80] All these disciplines have made "good contributions to the New Rhetoric."[81]

In "individual psychology," particularly the Freudian concern with the neuroses of individual patients, "there is a strongly rhetorical ingredient."[82] Burke asks the question, "Indeed, what could be more profoundly rhetorical than Freud's notion of a dream that attains expression by stylistic subterfuges designed to evade the inhibitions of a moralistic censor? What is this but the exact analogue of the rhetorical devices of literature under political or theocratic censorship? The *ego* with its *id* confronts the *super-ego* much as an orator would confront a somewhat alien audience, whose susceptibilities he must flatter as a necessary step toward persuasion. The Freudian psyche is quite a parliament, with conflicting interests expressed in ways variously designed to take the claims of rival factions into account."[83]

By considering the individual self as "audience" Burke brings morals and ethics into the realm of rhetoric. He notes that "a modern 'post-Christian' rhetoric must also concern itself with the thought that, under the heading of appeal to audiences, would also be included any ideas or images privately addressed to the individual self for moralistic or incantatory purposes. For you become your own audience, in some respects a very lax one, in some respects very exacting, when you become involved in psychologically stylistic subterfuges for presenting your own case to yourself in sympathetic terms (and even terms that seem harsh can often be found on closer scrutiny to be flattering, as with neurotics who visit sufferings upon themselves in the name of very high-powered motives which, whatever their discomfiture, feed pride." Therefore, the "individual person, striving to form himself in accordance with the communicative norms that match the cooperative

---

[78] *Ibid.*, p. 43.
[79] *Ibid.*, p. 44.
[80] *Ibid.*, pp. 43–44.
[81] *Ibid.*, p. 40.
[82] *Ibid.*, p. 37.
[83] *Ibid.*, pp. 37, 38.

ways of his society, is by the same token concerned with the rhetoric of identification."[84]

By considering style as essentially a mode of "ingratiation" or as a technique by which one gives the signs of identification and consubstantiality, Burke finds a rhetorical motive in clothes, pastoral, courtship, and the like.[85]

Burke links dialectics with rhetoric through a definition of dialectics in "its most general sense" as "linguistic transformation"[86] and through an analysis of three different levels of language, or linguistic terminology.[87] Grammatically, he discusses the subject from the point of view of linguistic merger and division, polarity, and transcendence, being aware that there are "other definitions of dialectics":[88] "reasoning from opinion"; "the discovery of truth by the give and take of converse and redefinition"; "the art of disputation"; "the processes of 'interaction' between the verbal and the non-verbal"; "the competition of coöperation or the coöperation of competition"; "the spinning of terms out of terms"; the internal dialogue of thought"; "any development . . . got by the interplay of various factors that mutually modify one another, and may be thought of as voices in a dialogue or roles in a play, with each voice or role in its partiality contributing to the development of the whole"; "the placement of one thought or thing in terms of its opposite"; "the progressive or successive development and reconciliation of opposites"; and "so putting questions to nature that nature can give unequivocal answer."[89] He considers all of these definitions as "variants or special applications of the functions"[90] of linguistic transformation conceived in terms of "Merger and division," "The three Major Pairs: action-passion, mind-body, being-nothing," and "Transcendence."[91]

Burke devotes 150 pages to the treatment of the dialectics of persuasion in the Rhetoric,[92] in addition to extensive treatment of it on the grammatical level.[93] Linguistic terminology is considered variously persuasive in its Positive, Dialectical, and Ultimate levels or orders.[94] "A positive term is most unambiguously itself when it names a visible and tangible thing which can be located in time and place."[95] Dialecti-

---

84 Ibid., pp. 38, 39.
85 Ibid., pp. 115–127; see also, p. xiv.
86 A Grammar of Motives, p. 402.
87 A Rhetoric of Motives, p. 183.
88 A Grammar of Motives, p. 402, 403.
89 Ibid., p. 403.
90 Ibid.
91 Ibid., p. 402.
92 A Rhetoric of Motives, pp. 183–333.
93 A Grammar of Motives, pp. 323–443.
94 A Rhetoric of Motives, p. 183.
95 Ibid.

cal terms "have no such strict location."[96] Thus terms like "Elizabethan-ism" or "capitalism" having no positive referent may be called "dia-lectical."[97] Often called "polar" terms,[98] they require an "opposite"[99] to define them and are on the level of "action," "principles," "ideas."[100] In an "ultimate order" of terminology, there is a "guiding idea" or "unitary principle."[101]

From the point of view of rhetoric, Burke believes that the "differ-ence between a merely 'dialectical' confronting of parliamentary con-flict and an 'ultimate' treatment of it would reside in this: The 'dialectical' order would leave the competing voices in a jangling rela-tion with one another (a conflict solved *faute de mieux* by 'horse-trading'); but the 'ultimate' order would place these competing voices themselves in a *hierarchy*, or *sequence*, or *evaluating series*, so that, in some way, we went by a fixed and reasoned progression from one of these to another, the members of the entire group being arranged *developmentally* with relation to one another."[102] To Burke "much of the *rhetorical* strength in the Marxist dialectic comes from the fact that it is 'ultimate' in its order,"[103] for a "spokesman for the proletariat can think of himself as representing not only the interests of that class alone, but the grand design of the entire historical sequence. . . ."[104]

In his concept of a "pure persuasion," Burke seems to be extending the area of rhetoric beyond its usual scope. As a metaphysician he attempts to carry the process of rhetorical appeal to its ultimate limits. He admits that what he means by "pure persuasion" in the "absolute sense" exists nowhere, but believes that it can be present as a motiva-tional ingredient in any rhetoric, no matter how "advantage-seeking such a rhetoric may be."[105] Pure persuasion involves the saying of something, not for an extraverbal advantage to be got by the saying, but because of a satisfaction intrinsic to the saying. It summons be-cause it likes the feel of a summons. It would be nonplused if the summons were answered. It attacks because it revels in the sheer syllables of vituperation. It would be horrified if, each time it finds a way of saying, 'Be damned,' it really did send a soul to rot in hell. It intuitively says, 'This is so,' purely and simply because this is so."[106]

---

[96] *Ibid.*, p. 184.
[97] *Ibid.*
[98] *Ibid.*
[99] *The Philosophy of Literary Form*, n. 26, p. 109.
[100] *A Rhetoric of Motives*, p. 184.
[101] *Ibid.*, p. 187
[102] *Ibid.*
[103] *Ibid.*, p. 190.
[104] *Ibid.*, pp. 190, 191.
[105] *Ibid.*, p. 269.
[106] *Ibid.*

With such a concept Burke finds himself at the "borders of meta-physics, or perhaps better 'meta-rhetoric'. . . ."[107]

III

Of great significance to the rhetorician is Burke's consideration of the general problem of motivation. Concerned with the problem of motivation in literary strategy,[108] he nevertheless intends that his observations be considered pertinent to the social sphere in general.[109] He had observed that people's conduct has been explained by an "endless variety of theories: ethnological, geographical, sociological, physiological, historical, endocrinological, economic, anatomical, mystical, pathological, and so on."[110] The assigning of motives, he concludes, is a "matter of *appeal*,"[111] and this depends upon one's general orientation. "A motive is not some fixed thing, like a table, which one can go to and look at. It is a term of interpretation, and being such it will naturally take its place within the framework of our *Weltanschauung* as a whole."[112] "To explain one's conduct by the vocabulary of motives current among one's group is about as self-deceptive as giving the area of a field in the accepted terms of measurement. One is simply interpreting with the only vocabulary he knows. One is stating his orientation, which involves a vocabulary of ought and ought-not, with attendant vocabulary of praiseworthy and blameworthy."[113] "We discern situational patterns by means of the particular vocabulary of the cultural group into which we are born."[114] Motives are "distinctly linguistic products."[115]

To Burke, the subject of motivation is a "philosophic one, not ultimately to be solved in terms of empirical science."[116] A motive is a "shorthand" term for "situation."[117] One may discuss motives on three levels, rhetorical, symbolic, and grammatical.[118] One is on the "grammatical" level when he concerns himself with the problem of the "intrinsic," or the problem of "substance."[119] "Men's conception of

107 *Ibid.*, p. 267.
108 *The Philosophy of Literary Form*, p. 78.
109 *Ibid.*, p. 105.
110 *Permanence and Change,* p. 47.
111 *Ibid.*, p. 38.
112 *Ibid.*
113 *Ibid.*, p. 33.
114 *Ibid.*, p. 52.
115 *Ibid.*
116 *A Grammar of Motives*, p. xxiii.
117 *Permanence and Change*, p. 44.
118 *A Grammar of Motives*, p. 465.
119 *Ibid.*

motive . . . is integrally related to their conception of substance. Hence, to deal with problems of motive is to deal with problems of substance."[120]

On the "grammatical" level Burke gives his most profound treatment of the problem of motivation. Strongly allied with the classicists throughout all his works in both his ideas and his methodology, Burke shows indebtedness to Aristotle for his treatment of motivation. Taking a clue from Aristotle's consideration of the "circumstances" of an action,[121] Burke concludes that "In a rounded statement about motives, you must have some word that names the *act* (names what took place, in thought or deed), and another that names the *scene* (the background of the act, the situation in which it occurred); also, you must indicate what person or kind of person (*agent*) performed the act, what means or instruments he used (*agency*), and the *purpose*."[122] Act, Scene, Agent, Agency, Purpose become the "pentad" for pondering the problem of human motivation.[123] Among these various terms grammatical "ratios" prevail which have rhetorical implications. One might illustrate by saying that, for instance, between *scene* and *act* a logic prevails which indicates that a certain quality of scene calls for an analogous quality of act. Hence, if a situation is said to be of a certain nature, a corresponding attitude toward it is implied. Burke explains by pointing to such an instance as that employed by a speaker who, in discussing Roosevelt's war-time power exhorted that Roosevelt should be granted "unusual powers" because the country was in an "unusual international situation." The scene-act "ratio" may be applied in two ways. "It can be applied deterministically in statements that a certain policy *had* to be adopted in a certain situation, or it may be applied in hortatory statements to the effect that a certain policy *should be* adopted in conformity with the situation."[124] These ratios are "principles of determination."[125] The pentad would allow for ten such ratios: scene-act, scene-agent, scene-agency, scene-purpose, act-purpose, act-agent, act-agency, agent-purpose, agent-agency, and agency-purpose.[126] Political commentators now generally use *situation* as their synonym for *scene*, "though often without any clear concept of its function as a statement about motives."[127]

Burke draws his key terms for the study of motivation from the

[120] *Ibid.,* p. 337.
[121] *Ethica Nicomachea,* tr. by W. D. Ross, III, i, 16.
[122] *A Grammar of Motives,* p. xv.
[123] *Ibid.*
[124] *Ibid.,* p. 13.
[125] *Ibid.,* p. 15.
[126] *Ibid.*
[127] *Ibid.,* p. 13.

analysis of drama. Being developed from the analysis of drama, his pentad "treats language and thought primarily as modes of action."[128] His method for handling motivation is designed to contrast with the methodology of the physical sciences which considers the subject of motivation in mechanistic terms of "flat cause-and-effect or stimulus-and-response."[129] Physicalist terminologies are proper to non-verbalizing entities, but man as a species should be approached through his specific trait, his use of symbols. Burke opposes the reduction of the human realm to terms that lack sufficient "coordinates"; he does not, however, question the fitness of physicalist terminologists for treating the physical realm. According to Burke, "Philosophy, like common sense, must think of human motivation dramatistically, in terms of action and its ends."[130] "Language being essentially human, we should view human relations in terms of the linguistic instrument."[131] His "vocabulary" or "set of coordinates" serves "for the integration of all phenomena studied by the *social* sciences."[132] It also serves as a "perspective for the analysis of history which is a 'dramatic' process. . . ."[133]

One may wonder with Charles Morris whether "an analysis of man through his language provides us with a full account of human motives."[134] One strongly feels the absence of insights into motivation deriving from the psychologists and scientists.

IV

Burke is not only philosopher and theorist; he has applied his critical principles practically to a great number of literary works. Of these, three are of particular interest to the rhetorician. In two instances, Burke attempts to explain the communicative relationship between the writer and his audience. Taking the speech of Antony from Shakespeare's *Julius Caesar*,[135] Burke examines the speech from "the standpoint of the rhetorician, who is concerned with a work's processes of appeal."[136] A similar operation is performed on a scene from *Twelfth Night*.[137]

[128] *Ibid.*, p. xxii.
[129] *The Philosophy of Literary Form*, pp. 103, 106.
[130] *A Grammar of Motives*, pp. 55, 56.
[131] *Ibid.*, p. 317.
[132] *The Philosophy of Literary Form*, p. 105.
[133] *Ibid.*, p. 317.
[134] Charles Morris, "The Strategy of Kenneth Burke," *The Nation*, CLXIII (July 27, 1946), 106.
[135] "Antony in Behalf of the Play," *Philosophy of Literary Form*, pp. 329–343.
[136] *Ibid.*, p. 330.
[137] "Trial Translation" (from *Twelfth Night*), *Ibid.*, pp. 344–349.

Undoubtedly one of his most straightforward attempts at analysis of a work of "literature for use," occurs in an essay on "The Rhetoric of Hitler's 'Battle.' "[138] "The main ideal of criticism, as I conceive it," Burke has observed, "is to use all that there is to use."[139] "If there is any slogan that should reign among critical precepts, it is that 'circumstances alter occasions.' "[140] Considering *Mein Kampf* as "the well of Nazi magic,"[141] Burke brings his knowledge of sociology and anthropology to bear in order to "discover what kind of 'medicine' this medicine-man has concocted, that we may know, with greater accuracy, exactly what to guard against, if we are to forestall the concocting of similar medicine in America."[142] He considers Hitler's "centralizing hub of *ideas*"[143] and his selection of Munich as a "mecca geographically located"[144] as methods of recruiting followers "from among many discordant and divergent bands. . . ."[145] He examines the symbol of the "international Jew"[146] as that "of a *common enemy*,"[147] the " 'medicinal' appeal of the Jew as scapegoat. . . ."[148]

His knowledge of psychoanalysis is useful in the analysis of the "sexual symbolism" that runs through the book: "Germany in dispersion is the 'dehorned Siegfried.' The masses are 'feminine.' As such, they desire to be led by a dominating male. This male, as orator, woos them—and, when he has won them, he commands them. The rival male, the villainous Jew, would on the contrary 'seduce' them. If he succeeds, he poisons their blood by intermingling with them. Whereupon, by purely associative connections of ideas, we are moved into attacks upon syphilis, prostitution, incest, and other similar misfortunes, which are introduced as a kind of 'musical' argument when he is on the subject of 'blood poisoning' by intermarriage or, in its 'spiritual' equivalent, by the infection of 'Jewish' ideas. . . ."[149]

His knowledge of history and religion is employed to show that the "*materialization*" of a religious pattern" is "one terrifically effective weapon . . . in a period where religion has been progressively weakened by many centuries of capitalist materialism."[150]

[138] *Ibid.*, pp. 191–220.
[139] *Ibid.*, p. 23.
[140] *Ibid.*
[141] *Ibid.*, p. 192.
[142] *Ibid.*, p. 191.
[143] *Ibid.*, p. 192.
[144] *Ibid.*
[145] *Ibid.*
[146] *Ibid.*, p. 194.
[147] *Ibid.*, p. 193.
[148] *Ibid.*, p. 195.
[149] *Ibid.*
[150] *Ibid.*, p. 194.

Conventional rhetorical knowledge leads him to call attention to the "power of endless repetition";[151] the appeal of a sense of "community";[152] the appeal of security resulting from "a world view" for a people who had previously seen the world only "piecemeal";[153] and the appeal of Hitler's "inner voice"[154] which served as a technique of leader-people "identification."[155]

Burke's analysis is comprehensive and penetrating. It stands as a superb example of the fruitfulness of a method of comprehensive rhetorical analysis which goes far beyond conventional patterns.

CONCLUSION

Burke is difficult and often confusing. He cannot be understood by casual reading of his various volumes. In part the difficulty arises from the numerous vocabularies he employs. His words in isolation are usually simple enough, but he often uses them in new contexts. To read one of his volumes independently, without regard to the chronology of publication, makes the problem of comprehension even more difficult because of the specialized meanings attaching to various words and phrases.

Burke is often criticized for "obscurity" in his writings. The charge may be justified. However, some of the difficulty of comprehension arises from the compactness of his writing, the uniqueness of his organizational patterns, the penetration of his thought, and the breadth of his endeavor. "In books like the *Grammar* and the *rhetoric*," observed Malcolm Cowley, "we begin to see the outlines of a philosophical system on the grand scale. . . . Already it has its own methodology (called 'dramatism'), its own esthetics (based on the principle that works of art are symbolic actions), its logic and dialectics, its ethics (or picture of the good life) and even its metaphysics, which Burke prefers to describe as a meta-rhetoric."[156]

One cannot possibly compress the whole of Burke's thought into an article. The most that one can achieve is to signify his importance as a theorist and critic and to suggest the broad outlines of his work. Years of study and contemplation of the general idea of effectiveness in language have equipped him to deal competently with the subject of rhetoric from its beginning as a specialized discipline to the present

[151] *Ibid.*, p. 217.
[152] *Ibid.*
[153] *Ibid.*, p. 218.
[154] *Ibid.*, p. 207.
[155] *Ibid.*
[156] Malcolm Cowley, "Prolegomena to Kenneth Burke," *The New Republic,* CXXII (June 5, 1950), 18, 19.

time. To his thorough knowledge of classical tradition he has added rich insights gained from serious study of anthropology, sociology, history, psychology, philosophy, and the whole body of humane letters. With such equipment, he has become the most profound student of rhetoric now writing in America.

PART III IVOR A. RICHARDS

8 THE PHILOSOPHY OF RHETORIC

I. A. RICHARDS

Richards urges restoration of rhetorical study to a position of respectability. The proper province of rhetorical inquiry, according to Richards, is "a study of misunderstanding and its remedies." In contrast to some treatises on rhetoric that discuss "just a set of dodges that will be found to work sometimes," Richards contends that a theory of rhetoric must probe the "fundamental laws of the use of language."

Instead of a macroscopic viewpoint, Richards proposes a "microscopic inquiry which endeavors to look into the structure of the meaning with which discourse is composed, not merely into the effects of various large-scale disposals of these meanings." Rhetorical theory as an analysis of "verbal understanding and misunderstanding" and of "how words work in discourse" should be capable of ministering "successfully to important needs." (See *Philosophy of Rhetoric*, 3, 5, 7, 23.)

Following the introductory chapter of *The Philosophy of Rhetoric* reprinted below, Richards offers five chapters that discuss some of his basic concepts: the aims of discourse, the "context" theory of meaning, the process of abstraction, and the central role of metaphor. In fact, one of his purposes is to "put the theory of metaphor in a more important place than it has enjoyed in traditional Rhetoric."

Source: *The Philosophy of Rhetoric* by I. A. Richards. Copyright 1936 by Oxford University Press, Inc. Renewed 1964 by I. A. Richards. Reprinted by permission.

These lectures are an attempt to revive an old subject. I need spend no time, I think, in describing the present state of Rhetoric. Today it is the dreariest and least profitable part of the waste that the unfortunate travel through in Freshman English! So low has Rhetoric sunk that we would do better just to dismiss it to Limbo than to trouble ourselves with it—unless we can find reason for believing that it can become a study that will minister successfully to important needs.

As to the needs, there is little room for doubt about them. Rhetoric,

I shall urge, should be a study of misunderstanding and its remedies. We struggle all our days with misunderstandings, and no apology is required for any study which can prevent or remove them. Of course, inevitably *at present,* we have no measure with which to calculate the extent and degree of our hourly losses in communication. One of the aims of these lectures will be to speculate about some of the measures we should require in attempting such estimates. "How much and in how many ways may good communication differ from bad?" That is too big and too complex a question to be answered as it stands, but we can at least try to work towards answering some parts of it; and these explanations would be the revived subject of Rhetoric.

Though we cannot measure our losses in communication we can guess at them. We even have professional guessers: teachers and examiners, whose business is to guess at and diagnose the mistakes other people have made in understanding what they have heard and read and to avoid illustrating these mistakes, if they can, themselves. Another man who is in a good position from which to estimate the current losses in communication is an author looking through a batch of reviews, especially an author who has been writing about some such subject as economics, social or political theory, or criticism. It is not very often that such an author must honestly admit that his reviewers —even when they profess to agree with him—have seen his point. That holds, you may say, only of bad writers who have written clumsily or obscurely. But bad writers are commoner than good and play a larger part in bandying notions about in the world.

The moral from this comes home rather heavily on a Lecturer addressing an audience on such a tangled subject as Rhetoric. It is little use appealing to the hearer as Berkeley did: "I do . . . once for all desire whoever shall think it worth his while to understand . . . that he would not stick in this or that phrase, or manner of expression, but candidly collect my meaning from the whole sum and tenor of my discourse, and laying aside the words as much as possible, consider the bare notions themselves. . . ."

The trouble is that we *can* only "collect the whole sum and tenor of the discourse" from the words, we cannot "lay aside the words"; and as to considering "the bare notions themselves," well, I shall be considering in a later lecture various notions of a notion and comparing their merits for a study of communication. Berkeley was fond of talking about these "bare notions," these "naked undisguised ideas," and about "separating from them all that dress and encumbrance of words." But an idea or a notion, when unencumbered and undisguised, is no easier to get hold of than one of those oiled and naked thieves who infest the railway carriages of India. Indeed an idea, or a notion, like the physicist's ultimate particles and rays, is only known by what it does. Apart from its dress or other signs it is not identifiable. Berkeley himself, of course, has his doubts: "laying aside the words as much as possible, consider . . ." That "as much as possible" is not very much; and is not nearly enough for the purposes for which Berkeley hoped to trust it.

We have instead to consider much more closely how words work in discourse. But before plunging into some of the less whelming divisions of this world-swallowing inquiry, let me glance back for a few minutes at the traditional treatment of the subject; much might be learnt from it that would help us. It begins, of course, with Aristotle, and may perhaps be said to end with Archbishop Whately, who wrote a treatise on Rhetoric for the *Encyclopaedia Metropolitana* that Coleridge planned. I may remark, in passing, that Coleridge's own *Essay on Method,* the preface to that Encyclopaedia, has itself more bearing on a possible future for Rhetoric than anything I know of in the official literature.

Whately was a prolific writer, but he is most often remembered now perhaps for an epigram. "Woman," he said, "is an irrational animal which pokes the fire from the top." I am not quoting this, here at Bryn Mawr, to prejudice you against the Archbishop: any man, when provoked, might venture such an unwarrantable and imperceptive generalization. But I do hope to prejudice you further against his modes of treating a subject in which he is, according to no less an authority than Jebb, the best modern writer. Whately has another epigram which touches the very heart of our problem, and may be found either comforting or full of wicked possibilities as you please: here it is. "Preachers nobly aim at nothing at all and hit it!" We may well wonder just what the Archbishop meant by that.

What we have to surmise is how Whately, following and summing up the whole history of the subject, can proceed as he did! He says quite truly that "Rhetoric is not one of those branches of study in which we can trace with interest a progressive improvement from age to age"; he goes on to discuss "whether Rhetoric be worth any diligent cultivation" and to decide, rather half-heartedly, that it is— provided it be taken not as *an* Art of discourse but as *the* Art—that is to say, as a philosophic discipline aiming at a mastery of the fundamental laws of the use of language, not just a set of dodges that will be found to work sometimes. That claim—that Rhetoric must go deep, must take a broad philosophical view of the principles of the Art—is the climax of his Introduction; and yet in the treatise that follows nothing of the sort is attempted, nor is it in any other treatise that I know of. What we are given by Whately instead is a very ably arranged and discussed collection of prudential Rules about the best sorts of things to say in various argumentative situations, the order in which to bring out your propositions and proofs and examples, at what point it will be most effective to disparage your opponent, how to recommend oneself to the audience, and like matters. As to all of which, it is fair to remark, no one ever learned about them from a treatise who did not know about them already; at the best, the treatise may be an occasion for realizing that there is skill to be developed in discourse, but it does not and cannot teach the skill. We can turn on the whole endeavour the words in which the Archbishop derides his arch-enemy Jeremy Bentham: "the proposed plan for the ready exposure of each argument resembles that by which children are deluded, of catching a bird by laying salt on its tail; the existing doubts and difficulties of debate being no greater than, on the proposed system, would be found in determining what Arguments were or were not to be classified" in which places in the system.

Why has this happened? It has happened all through the history of the subject, and I choose Whately because he represents an inherent tendency in its study. When he proceeds from these large-scale questions of the Ordonnance of arguments to the minute particulars of discourse—under the rubric of Style—the same thing happens. Instead of a philosophic inquiry into how words work in discourse, we got the usual postcard's-worth of crude common sense:—be clear, yet don't be dry; be vivacious, use metaphors when they will be understood not otherwise; respect usage; don't be long-winded, on the other hand don't be graspy; avoid ambiguity; prefer the energetic to the elegant; preserve unity and coherence. . . I need not go over to the other side of the postcard. We all know well enough the maxims that can be extracted by patient readers out of these agglomerations and how helpful we have all found them!

What is wrong with these two familiar attempts to discuss the working of words? How words work is a matter about which every user of language is, of necessity, avidly curious until these trivialities choke the flow of interest. Remembering Whately's recommendation of metaphor, I can put the mistake best perhaps by saying that all they do is to poke the fire from the top. Instead of tackling, in earnest, the problem of how language works at all, they assume that nothing relevant is to be learnt about it; and that the problem is merely one of disposing the given and unquestioned powers of words to the best advantage. Instead of ventilating by inquiry the sources of the whole action of words, they merely play with generalizations about their effects, generalizations that are uninstructive and unimproving unless we go more deeply and by another route into these grounds. Their conception of the study of language, in brief, is frustratingly distant or macroscopic and yields no return in understanding—either practical or theoretical

—unless it is supplemented by an intimate or microscopic inquiry which endeavours to look into the structure of the meanings with which discourse is composed, not merely into the effects of various large-scale disposals of these meanings. In this Rhetoricians may remind us of the Alchemists' efforts to transmute common substances into precious metals, vain efforts because they were not able to take account of the internal structures of the so-called elements.

The comparison that I am using here is one which a modern writer on language can hardly avoid. To account for understanding and misunderstanding, to study the efficiency of language and its conditions, we have to renounce, for a while, the view that words just have their meanings and that what a discourse does is to be explained as a composition of these meanings—as a wall can be represented as a composition of its bricks. We have to shift the focus of our analysis and attempt a deeper and more minute grasp and try to take account of the structures of the smallest discussable units of meaning and the ways in which these vary as they are put with other units. Bricks, for all practical purposes, hardly mind what other things they are put with. Meanings mind intensely—more indeed than any other sorts of things. It is the peculiarity of meanings that they do so mind their company; that is in part what we mean by calling them meanings! In themselves they are nothing—figments, abstractions, unreal things that we invent, if you like—but we invent them for a purpose. They help us to avoid taking account of the peculiar way in which any part of a discourse, in the last resort, does what it does only because the other parts of the surrounding, uttered or unuttered discourse and its conditions are what they are. "In the last resort"—the last resort here is mercifully a long way off and very deep down. Short of it we are aware of certain stabilities which hide from us this universal relativity or, better, interdependence of meanings. Some words and sentences still more, do seem to mean what they mean absolutely and unconditionally. This is because the conditions governing their meanings are so constant that we can disregard them. So the weight of a cubic centimeter of water seems a fixed and absolute thing because of the constancy of its governing conditions. In weighing out a pound of tea we can forget about the mass of the earth. And with words which have constant conditions the common sense view that they have fixed proper meanings, which should be learned and observed, is justified. But these words are fewer than we suppose. Most words, as they pass from context to context, change their meanings; and in many different ways. It is their duty and their service to us to do so. Ordinary discourse would suffer anchylosis if they did not, and so far we have no ground for complaint. We are extraordinarily skilful in some fields with these shifts of sense—especially when they are of the kind we recognize officially as metaphor. But our skill fails; it is patchy and fluctuant; and, when it fails, misunderstanding of others and of ourselves comes in.

A chief cause of misunderstanding, I shall argue later, is the Proper Meaning Superstition. That is, the common belief—encouraged officially by what lingers on in the school manuals as Rhetoric—that a word has a meaning of its own (ideally, only one) independent of and controlling its use and the purpose for which it should be uttered. This superstition is a recognition of a certain kind of stability in the meanings of certain words. It is only a superstition when it forgets (as it commonly does) that the stability of the meaning of a word comes from the constancy of the contexts that give it its meaning. Stability in a word's meaning is not something to be assumed, but always something to be explained. And as we try out explanations, we discover, of course, that—as there are many sorts of constant contexts —there are many sorts of stabilities. The stability of the meaning of a word like *knife*, say, is different from the stability of a word like *mass* in its technical use, and then again both differ from the stabilities of such words, say, as *event, ingression, endurance, recurrence,* or *object,* in the paragraphs of a very distinguished predecessor in this Lectureship. It will have been noticed perhaps that the way I propose to treat meanings has its analogues with Mr. Whitehead's treatment of things. But indeed no one to whom Berkeley has mattered will be very confident as to which is which.

I have been suggesting—with my talk of macroscopic and microscopic inquiries—that the theory of language may have something to learn, not much but a little, from the ways in which the physicist envisages stabilities. But much closer analogies are possible with some of the patterns of Biology. The theory of interpretation is obviously a branch of biology—a branch that has not grown very far or very healthily yet. To remember this may help us to avoid some traditional mistakes—among them the use of bad analogies which tie us up if we take them too seriously. Some of these are notorious; for example, the opposition between form and content, and the almost equivalent opposition between matter and form. These are wretchedly inconvenient metaphors. So is that other which makes language a dress which thought puts on. We shall do better to think of a meaning as though it were a plant that has grown—not a can that has been filled or a lump of clay that has been moulded. These are obviously inadequacies; but, as the history of criticism shows, they have not been avoided, and the perennial efforts of the reflective to amend or surpass them—Croce is the extreme modern example—hardly help.

More insidious and more devastating are the oversimple mechanical analogies which have been brought in under the heading of Associationism in the hope of explaining how language works. And thought as well. The two problems are close together and similar and neither can be discussed profitably apart from the other. But, unless we drastically remake their definitions, and thereby dodge the main problems, Language and Thought are not—need I say?—one and the same. I suppose I must, since the Behaviorists have so loudly averred that Thought is sub-vocal talking. That however is a doctrine I prefer, in these lectures, to attack by implication. To discuss it explicitly would take time that can, I think, be spent more fruitfully. I will only say that I hold that any doctrine identifying Thought with *muscular* movement is a self-refutation of the observationalism that prompts it— heroic and fatal. And that an identification of Thought with an activity of the nervous system is to me an acceptable hypothesis, but too large to have interesting applications. It may be left until more is known about both; when possibly it may be developed to a point at which it might become useful. At present it is still Thought which is most accessible to study and accessible largely through Language. We can all detect a difference in our own minds between thinking of a dog and thinking of a cat. But no neurologist can. Even when no cats or dogs are about and we are doing nothing about them except thinking of them, the difference is plainly perceptible. We can also say 'dog' and think 'cat.'

I must, though, discuss the doctrine of associations briefly, because when we ask ourselves about how words mean, some theory about trains of associated ideas or accompanying images is certain to occur to us as an answer. And until we see how little distance these theories take us they are frustrating. We all know the outline of these theories: we learn what the word 'cat' means by seeing a cat at the same time that we hear the word 'cat' and thus a link is formed between the sight and the sound. Next time we hear the word 'cat' an image of a cat (a visual image, let us say) arises in the mind, and that is how the word 'cat' means a cat. The obvious objections that come from the differences between cats; from the fact that images of a grey persian asleep and of a tabby stalking are very different, and from some people saying they never have any imagery, must then be taken account of, and the theory grows very complex. Usually, images get relegated to a background and become mere supports to something hard to be precise about—an idea of a cat—which is supposed then to be associated with the word 'cat' much as the image originally was supposed to be associated with it.

This classical theory of meaning has been under heavy fire from many sides for more than a century—from positions as different as those of Coleridge, of Bradley, of Pavlov and of the *gestalt* psychologists. In response it has elaborated itself, calling in the aid of the conditioned-reflex and submitting to the influence of Freud. I do not say that it is incapable, when amended, of supplying us with a workable theory of meaning—in fact, in the next lecture I shall sketch an outline theory of how words mean which has associationism among its obvious ancestors. And here, in saying that simple associationism does not go far enough and is an impediment unless we see this, I am merely reminding you that a clustering of associated images and ideas about a word in the mind does not answer our question: "How does a word mean?" It only hands it on to them, and the question becomes: "How does an idea (or an image) mean what it does?" To answer that we have to go outside the mind and inquire into its connections with what are not mental occurrences. Or (if you prefer, instead, to extend the sense of the word 'mind') we have to inquire into connections between events which were left out by the traditional associationism. And in leaving them out they left out the problem.

For our purposes here the important points are two. First, that ordinary, current, undeveloped associationism is ruined by the crude inapposite physical metaphor of impressions stamped on the mind (the image of the cat stamped by the cat), impressions then linked and combined in clusters like atoms in molecules. That metaphor gives us no useful account either of perception or of reflection, and we shall not be able to think into or think out any of the interesting problems of Rhetoric unless we improve it.

Secondly the appeal to *imagery* as constituting the meaning of an utterance has, in fact, frustrated a large part of the great efforts that have been made by very able people ever since the 17th Century to put Rhetoric back into the important place it deserves among our studies. Let me give you an example. Here is Lord Kames—who, as a Judge of the Court of Session in Scotland, was not without a reputation for shrewdness—being, I believe, really remarkably silly.

In *Henry V* (Act IV, scene I) Williams in a fume says this of what "a poor and private displeasure can do against a monarch": "You may as well go about to turn the sun to ice with fanning in his face with a peacock's feather." Lord Kames comments, "The peacock's feather, not to mention the beauty of the object, completes the image: an accurate image cannote be formed of that fanciful operation without conceiving a particular feather; and one is at a loss when this is neglected in the description." (*Elements of Criticism*, p. 372.)

That shows, I think, what the imagery obsession can do to a reader. Who in the world, apart from a theory, would be "at a loss" unless the sort of feather we are to fan the sun's face with is specified? If we cared to be sillier than our author, we could pursue him on his theory, by asking whether it is to be a long or a short feather or whether the sun is at its height or setting? The whole theory that the point of Shakespeare's specification is to "complete the image," in Kames' sense, is utterly mistaken and misleading. What *peacock* does, in the context there, is obviously to bring in considerations that heighten the idleness, the vanity, in Williams' eyes, of "poor and private displeasures against a monarch." A peacock's feather is something one might flatter oneself with. Henry has said that if the King lets himself be ransomed he will never trust his word after. And Williams is saying, "You'll never trust his word after! What's that! Plume yourself upon it as much as you like, but what will that do to the king!"

Lord Kames in 1761, blandly enjoying the beauty and completeness of the lively and distinct and accurate image of the feather he has produced for himself, and thereby missing, it seems, the whole tenor of the passage, is a spectacle worth some attention.

I shall be returning to Lord Kames, in a later lecture, when I discuss metaphor. His theories about trains of ideas and images are typical 18th Century Associationism—the Associationism of which David Hartley is the great prophet—and the applications of these theories in the detail of Rhetoric are their own refutation. We have to go beyond these theories, but however mistaken they may be, or however absurd their outcome may sometimes seem, we must not forget that they are beginnings, first steps in a great and novel venture, the attempt to explain in detail how language works and with it to improve communication. As such, these attempts merit the most discerning and the most sympathetic eye that we can turn upon them. Indeed, it is impossible to read Hartley, for example, without deep sympathy if we realize what a task it was that he was attempting. Not only when he writes, in his conclusion, in words which speak the thoughts of every candid inquirer: "This is by no means a full or satisfactory Account of the Ideas which adhere to words by Association. For the Author perceives himself to be still a mere novice in these speculations; and it is difficult to explain Words to the Bottom by Words; perhaps impossible." (On Man, 277.) But still more when he says: "All that has been delivered by the Ancients and Moderns, concerning the power of Habit, Custom, Example, Education, Authority, Party-prejudice, the Manner of learning the manual and liberal Arts, Etc., goes upon this Doctrine as its foundation, and may be considered as the detail of it, in various circumstances. I hope here to begin with the simplest case, and shall proceed to more and more complex ones continually, till I have exhausted what has occurred to me on this Subject." (On Man, p. 67.)

The man who wrote that was not 'poking the fire from the top.' His way of ventilating the subject may not have been perfectly advised, but he saw what needed doing and it is no wonder that Coleridge for a while admired Hartley beyond all other men. For upon the formation and transformations of meanings—which we must study with and through words—all that Hartley mentions, and much more, goes as its foundation. For it is no exaggeration to say that the fabrics of all our various worlds are the fabrics of our meanings. I began, you recall, with Berkeley, with—to use Mr. Yeats' noble lines—

God appointed Berkeley who proved all things a dream,
That this preposterous pragmatical pig of a world, its farrow that so solid seem,
Must vanish on the instant did the mind but change its theme.

Whatever we may be studying we do so only through the growth of our meanings. To realize this turns some parts of this attempted direct study of the modes of growth and interaction between meanings, which might otherwise seem a niggling philosophic juggle with distinctions, into a business of great practical importance. For this study is theoretical only that it may become practical. Here is the paragraph in which Hobbes condenses what he had learnt from his master, Bacon:

The end or scope of philosophy is, that we may make use to our benefit of effects formerly seen, or that, by the application of bodies to one another, we may produce the like effects of those we conceive in our mind, as far forth as matter, strength and industry, will permit, for the commodity of human life. For the inward glory and triumph of mind that a man may have for the mastery of some difficult and doubtful matter, or for the discovery of some hidden truth, is not worth so much pains as the study of Philosophy requires; nor need any man care much to teach another what he knows himself, if he think that will be the only benefit of his labour. The end of knowledge is power; and the use of theorems (which, among geometricians, serve for the finding out of properties) is for the construction of problems; and, lastly, the scope of all speculation is the performance of some action, or thing to be done.

I shall go on then, in the next Lecture, by the use of theorems to the construction of problems, without further insisting that these problems are those upon which, wittingly and unwittingly, we spend our whole waking life.

9
I. A. RICHARDS
AND THE "NEW RHETORIC"

MARIE HOCHMUTH NICHOLS

Like Kenneth Burke, who sees the genesis of rhetoric in man's state of apartness, Richards views communication as starting from the "natural isolation and severance of minds." Marie Nichols examines Richards' writings to analyze his view of the nature and function of rhetoric. Unlike Burke, who equates rhetoric and persuasion, Richards contends that exposition also is a rhetorical aim. More important, Richards claims as rhetoric's central function the "study of misunderstanding and its remedies." Richards' new rhetoric, says Nichols, "is concerned with the differentiation of referential and emotive language functions in order to produce understanding or to explain misunderstanding in any type of discourse."

Nichols calls attention to Richards' notion that language can best be viewed as an instrument, as an extension of our sense organs. Richards' view thus precedes by at least several decades Marshall McLuhan's now famous analysis of media as sensory extensions of man. As a supplement to the sources upon which Nichols bases her essay, you may wish to consult two of Richards' later books: *So Much Nearer* and *Design for Escape*. Also compare Nichols' treatment with that of Daniel Fogarty. (See Fogarty, *Roots for a New Rhetoric*, Chap. 2.)

Source: Quarterly Journal of Speech, XLIV (February 1958), 1–16. Reprinted with permission of the author and the publisher.

"No one, I imagine, migrates from Literature to Education for fun," wrote I. A. Richards in 1955, "but through a feeling as to what will happen if we do not develop improved teaching soon enough."[1] To approach Richards merely as a literary man concerned with literary problems is to lose sight of the sense of urgency that runs through all his writings. As a literary man he found himself dealing with a verbal medium, and he became profoundly concerned with the influence of the medium upon thought in all its forms. Conceiving of the language

[1] I. A. Richards, *Speculative Instruments* (Chicago, 1955), p. xi.

medium as the "instrument of all distinctively human development,"[2] he became persistent in a search for a sounder theoretical approach to language, a method for comprehending it in its various forms and multifarious uses, and the efficiency of language as an instrument. His twin interests have produced a stream of books that begins in 1922 and continues undiminished. Problems once comprehended under the ancient trivium—logic, grammar, and rhetoric—have reappeared under many titles, *The Foundations of Aesthetics* (with C. K. Ogden and James Wood, 1922), *The Meaning of Meaning* (with C. K. Ogden, 1923), *Principles of Literary Criticism* (1924), *Science and Poetry* (1926), *Practical Criticism* (1929), *Mencius on the Mind* (1932), *Basic Rules of Reason* (1933), *Coleridge on the Imagination* (1934), *Philosophy of Rhetoric* (1936), *Interpretation in Teaching* (1938), *How to Read a Page* (1942), *Speculative Instruments* (1955), and other works dealing with Basic English.

In 1936, Richards opened his *Philosophy of Rhetoric* with the remark: "These lectures are an attempt to revive an old subject. I need spend no time, I think, in describing the present state of Rhetoric. . . . So low has Rhetoric sunk that we would do better just to dismiss it to Limbo than to trouble ourselves with it—unless we can find reason for believing that it can become a study that will minister successfully to important needs."[3]

Even if Richards had never written a book under the caption of *The Philosophy of Rhetoric,* his other works would have considerable relevance for the student of rhetoric. His lifelong concern has been with the working of words in their many functions, and none of his works leaves any doubt that he is aware of a rhetorical function.

My purpose is primarily to examine Richards' attempt to revive an old subject. Although a central concern will be with his *Philosophy of Rhetoric,* I shall range freely over all his writings in order to determine his guiding principles. I shall be concerned with his conception of language, his theory of communication in general, his attempt to reorient rhetoric, his critical principles. I shall also be concerned with his place in the great tradition of rhetoric.

1

In 1923, when Richards' first important book, *The Meaning of Meaning,* was published with C. K. Ogden as collaborator, the authors voiced their conviction of an urgency which existed for a stricter examination of language from a point of view then not receiving attention.[4] Their

[2] *The Philosophy of Rhetoric* (New York, 1936), p. 131.
[3] *Ibid.,* p. 3.
[4] *The Meaning of Meaning,* New impression (New York, 1953), p. x.

timing was based upon two considerations: (1) the "readiness amongst psychologists to admit the importance of the problem" of language; and (2) the "realization that men of learning and sincerity are lamentably at the mercy of forms of speech."[5] Thus, in the preface, they suggested a psychological approach to the problems of language and trusted that dividends from such an approach might be seen in the lives of men of the work-a-day world.

As the authors turned to the matter of the fundamental nature of language, they concluded that "though often spoken of as a medium of communication," it is "best regarded as an instrument; and all instruments are extensions, or refinements, of our sense-organs."[6] Although language is to be considered a "system of signs,"[7] it is "no mere signalling system"[8] or "code";[9] it is an "organ—the supreme organ of the mind's self-ordering growth."[10] It is an "instrument for controlling our becoming."[11]

What, precisely, a sign is, and how language might be thought to be a member of the family of signs have long been problems to psychologists and students of language. In attempting to definitize the concept of sign, the authors concluded that anything which can be experienced or enjoyed and is understood to refer to something else is to be regarded as a sign.[12] Sign experience comes about as the result of the recurrence of experiences in partial uniformity.[13] Signs function by virtue of previous membership in a context or configuration that once affected us as a whole.[14] Even when part of the context reappears, that part affects us as though the whole context were present. Thus, that part of the context may be said to have sign or referential function. For instance, dark skies, thunder, lightning, and rain may once have constituted for us a configuration or context. Thereafter, if thunder or any of the other constituents of the configuration are noted, they affect us as though the rest of the context were present, and we take them as a sign of rain necessitating appropriate adaptive responses. A sign is "always a stimulus similar to some part of an original stimulus and sufficient to call up" an engram or residual trace left by the preceding experience.[15]

Words in language share the referential nature and work by the same

---

5 *Ibid.,* pp. x, xi.
6 *Ibid.,* p. 98.
7 *Ibid.,* p. vii.
8 *The Philosophy of Rhetoric,* p. 131.
9 *Speculative Instruments,* p. 9.
10 *Ibid.,* p. 9.
11 *Ibid.,* p. 9.
12 *The Meaning of Meaning,* p. 21; see also, p. 50.
13 *Principles of Literary Criticism,* 13th impression (New York, 1952), p. 90.
14 *The Meaning of Meaning,* p. 55.
15 *Ibid.,* p. 53.

mechanism as do all signs. However, since those signs that are used for purposes of communication and as instruments of thought occupy a peculiar place in the family of signs, and, according to Richards, in human experience generally, they may, for convenience, be referred to as *symbols*. Words, arrangements of words, images, gestures, drawings, and mimetic sounds are all to be considered instruments of thought and communication. These devices are all used to direct and organize, record and communicate; consequently they are to be referred to as symbols.[16]

In stating what symbols direct and organize, or what they record and communicate, Richards distinguishes between Thoughts and Things. It is Thought, or as Richards says, *reference* which is directed and organized; it is also Thought which is recorded and communicated. Language may trick us into believing that things are recorded and communicated; however, it is really thought about things or reference to things which is symbolized. Although we say that "the gardener mows the lawn when we know that it is the lawn-mower which actually does the cutting, so, though we know that the direct relation of symbols is with thought, we also say that symbols record events and communicate facts."[17]

When language is used to make a statement, three factors are involved: (1) the symbol; (2) thought or reference; and (3) the object of thought, or referent. Between the thought and a symbol, "causal relations hold." When we speak, we employ symbolism caused partly by reference and partly by social and psychological factors, including the purpose for which we make the reference, an intended effect upon other persons, and our attitude. When we listen, the symbols that we hear cause us to perform acts of reference and to assume attitudes which will be more or less similar to the act and attitude of the speaker.[18]

Richards' famous triangle showing the relations among symbols, reference, and referent has become a useful tool among psychologists. In addition to revealing a causal relation between a symbol and reference, it reveals that between thought and referent there is also a relation, "more or less direct," as when we think about or attend to a painting which we see, or "indirect," as when we think of or refer to Hitler. Between the symbol and the referent, there is no really relevant relation other than an indirect one resulting from its being used by someone to stand for some referent.[19]

Thus, one notes that, according to Richards' analysis of language,

[16] *Ibid.*, pp. 23, 9.
[17] *Ibid.*, p. 9.
[18] *Ibid.*, pp. 10, 11.
[19] *Ibid.*, p. 11.

"thinking or reference is reducible to causal relations." When one speaks of a reference, he is, in fact, speaking of external and psychological contexts by which a sign is linked to its referent. The mental events that take place in an act of reference to produce the symbol, Richards calls "psychological context." "All thinking, all reference," he maintains, "is adaptation due to psychological contexts which link together elements in external contexts." The contextual theory of reference covers all "beliefs, ideas, conceptions and 'thinkings of' " which relate the symbol to the referent. It asserts the recurrence of mental events in the main features with partial uniformity.[20]

Let us take the following three sets of symbols to illustrate Richards' analysis of language and the classification of its uses:

1. Winston Churchill is eighty-three years old.
2. The grand old man who occupied 10 Downing Street during the Second World War is eighty-three years old.
3. Four-score and three he counts his years, proud England's mighty son.

The first sentence Richards would identify as a purely referential statement, and, therefore, a *scientific* use of language. The context out of which the symbol grew would include recurrent experiences with the process of explicit naming and counting. The referent is the person bearing the name and having those years.

The second sentence represents a change in symbolization. The references, or psychological context, out of which the symbols were composed might include an affectionate attitude on the part of the composer of the symbol, a remembering of the events of the war, a recollection of others who had occupied the house at 10 Downing Street, in addition to a strict reference to the number of years of life. The referent is still to a person. The symbol, however, has not been produced for merely referential uses. Attitudes, reminiscences, and perhaps other factors have exerted strong influence. This use of language Richards labels "emotive" or "mixed," hence, "rhetorical."[21]

The third set of symbols represents still further change in symbolization. The purely referential function of language has almost completely vanished. Who is being talked about is no longer definite. The psychological context out of which this symbolization grew might contain feelings about age and England and some queries about relations, sonship, fatherhood. It might even include feelings about Lincoln at Gettysburg. This use of language represents almost completely the "emotive" function of language and would be regarded as poetry, good or bad.

When Richards and his collaborator published *The Meaning of Meaning,* they claimed among their peculiar contributions the follow-

---

[20] *Ibid.,* pp. 73, 68, 200, 57.
[21] *Ibid.,* p. 234.

ing: "An account of interpretation in causal terms by which the treatment of language as a system of signs becomes capable of results,"
and second, "A division of the functions of language into two groups,
the symbolic and the emotive." The symbolic use of words is *"statement;* the recording, the support, the organization and the communication of references." The emotive use of words is the "use of words to
express or excite feelings and attitudes."[22] There are, in other words,
"two totally distinct uses of language."[23]

2

Communication, according to Richards, starts from the "natural isolation and severance of minds." The experience of any two people
can be but similar.[24] There can be no such thing as transference of
experience or participation in identical experience.[35] By the use of
symbols one may provoke experience in another. A "language transaction or a communication" may be defined as "a use of symbols in
such a way that acts of reference occur in a hearer which are similar in
all relevant respects to those which are symbolized by them in the
speaker."[26] Accordingly, communication takes place "when one mind
so acts upon its environment that another mind is influenced, and in
that other mind an experience occurs which is like the experience in
the first mind, and is caused in part by that experience." This is a
complicated process and capable of degrees in at least two respects.
In the first place, two experiences may be more or less similar, and
in the second, one experience may be more or less dependent upon
the other. All that occurs is that "under certain conditions, separate
minds have closely similar experiences."[27]

Richards recognizes certain favorable conditions for communication.
Courage or audacity, freedom from pride and conceit, honesty,
humaneness, humility, humor, tolerance, good health—the Confucian
characteristics of the "superior man"—all these favor communication.[28]

In the absence of special communicative gifts, there is needed a fund
of common experience, long and varied acquaintanceship, close familiarity. Even when one possesses special communicative ability, the
success of communication in difficult circumstances depends upon the
extent to which one may make use of past similarities in experience.

22 *Ibid.,* pp. vii, viii, 149.
23 *Principles of Literary Criticism,* p. 261; see, T. C. Pollock, "A Critique of I. A.
Richards' Theory of Language and Literature," in *A Theory of Meaning Analyzed* (Chicago, 1942), pp. 1–25.
24 *Principles of Literary Criticism,* p. 177.
25 *Ibid.,* p. 176.
26 *The Meaning of Meaning,* pp. 205, 206.
27 *Principles of Literary Criticism,* pp. 177, 176.
28 *Ibid.,* p. 180.

Often in difficult circumstances the speaker must supply and control a large part of the causes of the listener's experiences, and correspondingly, the listener must try to block out intrusive, irrelevant elements from his past experiences.[29]

Richards' division of the functions of language yields two types of communication, that which he calls *scientific* and that which he calls *emotive*. Into the first type of communication go those language transactions concerned with strict attention to the symbolization of references. Outside the sciences this form of communication is rare.

In all discussions one finds that what is said is only in part determined by reference, Richards remarks.[30] Preoccupations with things other than referencing often determine the use of words, and unless one is aware of preoccupations, purposes, and interests of the moment, one will not really know what another may be talking about.[31] "When we speak, the symbolism . . . is caused partly by the reference we are making and partly by social and psychological factors—the purpose for which we are making the reference, the proposed effect of our symbols on other persons, and our own attitude."[32] Presumably to a much greater extent than we realize, we communicate through "offerings of Choices," not through presentation of fact.[33]

Communication may be classified on the basis of the degree to which emotive elements of language usage enters, ranging from strict referential use to poetic use, where the referential purpose is absent altogether or occupies a clearly subordinate position. Poetry, says Richards, affords the clearest examples of the "subordination of reference to attitude. It is the supreme form of *emotive* language."[34] The statements used in poetic discourse are "pseudo-statements." These statements are not justified by their truth or falsity as are the scientific statements; they are justified by their "effect in releasing or organizing our impulses and attitudes."[35] The difference between "emotive beliefs and scientific beliefs" is "not one of degree, but of kind." Thus, there is a truth of "reference" and a truth of "acceptability" of attitude.[36]

In considering the arrangements of words in various kinds of discourse Richards points out that in scientific uses of language not only must the references be correct for success, but the relations of references to one another must be logical. In emotive communications, logical arrangements are not necessary and may actually be an obstacle.

[29] *Ibid.,* p. 178.
[30] *The Meaning of Meaning,* p. 126.
[31] *Ibid.,* p. 126.
[32] *Ibid.,* pp. 10, 11.
[33] *Speculative Instruments,* p. 139.
[34] *Principles of Literary Criticism,* p. 273.
[35] *Science and Poetry* (New York, 1926), pp. 70, 71.
[36] *Principles of Literary Criticism,* pp. 278, 268, 269.

Attitudes have their own proper organization, their own emotional interconnection which must be respected.[37]

Since, in the main, Richards is not concerned with specific ends and practices in discourse, his theory of communication presents no theoretical basis for the classification and differentiation of "mixed" uses of language in communication, as, for instance, the sermon, the advertisement, the political speech, the poem. One should note, however, that he has no objection to classifications that serve useful purposes. He does not deny that older classifications of expository communication or persuasive communication, the machinery of epideictic, deliberative, or forensic communications, or lyric and epic poetry have their uses.[38] He simply denies that such classifications are useful where theoretical considerations of language are uppermost. Language has as many jobs as we find "convenient to distinguish for a purpose,"[39] he observes. Linguistic conveniences, so long as they are not taken to be a description of reality or to "apply directly to the make-up of the mind," are "useful, indispensable for their special purposes."[40]

The student of rhetoric may avoid confusion by remembering that according to Richards, communication which is partly emotive and partly referential, that is, communication which is classed as "mixed," is rhetorical communication. Into the class would go historical writing, most philosophical writing, some poetry, speeches, and discourse of any kind.

3

When Richards turns explicitly to the subject of Rhetoric, he does so with considerable complaint and suspicion, finding one of the general themes of the old Rhetoric especially pertinent to his discussion. "The old Rhetoric was an offspring of dispute," he remarks; "it developed as the rationale of pleadings and persuadings; it was the theory of the battle of words and has always been itself dominated by the combative impulse. Perhaps what it has most to teach us is the narrowing and blinding influence of that preoccupation, that debater's interest."[41]

Thus, in effect, does Richards in Olympian fashion seem to dispose of the theory underlying the practice of a Pericles, a St. Augustine, a Fenélon, a Burke, a Churchill, a Roosevelt. Nor does he stop there. Outside of some reading in educational theory which leans on psychol-

---

[37] *Ibid.,* p. 268.
[38] *How to Read a Page* (New York, 1942), p. 100.
[39] *Ibid.,* p. 100.
[40] *Ibid.,* p. 100; see also, *The Meaning of Meaning,* p. 95.
[41] *The Philosophy of Rhetoric,* p. 24.

ogy, he can find no more disheartening reading than "the dreary pages of those masters of Rhetoric who thought themselves perfectly acquainted with the subject when they had learnt only to name some of its tools."[42] Thus, seemingly, is dismissed any theory of rhetoric from Aristotle to Whately which had concern with "observing in any given case the available means of persuasion,"[43] or "influencing the *Will*."[44] What sorts of persuasions are there? and to what ends may we reasonably employ them? he asks in derision. "This is a question we all hope to dodge."[45] "Persuasion is only one among the aims of discourse. It poaches on the others—especially on that of *exposition*, which is concerned to state a view, not to persuade people to agree or to do anything more than examine it."[46]

Richards roundly condemns most of the theory and the practices of the past. From the time of the *Gorgias* onwards the literature of rhetoric has been "sales-talk selling sales-talk"; for good reasons, we should today be more interested in defenses against eloquent persuasion, not in aids to it.[47]

Although he finds the art of controlled interrogation man's best hope, it becomes man's worst bane when it turns, as it so often does, into a "technique of purblind disputation."[48] Logic-chopping at Cambridge had not convinced him that discussion was very profitable. Finding the traditional vogue of the disputation to be immense, he feels impelled to assert his opposition. "No verbal institution," he remarks, "has done more than disputation to frustrate man, to prevent the referential and emotive functions coming to terms, and to warp the conduct of language—in its highest self-administrating activities most of all." He would take a stand against the "puppy war with words" which has been fought ever since Plato's time. Since immediate specific purpose controls the disputant's interpretations, the disputant is usually too busy making his points to see what the points are.[49] A controversy, says Richards, is "normally an exploitation of a systematic set of misunderstandings for war-like purposes."[50]

According to Richards, the old Rhetoric begins with Aristotle and "may perhaps be said to end with Archbishop Whately." Not chiefly Aristotle, but Whately becomes representative of the old mode of

[42] *Interpretation in Teaching* (New York, 1938), p. 11.

[43] Rhetorica, tr. W. Rhys Roberts, *The Works of Aristotle*, ed. W. D. Ross (Oxford, 1924), XI, Bk. I, 2, 1355b.

[44] Richard Whately, *Elements of Rhetoric*, reprinted from the 7th ed. (London, 1866), p. 113.

[45] *Speculative Instruments*, p. 159.

[46] *The Philosophy of Rhetoric*, p. 24.

[47] *Speculative Instruments*, p. 166.

[48] *Ibid.*, p. 131.

[49] *Ibid.*, p. 52.

[50] *The Philosophy of Rhetoric*, p. 39.

dealing with rhetorical matters, and thus become Richards' chief target. Whately, who, according to Richards, begins by urging that "Rhetoric must go deep," ends with merely a "collection of prudential Rules about the best sorts of things to say in various argumentative situations, the order in which to bring out your propositions and proofs and examples, at what point it will be most effective to disparage your opponent, how to recommend oneself to the audience, and like matters." As to all of this, Richards concludes, "no one ever learned about them from a treatise who did not know about them already; at the best, the treatise may be an occasion for realizing that there is skill to be developed in discourse, but it does not and cannot teach the skill." So far as Whately treats style, Richards complains, it is no better. No philosophic inquiry into how words work in discourse emerges; there is nothing more than the "usual postcard's worth of crude common sense" about being clear, being vivacious, not being dry, using metaphors, avoiding ambiguity, etc. The ancients, Richards remarks, merely "play with generalizations" about the effects of words. Such generalizations he finds unimportant unless one goes more deeply and, more particularly, "by another route."[51]

Thus, Richards dismisses the old theory of rhetoric considered as the rationale of persuasive discourse and suggests an approach by another route. A "macroscopic" approach yields neither theoretical nor practical value unless it is supplemented by "an intimate or microscopic inquiry which endeavours to look into the structure of the meanings with which discourse is composed, not merely into the effects of various large-scale disposals of these meanings." He admits that there may be much in the old Rhetoric that the new Rhetoric will find useful and advantageous, at least "until man changes his nature, debates and disputes, incites, tricks, bullies and cajoles his fellows less."[52]

Richards appears not to have labored long over the old rhetorical doctrines, particularly the *Inventio* and *Dispositio* phases of ancient doctrine. One does not always find his complaints convincing. To equate *invention* with "finding matters for speech or writing," he remarks, oversimplifies and "narrows interpretation unduly."[53] "It is a very frequent meaning, without doubt," he continues, "but neither the only meaning nor the most active meaning in Tarquin's cry, 'O what excuse can my invention make?' "[54] He finds that the "senses of devising, fabricating, discovering, and originating were all current in Shakespear's time."[55] He complains of Dryden's equating of imagination with

[51] *Ibid.*, pp. 5, 7, 8, 9.
[52] *Ibid.*, pp. 9, 24.
[53] *Speculative Instruments,* p. 157.
[54] *Ibid.*, p. 157; see, Shakespeare, *The Rape of Lucrece,* Line 225.
[55] *Ibid.*, p. 157.

Invention, as one of the "humdrum senses of imagination."[56] He presumably is unaware of the adaptations to poetic theory of the classical conception of Invention in the Renaissance. According to Marvin Herrick, "The sixteenth-century commentators and critics, by combining . . . [the] Aristotelian imitation with theories found in Plato, Cicero, Horace, and Quintilian, arrived at a concept of imitation that closely corresponded to the traditional invention of logic and rhetoric. In fact, by the middle of the century, *imitatio, inventio, fictio,* and *fabula* were corollary terms, often used as synonyms."[57] Richards' complaint that the standard classical conception of Invention "narrows interpretation unduly" may well be the case; but such a judgment could appropriately be made only after full awareness of the inclusiveness of the meaning of the ancient canon.

Richards' misinterpretation follows naturally from his conception of the classical rhetoric. "Rhetorical theory," he observes, "in its entire scope is after all no more than a somewhat chaotic collection of observations made on the ways of lively, venturesome speech and writing."[58] Sections in the old rhetorics which dealt with audiences or with "Hearers as Men, in General," Richards remarks facetiously, "should favour mercy."[59] His cavalier handling of ancient doctrines causes R.S. Crane to reprimand him for dismissing "rival" doctrines and substituting others "prior to any inquiry";[60] and H. M. McLuhan ascribes too quickly, no doubt, the label "true nominalist son of . . . Agricola, and Ramus."[61]

In Richards, what was first proposed as a supplement becomes the entire rationale for his philosophy of rhetoric. The new rhetoric which arises is a rhetoric concerned, not with persuasion as a specific end, but with the meanings of statements in any type of discourse. The new rhetoric, Richards urges, "should be a study of misunderstanding and its remedies." It should concern itself with "How much and in how many ways may good communication differ from bad?"[62]

"Rhetoric I take to be 'the art by which discourse is adapted to its end.' " says Richards, echoing the well-known definition of George Campbell's eighteenth-century *The Philosophy of Rhetoric.*[63] What

[56] *Coleridge on the Imagination* (New York, 1950), p. 27.

[57] Marvin T. Herrick, "The Place of Rhetoric in Poetic Theory," *The Quarterly Journal of Speech,* XXXIV (February 1948), 13.

[58] *Speculative Instruments,* p. 158.

[59] *Interpretation in Teaching,* p. 13; see, George Campbell, *The Philosophy of Rhetoric,* 7th edn. (London, 1823), Bk. I, Ch. vii, p. 87.

[60] R. S. Crane, "I. A. Richards on the Art of Interpretation," *Critics and Criticism,* ed. R. S. Crane (Chicago, Illinois: University of Chicago Press, 1952), p. 44.

[61] H. M. McLuhan, "Poetic vs. Rhetorical Exegesis," *Sewanee Review,* 52 (Winter 1944,) pp. 266–276.

[62] *The Philosophy of Rhetoric,* p. 3.

[63] *Interpretation in Teaching,* p. 12; Cf. Campbell, Bk. I, Ch. 1, p. 13.

should be among its topics may be seen from the contents of Campbell's book, he says, "a book which deserves more attention than it is likely ever again to receive."[64] He does not believe that Campbell fulfilled his promise, but had he done so, he would have given us "all we need to know."[65]

As Richards turns to the general task of a new rhetoric, he is concerned both with the task and the mode of presentation of principles. One should teach rhetoric, "not by dogmatic formula but *by exercises in comparison*." Such exercises should give an understanding of the different modes of speech, their changing forms, and their disguises. The chief divisions of the field for comparison may be "statement, full and explicit, or condensed (by abstraction, ambiguity or implication, the hint, the aposiopesis); statement literal or direct, and indirect (by metaphor, simile, comparison, parallel etc.); suasion, open (from appeal to cajolery) or concealed (either as mere statement or as mere ornament) and so on." The more particular problems of rhetoric he believes to be problems concerning the Figures of Speech, about which present practice is deceiving and out of date.[66]

The art of rhetoric, says Richards, should be a "philosophic discipline aiming at a mastery of the fundamental laws of the use of language, not just a set of dodges that will be found to work sometimes."[67] Philosophy he takes to be a critique of assumptions; hence, a philosophy of rhetoric would have as its concern assumptions about the nature of language.

"To account for understanding and misunderstanding, to study the efficiency of language and its conditions," which he believes to be the role of the new rhetoric, is to face squarely the fact that meanings do not reside in words, but in responders to words, that ambiguity, instead of being a fault of language, is its inevitable condition, that metaphor, instead of being a "happy extra trick," is the constitutive nature of language, thought itself being metaphoric. Richards urges that we renounce the view "that words just have their meanings and that what a discourse does is to be explained as a composition of these meanings as a wall can be represented as a composition of its bricks." The focus of analysis, he argues, should be shifted in order to attempt a more minute grasp of the structures of the smallest discussable units of meaning, and the ways in which these units vary when they are put with other units.[68]

Richards' contextual theory of meaning, thus, paves the way for his

[64] *Interpretation in Teaching*, p. 12.
[65] *Ibid.*, p. 13.
[66] *Ibid.*, pp. 14, 15.
[67] *The Philosophy of Rhetoric*, p. 7.
[68] *Ibid.*, pp. 9, 10, 90, 93.

conception of the new rhetoric and suggests its role as being that of separating the referential function of language from the other language functions.[69]

After pondering the question, What is the relationship of rhetoric, grammar, and logic? Richards concludes that these three ways to intelligence cannot be separated without frustration. "By Definition things arise," giving us "things-to-be-thought-of." When things are thought of, those things are determined both by references and by other psychological factors. This intermingling of language functions makes for inconstancy. Richards urges a frank recognition of the fact that how any word is used is a matter of choice and consent and not a matter of regimentation or compulsion. Meanings are to be determined by how words are used in a sentence and not by any discrete senses they are imagined to possess.[70] Logic must be the systematizer. Logic, which has been "preoccupied either with judgments which are psychological, or with 'propositions,' which were treated as objects of thought, distinct from symbols and not psychological," should be concerned with "the systematization of symbols."[71] "All thought is sorting."[72] Logic is the "Art or discipline of managing our sortings." It is the "ethics of thinking."[73]

The relationship of grammar to rhetoric and logic is that grammar is pervasive. Since words do not have proper meanings, but meanings only in relation to a context, grammar is the *study of the co-operation of words with one another in their contexts.*"[74]

Richards' conception of the relation of rhetoric to logic and grammar may be revealed by his formulary statement: "The Optative view of Definition (which is the central problem of Logic) makes the creation of the things-to-be-thought-of, that is, the demarcation of Sense from the other language functions (which is the central problem of Rhetoric) a matter of our choice—subject, however, always to the exigencies of communication, that is the provision of sufficiently stable inter-verbal action (which is the central problem of Grammar)."[75]

This, then, is the new Rhetoric. It is concerned with the differentiation of referential and emotive language functions in order to produce understanding or to explain misunderstanding in any type of discourse. It assumes that if one understands the language functions, appropriate uses of language may be chosen for whatever end one may want to advance, be it to state a view clearly, to establish a right relationship

[69] *Interpretation in Teaching*, p. 395.
[70] *Ibid.*, pp. 3, 393, 395.
[71] *The Meaning of Meaning*, p. 87.
[72] *Interpretation in Teaching*, p. 359.
[73] *Ibid.*, p. 16.
[74] *Ibid.*, p. 16.
[75] *Ibid.*, p. 395.

with an audience, a right relationship with a subject, win an election, or record one's feelings about things in poetry. It is a study of language behavior and reveals how discourse in being adapted to its end reflects the referential and emotive language functions, the many manoeuverings of which language guided by purpose is capable. It is concerned with the smallest structural units of discourse and not with the large-scale ordonnance of argument.

4

The theoretical position of Richards with reference to rhetoric and communication has been strongly felt in the field of criticism. With care and precision equal to that manifested in his articulation of a theory of communication and meaning, Richards has articulated a critical theory that has given him significance in modern times.

John Crowe Ransom, long-time editor of the *Kenyon Review,* has remarked that "Discussion of the new criticism must start with Mr. Richards. The new criticism very nearly began with him."[76] With this statement few would disagree. Whereas one may find difficulty in defining the precise nature of the New Criticism, he would find the direction of the critical movement clear enough. Criticism simply shifted from a poet-poem or speaker-speech relationship to a poem-audience or speech-audience relationship. Finding metaphysical concern with such questions as What is poetry? or What is a poet? unfruitful, Richards turned to explore what the reader or listener gets from discourse. Poetry became for him an instrument by which experience of some kind is communicated to a reader or listener. To a generation accustomed to contemplating the beauties of poetry as aesthetic object, he asserted in somewhat lowly fashion, "But poetry itself is a mode of communication."[77] "What it communicates and how it does so and the worth of what is communicated form the subject-matter of criticism. It follows that criticism . . . is very largely, though not wholly, an exercise in navigation."[78] Thus was paved the introduction of a psychological approach to criticism to oppose metaphysical approaches.

We are not concerned with the influence of Richards on the new critical movement, although with Cleanth Brooks we may agree that he may be regarded as the critic "through whose mediation psychology was to make its greatest impact upon literary criticism."[79] We are

[76] John Crowe Ransom, *The New Criticism* (Norfolk, Connecticut, 1941), p. 3.
[77] *Practical Criticism,* New Impression (New York, 1954), p. 11.
[78] *Ibid.,* p. 11.
[79] William K. Wimsatt, Jr. & Cleanth Brooks, *Literary Criticism* (New York, 1957), p. 613; see also, Stanley Hyman, "I. A. Richards and the Criticism of Interpretation," *The Armed Vision* (New York, 1948), p. 308.

concerned with the relevance of Richards to the student of rhetoric, for whatever else rhetoric may be, its concern is with communication. Since Richards does not view literature as a private haven for aesthetes, his remarks may be generalized. In truth, he generalizes them himself. "The world of poetry," he remarks, "has in no sense any different reality from the rest of the world and it has no special laws and no other-worldly peculiarities. It is made up of experiences of exactly the same kinds as those that come to us in other ways."[80]

The chief weakness of our best criticism today, Richards remarks, "is the pretense that fundamental matters can be profitably discussed without prolonged and technical thinking." Accordingly, "Most evaluative criticism is not statement or even attempted statement. It is either suasion, which is politics, or it is social communion."[81] Critics and even theorists in criticism currently assume, he remarks, "that their first duty is to be moving, to excite in the mind emotions appropriate to their august subject-matter."[82] Nor will case-history studies of utterances as socio-economic-political products solve current critical problems. Although we should encourage them, since they "feed the scholars who make them," these critical studies, which may tell us *"why* something was said," do not in their present form tell *"what it was"* that was said.[83] Critics, he believes, have hardly begun to ask the question what they are doing and under what conditions they are working.[84]

As Richards understands it, criticism is "the endeavour to discriminate between experiences and to evaluate them." This cannot be done, he believes, without an understanding of the nature of experience, or without theories of value and communication. The principles which apply to criticism must be taken from more fundamental studies. So far as he can see, "critical remarks are merely a branch of psychological remarks."[85]

On the foundation of his theory of language and communication Richards raises his critical structure. Criticism is the "science of . . . meanings and the meanings which larger groups of words may carry." It is not a mere account of what men have written or how they have written, with answers to such questions being determined by borrowed standards, often applied without reference to the nature of the mind or to our growing outlook on the world.[86]

To Richards the critic must have three qualifications. He must be first "an adept at experiencing, without eccentricities, the state of mind

---

[80] *Principles of Literary Criticism,* p. 78.
[81] *Coleridge on the Imagination,* pp. 5, xiii.
[82] *Principles of Literary Criticism,* p. 3.
[83] *Speculative Instruments,* p. 82.
[84] *Principles of Literary Criticism,* p. 227.
[85] *Ibid.,* pp. 2, 23.
[86] *Coleridge on the Imagination,* pp. 231, 232.

relevant to the work of art he is judging. Secondly, he must be able to distinguish experiences from one another as regards their less superficial features. Thirdly, he must be a sound judge of values."[87]

Criticism has only one goal. All critical endeavor, all interpretation, appreciation, exhortation, praise, or abuse has as its goal "improvement in communication." Although he is aware that such a conception may appear to be an exaggeration, nevertheless he asserts that in practice this is true. Critical rules and principles are but means to the end of attaining more precise and more discriminating communication. There is, he admits, "a valuation side of criticism," but he asserts that "When we have solved, completely, the communication problem, when we have got, perfectly, the experience, *the mental condition* relevant," the problem of worth "nearly always settles itself; or rather, our own inmost nature and the nature of the world in which we live decide it for us." Value, he believes, cannot be demonstrated except through the communication of what is valuable.[88]

As Richards begins his critical theory he announces that there are two pillars upon which a theory of criticism must rest. These are an account of value and an account of communication.[89] The judgment "that a passage is good is an act of living. The examination and description of its merits is an act of theory."[90] A full critical statement, accordingly, consists of two parts. The part which describes the value of the experience Richards refers to as the *critical* part. The part dealing with a description of the object arousing the experience he refers to as the *technical* part.[91]

His critical system presents the theory underlying the judgment of both sides of the coin. His first concern is with the question, What kind of experiences are good? "What is good or valuable," he remarks, "is the exercise of impulses and the satisfaction of their appetencies." An impulse, he defines as the "process in the course of which a mental event may occur, a process . . . beginning in a stimulus and ending in an act." An appetency is a "seeking after." He admits that the word *desire* might serve as well as appetency, were it not for the fact that one cannot easily avoid the implication of accompanying conscious beliefs with references to what is sought and a further restriction to felt and recognized longings. For him, the term *want* has similar disadvantages. "Appetencies may be, and for the most part are, unconscious, and to leave out those which we cannot discover by introspection would involve extensive errors." For the same reason it is wiser not

[87] *Principles of Literary Criticism*, p. 114.
[88] *Practical Criticism*, pp. 11, 12.
[89] *Principles of Literary Criticism*, p. 25.
[90] *Coleridge on the Imagination*, p. 140.
[91] *Principles of Literary Criticism*, p. 23.

to start from *feeling*. He extends his conception of what is good or valuable by concluding, "Anything is valuable which will satisfy an appetency without involving the frustration of some equal or *more important* appetency; in other words, the only reason which can be given for not satisfying a desire is that more important desires will thereby be thwarted." The most valuable states of mind are those "which involve the widest and most comprehensive co-ordination of activities and the least curtailment, conflict, starvation, and restriction." The most valuable effects of communicative activity are those to be described in terms of *attitudes*, "the resolution, inter-inanimation, and balancing of impulses." In a well-developed person imaginal action and incipient action, that is, action which does not go so far as actual movement, is more important than overt action.[92]

As Richards turns to the matter of communication, he remarks that the important fact for the study of literature or any mode of communication is that several kinds of meaning are to be differentated. Either in speaking and writing or in reading and listening, the "Total Meaning we are engaged with is, almost always, a blend, a combination of several contributory meanings of different types." A critic, therefore, concerned with the matter of discrimination, must first discern what meanings are being communicated, and thereafter, how successfully these are being communicated.[93]

Most human utterance and nearly all articulate speech, he believes, can be profitably regarded from four points of view. The four aspects which are distinguishable he calls Sense, Feeling, Tone, and Intention. "We speak to say something," he remarks, "and when we listen we expect something to be said. We use words to direct our hearers' attention upon some state of affairs, to present to them some items for consideration and to excite in them some thoughts about these items." This is what Richards means by *Sense*, and, as may be readily recognized, it pertains to the matter of making references. Secondly, we have some "feelings *about these items*." We have attitudes, biases, and interests with respect to these items, and we use language to reflect these attitudes, interests, and feelings. Thus, *Feeling*, or attitude towards referents, becomes another dimension of meaning. Thirdly, the speaker ordinarily has *"an attitude to his listener."* His word choice and arrangement is largely governed by audience variation in automatic or deliberate "recognition of his relation to them." This is the *Tone* dimension of meaning, in terms of which Richards believes many of the secrets of style could be shown to reside. Finally, speakers have intentions or aims, conscious or unconscious; they desire to secure effects. Purpose modifies one's speech. An understanding of this dimension of

[92] *Ibid.,* pp. 58, 86, 47, 48, 59, 113, 111.
[93] *Practical Criticism*, p. 180.

meaning, purpose or intention, is "part of the whole business of appre-
hending . . . meaning." According to Richards, unless we know what a
speaker is trying to do, we are unable to estimate the measure of success. Sometimes, Richards notes, a speaker will "purpose no more than
to state his thoughts (1), or to express his feelings about what he is
thinking of, e.g. Hurrah! Damn! (2), or to express his attitude to his
listener (3)." "Frequently his intention operates through and satisfies
itself in a combination of the other functions. Yet it has effects not
reducible to their effects. It may govern the stress laid upon points in
an argument for example, shape the arrangement, and even call attention to itself in such phrases as 'for contrast's sake' or 'lest it be supposed.' " Nevertheless, it "controls the 'plot' in the largest sense of the
word, and is at work whenever the author [or speaker] is 'hiding his
hand.' "[94]

The difference between better or worse utterances, says Richards, is
in "design." Poor speech and poor writing is poor "either because it is
not attempting anything worth trying or because it is inefficient."[95]
Critics often demonstrate unmistakable confusion between value and
communicative efficacy.[96] A complete critical statement would be a
statement about the value of experience and also a statement about
communicative efficacy through which the experience is revealed.
Thus, Richards' critical theory and practice represent an attempt to be
microscopic in approach, just as does his rhetorical theory and practice.

CONCLUSION

"We struggle all our days with misunderstandings," remarks Richards
as he contemplates the process of reviving an old subject, and "no
apology is required for any study which can prevent or remove
them."[97] That rhetoric as a term has been equivocal throughout its
lifetime can scarcely be gainsaid. It has been a term of abuse as well
as a virtue word, a term referring to the whole rationale of persuasive
discourse, and a term referring to means. Has Richards clarified or
confused the concept?

When *The Meaning of Meaning* emerged from the press in 1923,
Richards and his collaborator announced a new "science of symbolism." By making the "beginning of a division between what cannot be
intelligibly talked of and what can" the authors believed the new
science to be in a position to "provide a new basis for Physics,"[98] to

94 *Ibid.,* pp. 181, 182, 207, 182, 183.
95 *Speculative Instruments,* p. 122.
96 *Principles of Literary Criticism,* p. 255.
97 *The Philosophy of Rhetoric,* p. 3.
98 *The Meaning of Meaning,* pp. vii, 85.

solve the most important problems of the theory of knowledge, to dispose of the problem of Truth, and to provide a definitive basis for scientific aesthetics.[99] These were considerably pretentious claims which, of course, have not completely yielded the harvest expected. That the few topics discussed in *The Philosophy of Rhetoric* are to be regarded as solving the problem of understanding and misunderstanding is doubtful. One feels considerable sympathy with the remark of F. R. Leavis, "had the ambition been less the profit might very well have been greater." The "largeness of promise and an impressiveness of operation [are] quite disproportionate to anything that emerges."[100]

As has sometimes been remarked, the importance of Richards' work on communication has been obscured for many people by their annoyance at a too frequent outcropping of the "amateur spirit." A romantic inflation about the significance of the topic, dark hints about the extent of our ignorance, the cataclysm that awaits us unless we accept his new theories, the ready dismissal of all who have gone before him—all these intrude upon the reader to make him suspicious of the performance. "No matter what a man's standing, and no matter how impressive the substance of his views, you can still regard him from an unassailable vantage-ground if only you happen to observe that he isn't capable of understanding what is said to him."[101]

Nevertheless, that Richards is a thoughtful man no one can doubt. Nor can one doubt that he has been a profound student of communication and rhetoric. R. S. Crane has posed a problem which may be seriously regarded by all students of rhetoric: "For what is the force of an appeal to the nature of things against rival doctrines of language or discourse when that nature itself has been determined by a decision, prior to any inquiry, to identify reality only with what can be signified in a particular fixed relationship among three equivocal words. And what is there to compel an abandonment of the distinctions of traditional grammar or logic in an argument which derives all its negative cogency from a metaphor so admirably adapted to the end of destroying such distinctions as that upon which Richards' system is based?"[102]

It would be easy to answer Crane's question with a resounding protest to the effect that there is nothing to compel an abandonment of traditional distinctions. The answer, I think, would not really be a response to Richards' theory. B. F. Skinner has reminded us that classical rhetoric might have been the forerunner of a science of verbal

---

[99] See Max Black, "Some Objections to Ogden and Richards' Theory of Interpretation," *The Journal of Philosophy*, XXXIX (May 21, 1942), 281.

[100] F. R. Leavis (Review of *The Philosophy of Rhetoric*), *Scrutiny*, VI (September 1937), 212.

[101] D. W. Harding, "I. A. Richards," *Scrutiny*, I (March 1933), 336.

[102] R. S. Crane, p. 44.

behavior. It began as an objective discipline, closer, perhaps, to a science than either the logic or grammar of the same period. Hundreds of technical terms were developed to describe linguistic features. As rhetoric came to be used for purposes of ornamentation and persuasion, it died as a pure science. "What is wanted is *an account of the events which occur when a man speaks or responds to speech.*"[103]

No one doubts that there is a rhetoric of practice and persuasion. Richards does not doubt this either. Indeed, without much casuistry, one could argue that Richards does not believe language communications are anything other than instances of persuasion, for he remarks that he "regards all discourse—outside the technicalities of science—as over-determined," that is, as having "multiplicity of meaning" due to the co-presence of referential and other functions of language.[104] Contemporary literary men have found Richards' theory distasteful on this point, that is, that he is willing to place his emphasis in poetry on external relations with an audience rather than on integrated structure to be contemplated for pleasure.[105]

Richards leans heavily upon George Campbell's conception of rhetoric, as the "adaptation of discourse to its ends," and Campbell has long been considered an eighteenth-century interpreter of the classical tradition in rhetoric. Furthermore, Richards has noted the disregard by contemporary scholars of their classical forbears. When, says he, "not long ago some of the very same concerns revived which had originally prompted the *Topica* and the *Rhetoric,* not many of those who set out, behind 'anti-metaphysical' or 'non-Aristotelian' banners, to teach us all how we should talk, evinced much curiosity about the ancient highways leading into their well-advertised new territory."[106]

One cannot easily make an anti-classicist out of Richards. One can far more easily make his work a vast subdivision of the classical tradition. When he opens his *Interpretation in Teaching,* he remarks: "Rhetoric, Grammar, and Logic—the first three liberal Arts, the three ways to intelligence and a command of the mind that met in the Trivium, meet here again." Neither "the general problem nor the plan of attack can be new."[107] "How to *make* minds clear as well as keep them clear," he says, "is . . . for us, as it was for Socrates, the key question."[108]

103 B. F. Skinner, *Verbal Behavior* (William James Lectures) (Harvard University, 1948), pp. 4, 5.
104 *The Philosophy of Rhetoric,* p. 39.
105 See H. M. McLuhan, "Poetic vs. Rhetorical Exegesis," *op. cit.,* pp. 266–276; also, Charles I. Glicksberg, "I. A. Richards and the Science of Criticism," *Sewanee Review,* XLVI (Oct.–Dec. 1938), 520–533; also, John Crowe Ransom, "A Psychologist Looks at Poetry," in *The World's Body* (New York, 1938), pp. 143–165; also, Christopher Isherwood, *Lions and Shadows* (London, 1933), pp. 121, 122.
106 *Speculative Instruments,* pp. 164, 165.
107 *Interpretation in Teaching,* p. 3.
108 *Speculative Instruments,* p. 71.

Allying the wisdom of the past with insights from all times, Richards has presented a "microscopic" supplement to ancient patterns, a gigantic supplement. His desire was to make language theory yield to experimental procedure, to refine and make precise that which has sometimes been cloudy or mystical. Significant scientists of language, including Charles Morris, have paid tribute to his "pioneer" work in the field of semeiotic, and a large segment of rhetorical scientists at work today testify to the helpfulness of the pioneering.[109]

Rhetoric and poetic severely separated in the nineteenth century meet again in the twentieth century through Richards in the ancient trivium, Rhetoric, Grammar, and Logic. This writer suspects that the future is in the direction of Richards. As understanding increases, a mere falling back upon tradition will not work. Sheer ecstasy and cults of the obscure will give way to ordered procedures and uses of the best tools for analysis that are available, whatever the field from which they come.

---

[109] Charles Morris, *Signs, Language and Behavior* (New York, 1946), pp. vii, 265.

10 I. A. RICHARDS' THEORY OF METAPHOR

MANUEL BILSKY

Clearly metaphor is a central concept in Richards' view of rhetoric. If, as he contends, all language and thought are metaphorical, and metaphor is the "omnipresent principle of language," then a theory of metaphor necessarily is basic to rhetorical theory. It is with this contention that Bilsky, a professor of philosophy, is concerned in the following essay. His purpose is to explain Richards' theory of metaphor and to evaluate the theory's shortcomings.

In his *Philosophy of Rhetoric* (90–91), Richards quotes from Percy Shelley's "Defense of Poetry" to support his view of metaphor's centrality. Shelley said, according to Richards, "Language is *vitally metaphorical*," implying that *all* language is so. Consult Shelley's essay to determine for yourself whether Shelley is describing the language of all men or only of those possessing a highly developed poetic faculty. (See, for example, Carl Grabo and Martin Freeman, eds., *The Reader's Shelley*, 474–478.)

For a more recent analysis of the place of metaphor in rhetorical theory see Michael Osborn and Douglas Ehninger, "The Metaphor in Public Address," *Speech Monographs*, XXIX (August 1962), 223–234.

Source: Modern Philology, 50 (1952), pp. 130–137. Reprinted with permission of the author and The University of Chicago Press.

According to the communication theory of art to which I. A. Richards subscribes, the work of art—the poem, say—is the medium for the transfer of an experience, predominantly emotional, from one mind to another. Successful communication of this sort, Richards urges, is contingent upon the fulfilment of certain conditions by both poet and reader. On the reader's side Richards suggests ten possible barriers to effective communication; these he discusses in detail in *Practical Criticism*. But a prior condition must be satisfied before communicative efficacy is insured. The poet himself must possess several characteristics, among which the "supreme agent" is the command of metaphor. Regarding its importance, Richards says that a study which "sketches the conditions of communication . . . has to put the Theory of Metaphor very much in the forefront."[1] Most of what he has written about the subject appears in *The Philosophy of Rhetoric* and *Interpretation in Teaching.*[2] But it is never far from his mind; he touches on it in most of his other books. In this paper I propose to set forth the main tenets of this theory, account for some of the discrepancies that appear in it, and finally point out some of its weaknesses. Four headings, it seems to me, cover the essential points in Richards' discussions: (1) his uses of the term "metaphor," (2) his distinction between a sense metaphor and an emotive metaphor, (3) his description of how a metaphor works, and (4) his concern with whether the command of metaphor is a unique gift of the poet.

I

Tentatively, Richards suggests a definition of "metaphor" which neither involves novelty nor occasions surprise: it is a comparison, he says, between two things, accomplished by a "carrying over of a word from its normal use to a new use."[3] The metaphor "in Johnson's phrase 'gives us two ideas for one.' . . . We compound different uses of the word into one, and speak of something as though it were another."[4] Thus the shift in "The lamp throws its light on the page" occurs in the word "throws," which is normally used to designate quite a different action from that attributed to the lamp: ordinarily, people throw objects. By combining "throw" with "lamp," therefore, we get two ideas for one, a person throwing an object and a lamp radiating light. Both uses of the word are compounded when "throw" is connected with "lamp"; we speak of the lamp as though it were a person.

Richards feels, however, that such a description is inadequate, partly because it leads to mistaken views as to the function of metaphor. The idea he opposes particularly is that metaphor "is a grace or added power of language."[5] He insists that it is not an ornament or embellishment. To show that such a view is mistaken, he distinguishes three senses of "metaphor," or, rather, he uses the term in three different senses. His distinctions, however, are implied rather than explicitly made: he leaves it to the reader to grasp the particular sense in which he is using the term.

His three uses can be distinguished on the basis of scope. In his first sense of the term, its scope is the least restricted; in the second sense,

---

[1] Hugh R. Walpole, *Semantics: The Nature of Words and Their Meanings* (New York, 1941), p. 11.

[2] I. A. Richards, *The Philosophy of Rhetoric* (New York, 1936); *Interpretation in Teaching* (London, 1938). These will be referred to hereafter as "P.R." and "I.T."

[3] I. A. Richards, *Practical Criticism* (New York, 1929), p. 221.

[4] *P.R.*, p. 117.

[5] *Ibid.*, p. 90.

more so; and in the third, still more highly restricted. It is in the first sense, the least restricted, or unrestricted, use of the term, that Richards expounds a doctrine that is radically different from most treatments of metaphor; and it is this sense which largely furnishes him the grounds for refuting those who hold some sort of embellishment view.

It is not too unusual, in the literature dealing with the subject, to find the view that language is largely metaphoric. But Richards carries this notion much further. He asserts not only that all language is of this character but that all thought is also: not only is "metaphor the omnipresent principle of language,"[6] but "thinking is [also] radically metaphoric."[7] Here is his argument for this view: All thinking is sorting. To think about anything is to take it as a member of a class and not merely as a particular. In order that it may be taken as a member of a class, the past must be operative. When we are presented with a lamp, say, recognition depends on our previous experiences with lamps and on our abstractive power which enables us to put the given object in the class of lamps; and it is in virtue of the comparison of the shared qualities that we apply "lamp" to the given presentation. In this sense James's polyp saying, "Hallo! Thingembob again!" is thinking. We start our thinking, therefore, not with particulars but with sortings, recognitions. These are the primitives in our thought-processes. Thus the word "lamp" is not a substitute for one discrete past impression; it represents a combination of the generalized features, or qualities, of all past and present impressions. But this is really an account of metaphor; for, when we use one, we support thoughts of two different things by one word or phrase. To take something as of a sort makes evident the parallel involved. If there are no qualities that the given object has in common with past objects, there would be no thinking; if there are no characteristics which the two terms of a metaphor have in common, there would be no metaphor, no comparison. Hence, all thought is metaphoric, and all thought is consequently expressed by means of linguistic metaphors; that is, all language is metaphoric.[8]

Richards calls this a theoretical justification for the claim that metaphor is the omnipresent principle of language. He also suggests an empirical justification, but this turns out to support, not the assertion that all language is metaphoric, but the more restricted notion, namely, that ordinary language contains a great many metaphors. Richards makes the switch from talking about metaphor in the unrestricted sense to talking about it in the restricted sense, without, apparently, being aware that he is making it. He says: "We cannot get through three sen-

[6] *Ibid.*, p. 92.
[7] *I.T.*, p. 48.
[8] *P.R.*, pp. 30–36; 93–94; also *I.T.*, pp. 48–49. This account presupposes a familiarity with Richards' context theory of meaning (see *I.T.*, pp. vii ff.).

tences of ordinary fluid discourse without [metaphor]. . . . Even in the rigid language of the settled sciences, we do not eliminate it or prevent it without great difficulty." This can be shown, he adds, by observation. But that "most sentences in free or fluid discourse turn out to be metaphoric" does not prove that all thought and all language are metaphoric. Thus his justification for the unrestricted use of the term must rest, not on this kind of empirical observation, but on his "theoretical" argument.

The second, or restricted, sense of "metaphor" is "a special type of the mode of operation of all language (and all signs)."[9] Richards does not make altogether clear what he has in mind for this second sense, but apparently he means by it those words, seemingly literal, which on close examination turn out to be metaphors: in these also, he says, "we range [the two terms, i.e., man's throwing a ball and the lamp's radiating light] together as examples of a class [and name] their common property."[10] Presumably this group contains what we would ordinarily call "dead," or "sleeping," metaphors.

The third sense which may be discriminated among Richards' remarks refers to what are commonly called "live" metaphors, those which make new and striking comparisons. Thus, whereas "the leg of a table" would be a second-sense metaphor, one so deeply ingrained in ordinary language that generally it is no longer considered metaphoric, Eliot's comparison of the evening sky to a "patient etherized upon a table" would be a third-sense metaphor. As has been suggested, Richards himself does not clearly distinguished these three senses, but they are implicit in what he says and must be kept separate if we are to understand what follows.

Richards draws an interesting distinction between a sense metaphor and an emotive metaphor. In the former, he says, the similarity is between sensations; in the latter it is between feelings. Richards' clearest statement of this distinction is the following:

In a sense metaphor a shift of the word is occasioned and justified by a similarity or analogy *between the object* it is usually applied to and the new object. In an emotive metaphor the shift occurs through some similarity *between the feelings* the new situation and the normal situation arouse. The same word may, in different contexts, be either a sense or an emotive metaphor. If you call a man a swine, for example, it may be because his features resemble those of a pig, but it may be because you have towards him something of the feeling you conventionally have towards pigs, or because you propose, if possible, to excite those feelings.[11]

Richards' terminology is slightly misleading, since both types of metaphor may function emotively, i.e., may express or evoke a range

---

[9] *I.T.*, p. 50 n.
[10] *Ibid.*, p. 59.
[11] *Practical Criticism*, pp. 221–22.

of emotions. It turns out, therefore, that metaphor (both types) is a species of emotive language. Hence everything Richards says in other contexts about emotive language—that it is a means of expressing or evoking an attitude or feeling—applies equally to metaphor. We get an intimation at this point of why Richards thinks the command of metaphor is such an asset to the poet. One further remark is perhaps in order. Since metaphor is a species of emotive language, what distinguishes it from other emotive languages? Richards suggests that, whereas metaphor is an indirect means of exciting emotions, things like the rhythm of poetry, tied imagery, or rhyme are more direct means.

To facilitate the description of how a metaphor best secures its effects, Richards introduces two terms, "tenor" and "vehicle," which are already so widely used that they scarcely need explanation. But, briefly, in the sentence, "The Oxford Movement is a spent wave," "Oxford Movement" is the tenor; "spent wave," the vehicle. The tenor, thus, is the main subject, while the vehicle is that to which the tenor is compared. Richards warns us, however, that we must not jump to the conclusion that one, the tenor, is central while the other is peripheral. This was the eighteenth-century notion which he rejects. The metaphor is not, for him, a mere embellishment. He suggests a scale of varying importance:

> With different metaphors the relative importance of the contributions of vehicle and tenor . . . varies immensely. At one extreme the vehicle may become almost a mere decoration or coloring of the tenor, at the other extreme, the tenor may become almost a mere excuse for the introduction of the vehicle, and so no longer be "the principal subject."[12]

Most of the problems about the effectiveness of a metaphor concern the relation of tenor to vehicle. One such question is whether the metaphor gets its effects mainly by means of the resemblances between tenor and vehicle, the disparities between them, or both. A second, and slightly different, question is whether many points of resemblance between tenor and vehicle are more effective than few. Should the reader be able to get the connection immediately, or should he have to struggle for it?

On the first of these, Richards' mature view seems to be:

> We must not, with the 18th Century, suppose that interactions of tenor and vehicle are to be confined to their resemblances. There is disparity action too. . . . In general, there are very few metaphors in which disparities between tenor and vehicle are not as much operative as the similarities.[13]

[12] *P.R.,* p. 100.
[13] *Ibid.,* p. 127. Earlier Richards expressed a somewhat different view (see I. A. Richards and C. K. Ogden, *The Meaning of Meaning* [New York, 1947], pp. 213–14).

One more quotation will perhaps make his point somewhat clearer. In discussing William James's "blotting paper voices," he says:

And often the operative ground of the metaphor is not a resemblance at all but some other relation. The relation may be obscure, as James thought it was here, even too obscure to be discovered. That does not prevent tenor and vehicle working together to produce the required resultant; and the extent, intimacy and adroitness of their co-operation does not necessarily at all depend upon our supposing that we know what the ground is.[14]

Our second question on the relation between tenor and vehicle is whether the poet should emphasize the resemblances or whether he should use a metaphor between whose tenor and vehicle there are but few similarities. Richards avoids either extreme. He rejects the "18th Century conception of the kind of comparison that metaphor should supply, the process of pointing out likenesses—perspicuously [sic] collecting particulars of resemblances."[15] His justification for rejecting this view may be found in the paragraph above. But he also rejects "the opposed conception of comparison—as a mere putting together of two things to see what will happen [as] a contemporary fashion, which takes an extreme case as the norm." He is referring to poets whose metaphors are so obscure that they leave most readers with a sense of bafflement. "This is," he tells us, "the opposite position from Johnson's, for . . . Johnson objected to comparisons being, like Cowley's 'far fetched.' "[16]

Perhaps the most important question and the one most closely related to Richards' central views on communication concerns the uniqueness of the poet's command of metaphor. In a sense all the foregoing has been preliminary to this. Is this metaphor-making ability a unique characteristic of the poet, something that distinguishes him from other people? Richards' answer emerges in the course of his criticism of the following Aristotelian dicta: "The greatest thing by far is to have a command of metaphor. . . . This alone cannot be imparted to another; it is the mark of genius, for to make good metaphors implies an eye for resemblances."[17] Richards questions three assumptions which he finds in the quotation.

The first is that " 'an eye for resemblances' is a gift that some men have but others have not." The grounds on which he denies this may be found above in the discussion of the unrestricted sense of "metaphor." Addressing himself directly to the assertion, Richards says: "But we all live, and speak, only through our eye for resemblances. Without

[14] *I.T.*, p. 133.
[15] *P.R.*, p. 122.
[16] *Ibid.*, p. 124.
[17] *Ibid.*, p. 89, quoting *Aristotle Poetics* 1459[a].

it we should perish early. Though some men may have better eyes than others, the differences between them are in degree only."[18]

In the second place, he doubts that "though everything else may be taught, 'this alone cannot be imparted to another.' " Richards holds that the differences in degree mentioned above "may be remedied, certainly in some measure, as other differences are, by the right kinds of teaching and study." It is possible to gain a command of metaphor, he says, "just as we learn whatever else makes us distinctively human. It is all imparted to us from others, with and through the language we learn, language which is utterly unable to aid us except through the command of metaphor which it gives."[19]

Third, Richards questions the assumption that "metaphor is something special and exceptional in the use of language, a deviation from its normal mode of working, instead of the omnipresent principle of all its free action."[20] Richards' answer to this may be found in the discussion of the first two senses of "metaphor," earlier in this paper. His conclusion, therefore, appears to be that the command of metaphor is not a gift which the poet and no one else has. Everyone who engages in any sort of language transaction, according to Richards, possesses it to some degree.

II

In his analysis Richards seems mainly concerned to refute Aristotle's view that the command of metaphor is a unique gift of the poet. We shall presently see how successful his refutation is. But several other interesting questions are suggested by Richards' discussion. Is there, for example, a contradiction between the tenor-vehicle distinction and the alleged metaphoric character of all language? Second, why is Richards so inconsistent on making every word a metaphor? Third, are there any consequences of this enterprise which Richards would be unwilling to accept? Before dealing specifically with the Richards-Aristotle controversy, I would like to make some remarks about each of these questions.

The first arises when we put the tenor-vehicle distinction alongside the assertion that all language is metaphoric.[21] To make such an assertion is equivalent to saying that any word in any context is a metaphor. If we ask how this applies to "river" in "I walked to the river," we learn

---

18 *Ibid.*, pp. 89–90.

19 *Ibid.*

20 *Ibid.*, p. 90. This point comes to much the same thing as the first.

21 Richards, it will be remembered, holds not only that all language is metaphoric but that the same is true for all thought. Either categorical assertion may be challenged on the same grounds, but for our purposes this will not be necessary. Nothing will be lost if we stick to the linguistic formulation of the problem.

from Richards' account that "river" is a metaphor in the first, or un-restricted, sense of the term. Granted that we accept this unusual doc-trine, a difficulty seems to arise when we ask how the tenor-vehicle distinction applies to such a metaphor. There is no problem when we are dealing with the second or third sense. If someone refers to his mind as "this river," "mind" is the tenor, "river" the vehicle. But in a first-sense metaphor, e.g., "river" in "I walked to the river," what is the tenor and what is the vehicle?

This question is very puzzling. Richards himself does not face it; but, if the tenor-vehicle distinction applies to all metaphors, surely it should apply to first-sense metaphors. If he were to try to answer the question, it seems as though he would have to resort to something like the following explanation. First let us see exactly how tenor and vehicle apply to a third-sense metaphor, namely, the mind-river collo-cation. A diagram will perhaps show more clearly what is involved (Fig. 1). On the basis of the resemblances, we substitute "river" for "mind"; thus we use "river" metaphorically.

Now let us use a similar diagram for the unrestricted sense of "meta-phor" (Fig. 2). Here again, on the basis of the resemblances, we sub-stitute "river$_2$" for "river$_1$"; thus, we are using "river$_2$" metaphorically. The difficulty, therefore, seems to disappear when we attach subscripts to the words in question.

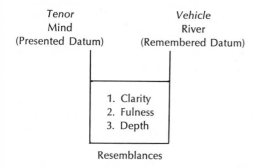

Tenor	Vehicle
Mind	River
(Presented Datum)	(Remembered Datum)

1. Clarity
2. Fulness
3. Depth

Resemblances

Figure 1

But does it really disappear? I have gone to extraordinary lengths to make Richards' tenor-vehicle distinction accord with his claim that all words are metaphors, as, it seems to me, Richards himself must, if his claim is to stand up. But if we examine a little more closely the mind-river collocation as compared with the river$_1$-river$_2$ collocation, some new difficulties appear.

In the first place, the second diagram makes sense only if the es-sence, the defining characteristic, of metaphor is resemblance. I do not wish, nor is it necessary, to get involved in the complexities of the theory of definition. But does not an appeal to usage justify our defining "metaphor" rather as a comparison between two things which are essentially different? Would it not then be a gross distortion of usage to apply the term "metaphor" in a case in which the two things being compared are essentially the same, as, for example, river₁ and river₂ are essentially the same?

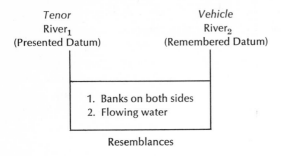

Figure 2

Furthermore, on Richards' own grounds, the function of an aesthetic experience is to provide synaesthesis, a balancing of opposed impulses. The chief instrument by which the poet accomplishes this is metaphor, and we can see how this theory is plausible when the metaphor involved is the mind-river collocation. We have opposed impulses to the two different ideas, and a balance is effected when the two are brought together by the metaphorical use of "river." But when "river₂" is alleged to be a metaphor, in what sense is there an opposition of impulses? The two ideas, river₁ and river₂, are essentially the same, and it becomes very difficult to see how there can be a balance of impulses when there is no opposition in the first place. Hence, even though Richards should be willing to accept the consequences of doing violence to ordinary usage, when we take synaesthesis into consideration, it hardly seems as though he is justified in applying the tenor-vehicle distinction to the river₁-river₂ collocation.

Why is Richards so insistent that all language is metaphoric? Nowhere does he state explicitly why he goes to such lengths to demonstrate the validity of this categorical statement. And if we confine our attention to his discussions of metaphor, we get no enlightenment from Richards. But if we consider his views on metaphor in conjunction with other parts of his aesthetic theory, we may get some explanation. It is true enough that his rejection of the eighteenth-century conception will be justified if he can show that metaphor is "the omnipresent principle of all language." He will have shown that metaphor is not ornamental but essential. But what we are at present concerned with is his reason for wanting to refute the eighteenth-century notion. And now, if we look briefly at some other views of Richards, we may perhaps see why he is so interested in making metaphor "the omnipresent principle of all language." In other words, I am suggesting that, while he may incidentally refute the eighteenth-century rhetoricians, his doctrine has more significant ramifications.

One of the cardinal principles of Richards' aesthetics is that aesthetic experience is continuous with ordinary experience. This means several things, among them (1) that generically one experiences the same emotions, whether perceiving aesthetically or practically; (2) that synaesthesis, or "balanced poise," is possible in any situation, not only in those involving what are commonly known as works of art; and (3) that there is no significant difference between aesthetic and ordinary experience—if we wish to study the former, we must first study the latter.

Hence it follows that the poet's experience, out of which the poem emerges, is not different in any significant sense from ordinary experience. If, therefore, Richards can show that the poet's language is not essentially different from that of the ordinary person, the claim for continuity is strengthened. Thus his views on metaphor become at the same time a buttress for, and an extension of, his position on this continuity. Whence it follows that his preoccupation with showing that metaphor, one of the chief devices of the poet, is generic to language is at least justifiable on Richards' part.

But suppose we accept Richards' views, as outlined above. Suppose we overlook the difficulties that have been pointed out. If we probe a little more deeply, it looks as though there is still another important objection. This arises in connection with certain consequences of his views. It is perfectly legitimate to ask whether the author of a position is willing to accept all the consequences entailed by it. If the answer is No, we have a right to reject what he asserts in the first place. Applying this criterion to Richards' first-sense metaphor, the unrestricted one, what do we find?

A definitive answer to whether Richards' holding that every word is a metaphor involves him in any consequences he would reject would carry us, metaphysically and epistemologically, far beyond the scope of this paper. But the outline and nature of the difficulty can be clearly sketched. In "I walked to the river," "river," it will be remembered, is a first-sense metaphor because it represents a comparison between the given datum and the remembered datum or data. If this is so, must not Richards account for his ability to apply "river" to any or all of the remembered data? If this process is continued, does it not lead to an infinite regress of remembered data, which must ultimately land Richrads in Plato's heaven of Ideas? How else can the regress get started? But how does this square with what someone has called Richards' "last-ditch nominalism," a view which may be found throughout his early writings and which he has nowhere expressly repudiated? Thus, on the one hand, we find Richards advocating a strongly nominalistic view in regard to universals while, in so far as metaphor is concerned, he expounds an analysis which seems to entail some sort of realism, some sort of belief in universals. To save his nominalism, he might resort to ostensive definition as a means of starting the series of re-membered data, but it is at least dubious whether this would get him out of his difficulties.

This brings us to Richards' attempted refutation of Aristotle. There seems to be two main points in his attempt. Aristotle says the com-mand of metaphor is a unique gift of the poet; Richards says it is not and that the use of language entails the use of metaphor, since all lan-guage is metaphoric. The command of metaphor, he concludes, is not a unique gift of the poet. As a corollary, Richards asserts, again in opposition to Aristotle, that the use of metaphor may be taught, that it is not an ineffable talent which cannot be passed from one man to another.

Does it not seem, however, that Richards, in trying to refute Aris-totle, is losing sight of the three senses in which "metaphor" may be used, in which, indeed, he himself uses it? If Richards had, as William James suggests, been "mindful of the scholastic adage that whenever you meet a contradiction you must make a distinction," there would have been no occasion for a dispute between him and Aristotle. Strangely enough, Richards has made the necessary distinctions; his dispute with Aristotle arises out of his failure to apply them. Let us try to see exactly where this failure lies.

As we have seen, there are three senses of "metaphor." Before we start arguing about whether Aristotle is correct, we should find out in which sense he is using the term. Consider the first statement of his which Richards questions: that " 'an eye for resemblances' is a gift that some men have but others have not." If we ask which sense of meta-phor is being used here, the answer is the third. Aristotle, in the con-text from which this statement is lifted, is discussing the characteristics of good style. It seems fairly obvious, therefore, that his "eye for re-semblances" covers live metaphor, the third sense of "metaphor." It is an open question whether Aristotle believes that metaphor in the first sense is a unique gift of the poet. Actually, it is highly unlikely that he would call it a metaphor at all.

Richards, however, in contradicting him, assumes that Aristotle is using the term in the first sense, an assumption which he has no right to make. "We all live and speak," says Richards, "through our eye for resemblances. Without it we should perish early." This is clearly an argument addressed to someone who holds that the command of metaphor is a unique gift, in the first sense of the term. But if Aristotle in asserting that some men have a knack, or natural ability, to construct *live* metaphors, is using "metaphor" in the third sense, Richards' argument is not germane. He himself does not have the ability to construct live metaphors to the extent that W. H. Auden does, but as yet there have been no reports of Richards' perishing early. It looks, therefore, as though Richards, in attempting to refute Aristotle, has set up a man of straw. As for the teaching of metaphor, we need not make a detailed examination of that, for the same considerations apply.

PART IV   RICHARD M. WEAVER

11 LANGUAGE IS SERMONIC

RICHARD M. WEAVER

Weaver contends that the nature of "man's image of man" influences man's conception of rhetoric's nature and function. Against the view of man as an austerely unemotional "logic machine," Weaver offers his view of man as a symbol-using animal and a classifying animal, who uses language to communicate his feelings, evaluations, and motivations as well as his inductions and deductions. Both I. A. Richards and Richard Weaver note the decline in respect for the study of rhetoric as an academic discipline. And both, in different ways, suggest means of restoring rhetorical study to a central place in education.

Weaver elaborates the advisory function of rhetoric in adapting an ethically ideal course of action to the needs and capacities of a specific audience. Since an "order of values" is the ultimate sanction of rhetoric," Weaver sees rhetoric as improving man's condition through advocacy of worthwhile values and ethically sound programs.

Note also several of Weaver's other contentions. He argues that language is sermonic rather than neutral; it inherently expresses choices, evaluations, and dispositions. He believes that potential lines of argument, such as definition, similitude, causality, consequence, and circumstance, can be ranked for preference in an ethical hierarchy determined by how closely the line of argument approximates the Platonic realm of the ideal and the essence.

Source: This essay was a public lecture delivered by Weaver at the University of Oklahoma in 1962. Reprinted with permission from Roger E. Nebergall, ed., *Dimensions of Rhetorical Scholarship* (Norman: University of Oklahoma Department of Speech, 1963), 49–64.

Our age has witnessed a decline of a number of subjects that once enjoyed prestige and general esteem, but no subject, I believe, has suffered more amazingly in this respect than rhetoric. When one recalls that a century ago rhetoric was regarded as the most important humanistic discipline taught in our colleges—when one recalls this fact and contrasts it with the very different situation prevailing today—he is forced to see that a great shift of valuation has taken place. In those days, in the not-so-distant Nineteenth Century, to be a professor of rhetoric, one had to be *somebody*. This was a teaching task that was thought to call for ample and varied resources, and it was recognized as addressing itself to the most important of all ends, the persuading of human beings to adopt right attitudes and act in response to them. That was no assignment for the plodding sort of professor. That sort of teacher might do a middling job with subject matter courses, where the main object is to impart information, but the teacher of rhetoric had to be a person of gifts and imagination who could illustrate, as the need arose, how to make words even in prose take on wings. I remind you of the chairs of rhetoric that still survive in title in some of our older universities. And I should add, to develop the full picture, that literature was then viewed as a subject which practically anyone could teach. No special gift, other than perhaps industry, was needed to relate facts about authors and periods. That was held to be rather pedestrian work. But the instructor in rhetoric was expected to be a man of stature. Today, I scarcely need point out, the situation has been exactly reversed. Today it is the teacher of literature who passes through a long period of training, who is supposed to possess the mysteries of a learned craft, and who is placed by his very specialty on a height of eminence. His knowledge of the intricacies of Shakespeare or Keats or Joyce and his sophistication in the critical doctrines that have been developed bring him the esteem of the academy. We must recognize in all fairness that the elaboration of critical techniques and special approaches has made the teaching of literature a somewhat more demanding profession, although some think that it has gone in that direction beyond the point of diminishing returns. Still, this is not enough to account for the relegation of rhetoric. The change has gone so far that now it is discouraging to survey the handling of this study in our colleges and universities. With a few honorable exceptions it is given to just about anybody who will take it. The "inferior, unlearned, mechanical, merely instrumental members of the profession"—to recall a phrase of a great master of rhetoric, Edmund Burke, have in their keeping what was once assigned to the leaders. Beginners, part-time teachers, graduate students, faculty wives, and various fringe people, are now the instructional staff of an art which was once supposed to require outstanding gifts and mature experience. (We must note that at the same time the course itself has been allowed to decline from one dealing philosophically with the problems of expression to one which tries to bring below-par students up to the level of accepted usage.) Indeed, the wheel of fortune would seem to have turned for rhetoric; what was once at the top is now at the bottom, and because of its low estate, people begin to wonder on what terms it can survive at all.

We are not faced here, however, with the wheel of fortune; we are faced with something that has come over the minds of men. Changes that come over the minds of men are not inscrutable, but have at some point their identifiable causes. In this case we have to deal with the most potent of cultural causes, an alteration of man's image of man. Something has happened in the recent past to our concept of what man is; a decision was made to look upon him in a new light, and from this decision new bases of evaluation have proceeded, which affect the public reputation of rhetoric. This changed concept of man is best described by the word "scientistic," a term which denotes the application of scientific assumptions to subjects which are not wholly comprised of naturalistic phenomena. Much of this is a familiar tale, but to understand the effect of the change, we need to recall that the great success of scientific or positivistic thinking in the Nineteenth Century induced a belief that nothing was beyond the scope of its method. Science, and its off-spring applied science, were doing so much to alter and, it was thought, to improve the material conditions of the world, that a next step with the same process seemed in order. Why should not science turn it apparatus upon man, whom all the revelations of religion and the speculations of philosophy seemed still to have left an enigma, with the promise of much better result? It came to be believed increasingly that to think validly was to think scientifically, and that subject matters made no difference.

Now the method of scientific investigation is, as T. H. Huxley reminded us in a lecture which does great credit to him as a rhetorician, merely the method of logic. Induction and deduction and causal inference applied to the phenomena of nature yielded the results with which science was changing the landscape and revolutionizing the modes of industry. From this datum it was an easy inference that men ought increasingly to become scientists, and again, it was a simple derivative from this notion that man at his best is a logic machine, or at any rate an austerely unemotional thinker. Furthermore, carried in the train of this conception was the thought, not often expressed of course, that things would be better if man did not give in so far to being human in the humanistic sense. In the shadow of the victories of science, his humanism fell into progressive disparagement. Just what comprises humanism is not a simple matter for analysis. Rationality is an indispensable part to be sure, yet humanity includes emotionality, or the capacity to feel and suffer, to know pleasure, and it includes the capacity for aesthetic satisfaction, and, what can be only suggested, a yearning to be in relation with something infinite. This last is his religious passion, or his aspiration to feel significant and to have a sense of belonging in a world that is productive of much frustration. These at least are the properties of humanity. Well, man had been human for some thousands of years, and where had it gotten him? Those who looked forward to a scientific Utopia were inclined to think that his humanness had been a drag on his progress; human qualities were weaknesses, except for that special quality of rationality, which might be expected to redeem him.

However curious it may appear, this notion gained that man should live down his humanity and make himself a more efficient source of those logical inferences upon which a scientifically accurate understanding of the world depends. As the impulse spread, it was the emotional and subjective components of his being that chiefly came under criticism, for reasons that have just been indicated. Emotion, and logic or science, do not consort; the latter must be objective, faithful to what is out there in the public domain and conformable to the processes of reason. Whenever emotion is allowed to put in an oar, it gets the boat off true course. Therefore emotion is a liability.

Under the force of this narrow reasoning, it was natural that rhetoric should pass from a status in which it was regarded as of questionable worth to a still lower one in which it was positively condemned. For the most obvious truth about rhetoric is that its object is the whole man. It presents its arguments first to the rational part of man, because rhetorical discourses, if they are honestly conceived, always have a basis in reasoning. Logical argument is the plot, as it were, of any speech or composition that is designed to persuade. Yet it is the very characterizing feature of rhetoric that it goes beyond this and appeals to other parts of man's constitution, especially to his nature as a pathetic being, that is, a being feeling and suffering. A speech intended to persuade achieves little unless it takes into account how men are reacting subjectively to their hopes and fears and their special circumstances. The fact that Aristotle devotes a large proportion of his *Rhetoric* to how men feel about different situations and actions is an evidence of how prominently these considerations bulked even in the eyes of a master theorist.

Yet there is one further fact, more decisive than any of these, to prove that rhetoric is addressed to man in his humanity. Every speech which is designed to move is directed to a special audience in its unique situation. (We could not except even those radio appeals to "the world." Their audience has a unique place in time.) Here is but a way of pointing out that rhetoric is intended for historical man, or for man as conditioned by history. It is part of the *conditio humana* that we live at particular times and in particular places. These are productive of special or unique urgencies, which the speaker has got to recognize and to estimate. Hence, just as man from the point of view of rhetoric is not purely a thinking machine, or a mere seat of rationality, so he is not a creature abstracted from time and place. If science deals with the abstract and the universal, rhetoric is near the other end, dealing in significant part with the particular and the concrete. It would be the height of wishful thinking to say that this ought not be so. As long as man is born into history, he will be feeling and responding to historical pressures. All of these reasons combine to show why rhetoric should be considered the most humanistic of the humanities. It is directed to that part of our being which is not merely rational, for it supplements the rational approach. And it is directed to individual men in their individual situations, so that by the very definitions of the terms here involved, it takes into account what science deliberately, to satisfy its own purposes, leaves out. There is consequently no need for wonder that, in an age that has been influenced to distrust and disregard what is characteristically human, rhetoric should be a prime target of attack. If it is a weakness to harbor feelings, and if furthermore it is a weakness to be caught up in historical situations, then rhetoric is construable as a dealer in weaknesses. That man is in this condition religion, philosophy, and literature have been teaching for thousands of years. Criticism of it from the standpoint of a scientistic Utopia is the new departure.

The incompleteness of the image of man as a creature who should make use of reason only can be demonstrated in another way. It is a truism that logic is a subject without a subject matter. That is to say, logic is a set of rules and devices which are equally applicable whatever the data. As the science of the forms of reasoning, it is a means of interpreting and utilizing the subject matters of the various fields which do have their proper contents. Facts from science or history or literature, for example, may serve in the establishment of an inductive generalization. Similar facts may be fed into a syllogism. Logic is merely the mechanism for organizing the data of other provinces of knowledge. Now it follows from this truth that if a man could convert himself into a pure logic machine or thinking machine, he would have no special relation to any body of knowledge. All would be grist for his mill, as the phrase goes. He would have no inclination, no partiality, no particular affection. His mind would work upon one thing as indifferently as upon another. He would be an eviscerated creature or a depassionated one, standing in the same relationship to the realities of the world as the thinking technique stands to the data on which it is employed. He would be a thinking robot, a concept which horrifies us precisely because the robot has nothing to think about.

A confirmation of this truth lies in the fact that rhetoric can never be reduced to a symbology. Logic is increasingly becoming "symbolic logic"; that is its tendency. But rhetoric always comes to us in well fleshed words, and that is because it must deal with the world, the thickness, stubbornness, and power of it.[1]

Everybody recognizes that there is thus a formal logic. A number of eminent authorities have written of rhetoric as if it were formal in the same sense and degree. Formal rhetoric would be a set of rules and devices for persuading anybody about anything. If one desires a certain response, one uses a certain device, or "trick" as the enemies of the art would put it. The set of appeals that rhetoric provides is analogized with the forms of thought that logic prescribes. Rhetoric conceived in this fashion has an adaptability and a virtuosity equal to those of logic.

But the comparison overlooks something, for at one point we encounter a significant difference. Rhetoric has a relationship to the world which logic does not have and which forces the rhetorician to kepe his eye upon reality as well as upon the character and situation of his audience. The truth of this is seen when we begin to examine the nature of the traditional "topics." The topics were first formulated by Aristotle and were later treated also by Cicero and Quintilian and by many subsequent writers on the subject of persuasion. They are a set of "places" or "regions" where one can go to find the substance for persuasive argument. Cicero defines a topic as "the seat of an argument." In function they are sources of content for speeches that are designed to influence. Aristotle listed a considerable number of them, but for our purposes they can be categorized very broadly. In reading or interpreting the world of reality, we make use of our four very general ideas. The first three are usually expressed, in the language of philosophy, as being, cause, and relationship. The fourth, which stands apart from these because it is an external source, is testimony and authority.

One way to interpret a subject is to define its nature—to describe the fixed features of its being. Definition is an attempt to capture essence. When we speak of the nature of a thing, we speak of something we expect to persist. Definitions accordingly deal with fundamental and unchanging properties.

Another way to interpret a subject is to place it in a cause-and-effect relationship. The process of interpretation is then to affirm it as the cause of some effect or as the effect of some cause. And the attitudes of those who are listening will be affected according to whether or not they agree with our cause-and-effect analysis.

A third way to interpret a subject is in terms of relationships of similarity and dissimilarity. We say that it is like something which we know

[1] I might add that a number of years ago the Mathematics Staff of the College at the University of Chicago made a wager with the English Staff that they could write the Declaration of Independence in mathematical language. They must have had later and better thoughts about this, for we never saw the mathematical rendition.

in fuller detail, or that it is unlike that thing in important respects. From such a comparison conclusions regarding the subject itself can be drawn. This is a very common form of argument, by which probabilities can be established. And since probabilities are all we have to go on in many questions of this life, it must be accounted a usable means of persuasion.

The fourth category, the one removed from the others by the fact of its being an external source, deals not with the evidence directly but accepts it on the credit of testimony or authority. If we are not in position to see or examine, but can procure the deposition of some one who is, the deposition may become the substance of our argument. We can slip it into a syllogism just as we would a defined term. The same is true of general statements which come from quarters of great authority or prestige. If a proposition is backed by some weighty authority, like the Bible, or can be associated with a great name, people may be expected to respond to it in accordance with the veneration they have for these sources. In this way evidence coming from the outside is used to influence attitudes or conduct.

Now we see that in all these cases the listener is being asked not simply to follow a valid reasoning form but to respond to some presentation of reality. He is being asked to agree with the speaker's interpretation of the world that is. If the definition being offered is a true one, he is expected to recognize this and to say, at least inwardly, "Yes, that is the way the thing is." If the exposition of cause-and-effect relationship is true, he may be expected to concur that X is the cause of such a consequence or that such a consequence has its cause in X. And according to whether this is a good or a bad cause or a good or a bad consequence, he is disposed to preserve or remove the cause, and so on. If he is impressed with the similarity drawn between two things, he is as a result more likely to accept a policy which involves treating something in the same way in which its analogue is treated. He has been influenced by a relationship of comparability. And finally, if he has been confronted with testimony or authority from sources he respects, he will receive this as a reliable, if secondary kind of information about reality. In these four ways he has been persuaded to read the world as the speaker reads it.

At this point, however, I must anticipate an objection. The retort might be made: "These are extremely formal categories you are enumerating. I fail to see how they are any less general or less indifferently applicable than the formal categories of logic. After all, definitions and so on can be offered of anything. You still have not succeeded in making rhetoric a substantive study."

In replying, I must turn here to what should be called the office of rhetoric. Rhetoric seen in the whole conspectus of its function is an art of emphasis embodying an order of desire. Rhetoric is advisory; it has the office of advising men with reference to an independent order of goods and with reference to their particular situation as it relates to these. The honest rhetorician therefore has two things in mind: a vision of how matters should go ideally and ethically and a consideration of the special circumstances of his auditors. Toward both of these he has a responsibility.

I shall take up first how his responsibility to the order of the goods or to the hierarchy of realities may determine his use of the topics.

When we think of rhetoric as one of the arts of civil society (and it must be a free society, since the scope for rhetoric is limited and the employment of it constrained under a despotism) we see that the rhetorician is faced with a choice of means in appealing to those whom he can prevail upon to listen to him. If he is at all philosophical, it must occur to him to ask whether there is a standard by which the sources of persuasion can be ranked. In a phrase, is there a preferred order of them, so that, in a scale of ethics, it is nobler to make use of one sort of appeal than another? This is of course a question independent of circumstantial matters, yet a fundamental one. We all react to some rhetoric as "untruthful" or "unfair" or "cheap," and this very feeling is evidence of the truth that it is possible to use a better or a worse style of appeal. What is the measure of the better style? Obviously this question cannot be answered at all in the absence of some conviction about the nature and destiny of man. Rhetoric inevitably impinges upon morality and politics; and if it is one of the means by which we endeavor to improve the character and the lot of men, we have to think of its methods and sources in relation to a scheme of values.

To focus the problem a little more sharply, when one is asking men to cooperate with him in thinking this or doing that, when is he asking in the name of the highest reality, which is the same as saying, when is he asking in the name of their highest good?

Naturally, when the speaker replies to this question, he is going to express his philosophy, or more precisely, his metaphysics. My personal reply would be that he is making the highest order of appeal when he is basing his case on definition or the nature of the thing. I confess that this goes back to a very primitive metaphysics, which holds that the highest reality is being, not becoming. It is a quasi-religious metaphysics, if you will, because it ascribes to the highest reality qualities of stasis, immutability, eternal perdurance—qualities that in Western civilization are usually expressed in the language of theism. That which is perfect does not change; that which has to change is less perfect. Therefore if it is possible to determine unchanging essences or qualities and to speak in terms of these, one is appealing to what is most real in so doing. From another point of view, this is getting people to see what is most permanent in existence, or what transcends the world of change and accident. The realm of essence is the realm above the flux of phenomena, and definitions are of essences and genera.

I may have expressed this view in somewhat abstruse language in order to place it philosophically, yet the practice I am referring to is everyday enough, as a simple illustration will make plain. If a speaker should define man as a creature with an indefeasible right to freedom and should upon this base an argument that a certain man or group of men are entitled to freedom, he would be arguing from definition. Freedom is an unchanging attribute of his subject; it can accordingly be predicated of whatever falls within the genus man. Stipulative definitions are of the ideal, and in this fact lies the reason for placing them at the top of the hierarchy. If the real progress of man is toward knowledge of ideal truth, it follows that this is an appeal to his highest capacity—his capacity to apprehend what exists absolutely.

The next ranking I offer tentatively, but it seems to me to be relationship or similitude and its subvarieties. I have a consistent impression that the broad resource of analogy, metaphor, and figuration is favored by those of a poetic and imaginative cast of mind. We make use of analogy or comparison when the available knowledge of the subject permits only probable proof. Analogy is reasoning from something we know to something we do not know in one step; hence there is no universal ground for predication. Yet behind every analogy lurks the possibility of a general term. The general term is never established as such, for that would change the argument to one of deductive reasoning with a universal or distributed middle. The user of analogy is hinting at an essence which cannot at the moment be produced. Or, he may be using an indirect approach for reason of tact; analogies not infrequently do lead to generalizations; and he may be employing this approach because he is respectful of his audience and desires them to use their insight.

I mentioned a moment earlier that this type of argument seems to be preferred by those of a poetic or non-literal sort of mind. That fact suggests yet another possibility, which I offer still more diffidently, asking your indulgence if it seems to border on the whimsical. The explanation would be that the cosmos *is* one vast system of analogy, so that our profoundest intuitions of it are made in the form of comparisons. To affirm that something is like something else is to begin to talk about the unitariness of creation. Everything is like everything else somehow, so that we have a ladder of similitude mounting up to the final one-ness—to something like a unity in godhead. Furthermore, there is about this source of argument a kind of decent reticence, a recognition of the unknown along with the known. There is a recognition that the unknown may be continuous with the known, so that man is moving about in a world only partly realized, yet real in all its parts. This is the mood of poetry and mystery, but further adumbration of it I leave to those more gifted than I.

Cause and effect appears in this scale to be a less exalted source of argument, though we all have to use it because we are historical men. Here I must recall the metaphysical ground of this organization and point out that it operates in the realm of becoming. Causes are causes having effect and effects are resulting from causes. To associate this source of argument with its habitual users, I must note that it is heard most commonly from those who are characteristically pragmatic in their way of thinking. It is not unusual today to find a lengthy piece of journalism or an entire political speech which is nothing but a series of arguments from consequence—completely devoid of reference to principle or defined ideas. We rightly recognize these as sensational types of appeal. Those who are partial to arguments based on effect are under a temptation to play too much upon the fears of their audience by stressing the awful nature of some consequence or by exaggerating the power of some cause. Modern advertising is prolific in this kind of abuse. There is likewise a temptation to appeal to prudential considerations only in a passage where things are featured as happening or threatening to happen.

An even less admirable subvariety of this source is the appeal to circumstance, which is the least philosophical of all the topics of argument. Circumstance is an allowable source when we don't know anything else to plead, in which cases we say, "There is nothing else to be done about it." Of all the arguments, it admits of the least perspicaciousness. An example of this which we hear nowadays with great regularity is: "We must adapt ourselves to a fast-changing world." This is pure argument from circumstance. It does not pretend, even, to offer a cause-and-effect explanation. If it did, the first part would tell us why we must adapt ourselves to a fast-changing world; and the second would tell us the result of our doing so. The usually heard formulation does neither. Such argument is preeminently lacking in understanding or what the Greeks called *dianoia*. It simply cites a brute circumstance and says, "Step lively." Actually, this argument amounts to a surrender of reason. Maybe it expresses an instinctive feeling that in this situation reason is powerless. Either you change fast or you get crushed. But surely it would be a counsel of desperation to try only this argument in a world suffering from aimlessness and threatened with destruction.

Generally speaking, cause and effect is a lower-order source of argument because it deals in the realm of the phenomenal, and the phenomenal is easily converted into the sensational. Sensational excitements always run the risk of arousing those excesses which we deplore as sentimentality or brutality.

Arguments based on testimony and authority, utilizing external sources, have to be judged in a different way. Actually, they are the other sources seen through other eyes. The question of their ranking involves the more general question of the status of authority. Today there is a widespread notion that all authority is presumptuous. ("Authority is authoritarian" seems to be the root idea); consequently it is held improper to try to influence anyone by the prestige of great names or of sanctioned pronouncements. This is a presumption itself, by which every man is presumed to be his own competent judge in all matters. But since that is a manifest impossibility, and is becoming a greater impossibility all the time, as the world piles up bodies of specialized knowledge which no one person can hope to command, arguments based on authority are certainly not going to disappear. The sound maxim is that an argument based on authority is as good as the authority. What we should hope for is a new and discriminating attitude toward what is authoritative, and I would like to see some source recognized as having moral authority. This hope will have to wait upon the recovery of a more stable order of values and the re-recognition of qualities in persons. Speaking most generally, arguments from authority are ethically good when they are deferential toward real hierarchy.

With that we may sum up the rhetorical speaker's obligation toward the ideal, apart from particular determinations. If one accepts the possibility of this or any other ranking, one has to concede that rhetoric is not merely formal; it is realistic. It is not a playing with counters; its impulses come from insights into actuality. Its topic matter is existential, not hypothetical. It involves more than mere demonstration because it involves choice. Its assertions have ontological claims.

Now I return to the second responsibility, which is imposed by the fact that the rhetorician is concerned with definite questions. These are questions having histories, and history is always concrete. This means that the speaker or writer has got to have a rhetorical perception of what his audience needs or will receive or respond to. He takes into account the reality of man's composite being and his tendency to be swayed by sentiment. He estimates the pressures of the particular situation in which his auditors are found. In the eyes of those who look sourly upon the art, he is a man probing for weaknesses which he means to exploit.

But here we must recur to the principle that rhetoric comprehensively considered is an art of emphasis. The definite situation confronts him with a second standard of choice. In view of the receptivity of his audience, which of the topics shall he choose to stress, and how?

If he concludes that definition should be the appeal, he tries to express the nature of the thing in a compelling way. If he feels that a cause-and-effect demonstration would stand the greatest chance to impress, he tries to make this linkage so manifest that his hearers will see an inevitability in it. And so on with the other topics, which will be so emphasized or magnified as to produce the response of assent.

Along with this process of amplification, the ancients recognized two qualities of rhetorical discourse which have the effect of impressing an audience with the reality or urgency of a topic. In Greek these appear as *energia* and *enargia,* both of which may be translated "actuality," though the first has to do with liveliness or animation of action and the second with vividness of scene. The speaker now indulges in actualization to make what he is narrating or describing present to the minds' eyes of his hearers.

The practice itself has given rise to a good deal of misunderstanding, which it would be well to remove. We know that one of the conventional criticisms of rhetoric is that the practitioner of it takes advantage of his hearers by playing upon their feelings and imaginations. He over-stresses the importance of his topics by puffing them up, dwelling on them in great detail, using an excess of imagery or of modifiers evoking the senses, and so on. He goes beyond what is fair, the critics often allege, by this actualization of a scene about which the audience ought to be thinking rationally. Since this criticism has a serious basis, I am going to offer an illustration before making the reply. Here is a passage from Daniel Webster's famous speech for the prosecution in the trial of John Francis Knapp. Webster is actualizing for the jury the scene of the murder as he has constructed it from circumstantial evidence.

"The deed was executed with a degree of steadiness and self-possession equal to the wickedness with which it was planned. The circumstances now clearly in evidence spread out the scene before us. Deep sleep had fallen upon the destined victim and all beneath his roof. A healthful old man, to whom sleep was sweet, the first sound slumbers of the night held him in their soft but strong embrace. The assassin enters, through a window already prepared, into an unoccupied apartment. With noiseless foot he paces the lonely hall, half-lighted by the moon; he winds up the ascent of the stairs, and reaches the door of the chamber. Of this, he moves the lock by soft and continued pressure, till it turns on its hinges without noise; and he enters, and beholds the victim before him. The room is uncommonly open to the admission of light. The face of the innocent sleeper is turned from the murderer, and the beams of the moon, resting on the gray locks of the aged temple, show him where to strike. The fatal blow is given! and the victim passes, without a struggle or a motion, from the repose of sleep to the repose of death! It is the assassin's purpose to make sure work; and he plies the dagger, though it is obvious that life has been destroyed by the blow of the bludgeon. He even raises the aged arm, that he may not fail in his aim at the heart, and replaces it again over the wounds of the poniard! To finish the picture, he explores the wrist for the pulse! He feels for it, and ascertains that it beats no longer! It is accomplished.

The deed is done. He retreats, retraces his steps to the window, passes out through it as he came in, and escapes. He has done the murder. No eye has seen him, no ear has heard him. The secret is his own, and it is safe!"

By depicting the scene in this fulness of detail, Webster is making it vivid, and "vivid" means "living." There are those who object on general grounds to this sort of dramatization; it is too affecting to the emotions. Beyond a doubt, whenever the rhetorician actualizes an event in this manner, he is making it mean something to the emotional part of us, but that part is involved whenever we are deliberating about goodness and badness. On this subject there is a very wise reminder in Bishop Whately's *Elements of Rhetoric:* "When feelings are strongly excited, they are not necessarily over-excited; it may be that they are only brought to the state which the occasion fully justifies, or even that they fall short of this." Let us think of the situation in which Webster was acting. After all, there is the possibility, or even the likelihood that the murder was committed in this fashion, and that the indicted Knapp deserved the conviction he got. Suppose the audience had remained cold and unmoved. There is the victim's side to consider and the interest of society in protecting life. We should not forget that Webster's "actualization" is in the service of these. Our attitude toward what is just or right or noble and their opposites is not a bloodless calculation, but a feeling for and against. As Whately indicates, the speaker who arouses feeling may only be arousing it to the right pitch and channeling it in the right direction.

To re-affirm the general contention: the rhetorician who practices "amplification" is not thereby misleading his audience, because we are all men of limited capacity and sensitivity and imagination. We all need to have things pointed out to us, things stressed in our interest. The very task of the rhetorician is to determine what feature of a question is most exigent and to use the power of language to make it appear so. A speaker who dwells insistently upon some aspect of a case may no more be hoodwinking me than a policeman or a doctor when he advises against a certain course of action by pointing out its nature or its consequences. He *should* be in a position to know somewhat better than I do.

It is strongly to be suspected that this charge against rhetoric comes not only from the distorted image that makes man a merely rationalistic being, but also from the dogma of an uncritical equalitarianism. The notion of equality has insinuated itself so far that it appears sometimes as a feeling, to which I would apply the name "sentimental plebeianism," that no man is better or wiser than another, and hence that it is usurpation for one person to undertake to instruct or admonish another. This preposterous (and we could add, wholly unscientific judgment, since our differences are manifold and provable) is propagated in subtle ways by our institutions of publicity and the perverse art of demagogic politics. Common sense replies that any individual who advises a friend or speaks up in meeting is exercising a kind of leadership, which may be justified by superior virtue, knowledge, or personal insight.

The fact that leadership is a human necessity is proof that rhetoric as the attempt through language to make one's point of view prevail grows out of the nature of man. It is not a reflection of any past phase of social development, or any social institution, or any fashion, or any passing vice. When all factors have been considered, it will be seen that men are born rhetoricians, though some are born small ones and others greater, and some cultivate the native gift by study and training, whereas some neglect it. Men are such because they are born into history, with an endowment of passion and a sense of the *ought*. There is ever some discrepancy, however slight, between the situation man is in and the situation he would like to realize. His life is therefore characterized by movement toward goals. It is largely the power of rhetoric which influences and governs that movement.

For the same set of reasons, rhetoric is cognate with language. Ever since I first heard the idea mentioned seriously it impressed me as impossible and even ridiculous that the utterances of men could be neutral. Such study as I have been able to give the subject over the years has confirmed that feeling and has led me to believe that what is sometimes held up as a desideratum—expression purged of all tend-ency—rests upon an initial misconception of the nature of language.

The condition essential to see is that every use of speech, oral and written, exhibits an attitude, and an attitude implies an act. "Thy speech bewrayeth thee" is aphoristically true if we take it as saying, "Your speech reveals your disposition," first by what you choose to say, then by the amount you decide to say, and so on down through the re-sources of linguistic elaboration and intonation. All rhetoric is a rhetoric of motives, as Kenneth Burke saw fit to indicate in the title of his book. At the low end of the scale, one may be doing nothing more than making sounds to express exuberance. But if at the other end one sits down to compose a *Critique of the Pure Reason*, one has the motive of refuting other philosophers' account of the constitution of being, and of substituting one's own, for an interest which may be universal, but which nonetheless proceeds from the will to alter some-thing.

Does this mean that it is impossible to be objective about anything? Does it mean that one is "rhetorical" in declaring that a straight line is the shortest distance between two points? Not in the sense in which the objection is usually raised. There are degrees of objectivity, and there are various disciplines which have their own rules for expressing their laws or their content in the most effective manner for their purpose. But even this expression can be seen as enclosed in a rhetorical intention. Put in another way, an utterance is capable of rhetorical function and aspect. If one looks widely enough, one can discover its rhetorical dimension, to put it in still another way. The scientist has some interest in setting forth the formulation of some recurrent feature of the physical world, although his own sense of motive may be lost in a general feeling that science is a good thing because it helps progress along.[2]

In short, as long as man is a creature responding to purpose, his linguistic expression will be a carrier of tendency. Where the modern semanticists got off on the wrong foot in their effort to refurbish language lay in the curious supposition that language could and should be outwardly determined. They were positivists operating in the linguistic field. Yet if there is anything that is going to keep on defying positivistic correlation, it is this subjectively born, intimate, and value-laden vehicle which we call language. Language is a system of imputation, by which values and percepts are first framed in the mind and are then imputed to things. This is not an irresponsible imputation; it does not imply, say, that no two people can look at the same clock face and report the same time. The qualities or properties have to be in the things, but they are not in the things in the form in which they are framed by the mind. This much I think we can learn from the great realist-nominalist controversy of the Middle Ages and from the little that contemporary semantics has been able to add to our knowledge. Language was created by the imagination for the purposes of man, but it may have objective reference—just how we cannot say until we are in possession of a more complete metaphysics and epistemology.

Now a system of imputation involves the use of predicates, as when we say, "Sugar is sweet" or "Business is good." Modern positivism and relativism, however, have gone virtually to the point of denying the validity of all conceptual predication. Occasionally at Chicago I purposely needle a class by expressing a general concept in a casual way, whereupon usually I am sternly reminded by some member brought up in the best relativist tradition that "You can't generalize that way." The same view can be encountered in eminent quarters. Justice Oliver

[2] If I have risked confusion by referring to "rhetoricians" and "rhetorical speakers," and to other men as if they were all non-rhetoricians, while insisting that all language has its rhetorical aspect, let me clarify the terms. By "rhetorician" I mean the deliberate rhetor: the man who understands the nature and aim and requirements of persuasive expression and who uses them more or less consciously according to the approved rules of the art. The other, who by his membership in the family of language users, must be a rhetorician of sorts, is an empirical and adventitious one; he does not know enough to keep invention, arrangement, and style working for him. The rhetorician of my reference is thus the educated speaker; the other is an untaught amateur.

Wendell Holmes was fond of saying that the chief end of man is to frame general propositions and that no general proposition is worth a damn. In the first of these general propositions the Justice was right, in the sense that men cannot get along without categorizing their apprehensions of reality. In the second he was wrong because, although a great jurist, he was not philosopher enough to think the matter through. Positivism and relativism may have rendered a certain service as devil's advocates if they have caused us to be more careful about our concepts and our predicates, yet their position in net form is untenable. The battle against general propositions was lost from the beginning, for just as surely as man is a symbol-using animal (and a symbol transcends the thing symbolized) he is a classifying animal. The morality lies in the application of the predicate.

Language, which is thus predicative, is for the same cause sermonic. We are all of us preachers in private or public capacities. We have no sooner uttered words than we have given impulse to other people to look at the world, or some small part of it, in our way. Thus caught up in a great web of inter-communication and inter-influence, we speak as rhetoricians affecting one another for good or ill. That is why I must agree with Quintilian that the true orator is the good man, skilled in speaking—good in his formed character and right in his ethical philosophy. When to this he adds fertility in invention and skill in the arts of language, he is entitled to that leadership which tradition accords him.

If rhetoric is to be saved from the neglect and even the disrepute which I was deploring at the beginning of this lecture, these primary truths will have to be recovered until they are a part of our active consciousness. They are, in summation, that man is not nor ever can be nor ever should be a depersonalized thinking machine. His feeling is the activity in him most closely related to what used to be called his soul. To appeal to his feeling therefore is not necessarily an insult; it can be a way to honor him, by recognizing him in the fulness of his being. Even in those situations where the appeal is a kind of strategy, it but recognizes that men—all men—are historically conditioned.

Rhetoric must be viewed formally as operating at that point where literature and politics meet, or where literatry values and political urgencies can be brought together. The rhetorician makes use of the moving power of literary presentation to induce in his hearers an attitude or decision which is political in the very broadest sense. Perhaps this explains why the successful user of rhetoric is sometimes in bad grace with both camps. For the literary people he is too "practical"; and for the more practical political people he is too "flowery." But there is nothing illegitimate about what he undertakes to do, any more than it would be illegitimate to make use of the timeless principles of aesthetics in the constructing of a public building. Finally, we must never lose sight of the order of values as the ultimate sanction of rhetoric. No one can live a life of direction and purpose without some scheme of values. As rhetoric confronts us with choices involving values, the rhetorician is a preacher to us, noble if he tries to direct our passion toward noble ends and base if he uses our passion to confuse and degrade us. Since all utterance influences us in one or the other of these directions, it is important that the direction be the right one, and it is better if this lay preacher is a master of his art.

12 RICHARD M. WEAVER ON THE NATURE OF RHETORIC: AN INTERPRETATION

RICHARD L. JOHANNESEN
RENNARD STRICKLAND
RALPH T. EUBANKS

In all of his writings on rhetoric, Richard Weaver seemed concerned with developing a philosophy of rhetoric more than a theory of rhetoric. Although he explored the workings of rhetorical lines of argument and stylistic techniques, his prime concern was an explication of the assumptions, values, and philosophical grounds that he felt should undergird a sound theory of rhetoric. He clearly took his stand with a specific philosophical view of reality and knowledge, namely Platonic idealism. And this metaphysical and epistemological starting point colored his conception of rhetoric. He argued, too, for a particular view of man's essential nature, a nature reflected in man's use of rhetoric.

In further developing his philosophy of rhetoric, Weaver isolated his conception of rhetoric's essence, explored the nature of language and meaning, commented on an ethical system for a sound rhetoric, and proposed a special cultural and societal role for rhetoric. The infusion of Weaver's philosophy of rhetoric into his theory of rhetoric bears out his premise that one's "conception of metaphysical reality finally governs our conception of everything else." (See Weaver, *Ideas Have Consequences*, 51.)

Source: Richard L. Johannesen, Rennard Strickland, and Ralph T. Eubanks, eds., *Language Is Sermonic: Richard M. Weaver on the Nature of Rhetoric* (Baton Rouge: Louisiana State University Press, 1970), 7–30. Reprinted with permission of the publisher.

Modern philosopher Eliseo Vivas uses the ancient term "rhetor" to describe the late Richard M. Weaver. Vivas contends that Weaver saw the importance of rhetoric, in its classical sense, as "no other thinker among us . . . has seen it."[1] Weaver remains, no doubt, one of the most stimulating and controversial rhetorical theorists of our time. From the

[1] Eliseo Vivas, "The Mind of Richard Weaver," *Modern Age,* VIII (Summer 1964), 309; Vivas, "Introduction," in Weaver, *Life Without Prejudice and Other Essays* (Chicago: Regnery, 1965), xiii–xiv. When Weaver died at age fifty-three, April 3, 1963, he was professor of English in the College of the University of Chicago.

outset of his career he has provided, as Paul Tillich observes of his first work, "philosophical shock—the beginning of wisdom." Over the years, Weaver's views on the nature of rhetoric have had increasing influence among rhetorical scholars.[2]

Weaver as a social critic has sought to clarify the role of rhetoric in improving a declining modern culture. At one point in *Visions of Order* he described a "kind of doctor of culture," a description which could also serve as a virtual self-portrait of his own function. Even though a member of the culture, this "doctor" in some degree had estranged himself from his culture through study and reflection. He had "acquired knowledge and developed habits of thought which enable him to see it in perspective and to gauge it."[3]

Although he wrote a large number of articles, essays, lectures, books, and book reviews both on academic and political subjects,[4] Weaver's views on rhetoric can be gleaned primarily from the following published sources: *Ideas Have Consequences*, a post-World War II critique of American society; *The Ethics of Rhetoric; Composition*, a college textbook; "Language Is Sermonic," a lecture delivered to a graduate speech seminar at the University of Oklahoma; *Visions of Order*, a posthumously published critique of our present society; *Life Without Prejudice and Other Essays*, a collection of previously published essays; "Relativism and the Use of Language"; "Concealed Rhetoric in Scientistic Sociology"; and "To Write the Truth."[5]

[2] For the influence of Weaver's ideas on other rhetorical theorists see Maurice Natanson, "The Limits of Rhetoric," *Quarterly Journal of Speech*, XLI (April, 1955), 133–39; Virgil Baker and Ralph Eubanks, *Speech in Personal and Public Affairs* (New York: David McKay, 1965), viii, 74, 80, 113; Ralph Eubanks and Virgil Baker, "Toward an Axiology of Rhetoric," *Quarterly Journal of Speech*, XLVIIII (April, 1962), 157–68; Walter R. Fisher, "Advisory Rhetoric: Implications for Forensic Debate," *Western Speech*, XXIX (Spring, 1965), 114–19; Donald Davidson, "Grammar and Rhetoric: The Teacher's Problem," *Quarterly Journal of Speech*, XXXIX (December, 1953), 424–36; Ralph T. Eubanks, "Nihilism and the Problem of a Worthy Rhetoric," *Southern Speech Journal*, XXXIII (Spring, 1968), 187–99; W. Ross Winterowd, *Rhetoric: A Synthesis* (New York: Holt, Rinehart, and Winston, 1968), 9–10, 13. Some of Weaver's essays now are being reprinted in anthologies on rhetoric. See, for example, Joseph Schwartz and John Rycenga (eds.), *The Province of Rhetoric* (New York: Roland Press, 1965), 275–92, 311–29; Dudley Bailey (ed.), *Essays on Rhetoric* (New York: Oxford University Press, 1965), 234–49; Maurice Natanson and Henry W. Johnstone (eds.), *Philosophy, Rhetoric, and Argumentation* (University Park: Pennsylvania State University Press, 1965), 63–79.

[3] Although most of his writings on rhetoric have this thrust, one of his most clearly focused essays was "The Cultural Role of Rhetoric," in *Visions of Order* (Baton Rouge: Louisiana State University Press, 1964), Chap. 4. See also page 7.

[4] The editors wish to acknowledge the cooperation of Louis Dehmlow, compiler of Weaver's papers, and the late Kendall Beaton, literary executor, in securing a bibliography of Weaver's writings and copies of some of Weaver's unpublished manuscripts. A complete bibliography of Weaver's published writings appears in his *The Southern Tradition at Bay*, edited by George Core and M. E. Bradford (New York: Arlington House, 1968), 401–18.

[5] *Ideas Have Consequences* (Chicago: University of Chicago Press, 1948); *The Ethics of Rhetoric* (Chicago: Regnery, 1953); *Composition: A Course in Writing and Rhetoric*

Weaver held two basic orientations that are of prime importance to an understanding of his rhetorical views.[6] First, politically he was a conservative of some note. Leading conservatives such as Russell Kirk and Willmoore Kendall held him in esteem.[7] Weaver was, for example, an associate editor of the conservative *Modern Age*, a contributor to *National Review*, a trustee of the Intercollegiate Society of Individualists, and a recipient in 1962 of a national award from the Young Americans for Freedom. In his public lectures, such as "How to Argue the Conservative Cause," he actively advocated rational conservatism.

In his mid-twenties Weaver had moved from arch-socialist to ardent conservative.[8] A product of Southern upbringing and education in North Carolina, Kentucky, Tennessee, and Louisiana, he defended Southern Agrarian traditions.[9] At Vanderbilt University he was exposed to the Southern Agrarian ideas of John Crowe Ransom, Robert Penn Warren, Donald Davidson, and Allen Tate.[10] Kendall contends that Weaver was more a commentator *on* Southern Agrarianism than a devotee of its ideals.[11] Weaver himself admitted that at Vanderbilt he felt a "powerful pull" toward the Agrarian ideals of the individual in contact with nature, the necessity of the small-property-holding class, and a pluralistic soci-

(New York: Holt, Rinehart and Winston, 1957); "Language Is Sermonic," in Roger E. Nebergall (ed.), *Dimensions of Rhetorical Scholarship* (Norman: University of Oklahoma Department of Speech, 1963); *Visions of Order; Life Without Prejudice and Other Essays;* "Relativism and the Use of Language," in H. Schoeck and J. W. Wiggins (eds.), *Relativism and the Study of Man* (New York: Van Nostrand, 1961), 236–54; "Concealed Rhetoric in Scientistic Sociology," *Georgia Review,* XIII (Spring, 1959), 19–32; "To Write the Truth," *College English,* X (October, 1948), 25–30.

[6] James Powell, "The Foundation of Weaver's Traditionalism," *New Individualist Review,* III (1964), 3–7; E. Victor Milione, "The Uniqueness of Richard M. Weaver," *Intercollegiate Review,* II (September, 1965), 67.

[7] Russell Kirk, "Richard Weaver, R I P," *National Review,* XIV (April 23, 1963), 308; Willmoore Kendall, "How to Read Richard Weaver," *Intercollegiate Review,* II (September, 1965), 77–86. In fact Kendall argues that Weaver was so unique that he was virtually the only true American conservative on the contemporary scene.

[8] Weaver discusses this transition in his autobiographical article, "Up from Liberalism," *Modern Age,* III (Winter, 1958–59), 21–32. Starting in 1932 he was a formal member of the American Socialist Party for at least two years.

[9] Weaver, "The Southern Tradition," *New Individualist Review,* III (1964), 7–17. Born in Weaverville, North Carolina, in 1910, he received his B.A. from the University of Kentucky in 1932, M.A. from Vanderbilt University in 1934, and Ph.D. from Louisiana State University in 1943.

[10] For statements of Southern Agrarian precepts, including those of Ransom, Warren, Davidson, and Tate, see *I'll Take My Stand: The South and the Agrarian Tradition,* by Twelve Southerners (New York: Harper, 1930); see also Herbert Agar and Allen Tate, *Who Owns America? A New Declaration of Independence* (Boston: Houghton Mifflin, 1936). Ransom, Warren, Davidson, and Tate, who led the influential literary group known as the "Nashville Fugitives," reflect on their participation in the Southern Agrarian movement in Rob Roy Purdy (ed.), *Fugitive's Reunion: Conversations at Vanderbilt* (Nashville: Vanderbilt University Press, 1959), 177–218. Ransom directed Weaver's M.A. thesis on "The Revolt Against Humanism." A recent analysis of the Southern Agrarian philosophy is Alexander Karanikas, *Tillers of a Myth: Southern Agrarians as Social and Literary Critics* (Madison: University of Wisconsin Press, 1966).

[11] Kendall, "How to Read Richard Weaver," 78.

ety.[12] He left Vanderbilt poised between the opposites of socialism and Southern Agrarianism and by the early 1940's, had firmly opted for conservatism generally and some particular facets of Southern Agrarianism.[13] For example, Weaver championed the Agrarian ideal of individual ownership of private property and disdain of science as inadequate to deal with values.[14] He desired in society law, order, and cohesive diversity. The just and ideal society, he believed, must reflect real hierarchy and essential distinctions. An orderly society following the vision of a Good purpose, with men harmoniously functioning in their proper stations in the structure, constituted Weaver's goal.[15]

Secondly, Weaver was a devoted Platonic idealist.[16] Belief in the reality of transcendentals, the primacy of ideas, and the view that form is prior to substance constituted his philosophical foundation.[17] While not a Platonist in all matters, he yet looked for societal and personal salvation to ideals, essences, and principles rather than to the transitory, the changing, and the expedient. His view was antipragmatic and antiutilitarian. While general semanticist S. I. Hayakawa attacks Weaver's Platonic idealism, Russell Kirk praises Weaver as a "powerful mind given to meditation upon universals."[18]

The ultimate "goods" in society were of central concern to Weaver.[19] Reality for him was a hierarchy in which the ultimate Idea of the Good constituted the value standard by which all other existents could be appraised for degree of goodness and truth. Truth to him was the degree to which things and ideas in the material world conform to their ideals, archetype, and essences. He contended that "the thing is not true and the act is not just unless these conform to a conceptual ideal."[20] What *the* ultimate Good was and how it is known through

---

[12] "Up from Liberalism," 23; Weaver, "The Confederate South, 1865–1910: A Study in the Survival of a Mind and Culture" (Ph.D. dissertation, Louisiana State University, 1943), 517. In a slightly revised form this dissertation has been published as *The Southern Tradition at Bay.*

[13] "Up from Liberalism," 23–24; Weaver, "The Tennessee Agrarians," *Shenandoah,* III (Summer, 1952), 3–10.

[14] *Who Owns America?,* 182–83, 325–26; *Ideas Have Consequences,* Chap. 7.

[15] *Ideas Have Consequences,* 20, 35–51, 74–75; *Visions of Order,* 13, 22–39.

[16] *Ideas Have Consequences,* 3–5, 12–17, 22–23, 34, 52, 60, 73, 119, 130–32, 146–47, 154; *Visions of Order,* 20–21, 38, 134–35; "Language Is Sermonic," 55; *Ethics of Rhetoric,* 3–26.

[17] Weaver, Foreword to *Ideas Have Consequences* (paperback, 1959), v; Weaver, *New York Times Book Review* (March 21, 1948), 29.

[18] S. I. Hayakawa, *Symbol, Status, and Personality* (New York: Harcourt, Brace, and World, 1963), 154–70, 182–85; Russell Kirk, "Ethical Labors," *Sewanee Review,* LXII (July–Sept., 1954), 489.

[19] *Ideas Have Consequences,* 17, 51–52; *Ethics of Rhetoric,* 211–32.

[20] *Ideas Have Consequences,* 130, 4. For many of the insights in the following paragraphs concerning Weaver's philosophy of reality and knowledge, the authors wish to acknowledge the research of Thomas D. Clark. See Thomas D. Clark, "The Philosophical Bases of Richard M. Weaver's View of Rhetoric," M.A. thesis, Indiana University, 1969.

intuition, Weaver never really made clear. What comprised *his* ultimate Good was likewise unclear. But he viewed freedom, justice, and order as ideals toward which men and cultures must strive. The reality of nature he saw as a dualistic paradox of essences and transformations. "Whatever the field we gaze upon," he observed, "we see things maintaining their identity while changing. Things both *are* and *are becoming*. They are because the idea or general configuration of them persists; and they are becoming because with the flowing of time, they inevitably slough off old substance and take on new."[21]

Weaver held a complex conception of the nature of knowledge. He partially agreed with Mortimer Adler that there are three "orders" of knowledge. First is the level of particulars and individual facts, the simple data of science. Second is the level of theories, propositions, and generalizations about these facts. Third is the level of philosophic evaluations and value judgments about such theories.[22] At this third level, Ideas, universals, and first principles function as judgmental standards. Knowledge based on particulars alone and on raw physical sensations is suspect since it is incomplete knowledge. True knowledge is of universals and first principles. Weaver adopted at one point the absolute position that "there is no knowledge at the level of sensation, and that therefore knowledge is of universals. . . . the fewer particulars we require in order to arrive at our generalization, the more apt pupils we are in the school of wisdom."[23] In two other books he suggested that knowledge of universals comes through dialectic, the ability to differentiate existents into categories, and through intuition, the ability to grasp "essential correspondences."[24]

Weaver believed man's essential nature encompasses fixed elements, yet for him the good man seemed more an ideal than an actuality. He held that man's fundamental humanness is founded in four faculties, capacities, or modes of apprehension.[25] Man possesses a rational or cognitive capacity which gives him knowledge; an emotional or aesthetic capacity which allows him to experience pleasure, pain, and beauty; an ethical capacity which determines orders of goods and judges between right and wrong; and a religious capacity which provides yearning for something infinite and gives man a glimpse of his destiny and ultimate nature.

Weaver used a tripartite division of body, mind, and soul to further explain man's essential nature. The body, man's physical being, houses the mind and soul during life but extracts its due through a constant

---

21 *Visions of Order,* 23.
22 *Ethics of Rhetoric,* 30–31; *Ideas Have Consequences,* 18.
23 *Ideas Have Consequences,* 12–13, 3, 27.
24 *Visions of Order,* 12; *Ethics of Rhetoric,* 49–54, 56–57, 203–204.
25 *Visions of Order,* 85; "Language Is Sermonic," 50–51; *Life Without Prejudice,* 146.

downward pull toward indiscriminate and excessive satisfaction of sensory pleasure. The body is self-centered and disdainful of worthy goals.[26] Man's mind or intellect provides him with the potential to apprehend the structure of reality, define concepts, and rationally order ideas. While giving man the capacity for knowledge and order, the mind is guided toward good or evil by the disposition of the soul.[27] Man's soul or spirit—depending upon whether it has been trained well or ill—guides the mind and body toward love of the good or toward love of physical pleasure. Weaver found the concept of soul difficult to explain; it seemed for him to encompass man's ethical and religious capacities.[28] The elements of man's essential nature he viewed as fixed. Yet he implied that the dominance of one component over others is determined by man's training, environment, and culture.

Weaver underscored two additional concepts in his analysis of man's uniquely human characteristics.[29] Man's capacity for choice-making affords him his dignity—if judiciously exercised in selecting means and ends. And as the symbol-using animal—although the definition is a partial one—man rises above the sensate and can communicate knowledge, feeling, and values.

In readily accepting the label of conservative, Weaver emphasized that a conservative believes there is a structure of reality independent of his own will and desire and accepts some principles as given, lasting, and good.[30] The true conservative for Weaver was one "who sees the universe as a paradigm of essences, of which the phenomenology of the world is a sort of continuing approximation. Or, to put it another way, he sees it as a set of definitions which are struggling to get themselves defined in the real world."[31]

These two fundamental orientations, political conservatism and Platonic idealism, led Weaver in *Ideas Have Consequences and Visions of Order* to indict contemporary Western culture for having lost faith in an order of "goods." Among the societal weaknesses and vices he condemned were the following: scientism, nominalism, semantic positivism, doctrinaire democracy, uncritical homage to the theory of evolution, radical egalitarianism, pragmatism, cultural relativism, materialism, emphasis on techniques at the expense of goals, idolization

---

[26] *Visions of Order*, 9, 144; *Life Without Prejudice*, 146; *Ideas Have Consequences*, 18.

[27] *Visions of Order*, 24, 50, 85; *Ideas Have Consequences*, 19–20; *Life Without Prejudice*, 45–46.

[28] *Visions of Order*, 43–44, 47, 85, 144; *Ideas Have Consequences*, 19–20; *Ethics of Rhetoric*, 17, 23.

[29] *Visions of Order*, 135; *Ideas Have Consequences*, 167; *Life Without Prejudice*, 46–47. For Kenneth Burke's analysis of man as the symbol-using animal, see Burke, *Language as Symbolic Action* (Berkeley: University of California Press, 1966), 3–24.

[30] *Life Without Prejudice*, 157–59.

[31] *Ethics of Rhetoric*, 112.

of youth, progressive education, disparagement of historical consciousness, deleterious effects of the mass media, and degenerate literature,
music, and art.

Weaver outlined the program he thought necessary for the restoration of health to Western culture. Among his positive suggestions were
the development of a sense of history; balance between permanence
and change; reestablishment of faith in ideas, ideals, and principles;
maintenance of the "metaphysical right" of private property; education in literature, rhetoric, logic, and dialectic; respect for nature, the
individual, and the ideals of the past; reemphasis on traditional education; and control (but not elimination) of war.[32]

From this vantage point Weaver expounded his view of the nature,
function, and scope of rhetoric. As his writings on rhetoric show, he
was familiar with the ancient theories of Plato, Aristotle, Cicero, and
Quintilian.[33] And Plato's views on the subject held a special attraction
for him. The influence of Kenneth Burke is also clearly reflected in
Weaver's writings on rhetoric.[34] At one point Weaver views rhetoric
as a process of making identifications and he widens the scope of
rhetoric beyond linguistic forms to include a rhetoric of "matter or
scene," as in the instance of a bank's erecting an imposing office
building to strengthen its image.[35]

In Weaver's view, rhetoric makes convictions compelling by showing them in the contexts of reality and human values. Rhetoric, he
wrote, is "persuasive speech in the service of truth"; it should "create
an informed appetition for the good."[36] It affects us "primarily by setting forth images which inform and attract." And generally, rhetoric
involves questions of policy. It operates formally at the point "where
literary values and political urgencies" can be combined. "The rhetorician," he observed, "makes use of the moving power of literary presentation to induce in his hearers an attitude or decision which is political
in the very broadest sense."[37]

Weaver explained the "office" of rhetoric at some length: "Rhetoric

[32] Some of Weaver's positive suggestions were propounded in *Ideas Have Consequences* and *Visions of Order;* others were presented in some of his articles such as
"The Humanities in a Century of Common Man," *New Individualist Review,* III (1964),
17–24. See also *Life Without Prejudice,* 15–64, 99–120; *The Southern Tradition at Bay,*
29–44, 388–96.

[33] Wilma R. Ebbitt, "Richard M. Weaver, Teacher of Rhetoric," *Georgia Review,*
XVIII (Winter, 1963), 417. These ancient sources are reflected, for example, in *Ethics
of Rhetoric,* 128, 174, 203; *Composition,* 212; and "Language Is Sermonic," 62. Chapter
one of *Ethics of Rhetoric* is a perceptive analysis of Plato's *Phaedrus.*

[34] Weaver, "Concealed Rhetoric in Scientistic Sociology," 20–24, 28–30; *Ethics of
Rhetoric,* 12, 22, 128, 225; "Language Is Sermonic," 60–61; *Composition,* 43; *Visions
of Order,* 105; *Life Without Prejudice,* 46–47.

[35] "Concealed Rhetoric in Scientific Sociology," 20, 22.

[36] *Life Without Prejudice,* 116–18.

[37] *Ethics of Rhetoric,* 16, 17, 115; "Language Is Sermonic," 63.

seen in the whole conspectus of its function is an art of emphasis embodying an order of desire. Rhetoric is advisory; it has the office of advising men with reference to an independent order of goods and with reference to their particular situation as it relates to these. The honest rhetorician therefore has two things in mind: a vision of how matters should go ideally and ethically and a consideration of the special circumstances of his auditors. Toward both of these he has a responsibility."[38] The duty of rhetoric, then, is to combine "action and understanding into a whole that is greater than scientific perception." Weaver the Platonic idealist believed that "rhetoric at its truest seeks to perfect men by showing them better versions of themselves, links in that chain extending up toward the ideal which only the intellect can apprehend and only the soul have affection for."[39]

Rhetoric, held Weaver, is axiological; it kneads values into our lives.[40] Rhetoric is the cohesive force that molds persons into a community or culture. Because man is "drawn forward by some conception of what he should be," a proper order of values is the "ultimate sanction of rhetoric." Rhetoric involves the making and presenting of choices among "goods" and a striving toward some ultimate Good. By its very nature, he emphasized, "language is sermonic"; it reflects choices and urges a particular "ought." The "noble rhetorician," in Weaver's view, functions to provide a better vision of what we can become. The true rhetorician attempts to actualize an "ideal good" for a particular audience in a specific situation primarily through "poetic or analogical association." He demonstrates, for instance, how an action, urged as just, partakes of ideal justice.

Weaver, therefore, condemned most social scientists for pretending to avoid value judgments in their writings while actually making such judgments.[41] He particularly attacked general semantics for its relativistic "truth" and its attempt to denude language of all reflections of value tendencies.[42] He also realized that rhetoric can be perverted to

---

[38] "Language Is Sermonic," 54. Rhetoric must integrate the realms of Ideas and particulars, of Being and Becoming.

[39] *Ethics of Rhetoric*, 24–25. The infusion of Weaver's philosophy into his view of rhetoric bears out his premise that our "conception of metaphysical reality finally governs our conception of everything else." *Ideas Have Consequences*, 51.

[40] *Ethics of Rhetoric*, 18, 23, 24, 211; "Language Is Sermonic," 58, 60–63; *Ideas Have Consequences*, 3, 19–20, 153, 167; *Visions of Order*, 67–69, 135; *Life Without Prejudice*, 118. Weaver made a detailed analysis of ultimate "god terms" and "devil terms" which have potency in contemporary American discourse. See *Ethics of Rhetoric*, 211–32.

[41] "Concealed Rhetoric in Scientistic Sociology," 19–32. Weaver also analyzed the "sources of pervasive vices" in the rhetoric of social scientists, sources which make their prose difficult to understand and seemingly divorced from reality. See *Ethics of Rhetoric*, Chap. 8.

[42] *Ideals Have Consequences*, 4–5, 150–60; *Visions of Order*, 67–70; "Relativism and the Use of Language," 236–54; Weaver, "To Write the Truth," 25–30.

employ basic techniques and to serve base ends. Such perversion, he believed, occurs in much modern advertising. Against these possibilities Weaver strove in all his writings on rhetoric. For he was certain that "all things considered, rhetoric, noble or base, is a great power in the world."[43]

Like Aristotle, Weaver perceived a close relationship between dialectic and rhetoric.[44] Dialectic, he maintained, was a "method of investigation whose object is the establishment of truth about doubtful propositions." It is "abstract reasoning" upon the basis of propositions through categorization, definition, drawing out of implications, and exposure of contradictions. Dialectic involves analysis and synthesis of fundamental terms in controversial questions. Both dialectic and rhetoric operate in the realm of probability. Rhetoric is joined with "that branch of dialectic which contributes to choice or avoidance"—that branch of dialectic which examines ethical and political questions. Good rhetoric presupposes sound dialectic. A successful dialectic secures not actuality but possibility; "what rhetoric thereafter accomplishes is to take any dialectically secured position . . . and show its relationship to the world of prudential conduct."[45] Weaver's criticism of the semantic positivists suggests that dialectic alone, without a succeeding rhetoric, is "social agnosticism." With dialectic unaided by rhetoric, man "knows" only in a vacuum. Thus, as earlier noted, "the duty of rhetoric is to bring together action and understanding into a whole that is greater than scientific perception." Rhetoric seeks actualization of a dialectically secured position in the existential world.

Weaver knew that logos, pathos, and ethos must combine in sound rhetoric.[46] For him "the most obvious truth about rhetoric is that its object is the whole man." It presents its arguments first to the rational aspect of man. Yet a complete rhetoric goes beyond man's cognitive capacity and appeals to other facets of his nature, especially to his nature as an emotional being, "a being of feeling and suffering." In addition, he realized that a "significant part of every speech situation is the character of the speaker." For Richard Weaver, then, the function of rhetoric was to make men both feel and believe and to perceive order, first principles, and fundamental values.

He seemed committed to the proposition that as a man speaks, so

[43] Ethics of Rhetoric, 11–12, 18–24, 217, 232; Ideas Have Consequences, 135; Life Without Prejudice, 121–28.

[44] Ethics of Rhetoric, 15–22, 25, 27–29; Composition, 120–23; Visions of Order, 55–72. For an example of Weaver's use of dialectic see Visions of Order, 92–112. As a rhetorical critic, he analyzed the use of rhetoric and dialectics by John Randolph of Roanoke, Henry David Thoreau, Bryan and Darrow in the Scopes Trial, and Webster and Hayne. See Life Without Prejudice, 65–97; Ethics of Rhetoric, Chap. 2; Weaver, "Two Orators," Modern Age, 14 (Summer-Fall, 1970), 243–248.

[45] Ethics of Rhetoric, 27–28.

[46] "Language Is Sermonic," 51, 59–60; Ethics of Rhetoric, 134; Ideas Have Consequences, 19, 21, 165–67; Visions of Order, 70–72.

he is—or that style is the man. A person's typical modes of argument and his stylistic characteristics Weaver saw as keys to that person's philosophical orientation. An analysis of a person's rhetorical style, for example, illuminated his world view.[47] Frequent use of the conjunction "but" indicates, for example, a "balanced view" as a habit of mind. Again: A person's level of generality in word choice tells us something about his approach to a subject.

"A man's method of argument is a truer index of his beliefs than his explicit profession of principles," Weaver held as a basic axiom.[48] "A much surer index to a man's political philosophy," he felt, "is his characteristic way of thinking, inevitably expressed in the type of argument he prefers." Nowhere does a man's rhetoric catch up with him more completely than in "the topics he chooses to win other men's assent." At one point Weaver elaborated his fundamental view at some length:

In other words, the rhetorical content of the major premise which the speaker habitually uses is the key to his primary view of existence. We are of course excluding artful choices which have in view only *ad hoc* persuasions. Putting the matter now figuratively, we may say that no man escapes being branded by the premise that he regards as most efficacious in argument. The general importance of this is that major premises, in addition to their logical function as a part of a deductive argument, are expressive of values, and a characteristic major premise characterizes the user.[49]

From the Aristotelian *topoi* Weaver selected and ranked certain "topics" or regions of experience to which an advocate could turn for the substance of persuasive argument. These "topics" are the "sources of content for speeches that are designed to influence."[50] By ranking them from the most to least ethically desirable, based on his philosophic conception of reality and knowledge, he outlined a hierarchy of topics which a persuader might use and which a critic could employ to assess the rhetoric of others.[51]

A speaker would make the highest order of appeal by basing his argument on genus or definition.[52] Argument from genus involves

---

[47] *Ethics of Rhetoric,* 115–42, 167. As a rhetorical critic, Weaver used a stylistic analysis to probe the "heroic" prose of John Milton and to illuminate the "spaciousness" of American oratory in the 1840's and 1850's. See *Ethics of Rhetoric,* Chaps. 5 and 6.

[48] This and the following quotations are from *Ethics of Rhetoric,* 58, 112, 114, 55.

[49] *Ibid.,* 55–56. Although Weaver excludes "artful choices," the point can be raised that rhetoric by definition is artful in its adaptation to audience and situation and in its conscious effort at success. For an interesting attempt to test Weaver's axiom, without prior knowledge of Weaver's view, see Edwin S. Shneidmann, "The Logic of Politics," in Leon Arons and Mary May (eds.), *Television and Human Behavior* (New York: Appleton, Century, Crofts, 1963), 177–99.

[50] "Language Is Sermonic," 53; *Composition,* 124.

[51] "Language Is Sermonic," 55.

[52] *Ibid.,* 53, 55–56; *Composition,* 124–27; *Ethics of Rhetoric,* 27, 56, 112–14; *Visions of Order,* 6. For Weaver's own extensive use of argument from genus or definition see, for example, *Ideas Have Consequences,* 43–44, 101, 129, 172; *Visions of Order,* Chaps. 1, 2, and 8.

arguing from the nature or essence of things. It assumes that there are fixed classes and that what is true of a given class may be imputed to every member of that class. In the argument from genus the classification already is established, or it is one of the fixed concepts in the mind of the audience to which the argument is addressed. In argument from definition, the work of establishing the classification must be done during the course of the argument, after which the defined term will be used as would a genus. Further: Definitions should be rationally rather than empirically sustained. Good definitions should be stipulative, emphasizing what-ought-to-be, rather than operative, emphasizing what-is. Under argument from genus or definition, Weaver also included argument from fundamental principles and argument from example. An example, he felt, always implies a general class. He believed that arguments from genus or definition ascribe "to the highest reality qualities of stasis, immutability, eternal perdurance."

He admitted that his preference for this mode of argument derived from his Platonic idealism. This mode of argument, he felt, was also a mark of the true conservative. To argue from genus or definition was to get people "to see what is most permanent in existence, or what transcends the world of change and accident. The realm of essence is the realm above the flux of phenomena; and definitions are of essences and genera."[53]

Weaver applied this viewpoint in his evaluation of the rhetoric of Abraham Lincoln.[54] He explicitly cited over a dozen examples of Lincoln's rhetoric. Yet unfortunately he did not indicate whether he based his generalizations on a careful examination of the entire corpus of the martyred President's oratory. Weaver's analysis led him to conclude that, although sometimes arguing from similitude, as in the Gettysburg Address, and again from consequence and circumstance, Lincoln characteristically argued from genus, definition, and principle. His greatest utterances, for example, were "chiefly arguments from definition." And in Weaver's view, therefore, Lincoln was a true conservative.[55] In contrast, many of Lincoln's contemporary Whigs were conservative, Weaver argued, only in the negative sense that they opposed Democratic proposals. Naturally Weaver praised Lincoln's rhetoric and his philosophical position.

[53] "Language Is Sermonic," 55; *Life Without Prejudice,* 158–59.

[54] *Ethics of Rhetoric,* 85–114. The user of arguments from genus, principle, and definition often realizes that on some issues there is no middle ground, only right and wrong. Lincoln, for instance, knew that honesty and long-run political success on the slavery issue depended upon avoiding major middle-road positions. But the failure of Stephen Douglas on the slavery question, believed Weaver, was that he chose an untenable position in the "excluded middle." See *Ethics of Rhetoric,* 94–95, 105–107.

[55] Weaver saw George Washington as the "archetypal American conservative." *Life Without Prejudice,* 165.

As second in rank among the topics Weaver placed argument from similitude.[56] In this mode of argument are embraced analogy, metaphor, figuration, comparison, and contrast. Metaphor received focused attention from Weaver; to him it was often central to the rhetorical process.[57] Some of our profoundest intuitions concerning the world around us, he noted, are expressed in the form of comparisons. His Platonic idealism again helped him rank this topic. The user of an analogy hints at an essence he cannot at the moment produce. Weaver asserted that "behind every analogy lurks the possibility of a general term."

Argument from cause and effect stands third in Weaver's hierarchy of topics, and includes argument from consequences.[58] Although causal reasoning is a "less exalted" source of argument, we "all have to use it because we are historical men." This method of argument and its subvarieties, he felt, characterized the radical and the pragmatist. Causal argument operates in the realm of "becoming" and thus in the realm of flux. Argument from consequences attempts to forecast results of some course of action, either very desirable or very undesirable. These results are a determining factor for one in deciding whether or not to adopt a proposed action. Arguments from consequences, Weaver observed, usually are completely "devoid of reference to principle or defined ideas."

At the very bottom of Weaver's hierarchy stands argument from circumstances, another subvariety of causal reasoning.[59] This mode of argument, in his view, is the least "philosophical" of the topics because it admits of the least perspicaciousness and theoretically stops at the level of perception of fact. Argument from circumstances characterizes those who are easily impressed by existing tangibles, and such argument marks, he believed, the true liberal.[60] The arguers from circumstance, concerned not with "conceptions of verities but qualities of

[56] "Langauge Is Sermonic," 53, 56; *Ethics of Rhetoric,* 56–57; *Composition,* 129–32. For examples of Weaver's own use of argument from similitude see *Visions of Order,* Chaps. 2 and 7.

[57] *Ethics of Rhetoric,* 18, 23, 127–35, 150–52, 202–206; *Composition,* 248–58; *Visions of Order,* 142.

[58] "Language Is Sermonic," 53, 56; *Composition,* 127–28; *Ethics of Rhetoric,* 57; *Life Without Prejudice,* 142, 145; Weaver, "A Responsible Rhetoric" (Address delivered March 29, 1955, to a Great Issues Forum of students at Purdue University), 4. See *Visions of Order,* Chaps. 1 and 2, for examples of his use of causal reasoning. And to a degree his *Ideas Have Consequences* is an argument from consequences; violation of certain ideals, values, and principles has led to destructive consequences.

[59] "Language Is Sermonic," 57; *Ethics of Rhetoric,* 57–58; *Composition,* 128–29; *Ideas Have Consequences,* 151. An example of Weaver's infrequent personal usage is in *Ideas Have Consequences,* 134.

[60] "Weaver's major redefinition of the terms "liberal" and "conservative" seems to violate the type of linguistic covenant which he espouses as necessary in "Relativism and the Use of Language," 247–53.

perceptions," lack moral vision and possess only the illusion of reality. We are driven back upon this method of argument when a course of action cannot be vindicated by principle or when effects cannot be demonstrated. The argument simply cites brute circumstance; it suggests expediency. "Actually," he explains, "this argument amounts to a surrender of reason. Maybe it expresses an instinctive feeling that in this situation reason is powerless. Either you change fast or you get crushed. But surely it would be a counsel of desperation to try only this argument in a world suffering from aimlessness and threatened with destruction."[61]

Weaver employed this topic to analyze the rhetoric of Edmund Burke, commonly classified as a conservative.[62] He conceded that many of Burke's observations on society have a conservative basis. On the other hand, he contended that when Burke came to grips with concrete policies, his rhetoric reflected "a strong addiction to the argument from circumstance." Weaver concluded, "When judged by what we are calling aspect of argument," Burke was "very far from being a conservative."[63] Burke was at his best, Weaver argued, when defending immediate circumstances and "reigning" circumstances. And until the time of the French Revolution when he felt the need for "deeper anchorage," Burke's habitual argument from circumstances marked him philosophically as a liberal.[64] Weaver held Burke in low esteem as a conservative.

Again, while Weaver cited some dozen examples of Burke's rhetoric, he failed to indicate whether his generalizations rested on a scrutiny of all Burke's speeches, letters, and essays. It is in this connection also worthy of note that Russell Kirk has levied several objections to Weaver's evaluation of Burke.[65] First, the true conservative described by Weaver, contends Kirk, represents Weaver's *ideal* and ignores the historical fact that a true conservative is a follower of Edmund Burke, no matter what his typical mode of argument. Second, Kirk alludes to one of Burke's speeches to indicate that while Burke disdained "abstraction," he did praise genuine "principle." Here Kirk ignores Weaver's axiom that the important index is not what one says, but how one characteristically argues. Third, Kirk claims that although Abraham Lincoln often may have argued from principles and definition, he also often acted from circumstances and consequences. Finally, Kirk sees

---

61 "Language Is Sermonic," 57.

62 *Ethics of Rhetoric*, 55–84; Weaver, "The People of the Excluded Middle" (unpublished and undated manuscript), 12. Weaver felt that although circumstance was no more than a retarding factor in Lincoln's considerations, circumstance was for Burke the deciding factor. See *Ethics of Rhetoric*, 95.

63 *Ethics of Rhetoric*, 58.

64 "The People of the Excluded Middle," 12.

65 Russell Kirk, "Ethical Labor," 485–503.

Burke's prosecution of Warren Hastings and his attack on French errors during the Revolution as "instances of argument and action from definition."

Weaver's central premise of a typical pattern of argument for a speaker implies simple frequency of usage, as reflected in his use of the terms "characteristic" and "habitual." But some speakers may not have a clearly predominant mode of argument; they may blend a number of types of argument mentioned by Weaver. Judgment of the speaker is then more difficult. More important, some speakers may use arguments from consequences and circumstances more frequently than other types and yet use a few arguments from genus or principle as the fundamental arguments underlying all others.[66] Finally, Weaver fails to explain how a critic may determine whether a given line of argument is a metaphysical choice reflecting a speaker's philosophical stance or an "artful" choice necessitated by the practicalities of audience adaptation.

The use of characteristic mode of argument as the prime standard for rhetorical criticism represents an overly simplistic approach to evaluation of rhetorical practice. Such analysis promotes the slighting of other relevant factors in the rhetorical process. In the dramatistic terms proposed by Kenneth Burke, Weaver overemphasizes "agency" at the expense of "agent," "act," "scene," and "purpose." His typology of the "aspect" of argument can afford valuable insights, but it must not be taken as a well-rounded critical system. Yet in fairness to him it must be admitted that he did not intend his system to serve as the universal criterion for rhetorical criticism.

In addition to the hierarchy of "internal" sources of argument is the "external topic" of argument from authority and testimony.[67] Statements made by observers and experts take the place of direct or logical interpretation of evidence. Such testimony often embodies arguments from genus or definition, cause-effect, consequences, and circumstances, and thus can be judged by the standards appropriate to such arguments. But also involved is the more general question of the status of the authority. Thus a sound criterion, wrote Weaver, is that an argument from authority is only as good as the authority itself.

In his writing and teaching Weaver constantly strove to train his students in ethical rhetoric. Hence knowledge of rhetoric and skill in its use provided a defense against base rhetoric and propaganda.[68] In rhetorical education he placed prime emphasis on invention and style. Argumentation, including induction, deduction, and a modernized set

---

[66] See, for example, Richard L. Johannesen, "John Quincy Adams' Speaking on Territorial Expansion, 1836–1848" (Ph.D. dissertation: University of Kansas, 1964), 304–50.
[67] "Language Is Sermonic," 54, 57; Composition, 132–34.
[68] Composition, iii–iv; Ethics of Rhetoric, 232; "To Write the Truth," 25–30.

of *topoi* adapted from Aristotle, formed a crucial part of rhetorical education.[69] The enthymeme received focused attention in Weaver's philosophy of rhetoric.[70] The rhetorician, he observed, enters into a oneness with his audience by tacitly agreeing with one of its perceptions of reality. Weaver noted further that the enthymeme functions only when the "audience is willing to supply the missing proposition."[71]

In *Composition*, a college textbook, Weaver treated the following "topics": genus or definition, cause and effect, similitude, comparison, contraries, circumstance, testimony, and authority. As could be expected, a major part of Weaver's text was devoted to style, including grammar and composition. His persistent efforts stimulated introduction of units on logic and the revitalized "topics" into the freshman English course in the College of the University of Chicago.[72]

Edward P. J. Corbett credits the article by Bilsky, Weaver, and others in *College English* (in 1953)—"Looking for an Argument"—with providing "perhaps the first suggestion of the value of classical rhetoric for the Freshman Composition course." Corbett claims that the treatment of the *topoi* in Weaver's *Composition*" represented the first instance of the use of the topics in a freshman rhetoric since the appearance of Francis P. Donnelly's books in the 1930's."[73]

Weaver's writings on rhetoric emphasize the processes and techniques of invention and the elements of effective style, giving minor place to organization and none to the classical canons of delivery and memory. He aims indeed at revitalizing invention and argumentation. To Weaver true rhetoric involves choices among values and courses of action; it aims at showing men "better versions of themselves" and better visions of an ultimate Good. As Platonic idealist and political conservative, he praised the ideal, the essence, the unchangeable, and condemned the particular, the transitory, and the expedient. A speaker's characteristic use of argument from genus, definition, principle,

[69] *Composition*, 90–120, 123–34.

[70] *Ethics of Rhetoric*, 173–74; *Visions of Order*, 63–64; *Composition*, 118–20; "Concealed Rhetoric in Scientistic Sociology," 29–31.

[71] For a similar view see Lloyd Bitzer, "Aristotle's Enthymeme Revisited," *Quarterly Journal of Speech*, XLV (December, 1959), 399–408. American oratory in the 1840's and 1850's was characterized by the use of "uncontested terms" and ideas "fixed by universal consensus" as unstated premises already accepted by audiences. This characteristic marked the "spaciousness" of the rhetoric of that era. See *Ethics of Rhetoric*, 164–74.

[72] Ebbitt, "Richard M. Weaver, Teacher of Rhetoric," 417. Insight into argumentation and the *topoi* as taught to the freshman is gained from Manuel Bilsky, McCrea Hazlett, Robert Streeter, and Richard Weaver, "Looking for an Argument," *College English*, XIV (January, 1953), 210–16. Many of Weaver's personal classroom concerns are reflected in an unpublished paper, "The Place of Logic in the English Curriculum."

[73] Edward P. J. Corbett, "Rhetoric and Teachers of English," *Quarterly Journal of Speech*, LI (December, 1965), 380.

similitude, cause and effect, consequences, and circumstances, Weaver regarded as an index to the speaker's philosophical viewpoint and ethical stature.

By reaffirming and refining the essential connection between dialectic and rhetoric, Weaver illuminated the true province of rhetoric. Indeed, Weaver's theory pointed the way to the current rapprochement between philosophy and rhetoric.[74] Some of Weaver's political, philosophical, and rhetorical assumptions may be questioned in whole or in part. Still: There's little doubt that Weaver's theory, rooted as it was in a dialectic of the "true nature of things," has helped to reestablish rhetoric as a substantive discipline—a discipline concerned with matters of "the real world" and with the preservation of "the permanent things." Thus, the final challenge of Weaver's ideal practitioner of the art of rhetoric is "to perfect men by showing them better versions of themselves."

[74] Natanson, "The Limits of Rhetoric," 136–37. Witness the increased recent interest in scholarly scrutiny of philosophical-rhetorical issues. See, for example, Otis Walter, "On Views of Rhetoric, Whether Conservative or Progressive," *Quarterly Journal of Speech*, XLIX (December, 1963), 367–82, and the journal, *Philosophy and Rhetoric*, published by the Pennsylvania State University Press.

PART V CHAIM PERELMAN

13 THE NEW RHETORIC

CHAIM PERELMAN
L. OLBRECHTS-TYTECA

Until the 1960s the writings in rhetoric of Chaim Perelman, a Belgian professor of philosophy, were not well known to many American rhetorical scholars. *The New Rhetoric,* from which the following introductory excerpt is reprinted, was published in two volumes in French in 1958 and only translated into English in 1969. Perelman's *The Idea of Justice and the Problem of Argument* appeared in 1963.

Dissatisfied with the neglect of practical argumentation by modern logicians and philosophers, Perelman draws on classical and Renaissance sources in an attempt to revive an ancient discipline; such a revival is his new rhetoric. His rhetorical view is conscious in its audience orientation. Argumentation is audience oriented whether that audience be oneself, another individual, an immediate or distant group, a lay or specialized group, or the "universal audience." A strong argument satisfies the critical standards of a "universal audience," is relevant to the point at issue, and withstands refutation.

His theory of rhetoric examines the structure of verbal argument, both written and oral. The classical canons of style and organization receive creative attention as they directly function to strengthen argument. The canons of delivery and memory are omitted. His analysis centers on the types of proofs discussed in Aristotle's *Topics* and *Rhetoric.*

Perelman draws heavily on the following classical sources: Aristotle, Quintilian, Cicero, Isocrates, Demosthenes, Plato, and the *Rhetorica ad Herennium.* Among his more modern sources are Pascal, Jacques-Bénigne Bossuet, and Richard Whately. Often, however, he takes issue with sources he cites and always he adapts them to his own purposes. (See, for example, *The New Rhetoric,* 357–358.)

The three major parts of *The New Rhetoric* explore first the framework of argumentation, second the starting points of argument in agreement, choice of data, and presentation of data, and third the techniques of argumentation. The general categories of argumentative techniques examined are quasi-logical ones that approximate formal logic, ones based on the structure of reality, and ones involving dissociation of concepts.

For a more complete overview and assessment of *The New Rhetoric* see Carroll Arnold, "Perelman's New Rhetoric," *Quarterly Journal of Speech,* LVI (February 1970), 87–92.

Source: Chaim Perelman and L. Olbrechts-Tyteca, *The New Rhetoric,* trans. John Wilkinson and Purcell Weaver (South Bend, Ind.: University of Notre Dame Press, 1969), 1–26. Reprinted with permission of the University of Notre Dame Press.

INTRODUCTION

I

The publication of a treatise devoted to argumentation and this subject's connection with the ancient tradition of Greek rhetoric and dialectic constitutes a *break with a concept of reason and reasoning due to Descartes* which has set its mark on Western philosophy for the last three centuries.[1]

Although it would scarcely occur to anyone to deny that the power of deliberation and argumentation is a distinctive sign of a reasonable being, the study of the methods of proof used to secure *adherence* has been completely neglected by logicians and epistemologists for the last three centuries. This state of affairs is due to the noncompulsive element in the arguments adduced in support of a thesis. The very nature of deliberation and argumentation is opposed to necessity and self-evidence, since no one deliberates where the solution is necessary or argues against what is self-evident. The domain of argumentation is that of the credible, the plausible, the probable, to the degree that the latter eludes the certainty of calculations. Now Descartes' concept, clearly expressed in the first part of *The Discourse on the Method,* was to "take well nigh for false everything which was only plausible." It was this philosopher who made the self-evident the mark of reason, and considered rational only those demonstrations which, starting from clear and distinct ideas, extended, by means of apodictic proofs, the self-evidence of the axioms to the derived theorems.

Reasoning *more geometrico* was the model proposed to philosophers desirous of constructing a system of thought which might attain to the dignity of a science. A rational science cannot indeed be content with more or less probable opinions; it must elaborate a system of necessary propositions which will impose itself on every rational being, concerning which agreement is inevitable. This means that disagreement is a sign of error. "Whenever two men come to opposite decisions about the same matter," says Descartes, "one of them at least must certainly be in the wrong, and apparently there is not even one

[1] Cf. Perelman, "Raison éternelle, raison historique," *L'homme et l'histoire, Actes du VIᵉ Congrès des Sociétés de Philosophie de langue française,* pp. 347–354.

of them who knows; for if the reasoning of one was sound and clear he would be able so to lay it before the other as finally to succeed in convincing *his* understanding also."[2]

What is important to the partisans of the experimental and inductive sciences is not so much the necessity of propositions as their truth, *their conformity with facts.* The empiricist considers as evidence not "that which the mind does or must yield to, but that which it *ought to* yield to, namely, that, by yielding to which, its belief is kept conformable to fact."[3] The evidence which the empiricist recognizes is not that of rational but of sensible intuition, the method he advocates is not that of the deductive but of the experimental sciences, but he is nonetheless convinced that the only valid proofs are those recognized by the natural sciences.

What conforms to scientific method is rational, in the broader sense of the word. Works on logic devoted to the study of the methods of proof, essentially limited to the study of deduction, usually supplemented by some remarks on inductive reasoning which merely consider the means not of constructing, but of verifying hypotheses, seldom venture to examine the proofs used in human sciences. The logician is indeed inspired by the Cartesian ideal and feels at ease only in studying those proofs which Aristotle styled analytic, since all other methods do not manifest the same characteristic of necessity. This tendency has been strongly reinforced during the last century, a period in which, under the influence of mathematical logicians, logic has been limited to formal logic, that is to the study of the methods of proof used in the mathematical sciences. The result is that reasonings extraneous to the domain of the purely formal elude logic altogether, and, as a consequence, they also elude reason. This reason, which Descartes hoped would, at least in principle, solve all problems set to man the solution of which is already possessed by the divine mind, has become more and more limited in its jurisdiction, to the point that whatever eludes reduction to the formal presents it with unsurmountable difficulties.

Must we draw from this evolution of logic, and from the very real advances it has made, the conclusion that reason is entirely incompetent in those areas which elude calculation and that, where neither experiment nor logical deduction is in a position to furnish the solution of a problem, we can but abandon ourselves to irrational forces, instincts, suggestion, or even violence?

Pascal made an attempt to provide for the shortcomings of the geometrical method resulting from the fact that fallen man is no longer uniquely a rational being by opposing the will to the understanding,

[2] Descartes, *Rules for the Direction of the Mind,* GBWW, vol. 31, p. 2.
[3] Mill, *A System of Logic,* bk. III, chap. XXI, 1, p. 370.

the "esprit de finesse" to the "esprit de géométrie," the heart to the head, and the art of persuading to the art of convincing.

The Kantian opposition of faith and science and the Bergsonian antithesis of intuition and reason have a similar purpose. But, whether we consider rationalist or so-called "antirationalist" philosophers, they all carry on the Cartesian tradition by the limitation they impose on the concept of reason.

We feel, on the contrary, that just here lies a *perfectly unjustified and unwarranted limitation of the domain of action of our faculty of reasoning and proving.* Whereas already Aristotle had analyzed dialectical proofs together with analytic proofs, those which concern the probable together with those which are necessary, those which are used in deliberation and argumentation together with those which are used in demonstration, the post-Cartesian concept of reason obliges us to make certain irrational elements intervene every time the object of knowledge is not self-evident. Whether these elements consist of obstacles to be surmounted—such as imagination, passion, or suggestion—or of suprarational sources of certitude such as the heart, grace, "Einfuehlung," or Bergsonian intuition, this conception introduces a dichotomy, a differentiation between human faculties, which is completely artificial and contrary to the real processes of our thought.

It is the *idea of self-evidence* as characteristic of reason, which we must assail, if we are to make place for a theory of argumentation that will acknowledge the use of reason in directing our own actions and influencing those of others. Self-evidence is conceived both as a force to which every normal mind must yield and as a sign of the truth of that which imposes itself because it is self-evident.[4] The self-evident would connect the psychological with the logical and allow passage back and forth between these two levels. All proof would be reduction to the self-evident, and what is self-evident would have no need of proof: such is the immediate application by Pascal of the Cartesian theory of self-evidence.[5]

Leibniz rebelled against the limitation imposed in this way on logic. It was his wish "that means be shown or given to demonstrate all axioms which are not primitive; without distinction of whatever opinions men have of them, or being concerned with whether they yield assent to them or not."[6]

Now the logical theory of demonstration developed following Leibniz and not Pascal; it has never allowed that what was self-evident

---

[4] Perelman, "De la preuve en philosophie," in Perelman and Olbrechts-Tyteca, *Rhétorique et philosophie,* pp. 123 et seq.

[5] Pascal, *On Geometrical Demonstration,* Section II: *Concerning the Art of Persuasion,* GBWW, vol. 33, p. 443.

[6] Leibniz, *Die Philosophischen Schriften,* vol. V, *Nouveaux essais sur l'entendement,* p. 67.

had no need of proof. In the same way, the theory of argumentation cannot be developed if every proof is conceived of as a reduction to the self-evident. Indeed, the object of the theory of argumentation is the study of the discursive techniques allowing us *to induce or to increase the mind's adherence to the theses presented for its assent.* What is characteristic of the adherence of minds is its variable intensity: nothing constrains us to limit our study to a particular degree of adherence characterized by self-evidence, and nothing permits us to consider *a priori* the degrees of adherence to a thesis as proportional to its probability and to identify self-evidence with truth. It is good practice not to confuse, at the beginning, the aspects of reasoning relative to truth and those relative to adherence, but to study them separately, even though we might have to examine later their possible interference or correspondence. Only on this condition is it possible to develop a theory of argumentation with any philosophical scope.

II

Although during the last three centuries ecclesiastics have published works on problems of faith and preaching[7] and though the 20th century has even been described as the century of advertising and propaganda, and a large number of works have been devoted to that subject,[8] logicians and modern philosophers have become totally disinterested in our subject. It is for this reason that the present book is mostly related to the concerns of the Renaissance and, beyond that, to those of certain Greek and Latin authors, who studied the art of persuading and convincing, the technique of deliberation and of discussion. Our work, therefore, is presented as a *new rhetoric.*

Our analysis concerns the proofs which Aristotle termed "dialectical," which he examines in his *Topics,* and the utilization of which he indicates in his *Rhetoric.* This appeal to Aristotle's terminology would justify the "rapprochement" of the theory of argumentation with dialectic, conceived by Aristotle himself as the art of reasoning from generally accepted opinions (ευλογος).[9] However, a number of reasons have led us to prefer a "rapprochement" with rhetoric.

The first of these reasons is the confusion which a return to Aristotle's terminology might produce. Although the term *dialectic* served for centuries to designate logic itself, since the time of Hegel and under the influence of doctrines inspired by him, it has acquired a

---

[7] Cf. Whately's *Elements of Rhetoric,* first published in 1828; and Cardinal Newman's *Grammar of Assent,* which appeared in 1870.

[8] See Lasswell, Casey, and Smith, *Propaganda and Promotional Activities, An Annotated Bibliography;* and Smith, Lasswell, and Casey, *Propaganda, Communication, and Public Opinion. A Comprehensive Reference Guide.*

[9] Aristotle, *Topics,* I, 1, 100a.

meaning which is very remote from its original one and which has become generally accepted in contemporary philosophy. The same cannot be said for the term *rhetoric,* which has fallen into such desuetude that it is not even mentioned, for example, in A. Lalande's philosophical lexicon: we hope that our attempts will contribute to the revival of an ancient and glorious tradition.

A second reason, which we consider much more important, has motivated our choice: the very spirit in which Antiquity was concerned with dialectic and rhetoric. Dialectical reasoning is considered as running parallel with analytic reasoning, but treating of that which is probable instead of dealing with propositions which are necessary. The very notion that dialectic concerns opinions, i.e., theses which are adhered to with variable intensity, is not exploited. One might think that the status of that which is subject to opinion is impersonal and that opinions are not relative to the minds which adhere to them. On the contrary, this idea of adherence and of the minds to which a discourse is addressed is essential in all the ancient theories of rhetoric. Our "rapproachement" with the latter aims at emphasizing the fact that *it is in terms of an audience that an argumentation develops;* the study of the opinionable, as described in the *Topics,* will have a place in this framework.

It is clear, however, that our treatise on argumentation will, in certain respects, go far beyond the bounds of the ancient rhetoric and at the same time neglect certain aspects of the matter which drew the attention of the ancient masters of the art.

Their object was primarily the art of public speaking in a persuasive way: it was therefore concerned with the use of the spoken word, with discourse to a crowd gathered in a public square, with a view to securing its adherence to the thesis presented. It is evident that the aim of oratory, the adherence of the minds addressed, is that of all argumentation. We see, however, no reason to limit our study to the presentation of an argument by means of the spoken word and to restrict the kind of audience addressed to a crowd gathered in a square.

The rejection of the first limitation is due to the fact that our interests are much more those of logicians desirous of understanding the mechanism of thought than those of masters of eloquence desirous of making people practice their teaching. It is sufficient to cite the *Rhetoric* of Aristotle to show that our way of looking at rhetoric can take pride in illustrious examples. Our study, which is mainly concerned with the structure of argumentation, will not therefore insist on the way in which communication with the audience takes place.

If it is true that the technique of public speaking differs from that of written argumentation, our concern being to analyze argumentation, we cannot be limited to the examination of spoken discourse. Indeed, in view of the importance of and the role played by the modern printing press, our analyses will primarily be concerned with printed texts.

On the other hand, we shall completely neglect mnemonics and the study of delivery or oratorical effect. Such problems are the province of conservatories and schools of dramatic art, and we can dispense with examining them.

The result of our emphasis on written texts, since these latter occur in the most varied forms, is that our study is conceived with complete generality; it will not be confined to discourses considered as an entity of more or less conventionally admitted structure and length. In our opinion discussion with a single interlocutor, or even with oneself, falls under a general theory of argumentation, so that it is clear that our concept of the object of our study goes far beyond that of classical rhetoric.

What we preserve of the traditional rhetoric is the idea of the *audience,* an idea immediately evoked by the mere thought of a speech. Every speech is addressed to an audience and it is frequently forgotten that this applies to everything written as well. Whereas a speech is conceived in terms of the audience, the physical absence of his readers can lead a writer to believe that he is alone in the world, though his text is always conditioned, whether consciously or unconsciously, by those persons he wishes to address.

Thus, for reasons of technical convenience, and in order not to lose sight of the essential role played by the audience, when we use the terms "discourse," "speaker," and "audience," we shall understand by them, respectively, the argumentation, the one who presents the argument, and those to whom it is addressed. We shall not dwell on whether or not the presentation is spoken or written, or distinguish between formal discourse and the fragmentary expression of thought.

Among the ancients, rhetoric appeared as the study of a technique for use by the common man impatient to arrive rapidly at conclusions, or to form an opinion, without first of all taking the trouble of a preliminary serious investigation,[10] but we have no wish to limit the study of argumentation to one adapted to a public of ignoramuses. It is that aspect of rhetoric which explains why Plato opposed it so fiercely in his *Gorgias*[11] and which was propitious to its decline in the estimation of philosophers.

The orator indeed is obliged to adapt himself to his audience if he wishes to have any effect on it and we can easily understand that the discourse which is most efficacious on an incompetent audience is not necessarily that which would win the assent of a philosopher. But why not allow that argumentations can be addressed to every kind of

[10] Cf. Aristotle, *Rhetoric,* I, 2, 1357a.
[11] Plato, *Gorgias,* notably 455, 457a, 463, and 471d.

audience? When Plato dreams, in his *Phaedrus*,[12] of a rhetoric which would be worthy of a philosopher, what he recommends is a technique capable of convincing the gods themselves. A change in audience means a change in the appearance of the argumentation and, if the aim of argumentation is always to act effectively on minds, in order to make a judgment of its value we must not lose sight of the quality of the minds which the argument has succeeded in convincing.

This justifies the particular importance accorded by us to philosophical arguments, which are traditionally considered to be the most "rational," for the reason that they are supposed to be addressed to readers upon whom suggestion, pressure, or self-interest have little effect. We shall show that the same techniques of argumentation can be encountered at every level, at that of discussion around the family table as well as at that of debate in a highly specialized environment. If the quality of the minds which adhere to certain arguments, in highly speculative domains, is a guarantee of the value of these arguments, the community of structure between these arguments and those used in daily discussions explains why and how we succeed in understanding them.

Our treatise will consider only the *discursive* means of obtaining the adherence of minds: in the sequel, only the technique which uses language to persuade and convince will be examined.

This limitation, in our opinion, by no means implies that the technique in question is the most efficacious way of affecting minds. The contrary is the case—we are firmly convinced that the most solid beliefs are those which are not only admitted without proof, but very often not even made explicit. And, when it is a matter of securing adherence, nothing is more reliable than external or internal experience and calculation conforming to previously admitted rules. But, recourse to argumentation is unavoidable whenever these proofs are questioned by one of the parties, when there is no agreement on their scope or interpretation, on their value or on their relation to the problems debated.

Further, any action designed to obtain adherence falls outside the range of argumentation to the degree that the use of language is lacking in its support or interpretation: those who set an example for other people without saying anything, or those who make use of a stick or a carrot, can obtain appreciable results. We are interested in such procedures only when they are emphasized by way of language, for example, by resort to promises or threats. There are yet other cases—for example, blessing and cursing—in which language is utilized as a

[12] Plato, *Phaedrus*, 273e.

direct, magical means of action and not as a means of communication. Again, we shall not treat of such cases unless this action is integrated into the framework of an argumentation.

One of the essential factors of propaganda as it has developed above all in the 20th century, but the use of which was well known to Antiquity, and which the Roman Catholic Church has put to profitable use with incomparable art, is the conditioning of the audience by means of numerous and varied techniques that utilize anything capable of influencing behavior. These techniques have an undeniable effect in preparing the audience, in rendering it more accessible to the arguments presented to it. Our analysis will also neglect them: we shall treat of the conditioning of the audience by the discourse alone, which will result in certain considerations on the order in which arguments must be presented to exercise their maximum effect.

Finally, what Aristotle termed "extra-technical proofs"[13]—meaning those proofs which are not related to rhetorical technique—will enter into our study only when there is disagreement concerning the conclusions that can be drawn from them. For we are less interested in the complete development of a discussion than in the *argumentative schemes* coming into play. The term "extra-technical proofs" is well designed to remind us that whereas our civilization, characterized by a great ingenuity in the techniques intended to act on things, has completely forgotten the theory of argumentation, of action on minds by means of discourse, it was this theory which, under the name of rhetoric, was considered by the Greeks the τέχνη "par excellence."

III

The theory of argumentation which, with the aid of discourse, aims at securing an efficient action on minds might have been treated as a branch of psychology. Indeed, if arguments are not compulsive, if they are not to be necessarily convincing but only possessed of a certain force, which may moreover vary with the audience, is it not by their effect that we can judge of this force? This would make the study of argumentation one of the objects of experimental psychology, where varied arguments would be tested on varied audiences which are sufficiently well known for it to be possible to draw fairly general conclusions from these experiments. A number of American psychologists have become involved in such studies, the interest of which is incontestable.[14]

We shall however proceed differently. We seek, first of all, to characterize the different argumentative structures, the analysis of which

---

[13] Aristotle, *Rhetoric*, I, 2, 1355b.
[14] Cf. Hollingsworth, *The Psychology of the Audience;* Hovland, "Effects of the Mass Media of Communication," *Handbook of Social Psychology*, pp. 1062–1103.

must precede all experimental tests of their effectiveness. And, on the other hand, we do not think that laboratory methods can determine the value of argumentations used in the human sciences, law, and philosophy; and this for the reason that the methodology of psychologists is itself an object of controversy and lies within the scope of our study.

Our procedure will differ radically from that adopted by those philosophers who endeavor to reduce reasoning in social, political, and philosophical matters by taking their cue from the models provided by the deductive or experimental sciences, and who reject as worthless everything which does not conform to the schemes which were previously imposed. Quite the opposite: we will draw our inspiration from the logicians, but only to imitate the methods which they have used so successfully for the last century or so.

We must not indeed lose sight of the fact that logic, in the first half of the 19th century, enjoyed no prestige either in scientific circles or with the public at large. Whately[15] could write in 1828 that, if rhetoric no longer enjoyed the esteem of the public, logic was some degrees lower in popular estimation.

Logic underwent a brilliant development during the last century when, abandoning the old formulas, it set out to analyze the methods of proof effectively used by mathematicians. Modern formal logic became, in this way, the study of the methods of demonstration used in the mathematical sciences. One result of this development is to limit its domain, since everything ignored by mathematicians is foreign to it. Logicians owe it to themselves to complete the theory of demonstration obtained in this way by a theory of argumentation. We seek here to construct such a theory by analyzing the methods of proof used in the human sciences, law, and philosophy. We shall examine arguments put forward by advertisers in newspapers, politicians in speeches, lawyers in pleadings, judges in decisions, and philosophers in treatises.

Our field of study is immense and it has lain fallow for centuries. We hope that our first results will incite other researchers to complete and perfect them.

THE FRAMEWORK OF ARGUMENTATION

Demonstration and Argumentation

The special characteristics of argumentation and the problems inherent to its study cannot be better conveyed than by contrasting argumentation with the classical concept of demonstration and, more particularly, with formal logic which is limited to the examination of demonstrative methods of proof.

---

[15] Whately, Preface to *Elements of Rhetoric* (1893) p. iii.

In modern logic, the product of reflection on mathematical reasoning, the formal systems are no longer related to any rational evidence whatever. The logician is free to elaborate as he pleases the artificial language of the system he is building, free to fix the symbols and combinations of symbols that may be used. It is for him to decide which are the axioms, that is, the expressions considered without proof as valid in his system, and to say which are the rules of transformation he introduces which will make it possible to deduce, from the valid expressions, other expressions of equal validity in the system. The only obligation resting on the builder of formal axiomatic systems, the one which gives the demonstrations their compelling force, is that of choosing symbols and rules in such a way as to avoid doubt and ambiguity. It must be possible, without hesitation, even mechanically, to establish whether a sequence of symbols is admitted in the system, whether it is of the same form as another sequence of symbols, whether it is considered valid, because it is an axiom or an expression deducible from the axioms, in a manner consistent with the rules of deduction. Any consideration that has to do with the origin of the axioms or the rules of deduction, with the role that the axiomatic system is deemed to play in the elaboration of thought, is foreign to logic conceived in this manner, in the sense that it goes beyond the framework of the formalism in question. The search for unquestionable univocity has even led the formalistic logicians to construct systems in which no attention is paid to the meaning of the expressions: they are satisfied if the symbols introduced and the transformations concerning them are beyond discussion. They leave the interpretation of the elements of the axiomatic system to those who will apply it and who will have to concern themselves with its adequacy for the end pursued.

When the demonstration of a proposition is in question, it is sufficient to indicate the processes by means of which the proposition can be obtained as the final expression of a deductive series, which had its first elements provided by the constructor of the axiomatic system within which the demonstration is accomplished. Where these elements come from, whether they are impersonal truths, divine thoughts, results of experiment, or postulates particular to the author, these are questions which the logician considers foreign to his discipline. But when it is a question of arguing, of using discourse to influence the intensity of an audience's adherence to certain theses, it is no longer possible to neglect completely, as irrelevancies, the psychological and social conditions in the absence of which argumentation would be pointless and without result. For *all argumentation aims at gaining the adherence of minds, and, by this very fact, assumes the existence of an intellectual contact.*

For argumentation to exist, an effective community of minds must be realized at a given moment. There must first of all be agreement, in principle, on the formation of this intellectual community, and, after that, on the fact of debating a specific question together: now this does not come about automatically.

Even in the realm of inward deliberation, certain conditions are required for argumentation: in particular, a person must conceive of himself as divided into at least two interlocutors, two parties engaging in deliberation. And there is no warrant for regarding this division as necessary. It appears to be constructed on the model of deliberation with others. Hence, we must expect to find carried over to this inner deliberation most of the problems associated with the conditions necessary for discussion with others. Many expressions bear witness to this, but two examples may suffice. The first, relating to preliminary conditions as they affect persons, is such a saying as "Don't listen to your evil genius." The other, having to do with preliminary conditions as they affect the object of argumentation, is a saying like "Don't bring that up any more."

The Contact of Minds

A whole set of conditions is required for the formation of an effective community of minds.

The indispensable minimum for argumentation appears to be the existence of a common language, of a technique allowing communication to take place.

But the minimum is not enough. No one shows this better than the author of *Alice in Wonderland*. The beings inhabiting that country understand Alice's language, more or less, but her problem is to make contact and open a discussion, as in Wonderland there is no reason why discussions should begin. The inhabitants know no reason for speaking to one another. On some occasions Alice takes the initiative, as where she plainly addresses the mouse with the vocative, "O, Mouse."[16] And she considers it a success to have managed the exchange of a few rather pointless remarks with the Duchess.[17] However, in her earlier attempt at conversation with the caterpillar, a deadlock is reached immediately: "I think you ought to tell me who you are, first," she says. "Why?" says the caterpillar.[18] In our well-ordered world, with its hierarchies, there are generally rules prescribing how conversation may be begun; there is a preliminary agreement arising from the norms set by social life. Between Alice and the inhabitants of Wonderland, no hierarchy, precedence, or functions requires one to answer rather

[16] Carroll, *Alice's Adventures in Wonderland*, p. 41.
[17] *Ibid.*, p. 82.
[18] *Ibid.*, p. 65.

than another. Even those conversations which do begin are apt to break off suddenly. The lory, for instance, prides himself on his age:

This Alice would not allow without knowing how old he was, and as the lory positively refused to tell its age, there was no more to be said.[19]

The only preliminary condition fulfilled here is Alice's wish to enter into conversation with the beings of this new universe.

The set of those a speaker wishes to address may vary considerably. For any particular speaker it falls far short of all human beings. In the case of a child, however, to whom the adult world is in varying measure closed, the universe he wants to address is correspondingly extended by the inclusion of animals and all the inanimate objects he regards as his natural interlocutors.[20]

There are beings with whom any contact may seem superfluous or undesirable. There are some one cannot be bothered to talk to. There are others with whom one does not wish to discuss things, but to whom one merely gives orders.

To engage in argument, a person must attach some importance to gaining the adherence of his interlocutor, to securing his assent, his mental cooperation. It is, accordingly, sometimes a valued honor to be a person with whom another will enter into discussion. Because of the rationalism and humanism of the last few centuries, it seems a strange notion that the mere fact of being someone whose opinion is taken into account should constitute a quality; but in many societies a person will no more talk to just anybody than, in the past, a man would fight a duel with just anybody. It is also to be observed that wanting to convince someone always implies a certain modesty on the part of the initiator of the argument; what he says is not "Gospel truth," he does not possess that authority which would place his words beyond question so that they would carry immediate conviction. He acknowledges that he must use persuasion, think of arguments capable of acting on his interlocutor, show some concern for him, and be interested in his state of mind.

A person—whether an adult or a child—who wants to "count" with others, wishes that they would stop giving him orders and would, instead, reason with him and concern themselves with his reactions. He wants to be regarded as a member of a more-or-less equalitarian society. A man who does not cultivate this kind of contact with his fellows will be thought a proud, unattractive creature as compared with one who, however important his functions, takes pains to address

[19] *Ibid.*, p. 44.
[20] Cassirer, "Le langage et la construction du monde des objets," *Journal de Psychologie*, XXX (1933), 39.

the public in a manner which makes clear the value he attaches to its appreciation.

But, as has been said many times, it is not always commendable to wish to persuade someone: the conditions under which contact between minds takes place may, indeed, appear to be rather dishonorable. The reader will recall the story of Aristippus, who, when he was reproached for having abjectly prostrated himself at the feet of Dionysius the tyrant in order to be heard by him, defended himself by saying that the fault was not his, but that of Dionysius who had his ears in his feet. Is the position of the ears, then, a matter of indifference?[21]

The danger seen by Aristotle in carrying on discussion with some people is that the speaker may thereby destroy the quality of his argumentation:

A man should not enter into discussion with everybody or practice dialectics with the first comer as reasoning always becomes embittered where some people are concerned. Indeed, when an adversary tries by every possible means to wriggle out of a corner, it is legitimate to strive, by every possible means, to reach the conclusion; but this procedure lack elegance.[22]

It is not enough for a man to speak or write; he must also be listened to or read. It is no mean thing to have a person's attention, to have a wide audience, to be allowed to speak under certain circumstances, in certain gatherings, in certain circles. We must not forget that by listening to someone we display a willingness to eventually accept his point of view. There is great significance in the attitude of a Churchill forbidding British diplomats even to listen to any peace proposals German emissaries might try to convey or in the attitude of a political party when it makes known its willingness to hear any proposals of a politician engaged in forming a ministry, because they prevent the establishment or recognize the existence of the conditions preliminary to possible argumentation.

Achievement of the conditions preliminary to the contact of minds is facilitated by such factors as membership in the same social class, exchange of visits and other social relations. Frivolous discussions that are lacking in apparent interest are not always entirely unimportant, inasmuch as they contribute to the smooth working of an indispensable social mechanism.

The Speaker and His Audience

The authors of scientific reports and similar papers often think that if they merely report certain experiments, mention certain facts, or enunciate a certain number of truths, this is enough of itself to auto-

[21] Bacon, *Advancement of Learning*, GBWW, vol. 30, p. 11.
[22] Aristotle, *Topics*, VIII, 14, 164b.

matically arouse the interest of their hearers or readers. This attitude rests on the illusion, widespread in certain rationalistic and scientific circles, that facts speak for themselves and make such an indelible imprint on any human mind that the later is forced to give its adherence regardless of its inclination. An editor of a psychological journal, Katherine F. Bruner, likens such authors, who do not worry very much about their audience, to discourteous visitors:

They slouch into a chair, staring glumly at their shoes, and abruptly announce, to themselves or not, we never know, "It has been shown by such and such . . . that the female of the white rat responds negatively to electric shock."
  "All right, sir," I say. "So what? Tell me first why I should care; then I will listen."[23]

It is true that these authors when addressing a learned society, or publishing an article in a specialized journal, can afford to neglect the means of entering into contact with their public, for the indispensable link between speaker and audience is provided by a scientific institution, the society, or the journal. In such a case, the author has merely to maintain, between himself and the public, the contact already established by the scientific institution.

But not everyone is in such a privileged position. For argumentation to develop, there must be some attention paid to it by those to whom it is directed. The prime concern of publicity and propaganda is to draw the attention of an indifferent public, this being the indispensable condition for carrying on any sort of argumentation. It is true that in a large number of fields—such as those of education, politics, science, the administration of justice—any society possesses institutions which facilitate and organize this contact of minds. But the importance of this preliminary problem must not be underrated on that account.

Under normal circumstances, some quality is necessary in order to speak and be listened to. In our civilization, where the printed word has become a commodity and utilizes economic organization to draw attention to itself, this preliminary condition is seen clearly only in cases where contact between the speaker and his audience cannot be brought about by the techniques of distribution. It is accordingly best seen where argumentation is developed by a speaker who is orally addressing a specific audience, rather than where it is contained in a book on sale in a bookstore. This quality in a speaker, without which he will not be listened to, or even, in many cases, allowed to speak, will vary with the circumstances. Sometimes it will be enough for the speaker to appear as a human being with a decent suit of clothes,

[23] Brunner, "Of Psychological Writings," *Journal of Abnormal and Social Psychology,* 37 (1942), 62.

sometimes he is required to be an adult, sometimes he must be a rank and file member of a particular group, sometimes the spokesman of this group. Under certain circumstances or before certain audiences the only admissible authority for speaking is the exercise of particular functions. There are fields where these matters of qualification to speak are regulated in very great detail.

The contact between the speaker and his audience is not confined to the conditions preliminary to argumentation: it is equally necessary if argumentation is to develop. For since argumentation aims at securing the adherence of those to whom it is addressed, it is, in its entirety, relative to the audience to be influenced.

How may such an audience be defined? Is it just the person whom the speaker addresses by name? Not always: thus, a member of Parliament in England must address himself to the Speaker, but he may try to persuade those listening to him in the chamber, and beyond that, public opinion throughout the country. Again, can such an audience be defined as the group of persons the speaker sees before him when he speaks? Not necessarily. He may perfectly well disregard a portion of them: a government spokesman in Parliament may give up any hope of convincing the opposition, even before he begins to speak, and may be satisfied with getting the adherence of his majority. And on the other hand, a person granting an interview to a journalist considers his audience to be not the journalist himself but the readers of the paper he represents. The secrecy of deliberations, by modifying the speaker's opinion of his audience, may change the content of his speech. It is at once apparent from these few examples how difficult it is to determine by purely material criteria what constitutes a speaker's audience. The difficulty is even greater in the case of a writer's audience, as in most cases it is impossible to identify his readers with certainty.

For this reason we consider it preferable to define an audience, for the purposes of rhetoric, as *the ensemble of those whom the speaker wishes to influence by his argumentation*. Every speaker thinks, more or less consciously, of those he is seeking to persuade; these people form the audience to whom his speech is addressed.

The Audience as a Construction of the Speaker

The audience, as visualized by one undertaking to argue, is always a more or less systematized construction. Efforts have been made to establish its psychological[24] or sociological[25] origins. The essential con-

[24] Sullivan, *The Interpersonal Theory of Psychiatry*.
[25] Millioud, "La propagation des idées," *Revue philosophique*, 69 (1910), 580–600; 70 (1910), 168–191.

sideration for the speaker who has set himself the task of persuading concrete individuals is that his construction of the audience should be adequate to the occasion.

This does not hold for someone engaged in mere essay-making, without concern for real life. Rhetoric, which has then become an academic exercise, is addressed to conventional audiences, of which such rhetoric can afford to have stereotyped conceptions. However, it is this limited view of the audience, as much as artificiality of subject-matter, which is responsible for the degeneration of rhetoric.[26]

In real argumentation, care must be taken to form a concept of the anticipated audience as close as possible to reality. An inadequate picture of the audience, resulting from either ignorance or an unforeseen set of circumstances, can have very unfortunate results. Argumentation which an orator considers persuasive may well cause opposition in an audience for which "reasons for" are actually "reasons against." Thus, if one argues for a certain measure that it is likely to reduce social tension, such argument will set against the measure all those who would like to see disturbances.

Accordingly, knowledge of those one wishes to win over is a condition preliminary to all effectual argumentation.

Concern with the audience transforms certain chapters in the classical treatises on rhetoric into veritable studies in psychology. For instance, in the passage in the *Rhetoric* dealing with the factors of age and fortune in audiences, Aristotle includes many shrewd descriptions of a differential-psychological nature that are still valid today.[27] Cicero shows the necessity of speaking differently to the class of men which is "coarse and ignorant, always preferring immediate advantage to what is honorable," and to "that other, enlightened and cultivated, which puts moral dignity above all else."[28] Later, Quintilian dwells on character differences, which are important to the orator.[29]

The study of audiences could also be a study for sociology, since a man's opinions depend not so much on his own character, as on his social environment, on the people he associates with and lives among. As M. Millioud has said: "If you want an uncultivated man to change his views, transplant him."[30] Every social circle or milieu is distinguishable in terms of its dominant opinions and unquestioned beliefs, of the premises that it takes for granted without hesitation: these views form an integral part of its culture, and an orator wishing to persuade a particular audience must of necessity adapt himself to it. Thus the

[26] Marou, *Histoire de l'éducation dans l'Antiquité*, p. 278.
[27] Aristotle, *Rhetoric*, II, 12–17, 1388b–1391b. See also De Coster, "L'idéalisme des jeunes," *Morale et enseignement*, 1951–52, nos. 2, 3.
[28] Cicero, *Partitiones Oratoriae*, 90.
[29] Quintilian, III, viii, 38 et seq.
[30] Millioud, "La propagation des idées," *Revlue philosophique*, 70 (1910), 173.

particular culture of a given audience shows so strongly through the speeches addressed to it that we feel we can rely on them to a considerable extent for our knowledge of the character of past civilizations.

Among the sociological considerations of possible use to an orator are those bearing on a very definite matter: the social functions exercised by his listeners. It is quite common for members of an audience to adopt attitudes connected with the role they play in certain social institutions. This fact has been stressed by the originator of the psychology of form:

One can sometimes observe marvelous changes in individuals, as when some passionately biased person becomes a member of a jury, or arbitrator, or judge, and when his actions then show the fine transition from bias to an honest effort to deal with the problems at issue in a just and objective fashion.[31]

The same observation can be made of the mentality of a politician whose point of view changes when, after years spent in the opposition, he becomes a responsible member of the government.

The listener, then, in his new functions, assumes a new personality which the orator cannot afford to disregard. And what is true of the individual listener holds equally true of whole audiences, so much so that the theoreticians of rhetoric have found it possible to classify oratory on the basis of the role performed by the audience addressed. The writers of antiquity recognized three types of oratory, the deliberative, the forensic, and the epidictic, which in their view corresponded respectively to an audience engaged in deliberating, an audience engaged in judging, and an audience that is merely enjoying the unfolding of the orator's argument without having to reach a conclusion on the matter in question.[32]

We are presented here with a distinction of a purely practical order, whose defects and inadequacies are apparent. Particularly unsatisfactory is its characterization of the epidictic type of oratory, of which we shall have more to say later.[33] Though this classification cannot be accepted as such for the study of argumentation, it has nevertheless the merit of underlining the importance which a speaker must give to the functions of his audience.

It often happens that an orator must persuade a composite audience, embracing people differing in character, loyalties, and functions. To win over the different elements in his audience, the orator will have to use a multiplicity of arguments. A great orator is one who possesses

[31] Wertheimer, *Productive Thinking*, pp. 135–136.
[32] Aristotle, *Rhetoric*, I, 3, 1358b, 2–7; Cicero, *Orator*, 37; *Partitiones Oratoriae*, 10; Quintilian, III, iv.
[33] Cf. 11, infra: The Epidictic Genre.

the art of taking into consideration, in his argumentation, the composite nature of his audience. Examples of this art may be found on close reading of speeches made before parliamentary assemblies, a type of composite audience whose constituent elements are readily discernible.

However, an orator does not have to be confronted with several organized factions to think of the composite nature of his audience. He is justified in visualizing each one of his listeners as simultaneously belonging to a number of disparate groups. Even when an orator stands before only a few auditors, or indeed, before a single auditor, it is possible that he will not be quite sure what arguments will appear most convincing to his audience. In such a case, he will, by a kind of fiction, insert his audience into a series of different audiences. In *Tristram Shandy*—since argumentation is one of the main themes of this book, we shall often refer to it—Tristram describes an argument between his parents, in which his father wants to persuade his mother to have a midwife:

He . . . placed his arguments in all lights; argued the matter with her like a Christian, like a heathen, like a husband, like a father, like a patriot, like a man. My mother answered everything only like a woman, which was a little hard upon her, for, as she could not assume and fight it out behind such a variety of characters, 'twas no fair match: 'twas seven to one.[34]

Notice that it is not only the orator who so changes his mask: it is even more so his audience—his poor wife in this case—which his fancy transforms, as he seeks its most vulnerable points. However, as it is the speaker who takes the initiative in this "breaking down" of the audience, it is to him that the terms "like a Christian," like a heathen," and so on, are applied.

When a speaker stands before his audience, he can try to locate it in its social setting. He may ask himself if all the members fall within a single social group, or if he must spread his listeners over a number of different—perhaps even opposed—groups. If division is necessary, several ways of proceeding are always possible: he may divide his audience ideally in terms of the social groups—political, occupational, religious, for example—to which the individual members belong, or in terms of the values to which certain members of the audience adhere. These ideal divisions are not mutually independent; they can, however, lead to the formation of very different partial audiences.

The breaking down of a gathering into sub-groups will also depend on the speaker's own position. If he holds extremist views on a question, there is nothing to restrain him from considering all his

[34] Sterne, *The Life and Opinions of Tristram Shandy,* bk. I, chap. 18, p. 42.

218
CHAIM PERELMAN

interlocutors as forming a single audience. On the other hand, if he holds a moderate view, he will see them as forming at least two distinct audiences.[35]

Knowledge of an audience cannot be conceived independently of the knowledge of how to influence it. The problem of the nature of an audience is indeed intimately connected with that of its conditioning. This term implies, at first sight, factors extrinsic to the audience. And all study of this conditioning assumes that this conditioning is considered as applying to an entity which would be the audience itself. But, on a closer view, knowledge of an audience is also knowledge of how to bring about its conditioning, as well as of the amount of conditioning achieved at any given moment of the discourse.

Various conditioning agents are available to increase one's influence on an audience: music, lighting, crowd effects, scenery, and various devices of stage management. These means have always been known and have been used in the past by primitive peoples, as well as by the Greeks, Romans, and men of the Middle Ages. In our own day, technical improvements have fostered the development of these conditioners to the point that they are regarded by some as the essential element in acting on minds.

Besides conditioning of this kind, which is beyond the scope of this work, there is the conditioning by the speech itself, which results in the audience no longer being exactly the same at the end of the speech as it was at the beginning. This form of conditioning can be brought about only if there is a continuous adaptation of the speaker to his audience.

Adaptation of the Speaker to the Audience

Vico wrote, "the end sought by eloquence always depends on the speaker's audience, and he must govern his speech in accordance with their opinions."[36] In argumentation, the important thing is not knowing what the speaker regards as true or important, but knowing the views of those he is addressing. To borrow Gracian's simile, speech is "like a feast, at which the dishes are made to please the guests, and not the cooks."[37]

The great orator, the one with a hold on his listeners, seems animated by the very mind of his audience. This is not the case for the ardent enthusiast whose sole concern is with what he himself considers

---

[35] Cf. the observations of L. Festinger on the lesser tendency toward communication found in those who hold moderate viewpoints: "Informal Social Communication," *Psychological Review,* vol. 57, no. 5, Sept. 1950, p. 275.
[36] Vico, *Opere,* ed. Ferrari, vol. II, *De Nostri Temporis Studiorum Ratione,* p. 10.
[37] Gracian, *L'homme de Cour,* p. 85.

important. A speaker of this kind may have some effect on suggestible persons, but generally speaking his speech will strike his audience as unreasonable. According to M. Pradines, the enthusiast's speech, even if capable of some effect, does not yield a "true" sound, the emotional reality "bursts through the mask of logic," for, he says, "passion and reasons are not commensurable."[38] The apparent explanation for this viewpoint is that the man swayed by passion argues without taking sufficiently into account the audience he is addressing: carried away by his enthusiasm, he imagines his audience to be susceptible to the same arguments that persuaded him. Thus, passion, in causing the audience to be forgotten, creates less an absence than a poor choice of reasons.

Because they adopted the techniques of the clever orator, Plato reproached the leaders of the Athenian democracy with "flattering" the populace when they should have led them. But no orator, not even the religious orator, can afford to neglect this effort of adaptation to his audience. "The making of a preacher," wrote Bossuet, "rests with his audience."[39] In his struggle against the demagogues at Athens, Demosthenes calls on the people to improve themselves so as to improve the performance of the orators:

Your orators never make you either bad men or good, but you make them whichever you choose; for it is not you that aim at what they wish for, but they who aim at whatever they think you desire. You therefore must start with a noble ambition and all will be well, for then no orator will give you base counsel, or else he will gain nothing by it, having no one to take him at his word.[40]

It is indeed the audience which has the major role in determining the quality of argument and the behavior of orators.[41]

Although orators, in their relationship to the listeners, have been compared to cooks, and even to parasites who "almost always speak a language contrary to their sentiments in order to be invited to fine meals,"[42] It must not be overlooked that the orator is nearly always at liberty to give up persuading an audience when he cannot persuade it effectively except by the use of methods that are repugnant to him. It should not be thought, where argument is concerned, that it is always honorable to succeed in persuasion, or even to have such an intention. The problem of harmonizing the scruples of the man of honor with submission to the audience received special attention

[38] Pradines, *Traité de psychologie générale*, vol. II, pp. 324–325.
[39] Bossuet, *Sermons*, vol. II, *Sur la parole de Dieu*, p. 153.
[40] Demosthenes, *On Organization*, 36.
[41] Cf. 2, supra: The Contact of Minds.
[42] Saint-Évremond, vol. IX, p. 19, referring to Petronius, *The Satyricon*, chap. III, p. 3.

from Quintilian.[43] To him rhetoric as *scientia bene dicendi*[44] implies that the accomplished orator not only is good at persuading, but also says what is good. If, then, one allows the existence of audiences of corrupt persons, whom one nonetheless does not want to give up convincing, and, at the same time, if one looks at the matter from the standpoint of the moral quality of the speaker, one finds oneself led, in order to solve the difficulty, to make distinctions and dissociations that do not come as a matter of course.

The coupling of obligation on the orator to adapt himself to his audience, with limitation of the audience to an incompetent mob, incapable of understanding sustained reasoning, or of maintaining attention if in the least distracted, has had two unfortunate results. It has discredited rhetoric, and has introduced into the theory of speech general rules which actually seem only to be valid in particular cases. We do not see, for instance, why, as a matter of principle, use of technical argumentation should lead away from rhetoric and dialectic.[45]

There is only one rule in this matter: adaptation of the speech to the audience, whatever its nature. Arguments that in substance and form are appropriate to certain circumstances may appear ridiculous in others.[46]

If the same event is described in a work that claims to be scientific and in a historical novel, the same method of proving its reality need not be adopted in the two cases. A reader who would have found Jules Romains' proofs of the voluntary suspension of the action of the heart ridiculous, had they appeared in a medical journal, might consider them an interesting hypothesis when developed in a novel.[47]

The procedures to be adopted in arguing are to some extent conditioned by the size of the audience, independently of considerations relating to the area of agreement taken as a basis for the argument, which vary from audience to audience. In discussing style as affected by the occasion of the speech, J. Marouzeau has drawn attention to

a kind of deference and self-consciousness imposed by numbers, . . . as intimacy decreases, qualms increase, qualms about gaining the esteem of the listeners, about winning their applause or, at least, their approbation as expressed in looks and attitudes.[48]

[43] Quintilian, III, VIII; XII, I.
[44] Quintilian, II, XV, 34.
[45] Aristotle, *Rhetoric*, I, 2, 1357a, 1358a.
[46] Whately, *Elements of Rhetoric* (Harper), pt. III, chap. I, 2, pp. 179 et seq.
[47] Reyes, *El Deslinde*, p. 40. Romains, *Les hommes de bonne volonté*, vol. XII: *Les créateurs*, chap. I–VII. Cf. Belaval, *Les philosophes et leur langage*, p. 138.
[48] Marouzeau, *Précis de stylistique française*, p. 208.

Many other observations might pertinently be made on characteristics of audiences that influence a speaker's behavior and mode of argument. In our view, the value of our study depends on consideration being given to the many distinct aspects of particular audiences in as concrete a manner as possible.

14 THE PHILOSOPHICAL BASIS OF CHAIM PERELMAN'S THEORY OF RHETORIC

RAY D. DEARIN

Dearin's purpose in this article is "to ferret out the postulates and philosophical assumptions underlying Perelman's theory of rhetoric." To this end he examines Perelman's view of the contingent nature of philosophical discourse, his concept of knowledge, and his conception of the nature of language.

Perelman's model of practical argumentation is drawn from jurisprudence. And the notion of formal justice is central to his philosophical view. As a preface to Perelman's rhetorical theory, Dearin explores the distinction between logical reason and rhetorical reason. For his analysis Dearin draws extensively on Perelman's *An Historical Introduction to Philosophical Thinking* and on *The Idea of Justice and the Problem of Argument.*

Source: *Quarterly Journal of Speech,* LV (October 1969), 213–224. Reprinted with permission of the author and the publisher.

To think philosophically about any subject is to approach it rationally. As Henry W. Johnstone, Jr. puts the matter, "Philosophy is just the use of reason to examine each mode of human experience."[1] There are times when a close rational examination of a subject such as rhetoric becomes especially necessary. Johnstone continues:

The need for a philosophical examination of rhetoric is more acute and the examination most welcome when the orderly processes through which people are normally able to persuade one another suddenly go awry and can no longer be counted on. Aristotle's examination of rhetoric was carried out in just such a period of reversal. Individuals claiming to be able for a fee to persuade anyone of anything were making a mockery of the art of persuading. In so doing, they unwittingly called attention to the need for a philosophical scrutiny of the foundations of rhetoric. Aristotle supplied such a scrutiny, disengaging persuasiveness from dialectical shenanigans and associating it firmly with virtue.[2]

[1] "The Relevance of Rhetoric to Philosophy and of Philosophy to Rhetoric," *QJS,* LII (February 1966), 42.
[2] *Ibid.,* 44.

In addition to a disruption or perversion of normal communication processes, other crises have called forth reexaminations of rhetoric. The problems of integrating the contributions of the pagan writers on rhetoric into the pedagogy of Christian theology occupied the attention of Augustine. In the eighteenth century, current views about psychology and epistemology led George Campbell to write *The Philosophy of Rhetoric*. Today modern science, with its concomitant effects on every field of learning, provokes new inquires into the nature of rhetoric and into its relevance to present-day man and his problems.

Among the contributions of modern theoreticians of rhetoric, none stresses the interrelationship of philosophy and rhetoric more strongly nor reveals more clearly the relevance of rhetoric to twentieth-century man than does the theory espoused by modern Belgian philosopher Chaim Perelman. The seeds of thought scattered throughout Perelman's numerous writings on such diverse topics as law, ethics, epistemology, philosophy, sociology, and argumentation over a period of more than three decades have already borne fruit in his *nouvelle rhétorique*, a theory whose fullest explication is found in the *Traité de l'argumentation*, which was written in collaboration with Madame L. Olbrechts-Tyteca in 1958. Since the publication of that treatise, Perelman has amplified and refined his theory of rhetoric in many books and articles. Doubtless, further extensions and refinements remain to be made.

Although future modifications may be expected, the uniqueness of Perelman's contributions and their obvious importance as specimens of modern rhetorical scholarship justify a close analytical scrutiny by students of rhetoric. Before one makes such an examination, however, he should ferret out the postulates and philosophical assumptions underlying Perelman's theory of rhetoric. To conduct such an investigation is the purpose of this article.

Stated most generally, the philosophic thought of M. Perelman represents a quest for a nonformal logic, one which may play a role in the behavioral sciences and philosophy analogous to that of modern formal logic and empiricism in the exact sciences. Moreover, the presuppositions behind his theory of rhetoric are foundational to his philosophical goal. I propose to show that in opposition to classical rationalism, which sought unique truth and certitude about its conclusions, Perelman enlarges the domain of reason to encompass a rhetorical rationalism that allows for a pluralism of values and a multiplicity of ways of being reasonable.

In my attempt to clarify Perelman's philosophical assumptions, I shall present four aspects of his thought: his conception of the nature of philosophy; his epistemology, which forms the substructure of the *nouvelle rhétorique;* his search for a nonformal logic that led him to the judicial model; and finally, the concept of rhetorical reason, the culmination of his philosophic efforts.

One of Perelman's central concerns is to establish the philosophical method as a necessary mode of viewing man and his problems. For him, philosophy plays a role in the clarification of the human condition which science can never usurp. To be sure, at an early stage in his career, Perelman recognized certain similarities between the scientific method and philosophy. Thus, he wrote in 1940 that "the philosophical method has the same logical structure as that of science. It consists of deducing from certain principles and from certain definitions . . . a set of consequences, and of comparing, as far as possible, these consequences with the facts."[3] But the limitations of science in dealing with human problems are clearly set forth in Perelman's recent work, *An Historical Introduction to Philosophical Thinking.* In a critique of Auguste Comte's positivism, for example, he writes:

It cannot be denied that Comte's analysis is correct regarding certain areas of knowledge where scientific answers have completely replaced theological or philosophical concepts. But that is quite another thing from saying that *all* human problems can be solved by calling on the experimental or deductive methods of science alone. The study not of what is but of what ought to be, what has the greater value, what is preferable, and what should determine our choices and our conduct can be abandoned to scientific methods only when we are dealing with purely technical problems. But that is far from being the case. Not only does the solution of our fundamental problems elude science and technology; the very hypothesis that philosophy can be dispensed with is itself a philosophical hypothesis.[4]

So Perelman believes in the meaningfulness and importance of philosophy. His conception of the aim of philosophy, however, differs markedly from the views of earlier philosophers who attempted to base their systems on necesssary or self-evident theses. In fact, whereas traditional metaphysics has always sought to discover eternal and immutable principles, Perelman believes that philosophy should "elaborate principles of being, thought, and action that are humanly *reasonable.*"[5] He maintains that the proverbial controversies and interminable discussions that mark the whole history of philosophic thought are due not to the lack of lucidity or the positive errors of philosophers, but to the very nature of the enterprise itself.[6] Moreover, philosophy cannot rightly employ the methods of formal logic. "The goal of

---

[3] Ch. Perelman, "Une conception de la philosophie," *Revue de l'Institut de Sociologie* XX, (1940), 46. [Translation mine.]

[4] Trans. Kenneth A. Brown (New York, 1965), pp. 5–6.

[5] Ch. Perelman, "On Self-Evidence in Metaphysics," *International Philosophical Quarterly,* IV (February 1964), 5–6.

[6] *Ibid.*

philosophy," he writes, "is to influence the mind and win its agreement, rather than to perform purely formal transformations of propositions."[7] In effect, "whoever develops a philosophical system undertakes to address everyone and to convince everyone."[8] In Perelman's fundamental conception of philosophy, therefore, the contingent nature of the axioms of every metaphysical system necessitates a recourse to rhetoric. This reliance upon argument is obligatory. Even those philosophers who have despised rhetoric have been compelled to use it: "The metaphysical rationalists, who strive to eliminate every conflict of values from their vision of the universe, which explains their scorn for rhetoric, arrive at their ends only after having imposed, thanks to rhetoric, their fundamental principles. . . . Every metaphysician must furnish reasons for the superiority of his system and, so long as his system is not admitted, he can only resort to the processes of rhetorical argumentation."[9]

Just as the philosopher resorts to argumentation in his presentation of a defensible world view, he also employs it in making ethical judgments. In his recent treatise, *Justice*, Perelman states:

The specific role of philosophy is, in effect, to propose to humanity objective principles of action that will be valid for the will of all reasonable men. This objectivity . . . envisages . . . an attempt to formulate norms and values such as could be proposed to every reasonable being. But to *propose* does not mean to *impose*. This distinction must be maintained at all cost. Otherwise we run the risk of a philosopher-king who would use the political authority and power of the State to ensure the supremacy of his convictions, his values, and his norms.[10]

The problems involved in the "ideal of universality" and the notion of "all reasonable men" will be set aside for subsequent consideration in connection with Perelman's conception of reason. At present, it is sufficient to note that in proposing ethical values, as in elaborating a world view, every philosopher employs postulates whose contingent nature excludes them from the realm of scientific demonstration or from the domain of formal logic.

Even if the principles of a philosophical system are granted by everyone, its conclusions may possibly be accepted by only a certain number of men. Because proof in philosophy is not simply a transposition in the order of axioms and theorems as in the deductive sciences of mathematics or geometry, the "conclusions are quite different from the original premises, and the process of arriving at them can only

---

[7] Perelman, *An Historical Introduction to Philosophical Thinking*, p. 101.
[8] *Ibid.*, p. 99.
[9] Ch. Perelman, "Réflexions sur la justice," *Revue de l'Institut de Sociologie*, XXIV (1951), 280–281. [Translation mine.]
[10] (New York, 1967), p. 78.

be explained by a difference in the nature of the proof."[11] Hence, Spinoza's ideal of a geometric, deductive, rationalistic philosophy can never be attained. As Perelman says, "A philosophical system cannot be proved like a treatise in geometry."[12]

The direction of Perelman's own thought concerning the nature of philosophy is revealed most clearly in his distinction between primary philosophies and regressive philosophy. Most traditional systems have been of the former type. Each has attempted to construct an edifice of universal, immutable truths. No provision has been made for future modifications. Consequently, when a crack appears in its foundation, the philosopher has been forced to admit that he has been mistaken, to attribute his error to spurious evidence or to a fallacious view of necessity, and then, after making the required modifications, to rebuild the structure as solidly as possible, and to proceed again to defend it to the last assault.[13] Regressive philosophy, on the other hand, affirms that from the time the philosopher begins his reflection, he starts with "a set of facts which he considers neither necessary, nor absolute, nor definitive, but as sufficiently assured to permit him to ground his thought."[14] Unlike the primary philosophy, "every crisis in its foundations constitutes, for regressive philosophy, a confirmation, a deepening of thought, for which it can only rejoice."[15] When he must modify his system, the philosopher will choose from among alternative possibilities the modification he deems best. Of course, he then must justify his choice by presenting reasons why it seems preferable to him, if he wishes to obtain the agreement of his peers.[16] Perelman's preference for regressive philosophy may be explained succinctly in these words: Philosophizing is a *human* endeavor. He states: "It is man, in the final analysis, who is the judge of his choice, and other men, his collaborators and his adversaries, judge, at the same time, this choice and the man who has chosen."[17]

This brief account of Perelman's views about philosophy reveals his beliefs that philosophy is an essential activity whose function cannot be replaced by science, that its methods are rhetorical and argumentative, rather than deductive and mathematical, and that the philosopher should entertain no delusion that his premises and conclusions are necessary or irrefragable. Not surprisingly, this attitude toward philosophy engenders a distinctive theory of knowledge.

---

[11] Perelman, *An Historical Introduction to Philosophical Thinking,* p. 101.
[12] *Ibid.,* p. 140.
[13] Ch. Perelman, "Philosophies premières et philosophie régressive," *Dialectica,* III (1949), 190.
[14] *Ibid.,* 185–186. [Translation mine.]
[15] *Ibid.,* 190.
[16] *Ibid.,* 184–185.
[17] *Ibid.*

2

In 1950 Perelman and Olbrechts-Tyteca suggested that a revival of rhetoric ought to accompany the formulation of a modern epistemology: "We believe that a theory of knowledge which corresponds to this climate of contemporary philosophy needs to integrate into its structure the processes of argumentation utilized in every domain of human culture and that . . . a renewal of rhetoric would conform to the humanist aspect of the aspirations of our age."[18] The form a modern view of knowledge should take can be better understood when the deficiencies in earlier theories are pointed out.

In the first place, the rationalists, empiricists, and positivists all failed to understand that, unlike physical phenomena, mental phenomena are not susceptible to quantification. A new insight came when Immanuel Kant observed that intensive magnitude is of an entirely different order from extensive magnitude. Perelman says, "This distinction of Kant's blazed the trail for Bergson's analysis. Bergson showed that psychological phenomena are qualitatively different from each other and that we cannot apply calculation or measure to them."[19]

A second flaw in traditional epistemologies, especially those inspired by the Cartesian model of an eternal and unchanging reason, is their failure to account for historical and social conditions. According to Perelman, "The concrete problem of the theory of knowledge is to study the means which make it possible to describe and explain phenomena and to determine the influence which the objects of our knowledge exercise on the processes that make knowledge possible."[20] A study of the *means* used to describe and explain phenomena will doubtless entail a consideration of the role of language in the acquisition of knowledge. That possibility will be considered presently. But it is the other aspect of the problem, the influence exerted by the *objects* of our knowledge, that suggests the relevance of social and cultural factors in the theory of knowledge. These factors led Perelman to assign to rhetoric a fundamental role in epistemology. In effect, for him rhetoric becomes the methodology of the sociology of knowledge. He writes:

To determine the field of application of the sociology of knowledge, it would be necessary to study most closely this strange logic [rhetoric] and the reasons which make it undergo the influence of social and cultural factors. One would see upon analysis that the proofs which govern it are neither the evidence of calculus nor experimental evidence, but those which Aristotle called "dialectical proofs," and which he studied in his *Topics* and his *Rhetoric*. In effect,

[18] Ch. Perelman and L. Olbrechts-Tyteca, "Logique et rhétorique," *Revue philosophique*, CXL (January 1950), 35. [Translation mine.]
[19] Perelman, *An Historical Introduction to Philosophical Thinking*, p. 186.
[20] *Ibid.*, p. 205.

socially conditional knowledge concerns the beliefs, the agreements, the adhesions of men. . . . Only a detailed examination of rhetorical argumentation will permit the founding of the sociology of knowledge upon the most solid bases.[21]

Thus, Perelman believes that modern epistemology should deal with all the factors, including social and cultural elements, which condition the acquisition of ideas and beliefs.

As stated earlier, a study of the means used to describe and explain phenomena introduces the element of language into any modern theory of knowledge. Perelman has long been aware of the problems involved in the communication of "meaning" through linguistic symbols.[22] In recent years he has shown that a weakness in classical rationalism was its belief that self-evidence founded on the identity of subject and object can lay claim to the truth. "Every assertion," he says, "before it can be judged true or false, must first be meaningful. Linguistic statements are made up of symbols which, by definition, cannot coincide with what they designate. In this case, how is it possible to identify the truth of a judgment with the self-evidence of an intuition?"[23] The best that rationalists can do is to "make the intervention of language as inoffensive as possible in order to render perfectly transparent the veil that it cannot help but be."[24] Perelman states his own view flatly: "The choice of a linguistic form is neither purely arbitrary nor simply a carbon copy of reality. The reasons that induce us to prefer one conception of experience, one analogy, to another, are a function of our vision of the world. The form is not separable from the content; language is not a veil which one need only discard or render transparent in order to perceive the real as such; it is inextricably bound up with a point of view, with the taking of a position."[25]

These foregoing weaknesses in earlier epistemologies are most pronounced in classical rationalism, and Perelman's work is, in large part,

---

21 Ch. Perelman, "Sociologie de la connaissance et Philosophie de la connaissance," *Revue internationale de philosophie*, IV (July 1950), 315. [Translation mine].

22 In 1940 Perelman was concerned to show that philosophy could deal just as objectively with the emotive meanings of words as with their conceptual meanings. ["Une conception de la philosophie," p. 41.] He was familiar with these distinctions made by C. K. Ogden and I. A. Richards in *The Meaning of Meaning* (London, 1923).

23 Perelman, "On Self-Evidence in Metaphysics," 13.

24 *Ibid.*, 16–17.

25 Chaim Perelman, "Rhetoric and Philosophy," trans. Henry W. Johnstone, Jr., *Philosophy and Rhetoric*, I (January 1968), 17–18. Elsewhere M. Perelman amplifies the idea that language is neither a simple copy of preestablished structures nor an arbitrary creation of man: "Although language is a human artefact, it is not produced by any irrational decision of a single individual. It develops, normally, in the midst of a community, the members of which can modify it by the use they make of it as soon as they consider there are any reasons for promoting any change." [Ch. Perelman, *The Idea of Justice and the Problem of Argument*, trans. John Petrie (London, 1963), p. 123.]

devoted to the overthrow of the Cartesian theory of knowledge. The Cartesian view of science as a collection of facts that have been established and definitively remain so "is, in the end, a theory of knowledge which is not human, but divine; of knowledge acquired by a unique and perfect Being, without initiation, training, tradition or need to learn. On this view, the history of knowledge, on its positive side, becomes uniquely that of additions, not that of successive modifications."[26] Such a notion is, of course, antithetical to Perelman's conception of a regressive philosophy. In contrast to the *results* of the scientific method, the Belgian philosopher would stress the *process* by which scientific theories come to be accepted:

If we assume that the sciences develop on the basis of opinions previously accepted—and replaced by others either when difficulty results from some contradiction or in order to allow of new elements of knowledge being integrated in the theory—then the understanding of scientific methodology requires us to be concerned not with building the scientific edifice on the foundation of self-evident truths, but with indicating why and how certain accepted opinions come to be no longer regarded as the most probable and the most suitable to express our beliefs, and are replaced by others. The history of the evolution of scientific ideas would be highly revealing in this regard.[27]

In Perelman's way of looking at scientific activity, "neither the self-evident principles of the rationalists nor the irrefragable facts of the empiricists constitute clear and distinct elements of knowledge which no subsequent progress would later modify or make more specific."[28] Not only have the rationalistic and empiricist ideas "generated misconceptions about the role of language and the methodology of the sciences," but by conceiving knowledge as "a structure at the base of which is an indubitable experience of sense-given data," they have led to an altogether "misleading contrast between knowledge and opinion."[29] As will be observed, Perelman attempts to remove this unnecessary distinction in his enlarged concept of reason.

Perelman stresses the importance of the problem of justifying one's fundamental postulates. He writes:

For centuries logicians have been able to neglect the problem of the justification of one's choice of axioms, by considering the latter either as self-evident or as arbitrary. In the first case, since we must bow to the evidence, we have no choice and therefore no need to justify our acceptance. In the second case, since all choices are considered equally arbitrary, it is impossible

[26] Perelman, *The Idea of Justice and the Problem of Argument,* pp. 116–117.
[27] *Ibid.,* p. 94.
[28] *Ibid.,* p. 95.
[29] H. L. A. Hart, Introduction to *ibid,* p. xi. Professor Hart also remarks that "in this part of his work M. Perelman has reached, by an independent route, conclusions similar to those of contemporary English philosophers who have also been critical of both the rationalism and the empiricism of the past."

to justify any one by showing it to be preferable to any other. When we reject both of these extremes, so reminiscent of realism and nominalism, when we admit that a choice of axioms is possible and that it is not entirely arbitrary, then the justification of choice ceases to be a negligible problem.[30]

By rejecting the idea of a self-evident intuition and its opposite extreme, Perelman thus conceives of an epistemology that is not only the antithesis of the Cartesian view, but one that also blurs the dubious distinction between knowledge and opinion. He states plainly: "I shall grant the status of knowledge to a tested opinion, to an opinion, that is, which has survived all objections and criticisms and with regard to which we have a certain confidence, though no certainty, that it will resist all such future attacks."[31]

The whole effect of Perelman's theory of knowledge, it should be clear by now, is to assert the role of decision in the working out of our ideas. This point of view emphasizes the *reasons* we have for deciding in a particular way as well as the *techniques of reasoning* by which we arrive at those decisions. Perelman believes, then, that an epistemology should be "founded on what a theory of the nature of argumentation, as it actually is, can teach us."[32] The next stage of our investigation chronicles his search for a nonformal logic that can explain how decisions are actually made.

3

For over twenty-five years, Perelman has been intrigued by the idea of justice, and, if one does not miss the connection between justice and "justification," then the relevance of this aspect of the philosopher's thought to his theory of rhetorical argumentation is obvious. To begin with, Perelman sought to clear away from the concept of justice the extraordinary confusion surrounding the multiplicity of meanings that have been attached to the idea throughout history. He found at first that the varied meanings of the word "justice" appear irreconcilable. Currently, the term is used to designate at least six different ideas:

1. To each the same thing.
2. To each according to his merits.
3. To each according to his works.
4. To each according to his needs.
5. To each according to his rank.
6. To each according to his legal entitlement.[33]

---

[30] Perelman, *Justice*, p. 60.
[31] Perelman, *The Idea of Justice and the Problem of Argument*, p. 117.
[32] *Ibid.*, p. 122.
[33] *Ibid.*, p. 7. [This section of the book originally appeared in 1945 as *De la justice*.]

As Julius Stone correctly observes, when Perelman is confronted with these multifarious conceptions of justice, his method is to seek "a kind of nucleus of justice, which shall be independent of varying usage-associations, and of the ideological implications of such usage."[34] Indeed, Perelman finds that beneath all the various systems of concrete justice and running throughout all the various conceptions of justice is one formal, abstract principle. Stated simply, formal justice consists of "*a principle of action in accordance with which beings of one and the same essential category must be treated in the same way.*"[35] This principle, being purely formal and abstract, is never realized in any normative system of justice. As will be seen, an arbitrary element always intervenes to flout formal justice. But the utility of this general principle extends beyond the field of ethics to the problem of justification in general. "Justification," writes Perelman, "can deal with legality, morality, regularity (in the widest sense of the word), usefulness or expediency."[36] Moreover, since the idea of justification implies the "possibility of an unfavorable appraisal of what you are trying to justify,"[37] it follows that the matter under consideration is debatable. Under such conditions, rational argument ensues, and here Perelman's abstract principle becomes a *rule of justice* that may be applied, he thinks, to determine the relative strength of arguments: "It is useless to try to define rational argumentation the way we define a demonstrative technique, namely, by its conformity to certain prescribed rules. Unlike demonstrative reasoning, arguments are never correct or incorrect; they are either strong or weak, relevant or irrelevant. The strength or weakness is judged according to the Rule of Justice, which requires that essentially similar situations be treated in the same manner."[38] Thus, a principle derived from Perelman's analysis of justice constitutes a yardstick for determining the strength of arguments which, by their very nature, cannot be judged according to the rules of formal logic.

Doubtless, a principal reason for Perelman's preoccupation with the notion of justice is that it lies in an area where value judgments abound. As indicated earlier, there can be no perfect justice because an arbitrary element enters into every normative system. Indeed, that element is the *value* affirmed by the principles of the system which are themselves not justified. For example, the decision to follow the prin-

---

[34] *Human Law and Human Justice* (Stanford, Calif., 1965), p. 302.

[35] Perelman, *The Idea of Justice and the Problem of Argument*, p. 16.

[36] Ch. Perelman, "Value Judgments, Justifications and Argumentation," trans. Francis B. Sullivan, *Philosophy Today*, VI (Spring 1962), 46.

[37] *Ibid.*

[38] Perelman, *Justice*, p. 83. He goes on to say that "relevance and irrelevance are to be examined according to the rules and criteria recognized by the various disciplines and their particular methodologies."

ciple, "to each according to his works," rather than "to each according to his needs" affirms a value judgment that is not itself obviously justified. Says Perelman, "This latter touch of the arbitrary it is logically impossible to avoid."[39] The implications of Perelman's rejection of the notion of unique truth are felt most strongly in the realm of values. From his own pluralistic perspective, two different decisions about the same object can both be reasonable as long as they express coherent and philosophically founded points of view.[40] If statements of value can be neither true nor false, then how are we to reason concerning values? Clearly, some way is needed: "The need for a logic of value judgments has been felt in philosophic thought from the day when it was realized that truth or falsity is not a property that can be attributed to every proposition."[41] In a sense, Perelman's analysis of justice has led him to formulate his philosophical goal. Max Loreau, in a critical exposition of his philosophy, identifies this objective which colors all of Perelman's work: *"to produce an instrument capable of achieving in the realm of values results exactly analogous to those pursued by analytical reasoning in the domain of the exact sciences."*[42]

The search for a nonformal logic and the results of that endeavor are best reported in the philosopher's own words:

Ten years after the beginning of our project, we had not found the logic of value judgments that we were looking for. We did, however, rediscover a long-neglected logic which had been completely forgotten by contemporary logicians, although it had been treated at length in the ancient treatises on rhetoric and in the *Topics* of Aristotle. This was the study of what Aristotle called dialectical proofs in contrast to the analytical proofs that interest modern logicians exclusively. In an extended empirical and analytical study called *Traité de l'argumentation* Mme. Olbrechts-Tyteca and I were able to put forward this nonformal logic as a theory of argumentation, complementary to the theory of demonstration that is the object of formal logic. . . . The same techniques of reasoning which we use to criticize and to justify opinions, choices, claims, and decisions, are also used when it comes to criticizing and justifying statements that are usually qualified as value judgments. That is why the practical use of reason cannot be understood without first integrating it into a general theory of argumentation.[43]

Before considering this "practical use of reason," which is central in Perelman's thought, it is instructive to notice the model he uses to exemplify the nonformal mode of reasoning. That model is drawn

[39] Perelman, *The Idea of Justice and the Problem of Argument,* p. 60.
[40] See Ch. Perelman, "Désaccord et rationalité des décisions," *Logica e Analisi: Archivio di Filosofia* (1960), 93.
[41] Perelman, "Réflexions sur la justice," 269.
[42] "Rhetoric as the Logic of the Behavioral Sciences," trans. Lloyd I. Watkins and Paul D. Brandes, *QJS,* LI (December 1965), 456.
[43] Perelman, *Justice,* pp. 58–59.

from jurisprudence. He says, "A thorough investigation of proof in law, of its variations and evolution, can, more than any other study, acquaint us with the relations existing between thought and action."[44] In resorting to the judicial model, Perelman makes a choice similar to that of the English philosopher and logician, Stephen Toulmin. Toulmin, whose search for a "working logic" applicable to human decision-making closely parallels Perelman's quest, also turns to law for his paradigm. Toulmin remarks: "Logic (we may say) is generalised jurisprudence. Arguments can be compared with law-suits, and the claims we make and argue for in extra-legal contexts with claims made in the courts, while the cases we present in making good each kind of claim can be compared with each other."[45] Julius Stone points out that both Perelman and Toulmin use the judicial model as an aid for their philosophical tasks, rather than to make judicial tasks easier.[46] However, Perelman, who is trained in law as well as in philosophy, has more than an ordinary interest in the legal process.

The selection of courtroom reasoning as a model of nonformal logic offers certain advantages. First, the judge, under penalty of law in most legal systems, cannot avoid rendering and justifying a decision. Perelman says: "The techniques peculiar to the reasoning of jurists . . . all go hand in hand with the obligation laid on the judge to decide and to give reasons for his decision. His business is to draw up a judgment as consistent as possible with the provisions of the law, and such consistency cannot be determined by the criteria of formal logic alone. The obligation to take a reasoned decision is an essential element in the constitution of juridical knowledge."[47] Secondly, the logic of jurisprudence is completely ignored by modern formal logicians: "When the advocates accuse each other of not respecting *logic,* the word 'logic' does not designate . . . formal logic, the only logic practiced by the majority of professional logicians, but juridical logic, which modern logicians entirely ignore."[48] Thirdly, legal reasoning ordinarily recognizes that presumption favors the *status quo:* "Law teaches us . . . to abandon existing rules only if good reasons justify their replacement: Only change requires justification, presumption playing in favor of what exists, just as the burden of proof falls upon him who wants to change an established state of affairs."[49] A fourth advantage of the judicial model, closely allied with the third, is that law recognizes the

---

[44] Perelman, *The Idea of Justice and the Problem of Argument,* p. 108.

[45] *The Uses of Argument* (Cambridge, 1964), p. 7.

[46] *Legal System and Lawyers' Reasonings* (Stanford, Calif., 1964), p. 335.

[47] Perelman, *The Idea of Justice and the Problem of Argument,* p. 90.

[48] Ch. Perelman, Preface to *Introduction à la logique juridique,* by Georges Kalinowski (Paris, 1965), p. v. [Translation mine.]

[49] Perelman, *Justice,* p. 104.

role of precedent in human reasoning and conduct. And here we see how the generalized "rule of justice" is made to play a key role in all rational argumentation. Perelman states:

The historicity of reason is always closely connected with its becoming part of a tradition, in which innovation must always produce its letters of credence. That is why so often the best justification of a course of conduct . . . consists in showing that that course is in conformity with the recognized order, that it can avail itself of unquestioned precedents. Precedent plays a quite primary role in argumentation, the rationality of which is linked with the observance of the *rule of justice,* which demands equal treatment for similar situations. Now, the application of the rule of justice assumes the existence of precedents to teach us how situations similar to the one confronting us now have been dealt with in the past. These precedents, just like the models by which a society is inspired, make part of its cultural tradition, which can be reconstructed on the basis of the argumentations in which they have been employed.[50]

We see, then, how Perelman's analysis of justice reveals a principle of action, formalized as the rule of justice, which serves as a common element in all rational activity. Although Perelman and his colleague, Olbrechts-Tyteca, could find no special logic of value judgments, their rediscovery of the dialectical proofs of Aristotle, together with a thorough understanding of the juridical patterns of argument, leads to an enlarged view of reason.

4

In setting forth his vision of an enlarged reason, Perelman hopes to counteract the pernicious influence of two groups: the Cartesian rationalists and the modern mathematical logicians. Both groups share the responsibility for the narrow concept of reason that exists today. Perelman and Olbrechts-Tyteca say: "The logician, inspired by the Cartesian ideal, feels at home only in the study of the proofs that Aristotle qualified as analytic. . . . And this tendency is all the more strongly marked after a period in which, under the influence of the mathematical logicians, logic was reduced to formal logic, to a study of the means of proof used in the mathematical sciences. As a result, reasoning which is foreign to the purely formal domain escapes logic, and consequently escapes reason too."[51] Elsewhere Perelman expresses his disappointment over the reduction of logic to the study of formal reasoning: "We feel that this narrowing of the field of logic is dis-

---

[50] Perelman, *The Idea of Justice and the Problem of Argument,* p. 157.
[51] Ch. Perelman and L. Olbrechts-Tyteca, *Traité de l'argumentation,* 2 vols. (Paris, 1958), I, 3. [From a translation of the introduction of this work by Francis B. Sullivan, which appeared as "The New Rhetoric," *Philosophy Today,* I (March 1957), 5.]

astrous for the methodology of the human sciences, for law and for all branches of philosophy."[52] Again, Toulmin's thought runs in a similar direction. Toulmin writes: "In logic as in morals, the real problem of rational assessment—telling sound arguments from untrustworthy ones, rather than consistent from inconsistent ones—requires experience, insight and judgment, and mathematical calculations (in the form of statistics and the like) can never be more than one tool among others of use in this task."[53] Both Perelman and Toulmin believe, then, that formal logic has unduly restricted the concept of reason.

A student of Perelman's philosophy must be aware of the philosopher's distinction between two types of reason—the logical and the rhetorical. A logical system, for Perelman, is a set of propositions and rules that manages to remove itself from time, isolating its data from every context except itself and fixing the instruments which it uses. Those instruments are correct expressions and rules of inference. Rhetoric, on the other hand, explores the domain of concrete and situated reason. Concerning this rhetorical reason, Loreau writes: "Its investigation bears upon discourse which allows a place to the non-conventional, to the implicit, to the indeterminate; it aspires to the explication and to the structuration of the systems of reasoning used implicitly in the discursive exploitation of the margin of indetermination which affects ideas and which is manifested when the meaning attributed to these latter finds itself contested, either by a new truth or by a new situation."[54] Perelman hopes to reassert this second kind of reasoning, the rhetorical. He believes that reason serves not only to discover truth and error, in the narrow logical sense, but also to justify and to argue:

Besides demonstrative and calculating reason, there exists a reason that deliberates and argues. Without a broadened vision of reason, which would enable us to understand what is meant by deciding and making an enlightened choice, a rational concept of liberty and human responsibility remains impossible. Besides the Cartesian conception of liberty, adherence to evidence, there is room for a concept of liberty-responsibility where, being face to face with arguments pro and con, neither of which is compelling, we decide that one side has more weight, and in doing so we take a final step. . . .

This broadening of our concept of reason, which no longer limits the rational to the analytical, opens a new field of study to the investigations of the logicians; it is the field of those reasons which, according to Pascal and according to contemporary logicians, reason does not know.[55]

---

[52] Ch. Perelman, "Reply to Henry W. Johnstone, Jr.," *Philosophy and Phenomenological Research*, XVI (December 1955), 245.

[53] Toulmin, p. 188.

[54] Loreau, "Rhetoric as the Logic of the Behavioral Sciences," 457–458; see also Max Loreau, "Pour situer la nouvelle rhétorique," *Logique et analyse*, VI (December 1963), 104.

[55] Chaim Perelman, "How Do We Apply Reason to Values?" *Journal of Philosophy*, LII (December 22, 1955), 802.

When the full implications of this broadened idea of reason are felt, the traditional distinction between the will and the understanding, reminiscent of faculty psychology, will disappear. Along with it will go the conviction-persuasion dichotomy which has plagued rhetorical theory for so long. Perelman and Olbrechts-Tyteca suggest that this unhappy distinction may be traced back to Aristotle, who devoted his *Topics* to the theoretical discussion of theses and his *Rhetoric* to the peculiarities of audiences.[56] At any rate, the philosophers following Descartes, whether rationalist or antirationalist, have, for the most part, fallen into the same fundamental error. Pascal opposed will to understanding, insight to geometry, the heart to reason, and the art of persuading to that of convincing. In a similar fashion, Kant opposed faith to science, and Bergson opposed intuition to reason. As for Perelman, he believes that these dichotomies constitute a dilemma and are based on an egregious error: "The error is to conceive man as made up of completely separated faculties."[57] In an article reporting the results of their survey of the fields of logic and rhetoric, Perelman and Olbrechts-Tyteca conclude that "the conviction-persuasion opposition cannot suffice when one leaves the bounds of a strict rationalism and examines the diverse means of obtaining the adherence of minds."[58]

By extending the domain of reason, Perelman hopes, of course, to give a rational basis to law, ethics, philosophy, political debate, and other areas of human endeavor that "cannot be considered relevant to logic in the strict sense."[59] Thus, when he and his collaborator examine the processes of actual argument in their *Traité*, they avow their intention to examine "arguments presented by publicists in their newspapers, by politicians in their speeches, by advocates in their pleadings, by judges in their deliberations, by philosophers in their treatises."[60] Only a reason broad enough to manifest itself in all the areas of human activity where justifications have to be made can be a truly practical reason. Perelman asks: "Must we abandon all philosophical use of practical reason and limit ourselves to the technical use of reason in the domain of action? Must we use our reason only to adjust our means to totally irrational ends? Affirmative answers to these questions form the position of all positivist philosophers, from Hume to Ayer. . . . Are the search for a rational foundation for our individual and collective actions and the desire to elaborate an ethic, a philosophy of law, and

---

[56] Perelman and Olbrechts-Tyteca, *Traité de l'argumentation,* I, 62. [Translation mine.].

[57] *Ibid.*

[58] Perelman and Olbrechts-Tyteca, "Logique et rhétorique," 7. [Translation mine.]

[59] Ch. Perelman and L. Olbrechts-Tyteca, "Act and Person in Argument," *Ethics,* LXI (July 1951), 251.

[60] Perelman and Olbrechts-Tyteca, *Traité de l'argumentation,* I, 13.

a political philosophy nourished only on illusion and illogic?"[61] As we have seen, the whole tenor of Perelman's philosophic thought provides a negative answer to such questions. For him, there exists a reason whose function is not merely to verify and to demonstrate, but also to deliberate, to criticize, and to justify, to give reasons for and against. In short, the function of reason is also to argue.

5

The philosophical basis upon which Chaim Perelman develops his theory of rhetoric should now be tolerably clear. His predisposition to reject the Cartesian notions of self-evidence and the uniqueness of truth leads him to conceive the aim of philosophy to be the elaboration and the justification of a defensible world view. Perelman believes that since one's fundamental axioms are neither self-evident nor necessary, a philosopher must resort to rational argumentation in order to supply such justification.

As we have seen, the epistemology that results from these presuppositions emphasizes the role of decision in the acquisition and transmission of knowledge. The idea that our knowledge constitutes an edifice of immutable truths, an idea stemming from the erroneous doctrines of classical rationalism and empiricism, is shattered by the realization that the truth of our beliefs cannot be guaranteed once and for all. As Perelman maintains, such truths "are worked out, made specific and refined—and these truths constitute no more than the best tested of our opinions."[62] The principal effect of this revelation is to remove the misleading distinction between knowledge and opinion.

Further, in search of a principle of justification that can lay claim to being rational, Perelman finds in his analysis of justice a common, abstract element at the base of the various conceptions of justice—the principle that beings of the same essential category must be treated alike. The arbitrariness inherent in the selection of the "essential categories" renders absolute justice impossible and highlights the need for a logic of value judgments. Perelman's search for such a logic merely leads him back to a consideration of the techniques of argument analyzed by Aristotle in his *Topics* and his *Rhetoric*. Thus, the philosopher concludes that a general theory of argumentation inspired by classical rhetoric is needed.

Finally, Perelman's view of rationality greatly enlarges the concept of reason inherited from Descartes and his successors. This "rhetorical

[61] Perelman, *Justice*, pp. 57–58.
[62] Perelman, *The Idea of Justice and the Problem of Argument*, p. 133.

reason" operates in the realm of the probable, the contingent, and the plausible; in brief, it seems especially adaptable to the behavioral sciences, to law, and to philosophy. It is in the light of Perelman's entire philosophical enterprise, then, that one should approach his theory of rhetoric.

PART VI STEPHEN TOULMIN

15 TOULMIN ON ARGUMENT: AN INTERPRETATION AND APPLICATION

WAYNE E. BROCKRIEDE
DOUGLAS EHNINGER

Some might contend that Stephen Toulmin's framework for analysis of argument provides an interesting conversational subject for scholars of rhetoric but offers little of real use or fresh insight for argumentation. The following essay afforded the initial basic explication of Toulmin's approach upon which many American students of rhetoric and argument based their favorable or critical reactions.

Toulmin, a British professor of philosophy, shares with Chaim Perelman the aim of developing a practical, real-life logic of argumentation. And both draw inspiration from the argumentative procedures of jurisprudence. (See Toulmin, *The Use of Argument*, 1–2, 7–8.) Remember also that Toulmin does not intend his approach to be definitive; he seeks to provoke discussion by lofting "trial balloons designed to draw the fire of others."

As you develop an understanding of the Toulmin layout of argument, consider these questions: Can his layout be applied as easily to actual arguments in real speeches as to hypothetical examples of possible arguments? At what points in the Toulmin model might the traditional tests for soundness of evidence and reasoning function? How easily can a *post hoc* critic determine the suppressed warrant? Does qualifier (or rebuttal) more realistically relate to claim or to data and warrant? How might the model be improved by allowing for backing of data? How accurate is Brockriede and Ehninger's explanation of warrant-using and warrant-establishing arguments? (See Toulmin, *The Uses of Argument*, 120.) Does the model afford significant advantages over the enthymeme and epicheireme?

Source: Quarterly Journal of Speech, XLVI (February 1960), 44–53. Reprinted with permission of the authors and the publisher.

During the period 1917–1932 several books, a series of articles, and many Letters to the Editor of *QJS* gave serious attention to exploring the nature of argument as it is characteristically employed in rhetorical proofs.[1] Since that time, however, students of public address have shown comparatively little interest in the subject, leaving to philosophers, psychologists, and sociologists the principal contributions which have more recently been made toward an improved understanding of argument.[2]

Among the contributions offered by "outsiders" to our field, one in particular deserves more attention than it has so far received from rhetoricians. We refer to some of the formulations of the English logician Stephen Toulmin in his *The Uses of Argument,* published in 1958.[3]

Toulmin's analysis and terminology are important to the rhetorician for two different but related reasons. First, they provide an appropriate structural model by means of which rhetorical arguments may be laid out for analysis and criticism; and, second, they suggest a system for classifying artistic proofs which employs argument as a central and unifying construct. Let us consider these propositions in order.

1

As described by Toulmin, an argument is *movement* from accepted *data,* through a *warrant,* to a *claim.*

Data (D) answer the question, "What have you got to go on?" Thus *data* correspond to materials of fact or opinion which in our textbooks are commonly called *evidence.* Data may report historical or contemporary events, take the form of a statistical compilation or of citations from authority, or they may consist of one or more general declarative sentences established by a prior proof of an artistic nature. Without data clearly present or strongly implied, an argument has no informative or substantive component, no factual point of departure.

---

[1] E.g., such books as James M. O'Neill, Craven Laycock, and Robert L. Scales, *Argumentation and Debate* (New York, 1917); William T. Foster, *Argumentation and Debating* (Boston, 1917); and A. Craig Baird, *Public Discussion and Debate* (Boston, 1928); such articles as Mary Yost, "Argument from the Point of View of Sociology," *QJS,* III (1917); 109–24; Charles H. Woolbert, "The Place of Logic in a System of Persuasion," *QJS,* IV, (1918), 19–39; Gladys Murphy Graham, "Logic and Argumentation," *QJS,* X (1924), 350–363; William E. Utterback, "Aristotle's Contribution to the Psychology of Argument," *QJS,* XI (1925), 218–225; Herbert A. Wichelns, "Analysis and Synthesis in Argumentation," *QJS,* XI (1925), 266–272; and Edward Z. Rowell, "Prolegomena to Argumentation," QJS, XVIII (1932), 1–13, 224–248, 381–405, 585–606; such Letters to the Editor as those by Utterback, XI (1925), 175–177; Wichelns, XI (1925), 286–288; Ralph C. Ringwalt, XII (1926), 66–68; and Graham, XII (1925), 196–197.

[2] See, for example, Mortimer Adler, *Dialectic* (New York, 1927); Paul Edwards, *The Logic of Moral Discourse* (Glencoe, Ill., 1955); Carl I. Hovland, Irving L. Janis, and Harold W. Kelley, *Communication and Persuasion* (New Haven, Conn., 1953); Charles Perelman, *Traité de l'argumentation,* 2 vols. (Paris, 1958), and *La nouvelle rhétorique* (Paris, 1952); and John Cohen, "Subjective Probability," *Scientific American,* MCMVII (1957), 128–38.

[3] (Cambridge, Cambridge University Press). See especially the third of the five essays in the books. *Cf.* J. C. Cooley, "On Mr. Toulmin's Revolution in Logic," *The Journal of Philosophy,* LVI (1959), 297–319.

Claim (C) is the term Toulmin applies to what we normally speak of as a *conclusion*. It is the explicit appeal produced by the argument, and is always of a potentially controversial nature. A claim may stand as the final proposition in an argument, or it may be an intermediate statement which serves as data for a subsequent inference.

Data and claim taken together represent the specific contention advanced by an argument, and therefore constitute what may be regarded as its *main proof line*. The usual order is *data* first, and then *claim*. In this sequence the *claim* contains or implies "therefore." When the order is reversed, the *claim* contains or implies "because."

Warrant (W) is the operational name **Toulmin gives to** that part of an argument which authorizes the mental "leap" involved in advancing from data to claim. As distinguished from data which answer the question "What have you got to go on," the warrant answers the question "How do you get there." Its function is to *carry* the accepted data to the doubted or disbelieved proposition which constitutes the claim, thereby certifying this claim as true or acceptable.

The relations existing among these three basic components of an argument, Toulmin suggests, may be represented diagrammatically:

(D)ata————————Therefore (C)laim
|
|
Since (W)arrant

Here is an application of the method:

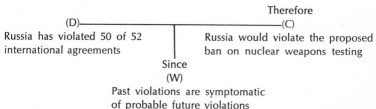

Therefore
(D)————————————————(C)
Russia has violated 50 of 52   Russia would violate the proposed
international agreements   ban on nuclear weapons testing
                    Since
                    (W)
          Past violations are symptomatic
          of probable future violations

In addition to the three indispensable elements of *data, claim,* and *warrant,* Toulmin recognizes a second triad of components, any or all of which may, but need not necessarily, be present in an argument. These he calls (1) *backing,* (2) *rebuttal,* and (3) *qualifier.*

Backing (B) consists of credentials designed to certify the assumption expressed in the warrant. Such credentials may consist of a single item, or of an entire argument in itself complete with data and claim. Backing must be introduced when readers or listeners are not willing to accept a warrant at its face value.

The rebuttal (R) performs the function of a safety valve or escape hatch, and is, as a rule, appended to the claim statement. It recognizes certain conditions under which the claim will not hold good or will hold good only in a qualified and restricted way. By limiting the area to which the claim may legitimately be applied, the rebuttal anticipates certain objections which might otherwise be advanced against the argument.

The function of the qualifier (Q) is to register the degree of force which the maker believes his claim to possess. The qualification may be expressed by a quantifying term such as "possibly," "probably," "to the five per cent level of confidence," etc., or it may make specific reference to an anticipated refutation. When the author of a claim regards it as incontrovertible no qualifier is appended.

These additional elements may be superimposed on the first diagram:

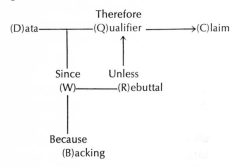

Therefore
(D)ata————(Q)ualifier ————→(C)laim

Since   Unless
(W)————(R)ebuttal

Because
(B)acking

We may illustrate the model as follows:

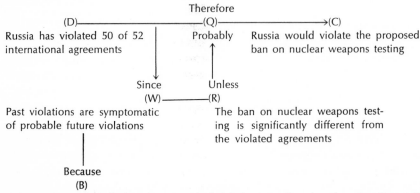

Therefore
(D)————————(Q)——————————→(C)
Russia has violated 50 of 52   Probably   Russia would violate the proposed
international agreements   ban on nuclear weapons testing

Since   Unless
(W)————(R)
Past violations are symptomatic   The ban on nuclear weapons test-
of probable future violations   ing is significantly different from
                                         the violated agreements

Because
(B)
Other nations which had such a record of violations continued such action/Expert X states that nations which have been chronic violators nearly always continued such acts/etc.

2

With Toulmin's structural model now set forth, let us inquire into its suitability as a means of describing and testing arguments. Let us compare Toulmin's method with the analysis offered in traditional logic, the logic commonly used as a basic theory of argumentation in current textbooks. We conceive of arguments in the customary fashion as (1) deriving from probable causes and signs, (2) proceeding more often by relational than implicative principles, (3) emphasizing material as well as formal validity, (4) employing premises which are often contestable, and (5) eventuating in claims which are by nature contingent and variable.

The superiority of the Toulmin model in describing and testing arguments may be claimed for seven reasons:

1. Whereas traditional logic is characteristically concerned with *warrant-using* arguments (i.e., arguments in which the validity of the assumption underlying the inference "leap" is uncontested), Toulmin's model specifically provides for *warrant-establishing* arguments (i.e., arguments in which the validity of the assumption underlying the inference must be established—through backing—as part of the proof pattern itself).[4]

2. Whereas traditional logic, based as it is upon the general principle of implication, always treats proof more or less as a matter of classification or compartmentalization, Toulmin's analysis stresses the inferential and relational nature of argument, providing a context within which all factors—both formal and material—bearing upon a disputed claim may be organized into a series of discrete steps.

3. Whereas in traditional logic arguments are specifically designed to produce universal propositions, Toulmin's second triad of backing, rebuttal, and qualifier provide, within the framework of his basic structural model, for the establishment of claims which are no more than probable. The model directs attention to the ways in which each of these additional elements may operate to limit or condition a claim.

4. Whereas traditional logic, with its governing principle of implication, necessarily results in an essentially static conception of argument, Toulmin by emphasizing *movement* from data, through warrant, to claim produces a conception of argument as dynamic. From his structural model we derive a picture of arguments "working" to establish and certify claims, and as a result of his functional terminology we are able to understand the role each part of an argument plays in this process.

5. Whereas the models based on the traditional analysis—enthymeme, example, and the like—often suppress a step in proof, Toulmin's model lays an argument out in such a way that each step may be examined critically.

---

[4] In traditional logic only the epicheirema provides comparable backing for premises.

6. Whereas in the traditional analysis the division of arguments into premises and conclusions (as in the syllogism, for example) often tends to obscure deficiencies in proof, Toulmin's model assigns each part of an argument a specific geographical or spatial position in relation to the others, thus rendering it more likely that weak points will be detected.

7. Whereas traditional logic is imperfectly equipped to deal with the problem of material validity, Toulmin makes such validity an integral part of his system, indicating clearly the role which factual elements play in producing acceptable claims.

In short, without denying that Toulmin's formulations are open to serious criticism at several points[5]—and allowing for any peculiarities in our interpretations of the character of traditional logic—one conclusion emerges. Toulmin has provided a structural model which promises to be of greater use in laying out rhetorical arguments for dissection and testing than the methods of traditional logic. For although most teachers and writers in the field of argumentation have discussed the syllogism in general terms, they have made no serious attempt to explore the complexities of the moods and figures of the syllogism, nor have they been very successful in applying the terms and principles of traditional logic to the arguments of real controversies. Toulmin's model provides a practical replacement.

3

Our second proposition is that Toulmin's structural model and the vocabulary he has developed to describe it are suggestive of a system for classifying artistic proofs, using argument (defined as *movement* from data through warrant, to claim) as a unifying construct.[6]

In extending Toulmin's analysis to develop a simplified classification of arguments, we may begin by restating in Toulmin's terms the traditional difference between *inartistic* and *artistic* proof. Thus, conceiving

[5] It may be charged that his structural model is merely "a syllogism lying on its side," that it makes little or no provision to insure the formal validity of claims, etc.

[6] Our suggestion as to the structural unity of artistic proofs is by no means novel. The ancients regularly spoke of *pathetic* and *ethical* enthymemes, and envisioned the *topoi* as applicable beyond the *pistis*. (See in this connection James H. McBurney, "The Place of the Enthymeme in Rhetorical Theory," *SM*, III [1936], 63.) At the same time, however, it must be recognized that especially since the advent of the faculty psychology of the seventeenth and eighteenth centuries, rhetorical thought has been profoundly and persistently influenced by the doctrine of a dichotomy between pathetic and logical appeals. (For significant efforts to combat this doctrine see Charles H. Woolbert, "Conviction and Persuasion: Some Considerations of Theory," *QJS*, III [1917], 249–264; Mary Yost, "Argument from the Point of View of Sociology," *QJS*, III [1917], 109–124; and W. Norwood Brigance, "Can We Redefine the James-Winans Theory of Persuasion?" *QJS*, XXI [1935], 19–26.)

of an argument as a movement by means of which accepted data are carried through a certifying warrant to a controversial claim, we may say that in some cases the data themselves are conclusive. They approach the claim without aid from a warrant—are tantamount to the claim in the sense that to accept them is automatically to endorse the claim they are designed to support. In such cases the proof may be regarded as *inartistic*. In another class of arguments, however, the situation is quite different. Here the data are not immediately conclusive, so that the role of the warrant in carrying them to the claim becomes of crucial importance. In this sort of argument the proof is directly dependent upon the inventive powers of the arguer and may be regarded as *artistic*.

If, then, the warrant is the crucial element in an artistic proof, and if its function is to carry the data to the claim, we may classify artistic arguments by recognizing the possible routes which the warrant may travel in performing its function.

So far as rhetorical proofs are concerned, as men have for centuries recognized, these routes are three in number: (1) an arguer may carry data to claim by means of an assumption concerning the relationship existing among phenomena in the external world; (2) by means of an assumption concerning the quality of the source from which the data are derived; and (3) by means of an assumption concerning the inner drives, values, or aspirations which impel the behavior of those persons to whom the argument is addressed.

Arguments of the first sort (traditionally called *logical*) may be called *substantive;* those of the second sort (traditionally called *ethical*) may be described as *authoritative;* and those of the third sort (traditionally called *pathetic*) as *motivational*.

Substantive Arguments

The warrant of a substantive argument reflects an assumption concerning the way in which things are related in the world about us. Although other orderings are possible, one commonly recognized, and the one used here, is six-fold. Phenomena may be related as cause to effect (or as effect to cause), as attribute to substance, as some to more, as intrinsically similar, as bearing common relations, or as more to some. Upon the first of these relationships is based what is commonly called argument from *cause;* on the second, argument from *sign;* on the third, argument from *generalization;* on the fourth, argument from *parallel case;* on the fifth, argument from *analogy;* and on the sixth, argument from *classification*.

Cause. In argument from cause the data consist of one or more accepted facts about a person, object, event, or condition. The warrant attributes to these facts a creative or generative power and specifies the nature of the effect they will produce. The claim relates these results to the person, object, event, or condition named in the data. Here is an illustration, from cause to effect:

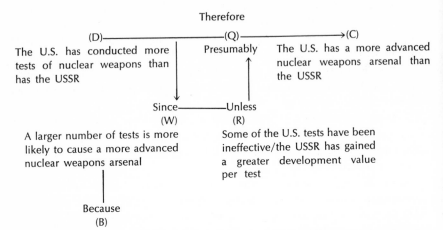

Therefore

(D)————————————(Q)————————————→(C)

The U.S. has conducted more tests of nuclear weapons than has the USSR

Presumably

The U.S. has a more advanced nuclear weapons arsenal than the USSR

Since————Unless
(W)   (R)

A larger number of tests is more likely to cause a more advanced nuclear weapons arsenal

Some of the U.S. tests have been ineffective/the USSR has gained a greater development value per test

Because
(B)

Our experience with parallel testing programs indicates this/Expert X testifies that many tests are more likely than fewer tests to create advanced nuclear weapons arsenals

When the reasoning process is reversed and the argument is from effect to cause, the data again consist of one or more facts about a person, object, event, or condition; the warrant asserts that a particular causal force is sufficient to have accounted for these facts; and the claim relates the cause to the person, object, event, or condition named in the data.

Sign. In argument from sign the data consist of clues or symptoms. The warrant interprets the meaning or significance of these symptoms. The claim affirms that some person, object, event, or condition possesses the attributes of which the clues have been declared symptomatic. Our first example concerning Russia's violation of international agreements illustrates the argument from sign.

Generalization. In argument from generalization the data consist of information about a number of persons, objects, events, or conditions, taken as constituting a representative and adequate sample of a given class of phenomena. The warrant assumes that what is true of the items constituting the sample will also be true of additional members of the class not represented in the sample. The claim makes explicit the assumption embodied in the warrant. The form can be diagrammed so:

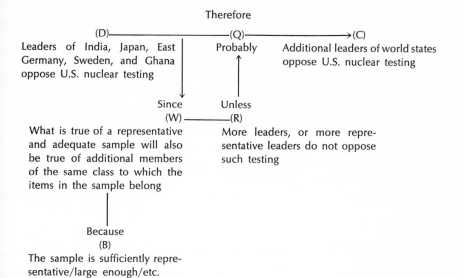

Parallel Case. In argument from parallel case the data consist of one or more statements about a single object, event, or condition. The warrant asserts that the instance reported in the data bears an essential similarity to a second instance in the same category. The claim affirms about the new instance what has already been accepted concerning the first. Here is an illustration:

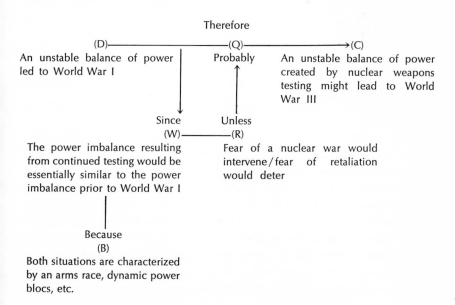

In argument from parallel cases a rebuttal will be required in either of two situations: (1) if another parallel case bears a stronger similarity to the case under consideration; or (2) if in spite of some essential similarities an essential dissimilarity negates or reduces the force of the warrant. The example illustrates the second of these possibilities.

Analogy. In argument from analogy the data report that a relationship of a certain nature exists between two items. The warrant assumes that a similar relationship exists between a second pair of items. The claim makes explicit the relationship assumed in the warrant. Whereas the argument from parallel case assumes a resemblance between two *cases,* the analogy assumes only a similarity of *relationship.* Analogy may be illustrated so:

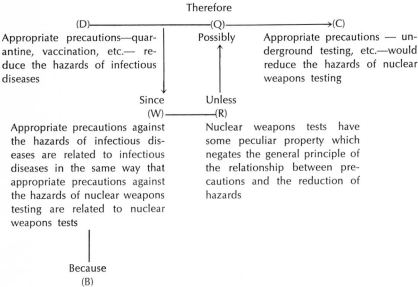

Therefore

(D)————————————————(Q)————————————→(C)

Appropriate precautions—quarantine, vaccination, etc.— reduce the hazards of infectious diseases

Possibly

Appropriate precautions — underground testing, etc.—would reduce the hazards of nuclear weapons testing

Since

(W)————————(R)

Unless

Appropriate precautions against the hazards of infectious diseases are related to infectious diseases in the same way that appropriate precautions against the hazards of nuclear weapons testing are related to nuclear weapons tests

Nuclear weapons tests have some peculiar property which negates the general principle of the relationship between precautions and the reduction of hazards

Because

(B)

Both participate in the general relationship between precautions and the reduction of hazards

In most cases the analogical relation expressed in an argument from analogy will require a strongly qualifying "possibly."

Classification. In argument from classification the statement of the data is a generalized conclusion about known members of a class of persons, objects, events, or conditions. The warrant assumes that what is true of the items reported in the data will also be true of a hitherto unexamined item which is known (or thought) to fall within the class there described. The claim then transfers the general statement which has been made in the data to the particular item under consideration. As illustrated, the form would appear:

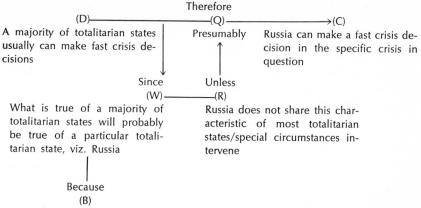

Therefore

(D)————————————(Q)————————————→(C)

A majority of totalitarian states usually can make fast crisis decisions

Presumably

Russia can make a fast crisis decision in the specific crisis in question

Since
(W)————————(R)

Unless

What is true of a majority of totalitarian states will probably be true of a particular totalitarian state, viz. Russia

Russia does not share this characteristic of most totalitarian states/special circumstances intervene

Because
(B)

The class "totalitarian states" is reasonably homogeneous, stable, etc./Russia generally shares the attributes of the totalitarian states class

Two kinds of reservations may be applicable in an argument from classification: (1) a class member may not share the particular attribute cited in the data, although it does share enough other attributes to deserve delineation as a member of the class; and (2) special circumstances may prevent a specific class member from sharing at some particular time or place the attributes general to the class.

Authoritative Arguments

In authoritative arguments the data consist of one or more factual reports or statements of opinion. The warrant affirms the reliability of the source from which these are derived. The claim reiterates the statement which appeared in the data, as now certified by the warrant. An illustration follows:

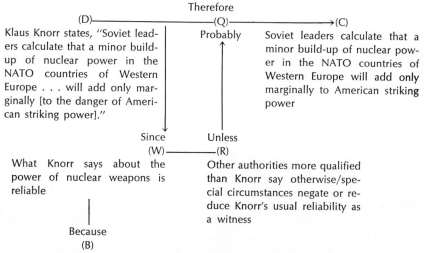

Therefore

(D)————————————(Q)————————————→(C)

Klaus Knorr states, "Soviet leaders calculate that a minor build-up of nuclear power in the NATO countries of Western Europe . . . will add only marginally [to the danger of American striking power]."

Probably

Soviet leaders calculate that a minor build-up of nuclear power in the NATO countries of Western Europe will add only marginally to American striking power

Since
(W)————————(R)

Unless

What Knorr says about the power of nuclear weapons is reliable

Other authorities more qualified than Knorr say otherwise/special circumstances negate or reduce Knorr's usual reliability as a witness

Because
(B)

Knorr is a professor at Princeton's Center of International Studies/is unbiased/has made reliable statements on similar matters in the past/etc.

The structure and function of an authoritative argument remains basically the same when the source of the data is the speaker or writer himself. The data is carried to claim status by the same sort of assumption embodied in the warrant. We may infer a claim from what Knorr says about nuclear weapons whether he is himself the speaker, or whether another speaker is quoting what Knorr has said. Thus the *ethos* of a speaker may be studied by means of the Toulmin structure under the heading of authoritative argument.

Motivational Arguments

In motivational arguments the data consist of one or more statements which may have been established as claims in a previous argument or series of arguments. The warrant provides a motive for accepting the claim by associating it with some inner drive, value, desire, emotion, or aspiration, or with a combination of such forces. The claim as so warranted is that the person, object, event, or condition referred to in the data should be accepted as valuable or rejected as worthless, or that the policy there described should or should not be adopted, or the action there named should or should not be performed. Illustrated the form would appear:

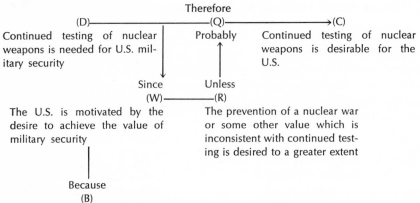

Therefore

(D)————————————————(Q)——————————→(C)

Continued testing of nuclear weapons is needed for U.S. military security

Probably

Continued testing of nuclear weapons is desirable for the U.S.

Since
(W)————————(R)

Unless

The U.S. is motivated by the desire to achieve the value of military security

The prevention of a nuclear war or some other value which is inconsistent with continued testing is desired to a greater extent

Because
(B)

Military security is related to self-preservation, the maintenance of our high standard of living, patriotism, the preservation of democracy, etc.

4

We have exhibited the structural unity of the three modes of artistic proof by showing how they may be reduced to a single invariant pattern using argument as a unifying construct. Let us as a final step explore this unity further by inquiring how artistic proofs, so reduced, may conveniently be correlated with the various types of disputable questions and the claims appropriate to each.

Let us begin by recognizing the four categories into which disputable questions have customarily been classified: (1) Whether something is? (2) What it is? (3) Of what worth it is? (4) What course of action should be pursued? The first of these queries gives rise to a question of *fact,* and is to be answered by what can be called a *designative claim;* the second, to a question of definition, to be answered by a *definitive claim;* the third, to a question of *value,* to be answered by an *evaluative claim;* and the fourth, to a question of *policy,* to be answered by an *advocative claim.*

Supposing, then, that an arguer is confronted with a question of fact, calling for a designative claim; or a question of policy, calling for an advocative claim, etc., what types of argument would be available to him as means of substantiating his claim statement? Upon the basis of the formulations developed in earlier sections of this paper, it is possible to supply rather precise answers.

Designative Claims. A designative claim, appropriate to answering a question of fact, will be found supportable by any of the six forms of substantive argument, or by authoritative argument, but not by motivational argument. That is, whether something exists or is so may be determined: (1) by isolating its cause or its effect (argument from cause); (2) by reasoning from the presence of symptoms to the claim that a substance exists or is so (argument from sign); (3) by inferring that because some members of a given class exist or are so, more members of the same class also exist or are so (argument from generalization); (4) by inferring because one item exists or is so, that a closely similar item exists or is so (argument from parallel case); (5) by reasoning that D exists or is so because it stands in the same relation to C that B does to A, when C, B, and A are known to exist or to be so (argument from analogy); and (6) by concluding that an unexamined item known or thought to fall within a given class exists or is so because all known members of the class exist or are so (argument from classification). Moreover, we may argue that something exists or is so because a reputable authority declares this to be the case. Motivational argument, on the other hand, may not be critically employed in designative claims, because values, desires, and feelings are irrelevant where questions of fact are concerned.

Definitive Claims. The possibilities for establishing definitive claims are more limited. Only two of the forms of substantive argument and authoritative argument are applicable. We may support a claim as to what something is: (1) by comparing it with a closely similar phenomenon (argument from parallel case); or (2) by reasoning that because it stands in the same relation to C as B does to A it will be analogous to C, where the nature of C, B, and A are known (argument from analogy). In addition, we may support a definition or interpretation by citing an acceptable authority. Among the substantive arguments, cause, sign, generalization, and classification are inapplicable; and once again motivational argument is irrelevant since emotions, wishes, and values cannot legitimately determine the nature of phenomena.

Evaluative Claims. Evaluative claims may be supported by generalization, parallel case, analogy, and classification, and by authoritative and motivational arguments. By generalization a class of phenomena may be declared valuable or worthless on the ground that a typical and adequate sample of the members of that class is so. By classification, in contrast, we infer from the worth of known members of a class the probable worth of some previously unexamined item known or thought to belong to that class. By parallel case, we infer goodness or badness from the quality of an item closely similar. By analogy, however, we infer value on the basis of a ratio of resemblances rather than a direct parallel. In authoritative argument our qualitative judgment is authorized by a recognized expert. In motivational argument, however, an item is assigned a value in accordance with its usefulness in satisfying human drives, needs, and aspirations. Arguments from cause and sign, on the other hand, are inapplicable.

Advocative Claims. Advocative claims may legitimately be established in only four ways. We may argue that some policy should be adopted or some action undertaken because a closely similar policy or action has brought desirable results in the past (argument from parallel case). We may support a proposed policy or action because it bears the same relation to C that B does to A, where B is known to have brought desirable results (argument from analogy). Or, of course, we may support our claim by testimony (authoritative argument), or by associating it with men's wishes, values, and aspirations (motivational argument).

This analysis concerning the types of arguments applicable to various sorts of claims may be summarized in tabular form:

	Designative	Definitive	Evaluative	Advocative
Substantive				
A. Cause	x			
B. Sign	x			
C. Generalization	x		x	
D. Parallel Case	x	x	x	x
E. Analogy	x	x	x	x
F. Classification	x		x	
Authoritative	x	x	x	x
Motivational			x	x

The world of argument is vast, one seemingly without end. Arguments arise in one realm, are resolved, and appear and reappear in others; and new arguments appear. If one assumes some rationality among men, a system of logical treatment of argument is imperative. The traditional logical system of syllogisms, of enthymemes, of middles distributed and undistributed, may have had its attraction in medieval times. The inadequacies of such a logic, however, have been described by experts; for example, see J. S. Mill on the syllogism and *petitio principii*.[7] The modern search has been for a method which would have some application in the dynamics of contemporary affairs.

Toulmin has supplied us with a contemporary methodology, which in many respects makes the traditional unnecessary. The basic theory has herein been amplified, some extensions have been made, and illustrations of workability have been supplied. All this is not meant to be the end, but rather the beginning of an inquiry into a new, contemporary, dynamic, and usable logic for argument.

[7] *A System of Logic,* I, chap. 3, Sec. 2.

16 ON TOULMIN'S CONTRIBUTION TO LOGIC AND ARGUMENTATION

PETER T. MANICAS

Manicas, a professor of philosophy, questions the utility of the model of argument proposed by Stephen Toulmin. The Toulmin framework, according to Manicas, not only lacks clarity and usefulness in itself but also offers no significant advantage over conventional methods of argumentative analysis.

In analyzing Toulmin's example of Harry's being born in Bermuda and being a British subject, Manicas contends that the qualifier, "presumably," and the rebuttal are not needed because lack of certainty already is implied by the term "generally" in the warrant. But consider whether Toulmin intends the qualifier to reflect the *strength* of probability and the rebuttal to specify the *circumstances* of exception. (See *The Uses of Argument*, 101.)

Evaluate the following contention of Manicas: "It seems more plausible to me to say that Toulmin's analysis of an argument consists of data, warrant, and conclusion (period). If the warrant *or* the data are challenged, then a *new* argument can be given which supports the challenged statement." Note that such a possibility concerning data already is implied by Toulmin. (See *Uses of Argument*, 97.)

For additional analyses critical of Toulmin's approach, see the journal articles by Jimmie Trent, J. C. Cooley, and J. L. Cowan listed in the bibliography at the end of this anthology.

Source: Journal of the American Forensic Association, III (September 1966), 83–94. Reprinted with permission of the author and the publisher.

It is lately becoming fashionable for books and articles on argumentation and debate to adopt the analysis of argument which was presented by Stephen E. Toulmin in his book, *The Uses of Argument*.[1] In what

[1] Cambridge University Press, Cambridge, 1958. All references to this book in this essay will be to the paperback edition of 1964.

For some recent discussions which use the Toulmin model, see Wayne Brockriede and Douglas Ehninger, "Toulmin on Argument: An Interpretation and Application," *Quarterly Journal of Speech*, 46 (February, 1960), 44–53; Ehninger and Brockriede, *Decision by Debate*, Dodd, Mead and Co., N.Y., 1963; Glen E. Mills, *Reason in Con-*

follows, the merits of this fashion will be examined with special reference to the particular utility of the Toulmin model for debaters. But insofar as debaters, like logicians and philosophers, are interested in what Toulmin calls "the rational process"—the setting out and clarification of argument—it will be necessary first to see to what extent Toulmin's discussion does shed light on argument. If, indeed, his layout is *not* illuminating, as I shall argue, then the utility of his model for debaters is already cast into doubt. Section I of this essay, then, discusses Toulmin's analysis of argument; Section II examines the special question: Is his analysis useful for debaters?

It may be noted, however, that Toulmin's book has some large philosophical goals. With his particular layout, he hopes to show that many of the traditional chestnuts of epistemology—those problems which involve justification of knowledge claims—dissolve into thin air. Though I am sympathetic with Toulmin's feelings toward (say) the "problem of induction" or the "problem of other minds" (and many of the others which he talks about), and though, to a large measure, I would agree with his overall conclusion, that, namely, we should demand of claims to knowledge standards commensurate with the inquiry (rather than strictly analytic, mathematical standards), I fail to see how his innovations help to show this. But this last point I shall not try to argue.[2]

I

It will be necessary first to sketch fairly clearly the main features of Toulmin's analysis of argument, to see what is distinctive about it and how it compares to the conventional analysis.[3]

We begin with his distinction between the *claim* or conclusion (C) which an argument seeks to establish and the "facts" which provide the

---

troversy, Allyn and Bacon, Inc., Boston, 1964; R. Windes, and A. Hastings, *Argumentation and Advocacy,* Random House, N.Y., 1965; James C. McCroskey, "Toulmin and the Basic Course," *The Speech Teacher,* 14 (March, 1965), 91–100; Austin J. Freeley, *Argumentation and Debate,* Wadsworth Publishing Co., San Francisco, 1966.

By contrast, there have been two highly critical appraisals of Toulmin's book by professional philosophers, namely, J. C. Cooley, "On Mr. Toulmin's Revolution in Logic," *The Journal of Philosophy,* 56 (March 26, 1959), 297–319; and J. L. Cowan, "The Uses of Argument—An Apology for Logic," *Mind,* 73 (January, 1964), 27–45.

[2] In general, I fail to see how Toulmin's criticism of Strawson's point that "inductive arguments are not deductive arguments" stands up. Once we take seriously this distinction, the quest for certainty and for "wholesale justification" of knowledge claims evaporates as surely as it does on Toulmin's grounds. (For the skeptics, the *same* philosophical difficulties emerge on either view.)

[3] I shall use the expression "the conventional analysis" to refer to (1) the definition of argument, as containing premises and a conclusion, (2) the distinction between deduction and induction, and (3) the distinction between truth, and validity and correctness.

"foundation" for the claim. The "facts" he calls the *data* (D). This much causes no difficulties. Even on the conventional analysis, we would distinguish conclusions from the evidence (premises) used in support of the conclusion.

It is then argued, however, that to make the move from (D) to (C) a third sort of statement is necessary, namely, "rules, principles, inference-licences," or what he decides to call "warrants." "What are needed," he says, "are general, hypothetical statements, which can act as bridges, and authorize the sort of step to which our particular argument commits us" (p. 98). It is very important to see that for Toulmin, warrants are to be sharply distinguished from data. On the conventional analysis, of course, "warrants" would simply be additional premises necessary for the correctness of the argument.

This much provides the "first skeleton." Every argument, to be an argument, *must* contain these three functional units. Warrants, however, confer different degrees of force upon the conclusions they justify. Modal qualifiers (Q), e.g., "probably," "presumably," "necessarily," etc., may then be attached to the conclusions. This presents no special innovations over the conventional analysis. In deductions, the conclusion may always be written: "So, necessarily so-and-so." In inductions, we would have: "So, probably so-and-so," etc.[4] Next, conditions of exception or rebuttal (R) may be included into the schema. These "unless clauses" serve to indicate the circumstances in which the general authority of the warrant would have to be set aside. The notion of "rebuttal" would not have a special place in the conventional analysis, but its usefulness in Toulmin's layout may be doubted. Consider his example:

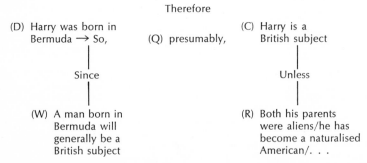

Therefore

(D) Harry was born in Bermuda → So,   (Q) presumably,   (C) Harry is a British subject

Since   Unless

(W) A man born in Bermuda will generally be a British subject   (R) Both his parents were aliens/he has become a naturalised American/. . .

It will be noted that the rebuttal (R) attaches to the modal qualifier (Q), and that the qualifier indicates the force of the warrant. But the conclusion of the argument quoted above has exactly the same force

---

[4] Toulmin devotes a full chapter to the discussion of probability and makes some innovations over what probability *means*. Since this is peripheral to our present problem we here ignore it. For a full criticism of Toulmin's ideas on this subject see Cooley, *op. cit.*, pp. 297–319.

with or without the rebuttal. This is so because the warrant itself implies that there are exceptions to the rule. If the warrant were stated as a categorical (A man born in Bermuda will be a British subject), no rebuttal would have been in order; the qualifier Q would have been "necessarily," and we would have had an old-fashioned deduction.

But isn't it more useful to think of a rebuttal in terms of the distinction between truth and correctness (validity being a special case of correctness)?[5] That is, an argument is rebuttable if the premises do not support the conclusion as stated or because the premises *themselves* are challengable. Thus the valid deduction, "(Some man) Harry was born in Bermuda; a man born in Bermuda will be a British subject; so, Harry is a British subject," is rebuttable by showing that Harry was born (say) in Jamaica *or* by showing that there are exceptions to the rule (by showing that being born in Bermuda is not sufficient for British citizenship). Either of these rebuttals, it must be noted, would involve a *new* argument and for reasons which will be stated later, nothing is gained by making *arguments* used to support premisses a part of the original argument.

On the other hand, consider this probable argument: "(Some man) Harry was born in Bermuda; A man born in Bermuda will generally be a British subject; so presumably, Harry is a British subject." When might we use such an argument? We might if we knew that being born in Bermuda was not sufficient for British citizenship, but were *unclear* as to precisely what were the appropriate provisos. But in this case we could *not* make explicit the rebuttal in Toulmin's sense. Were the appropriate provisos made available to us, they could then be included as part of the *premisses*. Then given additional premisses to the effect that neither of Harry's parents were alien/he has not become an American citizen, etc., the argument could be made considerably more cogent (if not deductively sound).[6] The point is, while the notion of rebuttal is a useful concept, Toulmin's special use of it is more restricting than the conventional analysis would allow.

The final distinction is that of the "backing" (B) of the warrants.

[5] By a "correct argument" I mean an argument in which the premisses provide good grounds for the conclusion.

[6] This argument could be put into form and proven:

"If Harry was born in Bermuda (p), then he is a British subject (q) unless his parents were aliens (r) or he has become a naturalized American citizen (s). Harry was born in Bermuda and his parents are not aliens and he has not become a naturalized American citizen; so, Harry is a British subject." which becomes:

$$\sim r.\sim s \rightarrow (p \rightarrow q)$$
$$p.\sim r.\sim s$$
$$\therefore q$$

(For simplicity, I have instantiated the universal premiss "A man born in Bermuda will be a British citizen.").

These are "assurances, without which the warrants themselves would possess neither authority, nor currency . . ." (p. 103). Thus the warrant, "A man born in Bermuda will generally be a British subject," may be backed by statutes and other legal provisions. Again, it is important for Toulmin that we not confuse warrants with their backings. But as with the distinction between data and warrant (to which we shall return) the distinction between warrant and backing is not one which grammatical tests can usually resolve, though, says Toulmin, grammar "hints at" the distinction (cf. p. 99). Before proceeding we should observe that it would not be cricket to insist that a meaningful distinction must have a grammatical reflection, though to be sure, to the extent that grammatical clues are lacking, to that extent making the distinction will be difficult. In any case, for Toulmin, his distinctions are functional; that is, data have a different function in argument than warrants, and warrants function differently than backings.

Before pressing the difficulties which do arise in making these distinctions, note first that backings are not *essential* to the argument and need not be made explicit. Warrants may be conceded without challenge; indeed, "if we demanded the credentials [backing] of all warrants at sight and never let one pass unchallenged, argument could scarcely begin" (p. 196). This is obviously true, but then isn't it arbitrary to say that the backing is *part* of the argument from data to conclusion? Why draw the line there? We might as well say that an argument to any conclusion necessarily involves us with an infinite regress. Moreover, aren't *data* challengeable? What are they supported with? Nothing, more data, or a different kind of backing? It seems more plausible to me to say that Toulmin's analysis of an argument consists of data, warrant and conclusion (period). If the warrant *or* the data are challenged, then a *new* argument can be given which supports the challenged statement. To be sure, the sort of argument used to justify a singular statement (Harry was born in Bermuda) and the sort of argument used to justify the warrant (A man born in Bermuda will generally be a British subject) will usually be different, but recognition of this did not await Toulmin and is not incompatible with any conventional analysis of argument.[7]

What then of the functional differences between data and warrant? Data (and backings) are *descriptive,* or reportive, statements of "categorical statements of fact," while warrants are permissive or entitling. Thus, in the argument quoted earlier, the statement "Harry was born in Bermuda" simply reports some fact. The warrant "A man born in Bermuda will be a British subject" tells you that given the data, *one*

---

[7] On the conventional analysis, an argument could never get started if each premiss were challenged. As I note, Toulmin suggests that data require no backing though warrants do. What is the ground for this?

may take it that Harry is a British subject. Note that both functional units, data and warrants, are essential to all argument. This distinction seems to work tolerably well with syllogisms in which (in the old analysis) one premiss is singular, one is universal and the conclusion is singular, although the reader may legitimately be puzzled as to how the warrant is *any less* a report of a "categorical statement of fact." The linguistic clues mentioned above are of *no* help since, to bring out the functional differences, grammatical transformations must sometimes be employed. For example, the warrant with which we have been dealing, "A man born in Bermuda will generally be a British citizen," may be expressed, says Toulmin, in either of these two ways: (1) "A man born in Bermuda may be taken to a British subject" or (2) "A man born in Bermuda will be found to be a British subject." (1) is entitling, so it must be a warrant. (2), however, is apparently reportative, so it can't be a warrant. And Toulmin points out that it isn't. It is a backing for the warrant, the original statement of the warrant being ambiguous. Now this is very subtle and interesting, but note that the same line of argument works with the singular statement. "Harry was born in Bermuda" may be taken as (1) "(It has been found that) Harry was born in Bermuda" or as (2) "(It may be taken that) Harry was born in Bermuda." (1) is reportive; (2) surely seems to me to be permissive. Put this together now: (D) a man born in Bermuda will be found to be a British subject, so, presumably, (C) Harry is a British subject, since (W) it may be taken that Harry was born in Bermuda!

Now Toulmin himself calls our attention to what he calls the ambiguities of the syllogism. On pages 107–113, he shows how a statement of the form "All A's are B's" may be construed as either warrant or backing. (For reasons which are not clear to me, he doesn't suggest that it might be construed as a datum). He observes that often enough the universal statement functions as *both* warrant and backing. But, however economical this telescoping may be, says Toulmin, "it leaves the effective structure or our arguments insufficiently candid" (p. 112). Thus, the syllogism, because of the "oversimple" form words, "All A's are B's" leaves room for ambiguity while his analysis does not. Two observations may here be made. (1) The (supposed) ambiguity was *created* by Toulmin's analysis. There need be no ambiguity in the argument: "All A's are B's; x is an A; so, x is a B," unless, of course, we *accept* Toulmin's distinctions. But why should we? Could the structure of this argument be any more *candid* than it now is? (2) The conventional analysis of argument need not be saddled with the oversimple "All A's are B's."[8] If we wish to distinguish taxonomic universals from

[8] As Cooley notes (*op. cit.,* p. 310), "the identity of the individuals who restrict themselves in this way remains obscure." As part II of the present essay suggests, Toulmin's analysis of argument gains stature through bad comparison.

statutes, from predictions, we can easily do so—without trying to make difficult, if not impossible, distinctions between data, warrants and backings.

Consider next this simple form of argument: "All M's are P's; All S's are M's; so, All S's are P's." This syllogism has no singular premiss and the conclusion is universal. What can Toulmin make of it? I suppose that there are several alternatives, but on pp. 127 ff., Toulmin himself suggests what might be involved. Unfortunately, he is content *throughout* his book to discuss *only* syllogisms with a singular premiss; and, if only in passing, this in itself should cause the reader to wonder how much of an advance has been made.

In any case, Toulmin proceeds to note that in "analytic arguments" the distinction between data and warrant-backing is much less sharp than it usually is (p. 127). Presumably, our Barbara[9] is an analytic argument, though we can't be positive. And we can't be positive since Toulmin *defines* analytic and substantial arguments in terms of the sort of information conveyed by the backing of the warrant authorizing the move from (D) to (C). Specifically, if the backing "includes, explicitly or implicitly, the information conveyed in the conclusion itself," the argument is analytic; otherwise it is substantial.

But consideration of the case in point raises this question: what is the warrant? If we can't locate the warrant, we can't locate the backing. Indeed, this is a problem. We are told that in analytic arguments the distinction between data and backing is anything but clear, but we can't even be sure if we have an analytic argument since we can't find the warrant.[10]

On the old (stick-in-the-mud) analysis of a *deductive* argument no such problem arises. If the premisses *entail* (necessarily imply) the conclusion, the argument is deductive, valid, necessary, etc. Something *approximating* Toulmin's definition of an analytic argument might be given: If the premisses "contain" explicitly or implicitly, the conclusion itself, the argument is deductive; otherwise, it is not. But I take it that one of the main points of Toulmin's analysis is to show that the conventional analysis mistakenly conflates four *different* distinctions into the deduction—induction distinction. But more on this later.

Let us assume, however, that Barbara is an analytic syllogism. Toulmin gives two alternative explications of analytic arguments with a singular premiss which we might apply to our case. We might, he says, be tempted to construe both premisses as data (Cf. p. 128). But then

---

[9] First figure syllogism, AAA (or three universal affirmative statements).

[10] The three "tests" for an analytic argument stated on p. 131 are of no help either for the same reasons. Each is stated in terms of data, backing and conclusion. Note that if instead of these distinctions, we substitute "premisses" for "data" and "backing," then on all three tests, Barbara is analytic.

surely we need *some* warrant, for, insists Toulmin, we can't move from data to a conclusion without some warrant. He asks: "what warrant, then, are we to say does authorize this particular step?" (p. 128). He notes that several different principles (in the checkered history of formal logic) have been put forward—the "principle of the syllogism" the *dictum de omni et nullo*," and others.

But this is simply nonsense. No one so far as I can see considered these principles as functioning as warrants in Toulmin's sense. It is by now generally agreed that for Aristotle, the principle of the "perfect" syllogism (called by Medieval logicians the *dictum de omni et nullo*), was an attempt to bring the three figures of the syllogism (Aristotle did not recognize the fourth) under *one* principle; that is, the principle was not employed to *justify* moves from premises to conclusions, but rather was thought of as a *generalization* of *all* syllogistic argument. Construed in any other way, Aristotle's doctrine of reduction makes little sense. The perfect syllogism (Barbara) needs no justification. As Aristotle said: "I call that a perfect syllogism which needs nothing other than what has been stated to make plain what necessarily follows" (*Prior Analytics,* 24b, 24, Jankinson translation). Toulmin gives an argument (on p. 130) which is very nearly summarized by Aristotle's remark and then concludes: "The suggestion that the principle really does a job for us, by serving as a warrant for all syllogistic arguments, is therefore implausible" (p. 130). Of course, it is; but whoever said that it did *that* job?

Toulmin then tries the alternative course. "Let us reject the request for a warrant to lend authority to all analytic syllogisms, instead insisting that one premise of every such syllogism provides all the warrant we need" (*ibid.*). Now this maneuver is plausible when we restrict ourselves to arguments of the form "All A's are B's; x is an A; so, x is a B;" but how does it work when *both* premises are universals? Which premise provides "all the warrant we need?" Nor does it seem that it will do to say that both premises are warrants, for then we have no data, and, on Toulmin's analysis, the data are the facts to which we must appeal if we are to have an argument at all.

I have not shown that Toulmin's analysis could not be rescued to "clarify the ambiguities of the syllogism."[11] Perhaps it can. But enough

---

[11] I choose the syllogism for discussion because Toulmin did. The going would have been rougher if his distinctions were brought to bear upon more complicated species of argument. Consider these few examples:

(a) If Robinson went to New York, then he took his wife, and if he went on business then he took his secretary. So if he went to New York on business, he took his wife and his secretary.

In this impeccable deduction the conclusion is hypothetical as are both premises. Are both premises warrants? Data? What?

(b) If I go to my first class tomorrow, I must get up very early, and if I go to the

may have been said to show that his version does beset us with gratu-itous problems. Even if these problems are soluble, one may legiti-mately wonder how much light has been shed.

Before moving to the second section of this essay, a few comments on the conventional deduction-induction distinction may be in order.

One of Toulmin's main points was to show that the deduction-induc-tion distinction illicitly conflates four or five different distinctions (Cf. p. 158). He does this, of course, by means of his particular layout of argument. Thus, it immediately follows that to the extent to which his distinctions between data, warrant, etc., cannot be made, then to that extent any new distinctions resting on them cannot be made. So there is a *prima facie* case (at least) that the distinction between (1) analytic and substantial arguments (see p. 8) and (2) warrant-using and warrant-establishing arguments (if we can't find the warrant, then what?) will be made with difficulty, if at all. The other distinctions which he wishes to enforce and separate from deduction-induction distinction are (3) the distinction between necessary arguments and probable arguments and (4) the distinction between arguments which are formally valid and those which are not.

(3), like (1) and (2), is defined in terms of Toulmin's apparatus. In a necessary argument the "warrant entitles us to argue unequivocally to the conclusion . . ." (p. 148). So again, in many cases we have here a problem. I think, however, that a great deal of the force of his critique of the deduction-induction dichotomy stems from his criticism of for-mal validity. So in addition to the brief remarks entered against distinc-tions (1) through (3) above, the discussion of validity seems to me to be most revealing.

There are several lines which might be taken against Toulmin on this issue: (A) He attacks a straw man conception of validity, (B) he fails

---

party tonight, I will stay up very late. If I stay up very late and get up early, I will have to get along on very little sleep. I can't get along on very little sleep; so, I must either miss my first class tomorrow or stay away from the party tonight.

In chain reasoning of this sort (which presumably is so important for debaters) nothing whatever is gained by trying to mark off warrants from data. Indeed, try it. (These two examples are from I. Copi, *Symbolic Logic*, Macmillan Co., N.Y. 1954).

(c) The cigarette butts in the ashtray had no lipstick on them, and were Pall Mall filters. The partner of the murdered man smoked Pall Mall filters and he knew that the murdered man knew that he was having an affair with his wife. So if we can show that the partner has no alibi, we have our man.

This textbook type Sherlock Holmes induction is a plausible argument with nothing but data. One might insist that the argument is telescoped and contains many sup-pressed premisses. No doubt a warrant authorizing the move from the data to the conclusion *could* be formulated. But how revealing would formulating it make the argument? It might go like this: We may take it that if unlipsticked Pall Mall filters are found at the scene of the crime and if someone with a motive has no alibi, but smokes Pall Mall filters, then we may suppose that he is the guilty party. It is always possible to frame a hypothetical which would make any argument *deductive*. (See below p. 17).

to utilize his own useful distinction between the features of arguments which are field-in-variant and those which are field-dependent, and (C) he relies too heavily on ordinary language.

To take these up in order: (A) Toulmin notes that "it is sometimes argued . . . that the validity of syllogistic arguments is a consequence of the fact that the conclusions of these arguments are simply 'formal transformations' of their premisses" (p. 118). There should be no problem sustaining this remark since if *one* logician discussed *syllogisms* in this way, it is true. But does this entitle Toulmin to treat *all* discussions of validity (in traditional *and* modern formal logic) in this cavalier way? I would acknowledge that there is some truth in saying that validity might be construed as resulting, as he puts it, "simply from shuffling the parts of the premisses and rearranging them in a new pattern" (*ibid.*); but even if construed in this way, the picture which emerges is a parody. He gives this example:

x is an A;
An A is certainly a B;
So, x is certainly a B.

He then asserts: "When the argument is put in this way, the parts of the conclusion are manifestly the same as the parts of the premisses, and the conclusion can be obtained simply by shuffling the parts of the premisses and rearranging them" (p. 119). He concludes: "If this is what is meant by saying that the argument has the appropriate 'logical form' and that it is valid on account of this fact, then this may be said to be a 'formally valid' argument" (*ibid.*).[12]

But is this what is meant by formal validity? Indeed, if this *is* what is meant, then it is an easy matter to show that many unexceptional, necessary, deductive arguments are not "formally valid." Toulmin gives this clinching counter-example:

Petersen is a Swede;
The recorded proportion of Roman Catholic Swedes is zero;
So, certainly, Petersen is not a Roman Catholic.

Now Toulmin is correct in saying that conventional discussions do **not** distinguish deductions from valid arguments (note here that I do *not* say "formally valid arguments." See below). That is, Q is deducible from P, if P entails (necessarily implies) Q, or if it is self-contradictory to assert P and deny Q or if the argument P, hence, Q is valid. Each of these formulations amounts to the same thing since, to speak very roughly, in *all* deductions the conclusion Q is "contained" in the premisses P. The expression "contained in" is, of course, a metaphor

---

[12] What is left out in this parody is that even in this simple case not any "shuffling" will do. What entitles one to replace the x, A and B in that particular way? Why not: "x is an A; an A is certainly a B; A is certainly an x?" This "shuffling" leads to an *invalid* argument.

and is philosophically very troubling. In some cases it may be understood quite literally, as in this example. "Johnson is President and Humphrey is Vice-President, so, necessarily Johnson is President." This sort of thing is, apparently, what Toulmin has in mind. Other sorts of deductions, however, simply do not fit this picture as, for example, "This rose is red, so necessarily, it is colored."

To be sure, anything which is red is colored; indeed, one might be tempted to add this as a suppressed premiss, but obviously one can always find a universal premiss to make *any* argument into a deduction. (Toulmin correctly observes this on p. 119). But in this particular argument the one stated premiss entails the conclusion, since from the very "meaning" of the *word* 'red' in English, that it is a "color-word," it necessarily follows that the rose is colored. To anyone who asserted the premiss and denied the conclusion, we would probably say: "my good man, you simply do not know the English language." Here validity involves *semantic* considerations, considerations about *meanings* and their entailments.

Still other arguments can be shown to be valid which fit neither simple picture. For example, "If today is Monday, then tomorrow is Tuesday, so, either today is Monday and tomorrow is Tuesday or today is not Monday and tomorrow is not Tuesday or today is not Monday and tomorrow is Tuesday." No "shuffling" will show this to be valid, nor is its validity a function of semantic considerations; yet the argument is indeed a deduction and is valid.[13]

With respect, then, to formal validity, the test of entailment (validity) is independent of any semantic considerations or considerations of "meaning," content and the like; that is, one can decide if an argument is valid or invalid solely on the basis of its logical form.[14] The

---

[13] Not only is it valid, but it is formally valid, as a truth-functional analysis will show. There is an important—indeed, fundamental—difference between a conclusion *being* one of the premises (A *petitio principii*) and a conclusion being *implied* by the premises. In all valid arguments the latter is true—only in some is the former true.

Consider this example:

If the U.S. Air Force bombs North Vietnam, then the Red Chinese will enter the war; the Red Chinese have not entered the war; so, either the U.S. Air Force has not bombed North Vietnam or the North Vietnamese do not want Chinese assistance.

This argument, too, is formally valid though no amount of shuffling will produce that part of the conclusion which does not appear, even implicity, in the premises.

[14] The Aristotelian analysis of form (which analyzes arguments by analysis of categorical statements) is perhaps misleading if taken as the paradigm. In the first place, it does suggest Toulmin's shuffling parody; but even then, the Aristotelian system must (and does) generate a kind of decision procedure for determining validity. Secondly, not any and all analyses of "form" will do. Aristotle's, of course, is successful for but a limited range of cases. Modern logic has been able to offer analyses which greatly enlarge the range of arguments which are formally provable. In addition to this greater power, it has been able to bring considerably more rigor to analysis.

It might be here mentioned that Toulmin's Roman Catholic Swede example is formally provable, though we cannot here develop it.

reason why logicians (since Aristotle) have concentrated on the formal aspects of argument is not hard to find; but this takes us to our second line of criticism.

(B) As Strawson (*Introduction to Logical Theory,* Methuen, London 1962, p. 40) has noted, the (formal) logician is not a lexicographer. He is not interested in listing all the "warrants" (Toulmin's sense) which could be used in the fantastically diversified contexts in which arguments appear. Indeed, he is interested primarily in those inference possibilities which are "field-in-variant" and not "field-dependent." But if this is so, he looks for the widest possible generality and attempts to arrive at an analysis which serves that end. Thus the argument: "Petersen is a Swede; A Swede is certainly not a Roman Catholic, so, Petersen is certainly not a Roman Catholic," is of no particular interest to him; but the *form* of that argument is.

Toulmin would seem to be aware of this.[15] What then does he have against formal logic?[16] Though several reasons might be given, I suspect that his distaste stems from his absolutely correct observation that the larger class of arguments with which we are concerned in ordinary life are simply not deductions subject to the standards of formal validity. But indeed, if this is his main objection, then the solution is not to *rename* validity to cover correct non-deductive arguments, but to look more carefully into those field-dependent features of correct non-deductive arguments which make them correct.

(C) Finally, Toulmin is convinced that if ordinary people *say* that they are making deductions when logicians insist that they are not and if astronomers and physicists continue to maintain that their conclusions *must* be so-and-so, when logicians point out that at best their conclusions are highly probable, then obviously, the logicians must be wrong!

It may well be that ordinary language preserves, reflects and reveals important distinctions, but is there any reason to believe that only those distinctions are worth making? With respect to those arguments

---

[15] But see his remarks, pp. 39–40, where he asks: ". . . can one hope, even as a matter of theory alone, to set out and criticize arguments in such a way that the form in which one sets out the arguments and the standards by appeal to which one criticizes them are both field-in-variant?" The answer to this question is an emphatic "yes" though of course there will be a large class of arguments which will not be provable by these means.

It may be observed that the way Toulmin puts his question is ambiguous. Does he mean all arguments or some? If he means can we set out and criticize all arguments by field-in-variant formal standards, the answer is still yes, but now many *correct* non-deductive arguments will be shown to be *formally* invalid. But so what? The predicate "valid" is not honorific. Obviously, if he means, can we set out and criticize some arguments in this way, the answer is positively yes, namely, the class of formally valid deductive arguments.

[16] Except his inordinate fear that university chairs in logic will be given to no one but mathematical logicians!

which are named substantial and conclusive by Toulmin, they are indeed deductions. But though their conclusions follow *necessarily,* the conclusions are not necessarily true. Applying Newtonian mechanics to a problem of stellar mechanics does of course yield "one single, unambiguous and unequivocal solution" (p. 137). But this solution must be so-and-so only if we are willing to accept the sum total of assumptions and presuppositions involved in Newtonian mechanics.[17]

II

Books and articles on argumentation and debate are not, it may be maintained, particularly interested in the questions of logical theory raised by Toulmin and discussed in section I above, nor are they interested in probability theory, the foundations of science, or the theory of knowledge. So that even if Toulmin's analysis is of little help in these areas, one may counter that it still may be useful for graphically displaying the features of "real-life" argument.

To say this would, I think, be a mistake, for insofar as debaters, like everyone else, require a clear and consistent picture of argument, their interests are coincident with the interests of philosophers, logicians and scientists. This is not to say that debaters have no special requirements, but these, after all, cannot be satisfied at the expense of those demands which are held in common. If, then, Toulmin's attempt to substitute for the deduction-induction distinction a new set of distinctions fails, and if his attempt to distinguish different "functions" of the statements used in arguments breaks down, then his model fails both for whatever purposes he may have had in mind and for those special purposes to which debaters have put his model.

In this context, it is worth noticing a chapter from R. R. Windes's and A. Hastings's recent book, *Argumentation and Advocacy* (Random House, N.Y. 1965). These writers assert that the traditional definition of an argument as consisting of "a statement (conclusion) which follows from other statements (premises) . . . is not precise enough," since, following Toulmin, "there are three functional elements in an argument" (p. 157). Enough has been said about these functional elements, but it is interesting to note that Windes and Hastings fail to see the problems located above because, like Toulmin, they all but chain

---

[17] Toulmin says: "If told that the wall is 6 ft. high and the sun at an angle of 30 degrees, a physicist will happily say that the shadow *must* have a depth of ten and a half feet" (p. 137).

But this is perfectly consistent with the conventional distinction between deduction and induction. The conclusion fails if there was a mistake in the calculation; *or,* if the wall is not exactly 6 feet, the sun is not exactly 30 degrees, the wall is not at right angles to the earth, the wall is not straight, the earth not level, light is not propagated rectilinearly, etc., etc.

their discussion to the simple quasi-syllogism. Secondly, their conception of the "traditional definition of argument" suggests that they have exclusively in mind *deduction*. At least conventionally, the expression "the conclusion follows from the premises" has been so employed. But why should we restrict ourselves in this way? This observation leads me to what I think is the main confusion underlying the ready acceptance of the Toulmin model.

W. Brockriede and D. Ehninger in their essay in the *Quarterly Journal of Speech* (see above) and in their book, *Decision by Debate* are strong advocates of the Toulmin layout. In both places they give several reasons why his analysis "seems more useful for debaters" (*Decision by Debate*, p. 98). But to say "Toulmin's analysis is more useful for debaters" raises this question: it is more useful than what?

The answer to this question is not hard to find. Brockriede and Ehninger compare Toulmin's analysis to, in the first place, "the apparatus derived from formal logic," and then they unpack this to refer to Aristotle's discussion of the rules, moods and figures of the syllogism. (See *Decision by Debate,* p. 98 and their article in *Quarterly Journal of Speech,* p. 46). But, I submit, this is very much like arguing that a modern physicist should employ Nicholas Oresme's laws of motion because they are "more useful" than those of Aristotle's![18] It is a little surprising to see that Brockriede and Ehninger make absolutely no mention of what has gone on in logic since Aristotle's day. Indeed, the textbooks of today[19] would have indicated that formal logic has taken vast strides forward since the 4th century B.C. Even the simple schema, "If p, then q; p; therefore q," which doesn't fit their

---

[18] Brockriede and Ehninger conclude their *Quarterly Journal of Speech* piece with these remarks: "The world of argument is vast, one seemingly without end. . . . The traditional logical system of syllogisms, of enthymemes, of middles distributed and undistributed, may have had its attraction in Medieval times. The inadequacies of such a logic, however, have been described by experts; for example, see J. S. Mill on the syllogism and *petitio principii*" (p. 53). This paragraph shows that my comparison is no exaggeration. Bringing Mill in as an "expert" is in itself remarkable. Mill's confusions on this point have by now been so thoroughly demonstrated that I can only refer the interested reader to one of several good discussions. See for example, R. M. Eaton, *General Logic,* Scribner's, N.Y., 1931 and 1959, pp. 140–150; M. R. Cohen and E. Nagel, *An Introduction to Logic and Scientific Method,* Harcourt, Brace and Co., N.Y., 1934, pp. 177–181. Just incidentally, Mill's objections were stated at least as early as 200 A.D. by Sextus Empiricus, and involve a confusion similar to the one discussed above on pp. 14 ff.

Paradoxically, when Aristotle came to discuss the "logic" of rhetoric, he did not restrict himself to syllogistic forms. See his *Rhetoric,* Book 1, Chapter II.

[19] In their bibliography in *Decision by Debate,* Brockriede and Ehninger refer to Alburey Castell's seldom used text of 1935 and to F. S. C. Schiller's confused and horribly dated discussion in his *Formal Logic* (1912). In addition to the works already cited they might have looked at W. V. O. Quine, *Methods of Logic,* Holt, Rinehart and Winston, N.Y., 1950; P. Suppes, *Introduction to Logic,* Van Nostrand & Co., N.J., 1957; R. B. Angell, *Reasoning and Logic,* Appleton-Century-Crofts, N.Y., 1964.

understanding of "traditional logic" was understood and well worked out by the Megaric philosopher Philo who lived around 320 B.C.!

But this is only half of the problem. As has been recognized for several centuries, most of the arguments which we encounter in everyday life must be judged for their correctness not on the basis of their logical form, but on the basis of extra-formal-logical considerations. As was suggested above, perhaps this is Toulmin's main concern and I suspect that this is properly the main concern of debaters. But here again, the solution is *not* to dismiss as totally irrelevant the highly illuminating machinery of formal logic (traditional and modern), to abandon the useful and important distinction between deduction and induction and to obfuscate argument analysis with fuzzy distinctions, but rather to seek more sophisticated treatments of the features of non-deductive arguments.[20]

This essay is not the place to get into such a possible treatment, but the following list of items would constitute at least a partial list of the problems and areas which such a discussion would include:

1. A discussion of the limits and strengths of modern formal logic with special emphasis on the use of the methods of analysis of formal logic in non-deductive argument.[21]

2. A treatment of the criteria of relevance regarding the premises of non-deductive arguments.

3. An attempt to delineate the special features of various types of non-deductive arguments including (a) analogical arguments (b) generalizations (c) causal arguments (d) arguments to conclusions about individuals and (e) arguments with value premises and conclusions.[22]

4. A consideration of the questions which arise over the acceptability of the premises which may be used to support conclusions.

5. A discussion of the typical informal fallacies, e.g., false cause, *ad hominem*, equivocation, etc.[23]

This essay may be concluded with the following statement: Toulmin seems to me to be mistaken in the way in which he wishes to bring logic into practice, but he is clearly right in insisting that logic must be brought into practice.

[20] Incidentally, of recently published texts on argumentation and debate, the only one which shows any real sophistication in its grasp of logic and its application to debate is Arthur N. Kruger's *Modern Debate: Its Logic and Strategy*, McGraw-Hill Book Co., Inc., N.Y., 1960.

[21] The reader may be recommended especially to R. B. Angell's excellent book, *Reasoning and Logic*. The items here listed were in a large way inspired by his illuminating discussion of many of these problems. In addition, Professor Angell has a special large section of his book devoted to "reasoning" which would be of great interest to debaters.

[22] This is not intended to be either exhaustive or exclusive.

[23] By far the best treatment of such problems and areas in a debate text is that found in Kruger's *Modern Debate (op. cit.)*.

PART VII MARSHALL McLUHAN

17 UNDERSTANDING MEDIA

MARSHALL McLUHAN

Civilization, in McLuhan's view of history, progressed from the age
of the tribal village, in which communication was largely oral and
sensory perception a unified Gestalt, through the ages of the
phonetic alphabet and printing press, in which writing and printing
dominated and perception became visual, linear, and sequential,
into the present electronic age, where the earlier oral mode and
mosaic perception have returned to form a global village. Each new
communication medium has altered the ratios of sense perception
of people exposed to it. Media have changed our views of reality
and rationality. A medium, as McLuhan defines it, is any extension
of one of the human sensory faculties. In arguing that "the medium
is the message" he claims that message is equatable with impact
on human sensory perception patterns and on our institutions. For
him, the medium, more than the content of communication, carries
the societally significant message.

McLuhan, a Canadian professor of English, sees his role, as well as
that of the artist in society, as one of creating awareness of the
often overlooked effects of media so that men can make enlightened
decisions about media. He strives to describe objectively the modern
situation, but expresses personal distaste for the movement from
print-oriented culture to the electronic age. (See Gerald Stearn, ed.,
McLuhan: Hot and Cool, 288.) His method of using tentative
"probes" rather than firm conclusions exasperates many critics.
In attempting to understand McLuhan, one might consider these
questions: What is the contemporary role of speech as a medium?
How important is content in the rhetorical process? How valid is
McLuhan's distinction between hot and cool media? What does
he mean by such concepts as Narcissus narcosis, rear-view mirror,
and anti-environment? In terms of Kenneth Burke's pentad, does
he overemphasize agency at the expense of act, scene, agent,
and purpose?

THE MEDIUM IS THE MESSAGE

In a culture like ours, long accustomed to splitting and dividing all things as a means of control, it is sometimes a bit of a shock to be reminded that, in operational and practical fact, the medium is the message. This is merely to say that the personal and social consequences of any medium—that is, of any extension of ourselves—result from the new scale that is introduced into our affairs by each extension of ourselves, or by any new technology. Thus, with automation, for example, the new patterns of human association tend to eliminate jobs, it is true. That is the negative result. Positively, automation creates roles for people, which is to say depth of involvement in their work and human association that our preceding mechanical technology had destroyed. Many people would be disposed to say that it was not the machine, but what one did with the machine, that was its meaning or message. In terms of the ways in which the machine altered our relations to one another and to ourselves, it mattered not in the least whether it turned out cornflakes or Cadillacs. The restructuring of human work and association was shaped by the technique of fragmentation that is the essence of machine technology. The essence of automation technology is the opposite. It is integral and decentralist in depth, just as the machine was fragmentary, centralist, and superficial in its patterning of human relationships.

The instance of the electric light may prove illuminating in this connection. The electric light is pure information. It is a medium without a message, as it were, unless it is used to spell out some verbal ad or name. This fact, characteristic of all media, means that the "content" of any medium is always another medium. The content of writing is speech, just as the written word is the content of print, and print is the content of the telegraph. If it is asked, "What is the content of speech?," it is necessary to say, "It is an actual process of thought, which is in itself nonverbal." An abstract painting represents direct manifestation of creative thought processes as they might appear in computer designs. What we are considering here, however, are the psychic and social consequences of the designs or patterns as they amplify or accelerate existing processes. For the "message" of any medium or technology is the change of scale or pace or pattern that it introduces into human affairs. The railway did not introduce movement or transportation or wheel or road into human society, but it accelerated and enlarged the scale of previous human functions, creating totally new kinds of cities and new kinds of work and leisure. This happened whether the railway functioned in a tropical or a northern environment, and is quite independent of the freight or content of the railway medium. The airplane, on the other hand, by accelerating the rate of transportation, tends to dissolve the railway form of city, politics, and association, quite independently of what the airplane is used for.

Let us return to the electric light. Whether the light is being used for brain surgery or night baseball is a matter of indifference. It could be argued that these activities are in some way the "content" of the electric light, since they could not exist without the electric light. This fact merely underlines the point that "the medium is the message" because it is the medium that shapes and controls the scale and form of human association and action. The content or uses of such media are as diverse as they are ineffectual in shaping the form of human association. Indeed, it is only too typical that the "content" of any medium blinds us to the character of the medium. It is only today that industries have become aware of the various kinds of business in which they are engaged. When IBM discovered that it was not in the business of making office equipment or business machines, but that it was in the business of processing information, then it began to navigate with clear vision. The General Electric Company makes a considerable portion of its profits from electric light bulbs and lighting systems. It has not yet discovered that, quite as much as A.T.&T., it is in the business of moving information.

The electric light escapes attention as a communication medium just because it has no "content." And this makes it an invaluable instance of how people fail to study media at all. For it is not till the electric light is used to spell out some brand name that it is noticed as a medium. Then it is not the light but the "content" (or what is really another medium) that is noticed. The message of the electric light is like the message of electric power in industry, totally radical, pervasive, and decentralized. For electric light and power are separate from their uses, yet they eliminate time and space factors in human association exactly as do radio, telegraph, telephone, and TV, creating involvement in depth.

A fairly complete handbook for studying the extensions of man could be made up from selections from Shakespeare. Some might quibble about whether or not he was referring to TV in these familiar lines from *Romeo and Juliet:*

But soft! what light through yonder window breaks?
It speaks, and yet says nothing.

In *Othello,* which, as much as *King Lear,* is concerned with the torment of people transformed by illusions, there are these lines that bespeak Shakespeare's intuition of the transforming powers of new media:

Is there not charms
By which the property of youth and maidhood
May be abus'd? Have you not read Roderigo,
Of some such thing?

In Shakespeare's *Troilus and Cressida,* which is almost completely devoted to both a psychic and social study of communication, Shakespeare states his awareness that true social and political navigation depend upon anticipating the consequences of innovation:

The providence that's in a watchful state
Knows almost every grain of Plutus' gold,
Finds bottom in the uncomprehensive deeps,
Keeps place with thought, and almost like the gods
Does thoughts unveil in their dumb cradles.

The increasing awareness of the action of media, quite independently of their "content" or programming, was indicated in the annoyed and anonymous stanza:

In modern thought, (if not in fact)
Nothing is that doesn't act,
So that is reckoned wisdom which
Describes the scratch but not the itch.

The same kind of total, configurational awareness that reveals why the medium is socially the message has occurred in the most recent and radical medical theories. In his *Stress of Life,* Hans Selye tells of the dismay of a research colleague on hearing of Selye's theory:

When he saw me thus launched on yet another enraptured description of what I had observed in animals treated with this or that impure, toxic material, he looked at me with desperately sad eyes and said in obvious despair: "But Selye, try to realize what you are doing before it is too late! You have now decided to spend your entire life studying the pharmacology of dirt!"

(Hans Selye, *The Stress of Life*)

As Selye deals with the total environmental situation in his "stress" theory of disease, so that latest approach to media study considers not only the "content" but the medium and the cultural matrix within which the particular medium operates. The older unawareness of the psychic and social effects of media can be illustrated from almost any of the conventional pronouncements.

In accepting an honorary degree from the University of Notre Dame a few years ago, General David Sarnoff made this statement: "We are too prone to make technological instruments the scapegoats for the sins of those who wield them. The products of modern science are not in themselves good or bad; it is the way they are used that determines their value." That is the voice of the current somnambulism. Suppose we were to say, "Apple pie is in itself neither good nor bad; it is the way it is used that determines its value." Or, "The smallpox virus is in itself neither good nor bad; it is the way it is used that determines its value." Again, "Firearms are in themselves neither good nor bad; it is the way they are used that determines their value." That is, if the slugs reach the right people firearms are good. If the TV tube fires the right ammunition at the right people it is good. I am not being perverse. There is simply nothing in the Sarnoff statement that will bear scrutiny, for it ignores the nature of the medium, of any and all media, in the true Narcissus style of one hypnotized by the amputation and extension of his own being in a new technical form. General Sarnoff went on to explain his attitude to the technology of print, saying that it was true that print caused much trash to circulate, but it had also disseminated the Bible and the thoughts of seers and philosophers. It has never occurred to General Sarnoff that any technology could do anything but *add* itself on to what we already are.

Such economists as Robert Theobald, W. W. Rostow, and John Kenneth Galbraith have been explaining for years how it is that "classical economics" cannot explain change or growth. And the paradox of mechanization is that although it is itself the cause of maximal growth and change, the principle of mechanization excludes the very possibility of growth or the understanding of change. For mechanization is achieved by fragmentation of any process and by putting the fragmented parts in a series. Yet, as David Hume showed in the eighteenth century, there is no principle of causality in a mere sequence. That one thing follows another accounts for nothing. Nothing follows from following, except change. So the greatest of all reversals occurred with electricity, that ended sequence by making things instant. With instant speed the causes of things began to emerge to awareness again, as they had not done with things in sequence and in concatenation accordingly. Instead of asking which came first, the chicken or the egg, it suddenly seemed that a chicken was an egg's idea for getting more eggs.

Just before an airplane breaks the sound barrier, sound waves become visible on the wings of the plane. The sudden visibility of sound just as sound ends is an apt instance of that great pattern of being that reveals new and opposite forms just as the earlier forms reach their peak performance. Mechanization was never so vividly fragmented or sequential as in the birth of the movies, the moment that translated us beyond mechanism into the world of growth and organic interrelation. The movie, by sheer speeding up the mechanical, carried us from the world of sequence and connections into the world of creative configuration and structure. The message of the movie medium is that of transition from lineal connections to configurations. It is the transition that produced the now quite correct observation: "If it works, it's obsolete." When electric speed further takes over from mechanical movie sequences, then the lines of force in structures and in media become loud and clear. We return to the inclusive form of the icon.

To a highly literate and mechanized culture the movie appeared as a world of triumphant illusions and dreams that money could buy. It was at this moment of the movie that cubism occurred, and it has been described by E. H. Gombrich (*Art and Illusion*) as "the most radical attempt to stamp out ambiguity and to enforce one reading of the picture—that of a man-made construction, a colored canvas." For cubism substitutes all facets of an object simultaneously for the "point of view" or facet of perspective illusion. Instead of the specialized illusion of the third dimension on canvas, cubism sets up an interplay of planes and contradiction or dramatic conflict of patterns, lights, textures that "drives home the message" by involvement. This is held by many to be an exercise in painting, not an illusion.

In other words, cubism, by giving the inside and outside, the top, bottom, back, and front and the rest, in two dimensions, drops the illusion of perspective in favor of instant sensory awareness of the whole. Cubism, by seizing on instant total awareness, suddenly announced that *the medium is the message*. Is it not evident that the moment that sequence yields to the simultaneous, one is in the world of the structure and of configuration? Is that not what has happened in physics as in painting, poetry, and in communication? Specialized segments of attention have shifted to total field, and we can now say, "The medium is the message" quite naturally. Before the electric speed and total field, it was not obvious that the medium is the message. The message, it seemed, was the "content," as people used to ask what a painting was *about*. Yet they never thought to ask what a melody was about, nor what a house or a dress was about. In such matters, people retained some sense of the whole pattern, of form and function as a unity. But in the electric age this integral idea of structure and configuration has become so prevalent that educational theory has taken up the matter. Instead of working with specialized "problems" in arithmetic, the structural approach now follows the lines of force in the field of number and has small children meditating about number theory and "sets."

Cardinal Newman said of Napoleon, "He understood the grammar of gunpowder." Napoleon had paid some attention to other media as well, especially the semaphore telegraph that gave him a great advantage over his enemies. He is on record for saying that "Three hostile newspapers are more to be feared than a thousand bayonets."

Alexis de Tocqueville was the first to master the grammar of print and typography. He was thus able to read off the message of coming change in France and America as if he were reading aloud from a text that had been handed to him. In fact, the nineteenth century in France and in America was just such an open book to de Tocqueville because he had learned the grammar of print. So he, also, knew when that grammar did not apply. He was asked why he did not write a book on England, since he knew and admired England. He replied:

One would have to have an unusual degree of philosophical folly to believe oneself able to judge England in six months. A year always seemed to me too short a time in which to appreciate the United States properly, and it is much easier to acquire clear and precise notions about the American Union than about Great Britain. In America all laws derive in a sense from the same line of thought. The whole of society, so to speak, is founded upon a single fact; everything springs from a simple principle. One could compare America to a forest pierced by a multitude of straight roads all converging on the same point. One has only to find the center and everything is revealed at a glance. But in England the paths run criss-cross, and it is only by travelling down each one of them that one can build up a picture of the whole.

De Tocqueville, in earlier work on the French Revolution, had explained how it was the printed word that, achieving cultural saturation in the eighteenth century, had homogenized the French nation. Frenchmen were the same kind of people from north to south. The typographic principles of uniformity, continuity, and lineality had overlaid the complexities of ancient feudal and oral society. The Revolution was carried out by the new literati and lawyers.

In England, however, such was the power of the ancient oral traditions of common law, backed by the medieval institution of Parliament, that no uniformity or continuity of the new visual print culture could take complete hold. The result was that the most important event in English history has never taken place; namely, the English Revolution on the lines of the French Revolution. The American Revolution had no medieval legal institutions to discard or to root out, apart from monarchy. And many have held that the American Presidency has become very much more personal and monarchical than any European monarch ever could be.

De Tocqueville's contrast between England and America is clearly based on the fact of typography and of print culture creating uniformity and continuity. England, he says, has rejected this principle and clung to the dynamic or oral common-law tradition. Hence the discontinuity and unpredictable quality of English culture. The grammar of print cannot help to construe the message of oral and non-written culture and institutions. The English aristocracy was properly classified as barbarian by Matthew Arnold because its power and status had nothing to do with literacy or with the cultural forms of typography. Said the Duke of Gloucester to Edward Gibbon upon the publication of his *Decline and Fall*: "Another damned fat book, eh, Mr. Gibbon? Scribble, scribble, scribble, eh, Mr. Gibbon?" De Tocqueville was a highly literate aristocrat who was quite able to be detached from the values and assumptions of typography. That is why he alone understood the grammar of typography. And it is only on those terms, standing aside from any structure or medium, that its principles and lines of force can be discerned. For any medium has the power of imposing its own assumption on the unwary. Prediction and control consist in avoiding this subliminal state of Narcissus trance. But the greatest aid to this end is simply in knowing that the spell can occur immediately upon contact, as in the first bars of a melody.

A Passage to India by E. M. Forster is a dramatic study of the inability of oral and intuitive oriental culture to meet with the rational, visual European patterns of experience. "Rational," of course, has for the West long meant "uniform and continuous and sequential." In other words, we have confused reason with literacy, and rationalism with a single technology. Thus in the electric age man seems to the conventional West to become irrational. In Forster's novel the moment of truth and dislocation from the typographic trance of the West comes in the Marabar Caves. Adela Quested's reasoning powers cannot cope with the total inclusive field of resonance that is India. After the Caves: "Life went on as usual, but had no consequences, that is to say, sounds did not echo nor thought develop. Everything seemed cut off at its root and therefore infected with illusion."

A Passage to India (the phrase is from Whitman, who saw America headed Eastward) is a parable of Western man in the electric age, and is only incidentally related to Europe or the Orient. The ultimate conflict between sight and sound, between written and oral kinds of perception and organization of existence is upon us. Since understanding stops action, as Nietzsche observed, we can moderate the fierceness of this conflict by understanding the media that extend us and raise wars within and without us.

Detribalization by literacy and its traumatic effects on tribal man is the theme of a book by the psychiatrist, J. C. Carothers, *The African Mind in Health and Disease* (World Health Organization, Geneva, 1953). Much of his material appeared in an article in *Psychiatry* magazine, November, 1959: "The Culture, Psychiatry, and the Written Word." Again, it is electric speed that has revealed the lines of force operating from Western technology in the remotest areas of bush, savannah, and desert. One example is the Bedouin with his battery radio on board the camel. Submerging natives with floods of concepts for which nothing has prepared them is the normal action of all of our technology. But with electric media Western man himself experiences exactly the same inundation as the remote native. We are no more prepared to encounter radio and TV in our literate milieu than the native of Ghana is able to cope with the literacy that takes him out of his collective tribal world and beaches him in individual isolation. We are as numb in our new electric world as the native involved in our literate and mechanical culture.

Electric speed mingles the cultures of prehistory with the dregs of industrial marketeers, the nonliterate with the semiliterate and the postliterate. Mental breakdown of varying degrees is the very common result of uprooting and inundation with new information and endless new patterns of information. Wyndham Lewis made this a theme of his group of novels called *The Human Age*. The first of these, *The Childermass*, is concerned precisely with accelerated media change as a kind of massacre of the innocents. In our own world as we become more aware of the effects of technology on psychic formation and manifestation, we are losing all confidence in our right to assign guilt. Ancient prehistoric societies regard violent crime as pathetic. The killer is regarded as we do a cancer victim. "How terrible it must be to feel like that," they say. J. M. Synge took up this idea very effectively in his *Playboy of the Western World*.

If the criminal appears as a nonconformist who is unable to meet the demand of technology that we behave in uniform and continuous patterns, literate man is quite inclined to see others who cannot conform as somewhat pathetic. Especially the child, the cripple, the woman, and the colored person appear in a world of visual and typographic technology as victims of injustice. On the other hand, in a culture that assigns roles instead of jobs to people—the dwarf, the skew, the child create their own spaces. They are not expected to fit into some uniform and repeatable niche that is not their size anyway. Consider the phrase "It's a man's world." As a quantitative observation endlessly repeated from within a homogenized culture, this phrase refers to the men in such a culture who have to be homogenized Dagwoods in order to belong at all. It is in our I.Q. testing that we have produced the greatest flood of misbegotten standards. Unaware of our typographic cultural bias, our testers assume that uniform and continuous habits are a sign of intelligence, thus eliminating the ear man and the tactile man.

C. P. Snow, reviewing a book of A. L. Rowse (*The New York Times Book Review*, December 24, 1961) on *Appeasement* and the road to Munich, describes the top level of British brains and experience in the 1930s. "Their I.Q.'s were much higher than usual among political bosses. Why were they such a disaster?" The view of Rowse, Snow approves: "They would not listen to warnings because they did not wish to hear." Being anti-Red made it impossible for them to read the message of Hitler. But their failure was as nothing compared to our present one. The American stake in literacy as a technology or uniformity applied to every level of education, government, industry, and social life is totally threatened by the electric technology. The threat of Stalin or Hitler was external. The electric technology is within the gates, and we are numb, deaf, blind, and mute about its encounter with the Gutenberg technology, on and through which the American way of life was formed. It is, however, no time to suggest strategies when the threat has not even been acknowledged to exist. I am in the position of Louis Pasteur telling doctors that their greatest enemy was quite invisible, and quite unrecognized by them. Our conventional response to all media, namely that it is how they are used that counts, is the numb stance of the technological idiot. For the "content" of a medium is like the juicy piece of meat carried by the burglar to distract the watchdog of the mind. The effect of the medium is made strong and intense just because it is given another medium as "content." The content of a movie is a novel or a play or an opera. The effect of the movie form is not related to its program content. The "content" of writing or print is speech, but the reader is almost entirely unaware either of print or of speech.

Arnold Toynbee is innocent of any understanding of media as they have shaped history, but he is full of examples that the student of media can use. At one moment he can seriously suggest that adult education, such as the Workers Educational Association in Britain, is a useful counterforce to the popular press. Toynbee considers that although all of the oriental societies have in our time accepted the industrial technology and its political consequences: "On the cultural plane, however, there is no uniform corresponding tendency." (Somervell, I. 267) This is like the voice of the literate man, floundering in a milieu of ads, who boasts, "Personally, I pay no attention to ads." The spiritual and cultural reservations that the oriental peoples may have toward our technology will avail them not at all. The effects of technology do not occur at the level of opinions or concepts, but alter sense ratios or patterns of perception steadily and without any resistance. The serious artist is the only person able to encounter technology with impunity, just because he is an expert aware of the changes in sense perception.

The operation of the money medium in seventeenth-century Japan had effects not unlike the operation of typography in the West. The penetration of the money economy, wrote G. B. Sansom (in *Japan*, Cresset Press, London, 1931) "caused a slow but irresistible revolution, culminating in the breakdown of feudal government and the resumption of intercourse with foreign countries after more than two hundred years of seclusion." Money has reorganized the sense life of peoples just because it is an *extension* of our sense lives. This change does not depend upon approval or disapproval of those living in the society.

Arnold Toynbee made one approach to the transforming power of media in his concept of "etherialization," which he holds to be the principle of progressive simplification and efficiency in any organization or technology. Typically, he is ignoring the *effect* of the challenge of these forms upon the response of our senses. He imagines that it is the response of our opinions that is relevant to the effect of media and technology in society, a "point of view" that is plainly the result of the typographic spell. For the man in a literate and homogenized society ceases to be sensitive to the diverse and discontinuous life of forms. He acquires the illusion of the third dimension and the "private point of view" as part of his Narcissus fixation, and is quite shut off from Blake's awareness or that of the Psalmist, that we become what we behold.

Today when we want to get our bearings in our own culture, and have need to stand aside from the bias and pressure exerted by any technical form of human expression, we have only to visit a society where that particular form has not been felt, or a historical period in which it was unknown. Professor Wilbur Schramm made such a tactical move in studying *Television in the Lives of Our Children*. He found areas where TV had not penetrated at all and ran some tests. Since he had made no study of the peculiar nature of the TV image, his tests were of "content" preferences, viewing time, and vocabulary counts. In a word, his approach to the problem was a literary one, albeit unconsciously so. Consequently, he had nothing to report. Had his methods been employed in 1500 A.D. to discover the effects of the printed book in the lives of children or adults, he could have found out nothing of the changes in human and social psychology resulting from typography. Print created individualism and nationalism in the sixteenth century. Program and "content" analysis offer no clues to the magic of these media or to their subliminal charge.

Leonard Doob, in his report *Communication in Africa*, tells of one African who took great pains to listen each evening to the BBC news, even though he could understand nothing of it. Just to be in the presence of those sounds at 7 P.M. each day was important for him. His attitude to speech was like ours to melody—the resonant intonation was meaning enough. In the seventeenth century our ancestors still shared this native's attitude to the forms of media, as is plain in the following sentiment of the Frenchman Bernard Lamy expressed in *The Art of Speaking* (London, 1696):

'Tis an effect of the Wisdom of God, who created Man to be happy, that whatever is useful to his conversation (way of life) is agreeable to him . . . because all victual that conduces to nourishment is relishable, whereas other things that cannot be assimilated and be turned into our substance are insipid. A Discourse cannot be pleasant to the Hearer that is not easie to the Speaker; nor can it be easily pronounced unless it be heard with delight.

Here is an equilibrium theory of human diet and expression such as even now we are only striving to work out again for media after centuries of fragmentation and specialism.

Pope Pius XII was deeply concerned that there be serious study of the media today. On February 17, 1950, he said:

It is not an exaggeration to say that the future of modern society and the stability of its inner life depend in large part on the maintenance of an equilibrium between the strength of the techniques of communication and the capacity of the individual's own reaction.

Failure in this respect has for centuries been typical and total for mankind. Subliminal and docile acceptance of media impact has made them prisons without walls for their human users. As A. J. Liebling remarked in his book *The Press,* a man is not free if he cannot see where he is going, even if he has a gun to help him get there. For each of the media is also a powerful weapon with which to clobber other media and other groups. The result is that the present age has been one of multiple civil wars that are not limited to the world of art and entertainment. In *War and Human Progress,* Professor J. U. Nef declared: "The total wars of our time have been the result of a series of intellectual mistakes . . ."

If the formative power in the media are the media themselves, that raises a host of large matters that can only be mentioned here, although they deserve volumes. Namely, that technological media are staples or natural resources, exactly as are coal and cotton and oil. Anybody will concede that a society whose economy is dependent upon one or two major staples like cotton, or grain, or lumber, or fish, or cattle is going to have some obvious social patterns of organization as a result. Stress on a few major staples creates extreme instability in the economy but great endurance in the population. The pathos and humor of the American South are embedded in such an economy of limited staples. For a society configured by reliance on a few commodities accepts them as a social bond quite as much as the metropolis does the press. Cotton and oil, like radio and TV, become "fixed charges" on the entire psychic life of the community. And this pervasive fact creates the unique cultural flavor of any society. It pays through the nose and all its other senses for each staple that shapes its life.

That our human senses, of which all media are extensions, are also fixed charges on our personal energies, and that they also configure the awareness and experience of each one of us, may be perceived in another connection mentioned by the psychologist C. G. Jung:

Every Roman was surrounded by slaves. The slave and his psychology flooded ancient Italy, and every Roman became inwardly, and of course unwittingly, a slave. Because living constantly in the atmosphere of slaves, he became infected through the unconscious with their psychology. No one can shield himself from such an influence. (*Contributions to Analytical Psychology,* London, 1928).

. . .

THE SPOKEN WORD: FLOWER OF EVIL?

A few seconds from a popular disk-jockey show were typed out as follows:

That's Patty Baby and that's the girl with the dancing feet and that's Freddy Cannon there on the David Mickie Show in the night time ooohbah scuba-doo how are you booboo. Next we'll be Swinging on a Star and sssshhh-wwoooo and sliding on a moonbeam.

Waaaaaaa how about that . . . one of the goodest guys with you . . . this is lovable kissable D.M. in the p.m. at 22 minutes past nine o'clock there, aahh-rightie, we're gonna have a Hitline, all you have to do is call WAlnut 5-1151, WAlnut 5-1151, tell them what number it is on the Hitline.

Dave Mickie alternately soars, groans, swings, sings, solos, intones, and scampers, always reacting to his own actions. He moves entirely in the spoken rather than the written area of experience. It is in this way that audience participation is created. The spoken word involves all of the senses dramatically, though highly literate people tend to speak as connectedly and casually [sic.; Ed.] as possible. The sensuous involvement natural to cultures in which literacy is not the ruling form of experience is sometimes indicated in travel guides, as in this item from a guide to Greece:

You will notice that many Greek men seem to spend a lot of time counting the beads of what appear to be amber rosaries. But these have no religious significance. They are *komboloia* or "worry beads," a legacy from the Turks, and Greeks click them on land, on the sea, in the air to ward off that insupportable silence which threatens to reign whenever conversation lags. Shepherds do it, cops do it, stevedores and merchants in their shops do it. And if you wonder why so few Greek women wear beads, you'll know it's because their husbands have pre-empted them for the simple pleasure of clicking. More aesthetic than thumb-twiddling, less expensive than smoking, this Queeg-like obsession indicates a tactile sensuousness characteristic of a race which has produced the western world's greatest sculpture . . .

Where the heavy visual stress of literacy is lacking in a culture, there occurs another form of sensuous involvement and cultural appreciation that our Greek guide explains whimsically:

. . . do not be surprised at the frequency with which you are patted, petted and prodded in Greece. You may end up feeling like the family dog . . . in an affectionate family. This propensity to pat seems to us a tactile extension of the avid Greek curiosity noted before. It's as though your hosts are trying to find out what you are made of.

The widely separate characters of the spoken and written words are easy to study today when there is ever closer touch with nonliterate societies. One native, the only literate member of his group, told of acting as reader for the others when they received letters. He said he felt impelled to put his fingers to his ears while reading aloud, so as not to violate the privacy of their letters. This is interesting testimony to the values of privacy fostered by the visual stress of phonetic writing. Such separation of the senses, and of the individual from the group, can scarcely occur without the influence of phonetic writing. The spoken word does not afford the extension and amplification of the visual power needed for habits of individualism and privacy.

It helps to appreciate the nature of the spoken word to contrast it with the written form. Although phonetic writing separates and extends the visual power of words, it is comparatively crude and slow. There are not many ways of writing "tonight," but Stanislavsky used to ask his young actors to pronounce and stress it fifty different ways while the audience wrote down the different shades of feeling and meaning expressed. Many a page of prose and many a narrative has been devoted to expressing what was, in effect, a sob, a moan, a laugh, or a piercing scream. The written word spells out in sequence what is quick and implicit in the spoken word.

Again, in speech we tend to react to each situation that occurs, reacting in tone and gesture even to our own act of speaking. But writing tends to be a kind of separate or specialist action in which there is little opportunity or call for reaction. The literate man or society develops the tremendous power of acting in any matter with considerable detachment from the feelings or emotional involvement that a nonliterate man or society would experience.

Henri Bergson, the French philosopher, lived and wrote in a tradition of thought in which it was and is considered that language is a human technology that has impaired and diminished the values of the collective unconscious. It is the extension of man in speech that enables the intellect to detach itself from the vastly wider reality. Without language, Bergson suggests, human intelligence would have remained totally involved in the objects of its attention. Language does for intelligence what the wheel does for the feet and the body. It enables them to move from thing to thing with greater ease and speed and ever less involvement. Language extends and amplifies man but it also divides his faculties. His collective consciousness or intuitive awareness is diminished by this technical extension of consciousness that is speech.

Bergson argues in *Creative Evolution* that even consciousness is an extension of man that dims the bliss of union in the collective unconscious. Speech acts to separate man from man, and mankind from the cosmic unconscious. As an extension or uttering (outering) of all our senses at once, language has always been held to be man's richest art form, that which distinguishes him from the animal creation.

If the human ear can be compared to a radio receiver that is able to decode electromagnetic waves and recode them as sound, the human voice may be compared to the radio transmitter in being able to translate sound into electromagnetic waves. The power of the voice to shape air and space into verbal patterns may well have been preceded by a less specialized expression of cries, grunts, gestures, and commands, of song and dance. The patterns of the senses that are extended in the various languages of men are as varied as styles of dress and art. Each mother tongue teaches its users a way of seeing and feeling the world, and of acting in the world, that is quite unique.

Our new electric technology that extends our senses and nerves in a global embrace has large implications for the future of language. Electric technology does not need words any more than the digital computer needs numbers. Electricity points the way to an extension of the process of consciousness itself, on a world scale, and without any verbalization whatever. Such a state of collective awareness may have been the preverbal condition of men. Language as the technology of human extension, whose powers of division and separation we know so well, may have been the "Tower of Babel" by which men sought to scale the highest heavens. Today computers hold out the promise of a means of instant translation of any code or language into any other code or language. The computer, in short, promises by technology a Pentecostal condition of universal understanding and unity. The next logical step would seem to be, not to translate, but to by-pass languages in favor of a general cosmic consciousness which might be very like the collective unconscious dreamt of by Bergson. The condition of "weightlessness," that biologists say promises a physical immortality, may be paralleled by the condition of speechlessness that could confer a perpetuity of collective harmony and peace.

18 RHETORIC AND / OF McLUHAN

BRUCE E. GRONBECK

In this essay Gronbeck undertakes a description and evaluation of assumptions and concepts integral to McLuhan's view of communication. This analysis leads to the conclusion that "one can take or leave but not neglect Marshall McLuhan."

Gronbeck contends that McLuhan's view is a meta-communication theory; that is, McLuhan uses his notion of media influence to explain changing communication habits throughout history and to explain changes in educational, economic, and political systems. Various critics in *McLuhan: Pro and Con* condemn McLuhan's selective use of historical evidence, simplistic technological determinism, esoteric definitions, and misunderstanding of Shakespeare and James Joyce as he carries out his meta-communication theorizing.

Of special interest is Gronbeck's suggestion that McLuhan and his followers place greater emphasis on understanding the human processes of sensory perception and information processing. He implies that this is the key line of research if any viable conclusions are to follow from the McLuhanite probes.

For another attempt to explicate many of the same notions with which McLuhan grapples, see Walter J. Ong, *The Presence of the Word*, 17–110.

Source: This essay was written by Gronbeck especially for this anthology. Many of the ideas contained in it were developed in two of his previous publications: "McLuhanism's Rhetorical Theory: An Exposition and Evaluation," *Ohio Speech Journal*, IV (1967), 44–50; and "Beyond the Flannel Graph: Mass Media and the Christian Message," *Event Magazine*, IX (March 1969), 3–13.

The twentieth century has seen many revolutions—in medicine, in aerodynamics, in urban affairs, in colonial policy, in nuclear physics, in ecumenicalism, in ideological dispute—but undoubtedly among the great revolutions of all history must be placed the Electronic Revolution. That bugaboo of the suburban parent, "New Math," in combination with the transistor and the photoelectric cell, has thrust this civilization into the Computer Age. Amazingly large portions of your life lay punched up on computer tapes capable of printing you out in microseconds if necessary.

The results of this electronic revolution are varied, but among the most important is the fact that we now live in a society dominated by a multi-media approach to communication. As technology has increased the number and kinds of products on the market and has provided higher wages for more consumers, the marketer has used every means possible to reach into your billfold. Radio and television advertising has taken on new hard-sell and soft-sell formats; billboards threaten you on every highway; neon lights flash "The Lowest Prices in Town"; junk mail triples your postman's daily burden; flyers are slipped under your windshield wipers at the supermarket; bull horns offer you the best fruit in the country; small aircraft trail banners pushing the Shrine Circus; young boys bring broadsides announcing tomorrow's shirt sale; marquees assure you of a good seat and air conditioning; telethons ask you to contribute to your alma mater; short films demand that you vote against daylight savings time; bumper stickers divulge everything from personal philosophy to spectacular views of the Grand Canyon. Then the bills come. You begin to feel that life is a window envelope.

Enter (Herbert) Marshall McLuhan (1911–   ), sociologist/political theorist/communicologist/critic/etc.

At least as early as 1945–1946, McLuhan revealed his interest in communication (then preferring the word "rhetoric"); he pictured the world's great philosophical struggles as the confrontation of the "grammarians" and the "dialecticians." He saw the grammarians (rhetoricians or Sophists) of the ancient world urging the life of action and persuasion, over against the dialecticians (à la Socrates), who prefered the life of contemplation and philosophy. McLuhan noted that the grammarians triumphed only briefly; much of the rest of history, he believed, was run by the dialecticians, those who patterned and constrained all values and ideas, locking them in philosophies and ideologies.[1]

As Compton suggests,[2] McLuhan even then was on the side of the grammarians, the men of eloquence, extroversion, and public life—the men who would interact with their world as it was. By the writing of *The Mechanical Bride* (1951), McLuhan was reacting pessimistically to the submersion of his grammarian. In this, his first major work on the American print culture (especially advertising), he visualized modern man in the grips of "a world of social myths or forms," "employed in an effort to paralyze the mind":

[1] Marshall McLuhan, "An Ancient Quarrel in Modern America," *The Classical Journal,* XLI (No. 4, January 1946). McLuhan makes further use of the grammarian/dialectician distinction in "The Southern Quality," *Sewanee Review,* LV (No. 1, July 1947). For a fuller discussion of both articles, see Neil Compton, "The Paradox of Marshall McLuhan," in *McLuhan: Pro & Con,* ed. Raymond Rosenthal (New York: Funk & Wagnalls, 1968), pp. 106–124.

[2] Compton, p. 108.

It is observable that the more illusion and falsehood [are] needed to maintain any given state of affairs, the more tyranny is needed to maintain the illusion and falsehood. Today the tyrant rules not by club or fist, but, disguised as a market researcher, he shepherds his flock in the ways of utility and comfort.[3]

The Mechanical Bride was a collage of ads, with commentaries destroying the *Readers' Digest, Time,* Coca Cola, most comics, soap operas, etc.

The pessimism and dejection revealed in this early venture into America's communication patterns, however, was softened in his next major work, *The Gutenberg Galaxy* (1962). In attempting to demonstrate how a communication medium—print—revolutionized the world, he touched briefly on the twentieth century and the electronic revolution, arguing that the discovery of curved space in 1905 "officially dissolved" the Gutenberg galaxy, for "with the end of lineal specialisms and fixed points of view, compartmentalized knowledge became an unacceptable as it had always been irrelevant."[4] He thus projected the coming of a new age, one wherein man again could sense fully his world rather than examining it through the partial filters of disciplinary and philosophical glasses.

And finally, it was almost with joy that McLuhan proclaimed that "the medium is the message" in his popularized *Understanding Media* (1964): The phrase indicated "that a totally new environment had been created" as "technologies begin to perform the function of art in making us aware of the psychic and social consequences of technology."[5] McLuhan's discovery of the "synesthetic" man—the man of the Electronic Age who used all of his senses in reacting to his environment—apparently reminded McLuhan of the ancient grammarian or man of action. The synesthetic man was celebrated in the kinescope-record-film, *The Medium is the Massage* (1967).

Beginning thus as a literary critic fascinated with a parallel between ancient Greece and modern America, McLuhan has progressed to his present position as Director of the Centre for Culture and Technology, University of Toronto, and to a reputation unparalleled among communicologists.

Through all of these (and other)[6] major works, McLuhan has talked

[3] Herbert Marshall McLuhan, *The Mechanical Bride; Folklore of Industrial Man* (New York: Vanguard Press, 1951), pp. v, vi.

[4] Marshall McLuhan, *The Gutenberg Galaxy; The Making of Typographic Man* (Toronto, Canada: Univ. of Toronto Press, 1962), p. 302.

[5] Marshall McLuhan, *Understanding Media: The Extensions of Man* (New York: McGraw-Hill, 1965), pp. vii, viii.

[6] McLuhan's bibliography through early 1967 may be found at the end of Gerald E. Stearn (ed.), *McLuhan: Hot & Cool; A Primer for the Understanding of & A Critical Symposium with a Rebuttal by McLuhan* (New York: Dial Press, 1967), pp. 305–312. Two new books, to be found neither in Stearn nor in this essay, should be added to complete his major works: *Counterblast* (1969) and *Culture Is Our Business* (1970).

in images and impulses at least generally familiar to the rhetorical theorist/critic. Following the trail of the Canadian economist Harold Adams Innis, whose major works, *The Bias of Communication* (1951) and *Empire and Communications* (1950), began to explore the effect of communication patterns upon cultural change,[7] McLuhan has made fashionable and fascinating a host of concepts rooted in basic communication theory. In a style which Christopher Ricks characterizes as a "viscous fog, through which loom stumbling metaphors" or which Samuel Becker in gentler motions terms "free association writing,"[8] McLuhan has explained the Generation Gap, the move toward "involvement" in all human activity, the disorientation visible in contemporary life, and even such phenomena as the death of baseball through his analysis of mass, and more personalized, media of communication.

At the risk of attempting the impossible and cognizant that much will remain unsaid, in this essay I seek to lay bare what apparently is McLuhan's underlying communication theory. Assuming that a "communication theory" generally proposes to delineate the relationships among the source, destination, message, and medium of exchange as it describes and critiques the rhetorical encounter, I will discuss that theory element by element. This communication theory is drawn from most of his principal works, and hence represents a kind of eclecticism that McLuhan himself seemingly appreciates. Once the basic theory is described, comments upon the theory as a whole and problems inherent to it will be offered.

HOT, COOL, AND MEDIUM

Source

Contrary to many observers, McLuhan does not begin his study with an analysis of the medium of communication, but rather takes his departure from a discussion of the perceptual process. Herein lies his originality:[9] He believes the actual process of perception controls information. The process has two steps: (1) Man takes in information through all of his senses, which allow the data-outside-his-brain to come into the central nervous system to form "ideas." If all of the senses are perceiving in consort, "synesthesia" or "totalism in the use

[7] For an admirable discussion of the influence of Innis upon McLuhan, see James W. Carey, "Harold Adams Innis and Marshall McLuhan," in *McLuhan: Pro & Con*, pp. 270–308.

[8] Christopher Ricks, "the style is a viscous fog, . . ." in *McLuhan: Hot & Cool*, p. 212; and Samuel L. Becker, "Understanding Media," *QJS*, LI (1965), p. 87.

[9] Actually, McLuhan is not unique among rhetorical theorists when he begins with epistemological considerations; Campbell, and even Burke, do likewise. What does set him apart on this account is that he carries his epistemology to its logical conclusion by concentrating on, rather than merely recognizing, his radical empiricism.

of the senses" is achieved.[10] To McLuhan, primitive man and perhaps this century's TV generation are the only people to attain "entire interplay among experiences."[11] (2) During the greater part of his history, man rather has used only some of his senses as his principal data-receptors. This partial employment of the senses means that "ideas" are determined by the particular "balance" or "ratio" among the senses absorbing data at a given time. The "ratio" controls what the "imagination" has to work with:

Imagination is that ratio among the perceptions and faculties which exists when they are not embedded or outered in material technologies. When so outered, each sense and faculty becomes a closed system. Prior to such outering there is entire interplay among experiences.[12]

The "imagination," then, is but a receptacle—or "ratio"—wherein sense-perceptions are somehow balanced and shaped into ideas; and, when one or more of the senses are "outered"—as with technological media (see below)—the imagination receives only partial data. Only when "our private senses are not closed systems but are endlessly translated into each other in that experience which we call consciousness"[13] can man benefit from a complete idea.

The source, therefore, for McLuhan is the imagination, traditionally a composite of fragmentary sense data representing only a partial construction of the "real" world for most people (unless they have achieved synesthesia). Precisely how the senses interact, however, is not laid open in any of his works.

Destination

Little need be said about the receivers of messages. McLuhan and his fellow theorists are concerned with audiences only in so far as they represent a fairly homogeneous set of perceiving habits. That is, just as the communicator's ideas are influenced by the senses used in absorbing information, so the audience's reception of ideas is affected by a culture's common means of information intake. On such a premise McLuhan discusses the methods of intake used by primitive African tribes and Eskimos; Riesman analyzes the perceptual characteristics of the Papago Indians; Lee invades the Ontong Java Islands for similar observations.[14]

[10] Marshall McLuhan et al., *Verbi-Voco-Visual Explorations* (New York: Something Else Press, 1967), Sec. 3. The bulk of this little anthology was originally printed as No. 8 of *Explorations*, the periodical edited by McLuhan and Edmund Carpenter through a grant from the Ford Foundation.
[11] *Gutenberg Galaxy*, p. 265.
[12] *Ibid.*
[13] *Ibid.*, p. 5.
[14] See, respectively, *Gutenberg Galaxy*, p. 37, and *Verbi-Voco-Visual Explorations*, Sec. 24; Edmund Carpenter and Marshall McLuhan (eds.), *Explorations in Communication; An Anthology* (Boston: Beacon Press, 1960), pp. 109–117; and *ibid.*, pp. 136–154.

In other words, in the tradition of Whorf-Sapir, the McLuhanites examine a given culture's perception of the world in order to explain that culture's patterns of communication: Transmittable ideas and reasoning patterns are determined by habitual procedures of perception, which in turn are governed by "ratios" among the senses used in that process.[15]

Message

Little more should be said about the message for now. To be sure, the theme of *Understanding Media* is "the medium is the message," but as his title indicates, his focus is the medium, not the message. McLuhan is concerned with messages only in so far as they demonstrate the influence of medial changes. The alphabet, print, the telegraph, and so on, each reshaped basic messages, and, McLuhan asserts, reoriented their very content.[16]

Perhaps his best illustrations here relate to the introduction of printing and television. In *Gutenberg Galaxy*, he takes pains to demonstrate (1) that the new media began by adopting the content of the old (and thus medieval manuscripts were the first printed texts and old movies were among the first television fare), but (2) that they soon developed their own messages (print, the equitone linear prose, and TV, the intimate personal plot). In other words, print began by adopting the "nonlinear" dialogue but soon produced "linear" essays, logically constructed idea-by-idea; and television started with the "linear" novel/movie plot, and only later experimented with "nonlinear" collages of images.[17]

While McLuhan's analysis of messages is captivating—particularly when he is discussing the linear/nonlinear dichotomy—it nevertheless leaves the reader with a puzzle: What *is* the message? Ideas? Simple medial characteristics? We will play with the puzzle in the last section.

---

[15] Even though McLuhan does appear at times in the clothing of a cultural- or sociolinguist, he has been attacked for not reading the *good* scholars in that field. See Dell Hymes, "The author's mode of reasoning is such that *involvement* and *importance* (particularly of print) is transformed into *primary characteristic* and *determinant*," *McLuhan: Hot & Cool*, p. 173.

[16] On the alphabet, see *Understanding Media*, pp. 84–85, *Gutenberg Galaxy*, pp. 22–23; on print, *Gutenberg Galaxy*, esp. pp. 135–164, *Explorations in Communication*, pp. 125–135; and on the telegraph, *Understanding Media*, pp. 206, 246–257.

[17] See *Gutenberg Galaxy*, esp. pp. 142–143, as well as *Explorations in Communication*, pp. 136–155, 162–180. The linear/nonlinear dichotomy is certainly the major emphasis of *Gutenberg Galaxy*. The impact of print and the consequent adjustments in perception, thought, and values are approached by an analysis of "nonlinear" manuscripts and dialogues and of "linear" prose. His contrast between "all-at-once" medieval writing and "thought-by-thought" Renaissance equitones is clear and perceptive. The conclusions he draws, however, are definitely questionable. See the last section of this essay.

Medium

Perhaps the clearest statement of McLuhan's central theme is seen in *Understanding Media:*

Each form of transport not only carries, but translates and transforms, the sender, the receiver, and the message. The use of any kind of medium or extension of man alters the patterns of interdependence among people, as it alters the ratios among our senses.[18]

Impacted in this quotation are two important notions: (1) Various media of communication "extend" man's senses, his physiological data-receptors. Thus, the pen is an extension of touch; the telephone is an extension of the voice; film and television are extensions of eyes; even clothing is an extension—of skin. (For example, the beads of a hippie, the collar of the minister, the uniform of a policeman, the new habit of a nun—each of these tells you something about the person.) Each of these extensions affects man's relationships with his fellow man and with his environment, and, as we saw earlier, can "outer" man's senses by overemphasizing one sense. Thus, if one only reads for his knowledge, his other senses are "outered" or excluded from the learning process.[19] (2) Not only do media "extend" man's senses, but they also control the knowledge gained in any exchange. Because each medium both selects from among the senses and extends man beyond his own physiology, a given medium will determine what kind and how much information is taken in by the mind. For example, during the Civil War, most Americans knew of Lincoln only by his words printed in newspapers; he was seen as a lofty thinker and writer of beautiful prose. Warren Harding (and most successfully, FDR) could communicate through both the printed and spoken word, for they had radio, which could send the warm nuances of voice to their publics. John F. Kennedy, in contrast, through the power of television could use his youthful vigor *in toto,* almost synesthetically, could strike both the ear and the eye as his audiences read, heard, and saw him offer the New Frontier. An audience could be more fully "informed" about Kennedy than perhaps about any previous president. This is why McLuhan can utter that famous epigram, "The Medium is the Message." The medium controls both the *amount* and the *configuration* of information, of ideas, of knowledge itself.

[18] *Understanding Media,* p. 90.
[19] McLuhan illustrates this idea with a reference to the Narcissus myth, wherein the Greek became a "servomechanism" because of self-hypnosis by a medium (a reflecting pool), and wherein Narcissus—as source, message, and destination—was destroyed consequently by that medium (*Understanding Media,* pp. 41–42). In effect, to McLuhan, Narcissus overextended a single sense to the destruction of his other senses and ultimately himself.
The idea of "extension" generally dominates the first half of Marshall McLuhan and Quentin Fiore, *The Medium is the Massage; An Inventory of Effects* (New York: Bantam Books, 1967).

The medium has received most of McLuhan's attention, therefore, not because it is necessarily the core of his communication theory—for I believe his understanding of the perceptual process holds the key—but because it can modify radically the source, the message, and the destination:

1. The source is affected in that the medium of intake necessarily determines the data received—"eye-data" yields different information than "ear-data," for example.[20] Further, the medium of exchange shapes the source's projected image, as is seen in one of McLuhan's paradoxes: "Speak that I may see you."[21]

2. The message, too, is affected by the medium. The message is partially determined by medial considerations—color, for example, is certainly better conveyed through a visual than through an aural medium.[22] The medium also reorients our perceptual processes, as the linear/nonlinear dichotomy emphasizes.

3. Finally, the destination is affected by the medium. That is, when taking in information through some media (e.g. a photograph), the receiver simply sits back and enjoys, while when exposing himself to others (e.g. a cartoon), he must fill in visual spaces. Print for McLuhan is "hot," while television is "cool," as are the telephone and human speech (where one fills in acoustical space). As McLuhan says in *Understanding Media:*

Hot media are, therefore, low in participation, and cool media are high in participation or completion by the audience. Naturally, therefore, a hot medium like radio has very different effects on the user from a cool medium like the telephone. . . . Any hot medium allows of less participation than a cool one, as a lecture makes for less participation than a seminar, and a book for less than dialogue.[23]

Hence, McLuhan and Fiore's metaphoric adjustment of the old phrase to read "the medium is the massage" is understandable. The medium "massages" the destination of a message, in that it controls how and with what he must work in decoding.

META-PHORWARD

The outlines of a McLuhanite rhetorical or communication theory thus far have been sketched. The emerging picture is one dominated by the medium because the medium radically alters the functioning of the

[20] See *Explorations in Communication* (pp. 160–182, and *Understanding Media,* pp 77–88.

[21] *Explorations in Communication,* p. 207. The same idea is seen in the frontispiece to *Verbi-Voco-Visual Explorations,* in which is pictured a face on which an ear is superimposed over the eyes.

[22] See *Explorations in Communication,* esp pp. 98–99.

[23] *Understanding Media,* p. 23.

source, the message, and the destination, and because, I suppose, it is McLuhan's focus upon media that brought him into the limelight.

What we have discovered, I think, is really a *meta-rhetorical* or *meta-communication theory*. That is, we have seen postulated a theory to explain communicative habits and the *evolution* of those habits through time. Essentially, McLuhan has advocated a theory in which the medium is seen as an *independent variable* surrounded by a host of dynamic, interacting *dependent variables*.

Perhaps we have inferred too much. McLuhan's occasional references to the history of rhetorical theory, however, would seem to justify the inference. McLuhan sees the figures of speech in Greek rhetoric as "archetypes or postures of individual minds," which became wholly routinized in Rome, or which in his terms became "archetypes or postures of collective consciousness."[24] He appears to mean that what had been devices occasionally employed by Greek orators were translated into an educational code—lists of schemes and tropes—and thus were engrained in the perceptual equipment of the Romans. He argues that the translation process involved was indicative of a new, codified medium for intake and output of information, of a fundamental shift in the perceptual habits of audiences. Rhetorical theory, however, changed again when Augustine, because of a desire to propagate Christianity via exegetical letters, stole *grammatica* and *philogia* for rhetoric, as he needed devices for literary analysis.[25] And, McLuhan notes, stylistic rhetorics, often couched in dialogue form, died because of the advent of linear print.[26] Further, the emphasis of logic returned with the visualization print afforded.[27] And finally, he argues, of course, that modern technology has destroyed the nineteenth-century forms of communication, replacing linearality with all-at-onceness and instantaneousness.[28]

In other words, working from his assumptions concerning the perceptual process and medial influence upon messages and destinations, and perhaps seeking to trace the rise, fall, and rebirth of his synesthetic "grammarian," McLuhan has attempted (at least implicitly) to explain variations in communicative habits through time. What is implied here, I think, is that given knowledge about (1) the senses involved in sending and receiving messages, and (2) the characteristics of available media, we can *account for* and *predict* the forms communication has and will take. In their predictive capacity as artists, the theorists of communication can project, warn, and adapt; in effect, serving as "an

24 *Gutenberg Galaxy*, p. 267.
25 *Ibid.*, p. 219.
26 *Ibid.*, p. 164.
27 *Ibid.*, p. 219.
28 *Understanding Media*, pp. 52–55, 56–59, 64–73.

early warning system,"[29] they can tell their societies what to expect when engaging in interpersonal and mass communication.

What is also implied is that a society's communication system affects its educational, economic, political, and even philosophical systems. Indeed, the purpose of *Gutenberg Galaxy*—to "elucidate a principal factor in social change"[30]—convincingly demonstrates McLuhan's belief that patterns of communication carry with them near-necessary patterns of social relationships, political structures, economic institutions, etc.[31] As illustrations, both *The Medium is the Massage* and *War and Peace in the Global Village* (1968) visualize America's two wholly different societies—the society of the older generation, raised in a print-dominated culture, and the society of the younger generation, raised in a "verbi-voco-visual" culture:

Today we're just beginning to realize that the new media aren't just mechanical gimmicks for creating worlds of illusion, but new languages with new and unique powers of expression.[32]

And those "new languages" have brought to their users new global values, global sympathies, and even global politics and economics.

McLuhan, therefore, has set forth much more than a traditional rhetorical theory, more than a rationale for the discourse of his age. He has swept through the history of man communicating with man, explained that history, and related that history to the sociological/political/economic progress of the race.

HOME ON THE STRANGE

Any attempt to evaluate the worth of McLuhan's ideas is almost doomed from the start. He insists, for example, that both *The Mechani-*

[29] *Ibid.*, p. x. McLuhan's new introduction to the paperback edition of *Understanding Media* serves two functions: He attempts to explain some apparently misunderstood concepts and also presents a case for considering "the arts as prophetic." To quote him at more length: "Art as a radar environment takes on the function of indispensable perceptual training rather than the role of a privileged diet for the elite. While the arts as radar feedback provide a dynamic and changing corporate image, their purpose may be not to enable us to change but rather to maintain an even course toward permanent goals, even amidst the most disrupting innovations. We have already discovered the futility of changing our goals as often as we change our technologies" (x). What is most intriguing about this idea of prophesy, I think, is the fact that whenever a new mass medium comes into existence, writers *do* attempt to predict changes in the communication process. See Robert E. Davis, "Response to Innovation: A Study of Popular Argument About New Mass Media" (unpub. Ph.D. dissert., Univ. of Iowa, 1965).

[30] *Gutenberg Galaxy*, p. 11.

[31] The influence of Innis on McLuhan is unmistakable in this argument. Again, see the Carey essay.

[32] Marshall McLuhan, "Classroom Without Walls," *Explorations* (No. 8, May 1957), reprinted in *McLuhan: Hot & Cool*, p. 111.

cal *Bride* and *Gutenberg Galaxy* can be read by starting at any point in the books and then reading around to where you began. His attempt to write in a "mosaic" makes evaluation difficult. And, too, McLuhan constantly insists that "I merely regard myself as a probe."[33] Presumably, as a probe he cannot be asked to account systematically for his claims. Nevertheless, if too much injustice has not been done him so far, the following judgments seem warranted:

1. McLuhan succumbs to gross *post hoc* arguments on one hand, and to many other apparently unwarranted assumptions on the other. These run from trivial matters—concerning nylons and city slickers, for example[34]—to more serious matters—the question of "hot" and "cool," the death of stylistics, the rise of nationalism, and the fundamental activity of human perception.[35] The importance of such matters is this: Unless you accept his divinations regarding the variations among media—as for example the idea that with film, man is a camera, and with TV, a screen, or that TV is "hot" because man fills in the spaces but that film is "cool" because he does not—you *cannot* accept the conclusions he draws. As one of his critics, Lieberman, says:

> McLuhan's message is that the media aren't what people think they are . . . Unfortunately, McLuhan is so full of jerry-built theory, dogmatic overgeneralizations, nonsequiturs, disorganized successions of parenthetical observations, and bewilderingly swift and large leaps among high peaks of misconception, that he makes little contribution himself to that understanding.[36]

His lack of clear, causal links is frustrating on one level, disastrous on another.

2. A second charge already has been mentioned: What IS the message? On the surface, McLuhan now is saying that the medium is the message, in that it modifies structure of thought, means of transmission, and habit of perception. But, certainly varying fields of study nevertheless do operate from sundry assumptions, do proceed with often con-

---

[33] *America*, (28 May 1966), p. 784. This disclaimer he has phrased in many ways. For example, in the introduction to *McLuhan: Hot & Cool* (p. xiii), he says: "I am an investigator. I make probes. I have no point of view. I do not stay in one position. . . . I don't explain—I explore." His use of Poe's "A Descent into the Maelstrom" in the preface to *The Mechanical Bride* (p. v) serves the same purpose.

[34] *Understanding Media*, pp. 29, 27.

[35] *Understanding Media*, pp. 22–40; *Gutenberg Galaxy*, pp. 192, 218, 265. Perhaps the prime example of his *post hoc* problems—most of which are of the chicken-or-the-egg variety—is his thesis on cultural determinism: Do communication patterns determine philosophical/economic/political/etc. institutions *or* do such institutions within a society call for communication channels of thus-and-so a kind? McLuhan, of course, takes his stand on the first half of this disjunction, but the second half certainly is just as defensible. One certainly could argue that America's full industrialization and emerging role in world politics in the twentieth century demanded faster communication, and hence fostered the utilization of radio and the development of television.

[36] Ben Lieberman, "The greatest defect of McLuhan's theory is the complete rejection of any role for the content of communication," in *McLuhan: Hot & Cool*, p. 225.

tradictory methods, and do apply their conclusions to discrete areas of human behavior—in effect, are separated conceptually, methodologically, and affectively. Ricks comments upon this paradox:

A newspaper is not *only* what McLuhan so effectively shows us that it is (a montage which replaces continuity by simultaneity, and so presents the globe in juxtaposition, "cramped into a planisphere"), but also actual news items, which say some things and not others. McLuhan's isolation of the medium (the front page itself, not the new item) may once have been a reasonable strategy. But he is now trapped in his strategy, so that he has practically nothing to say about the really difficult question: the *interplay* between what a medium does and what it says.[37]

The question "interplay" between the medium and the message—certainly in need of full explication in light of McLuhan's emphasis upon medial influence—simply has not been treated clearly in any of his books, with the possible exception of *The Mechanical Bride*, to which Ricks is referring. In that work—particularly in McLuhan's analysis of front pages and of certain ads—one feels that he is trying to illustrate the control a medium has in shaping and giving impact to a message, but it is only a feeling. The interplay never is demonstrated sharply.

The whole idea of interplay also forces one to remember his use of that term in *Gutenberg Galaxy*, wherein he discussed interplay in connection with the imagination. We again must ask: What IS the message? Is it the result of an interplay between medium and message (as in *Understanding Media*) or an interplay among bits of data in the imagination (as in *Gutenberg Galaxy*)? Boulding raises a similar question:

We are interested . . . not merely in the amount of information which can be transmitted per unit of time, but in the total information which can be transmitted and processed during the life of a system. There is no point in having an enormous intake of information through the senses for five minutes if it takes us five days to digest and process the information we have received. *It is probably the information-processing apparatus which is the real bottleneck, not the information-receiving apparatus.* The failure to realize this occasionally leads McLuhan astray. I suspect, for instance, that he puts too much stress on "synaesthesia," or the combination of the senses, and not enough on the fact that it is the processing of information in the human nervous system which is the really crucial process in the social system. In this sense it *is* the message, not the medium, which is important. The message is not just another medium, as McLuhan is continually saying, for the message consists of the processing of information into knowledge, and not the mere transmission of information through a medium.[38]

[37] Christopher Ricks, "McLuhanism," in *McLuhan: Pro & Con*, pp. 103–104.
[38] Kenneth E. Boulding, "It is perhaps typical of very creative minds that they hit very large nails not quite on the head," in *McLuhan: Hot & Cool*, pp. 62–63. As Boulding in this article is reviewing *Understanding Media* rather than *Gutenberg Galaxy*, he finds the emphasis upon media disturbing. Had he reviewed the earlier book, he probably could not have raised the same question. As I implicitly indicated in the

The pedants scream at McLuhan's lack of clear documentation, the products of our "linear" education find his style impossible to decode, and most readers discover many of his aphorisms are more engaging than enlightening—but of all the criticisms that can be leveled, that set out by Ricks and Boulding is easily the most damning. While McLuhan now tries to argue that the medium of exchange predetermines the message, he never specifies the actual "message" so constrained. Certainly the channels themselves are not "the" message—they are but carriers of "the" something-else, even given their ability to configure the "the." If, as in *Gutenberg Galaxy,* one argues that "the" message is the composite of sense-data stored in the "imagination" or whatever McLuhan wants to call the central nervous system, then as Boulding points out, it is that information-receiving apparatus and not the medium per se which is shaping "the" message. It seems to me, then, that the McLuhanite communication theorists are caught in a dilemma: Either they must return to a study of the perceptual process, continuing the work begun in *Gutenberg Galaxy* and *Explorations in Communication* (and thereby deemphasizing the more flashy medial studies per se) *or* they must carry their attack upon the message to its logical conclusion, arguing that messages themselves are of really no importance in the communicative exchange. As of this writing, the corpus of McLuhanism seemingly contains an unresolved theoretical tension: Should his epigram read "Perception is the message" or "The medium is communication"?

McLuhan may well be correct in insisting that communication theorists have done too little with medial effects upon the process of communication and upon the functioning of communications systems, but he has stretched a useful idea well beyond its elastic limits.

3. McLuhan himself has made but faint gestures (only in the new introduction to *Understanding Media*) toward a defense against these charges of unwarranted assumption, mosaic mesmerism, and over-extension/underdevelopment. While one can presume that the charges stand, one therefore cannot write him off as well-glossed pulp. In that he has set the world of communications to thinking of media in terms of the perceptual process and affectiveness; in that he has stimulated new approaches to old problems with his concepts of "ratios among senses," "hot," "cool," "linear," "nonlinear," "massage," etc.; and in that he has sought to capture his ideas in a near-poetic medium,

---

introductory section of this essay, McLuhan *must* be read in sequence—his move from pessimism to optimism is accompanied by a shift in focus.

As an interesting sidenote, the reader of McLuhan's critics is immediately impressed with the fact that almost without exception they like *The Mechanical Bride* and *Gutenberg Galaxy* much better than *Understanding Media* and all of the later works; the reading public and McLuhan himself, however, prefer those later works. The conclusions one may wish to draw from this observation could be interesting.

thereby forcing more reader-reaction than perhaps any other communication theorist, he has a place in the annals of contemporary rhetoric/communication. One can take or leave but not neglect Marshall McLuhan.

Boulding offers the definitive reaction to McLuhan when he says: "It is perhaps typical of very creative minds that they hit very large nails not quite on the head."[39]

---

[39] *Ibid.,* p. 56.

19 UNDERSTANDING McLUHAN

JOHN H. SLOAN

When discussing the linear, sequential logic that the print medium has imposed on man's perceptions, Sloan cites McLuhan's notion that only in print-oriented societies is it said that something "follows" from something. In *The Medium is the Massage* (p. 45), McLuhan contends that the phrase "I don't follow you" means "I don't think what you're saying is rational." How valid is this example of McLuhan's? Consider whether a more acceptable translation of the phrase would be "I don't understand you."

If, as McLuhan contends, the medium is the message, what is the role in communication of content? Some critics maintain that McLuhan completely ignores any role for content. (See, for example, Stearn, ed., *McLuhan: Hot and Cool,* 213, 225.) However, Mc-Luhan actually is saying only that previously scholars have placed too much emphasis on the effects of content while overlooking the pervasive effects of media. He states: "I'm not suggesting that content plays *no* role—merely that it plays a distinctly subordinate role." (See the interview with McLuhan in *Playboy,* March 1969, p. 61.)

For anthologies of both laudatory and critical comment on McLuhan see Gerald Stearn, ed., *McLuhan: Hot and Cool;* Raymond Rosenthal, ed., *McLuhan: Pro and Con,"* and Harry Crosby and George Bond, eds., *The McLuhan Explosion.*

Source: The Speech Teacher, XVII (March 1968), 140–144. Reprinted with permission of the author and the publisher.

Perhaps no contemporary communications critic and theorist has aroused greater controversy and more adulation in the 1960's than Marshall McLuhan. Especially since the publication of *Understanding Media* in 1964 the cult of McLuhanism has become widespread. In 1968 one sees McLuhan himself appearing on nation-wide TV as a critic; one reads popular essays by McLuhan in such unlikely sources as *Family Circle* and *TV Guide;* and one hears his praises sung by such varied authorities as television executives and Mayor Sam Yorty of Los

Angeles. One even sees McLuhan represented on the paperback counter of the local drug store: *Understanding Media* is now available in reprint as well as his latest "pop" effort, *The Medium is the Massage*.

What has precipitated this sudden popularity? One explanation is obvious: the very audacity of McLuhan's thinking. Because of his ready willingness to say the unusual, he is fresh, novel, appealing. He is also controversial. Thus, one finds him referred to as "the Oracle of the electric age"[1] as well as a writer of "impure nonsense, nonsense adulterated by sense."[2] Secondly, McLuhan's prose style is distinctive and curious. One feels that he delights in overstatement and over-simplification, while at the same time enjoying ambiguity and irony to the point of utter frustration. Depending upon the point of view one holds, he is either a prophet or a fool. It is difficult to find a middle ground.

In this paper I am not attempting to attack or defend McLuhan. What I do propose to do is to focus on several key concepts represented in *Understanding Media* and discuss some of their implications for the teacher and critic of speech. The purpose of the paper is admittedly exploratory; hopefully, it will lay the groundwork for further research on McLuhan.

ON THE TEACHING OF SPEECH

One of the earliest and certainly one of the most pervasive ideas expressed by McLuhan is that the invention of print revolutionized society. As such, this notion does not sound bizarre, but McLuhan adds his own unique rationale: that print as a *medium* has imposed a pseudo-logic upon man through its linear, step-by-step nature, and furthermore has produced a sense of detachment from the real all-at-onceness of interpersonal communication and actual events. McLuhan speculates that only in literate societies is it possible to say that something "follows" from something. He argues that there is no causality in sequence, that the sequential is merely additive, not causative. He concludes that ". . . The hidden cause of our Western bias toward sequence as 'logic' is in the all-pervasive technology of the alphabet."[3] McLuhan describes his "detachment" concept in this manner:

. . . In speech we tend to react to each situation that occurs, reacting in tone and gesture even to our own act of speaking. But writing tends to be a kind of specialist action in which there is little opportunity or call for reaction. The

[1] Cited in John M. Culkin, "A Schoolman's Guide to Marshall McLuhan," *Saturday Review of Literature,* L (March 18, 1967), 51.

[2] Cited in Richard Schickel, "Marshall McLuhan: Canada's Intellectual Comet," *Harper's Magazine,* 231 (November 1965), 66.

[3] Marshall McLuhan, *Understanding Media: The Extensions of Man* (New York: New American Library, Inc., 1966), p. 88.

literate man or society develops the tremendous power of acting in any matter with considerable detachment from the feelings or emotional involvement that a non-literate man or society would experience.[4]

McLuhan's conclusion about the Twentieth Century is that the electronic media have restored the missing elements to communication, and as a result, the world is becoming "a global village"[5] in terms of identification. He concludes: "We are as new in our electric world as the native involved in our literate and mechanical culture."[6]

McLuhan's distinction between written and oral media provides several important implications for the speech teacher. The spoken word, according to McLuhan, creates audience participation, the written word does not. The spoken word "involves all of the senses dramatically,"[7] the written word is dispassionate. Furthermore, although the written word is sequential and linear, the spoken word is not. McLuhan observes:

It helps to appreciate the nature of the spoken word to contrast it with the written form. Although phonetic writing separates and extends the visual power of words, it is comparatively crude and slow. There are not many ways of writing "tonight," but Stanislavsky used to ask his young actors to pronounce and stress it fifty different ways while the audience wrote down the different shades of meaning and feeling expressed. Many a page of prose and many a narrative has been devoted to expressing what was, in effect, a sob, a moan, a laugh, or a piercing scream. *The written word spells out in sequence what is quick and implicit in the spoken word.* (Italics mine)[8]

If it is true that it is the *aurality* of language which gives the oral message its unique impact and flavor, perhaps we should re-evaluate our emphasis upon such logical and grammatical "bases" as structure and syntax, for McLuhan would submit that they are not strictly appropriate to the oral mode. As Richard Schickel observes: "Logic as the organizing principle for the presentation of information is for McLuhan appropriate only to the printed page."[9] In other words McLuhan would undoubtedly object to the methods typically employed in the teaching of structure and style in the elementary speech class on three counts: (1) There is a fundamental distinction between oral and written style; (2) The "logic" of orderly point-development and sentence structure is not appropriate to oral discourse; (3) In trying to apply these "logical" elements of structure and grammar to speechmaking, we are actually doing our students a disservice. We are encouraging a "pseudo-logical"

[4] McLuhan, *Media,* p. 84.
[5] Marshall McLuhan, *The Gutenberg Galaxy* (Toronto: University of Toronto Press, 1962) p. 31.
[6] McLuhan, *Media,* p. 31.
[7] McLuhan, *Media,* p. 81.
[8] McLuhan, *Media,* p. 82.
[9] Schickel, p. 63.

artificiality which distorts the nature of oral rhetoric and subsequently diminishes its impact. Does McLuhan's thinking on language have validity? To this extent it does: it helps to explain the "text-book" speech with little appeal, and the "speech which breaks the rules" and has impact. It helps to support the view that a perfectly developed "motivated sequence" will not guarantee an artistic product. It encourages *creativity* when we so often stifle it in the classroom with our insistence upon adhering to "the rules" of structure and grammar. Although McLuhan's view does not mean that units on "structure" and "style" be deleted from public speaking classes, it suggests that these topics be treated in a manner which encourages student creativity and reflects the unique nature of oral discourse.

Another McLuhan concept which appears highly relevant to the teacher of speech is the classification of media as "hot" or "cool." This distinction has been criticized as ". . . one of the embellishments that seems to lead, via labyrinths of confusion, to a dead end."[10] It has also been praised as a major concept, "the most unique"[11] in *Understanding Media,* according to one reviewer. The theory, essentially, is that media can be described and categorized according to the *degree of participation* required by the audience. Thus, according to McLuhan, radio, the movies, print, and photography require little participation, and are *hot* media. TV, speech, cartoons, and the telephone require extensive participation, and are *cool* media.[12] Unfortunately, one must accept the categories on faith alone; McLuhan is quite arbitrary in his distinctions. The notion is further complicated by the less successful description of "hot" and "cool" cultures. Basically, literate cultures are "hot"; non-literate cultures are "cool." Again, one must accept a lack of real justification for the dichotomy, although it is easy to see another extension of McLuhan's notion that *print* causes detachment.

McLuhan does not extend his broad distinctions among media to specific analyses of individual media, but he urges that such applications be made. What relevance does the notion of audience *participation* have to the teaching of speech? Clearly, it is related to such topics as identification and common ground so prevalent in the literature of our discipline. If a system could be developed which described differences in audiences based on their degree of participation, it might be a very helpful adjunct to current ways of categorizing and stereotyping audiences. Such a system might well be based upon the traditional (and useful) scheme of classifying audiences as "hostile," "neutral" or "parti-

[10] Eric Barnouw, "McLuhanism Reconsidered," *Saturday Review of Literature,* XLIX (July 23, 1966), 21.

[11] Samuel Becker, rev. of *Understanding Media, Quarterly Journal of Speech,* LI (February 1965), 86.

[12] McLuhan, *Media,* p. 36 ff.

san." A "hostile" situation, for example, would typically demand that the speaker introduce cues which would encourage the audience to participate in his message, although he might well need to diminish the degree of participation if the situation were to get out of hand. The "partisan" audience already participates, and the speaker's task is generally to strengthen this predisposition. "Neutral" audiences might require high or low degrees of participation, depending upon the formality of the situation.

To summarize this section, we have seen that the extensions of two of McLuhan's most basic concepts have several implications for teachers of speech. McLuhan's notion of the "pseudo-logic" imposed by print gives us a refreshing distinction between written and oral language and suggests strongly that we are unrealistic and even distorted in our "traditional" approach to structure and style. Furthermore, the classification of media based upon the degree of auditor *participation* or involvement may provide us with a new perspective on describing speaker-audience relationships.

ON THE CRITICISM OF SPEECHMAKING

McLuhan's most often quoted phrase is the simple statement: "The medium is the message." In short, McLuhan feels that critics and commentators in the area of communication have missed the point when they refer exclusively to the "content" of the "message." It is the medium itself, according to McLuhan, that is meaningful. Content, he says, compares to "the juicy piece of meat carried by the burglar to distract the watchdog of his mind."[13] Distracted by thinking about "content," we slip into "subliminal and docile accepance of media impact."[14] Thus, media become "prisons without walls for their human users."[15] McLuhan's most telling point here is the one which seems to have generated the theory: the idea, previously discussed in this essay, that the total impact of all messages in print is not nearly so meaningful as the impact of the *medium* of print itself upon the thinking habits of Western Man. *Understanding Media* attempts to extend this thesis to such diverse "media" as money, housing, clocks, clothing, and the wheel. Although these topics seem far-removed from the main-stream of rhetorical theory, several important implications of the theory exist for the rhetorical critic.

Perhaps the most important application of "the medium is the message" is that rhetorical criticism, when it places primary emphasis upon the "message" of the speech, is distorted and unrealistic. In short the speech act is more than the sum total of its parts and must be looked

[13] McLuhan, *Media*, p. 32.
[14] McLuhan, *Media*, p. 34.
[15] McLuhan, *Media*, p. 34.

at as an organic whole or in its total context. Although one could hardly maintain that all "rules of rhetoric" be completely ignored, McLuhan's philosophy might help to justify the speaker who breaks rules and still has impact. In other words "appropriateness" in its highest sense would be the ultimate judgment of the effectiveness of a speech; an "appropriateness" which could only be perceived when looking at the medium operating in particular circumstances at a particular time.[16]

The notion that "the medium is the message," then, places a different focus on the observations and conclusions of the critic. Traditionally some rhetorical critics have placed their emphasis upon the speaker, by emphasizing "influences" on his effectiveness, or describing the type of speech training he received, or revealing the speaker's own views on his speaking abilities.[17] Other critics have approached the rhetorical process with primary attention to the speaker's message, urging that the primary goal of the critic is to establish the influence of the content upon the audience, the times, and subsequently, the course of history.[18] Finally, there are those who urge the critics to focus their attention upon the audience, either in terms of effect (the response to the message)[19] or as the audience shapes the "choices" or decisions made by the speaker.[20]

How do McLuhan's views differ from all these? Is McLuhan simply saying: "The speech must be adapted to the audience?" I believe he is saying more. He would urge that the medium be the primary concern of the critic, thus all considerations about the speaker, the message, and the audience would be made subordinate to the requirements imposed by the medium itself. In a sense, this notion comes closer than anything else to our view of occasion, but only in the broadest possible sense. It would analyze and describe all conditions existing in the "place" of the discourse and would make all considerations and observations subordinate to this focal point. By place I refer not only to the physical setting for the discourse but the metaphysical setting as well: the peculiar combination of conditions and interactions which shape the totality of the speaking situation.

[16] A similar interpretation about the implications of McLuhan's theory for the critic is made by Richard Schickel, "Marshall McLuhan: Canada's Intellectual Comet," p. 63. Schickel observes: "[The medium is the message] . . . imperils our conventional critical standards, as we have tried to apply them to the mass media."

[17] For examples of this type of criticism, see W. N. Brigance, ed., *A History and Criticism of American Public Address* (New York: McGraw-Hill Book Co., 1943).

[18] This point of view is advocated by Ernest W. Wrage in "Public Address: A Study in Social and Intellectual History," *Quarterly Journal of Speech*, XXXIII (December 1947), 451–457.

[19] This point of view is advocated by Lester Thonssen and A. Craig Baird in *Speech Criticism* (New York: Ronald Press, 1948).

[20] This point of view is advocated by Marie Hochmuth Nichols in her essay "The Criticism of Rhetoric," *A History and Criticism of American Public Address*, III (New York: Longman, Green and Co., 1955), 1–23.

The notion of place as an important element of rhetorical criticism is not a new one. Marie Hochmuth Nichols discusses it as bot'ı a physical condition and a metaphysical condition in her essay: "The Criticism of Rhetoric." She notes: "Place conditions both the speaker's method and the audience's reaction. People do not react in a smoke-filled room the way they do in the restrained atmosphere of the Senate gallery."[21] McLuhans' implication takes us one step further. Instead of being *an* important element of rhetorical criticism, "place" becomes *the* important element—the focal point.

McLuhan's thinking raises more serious questions about the nature of speech criticism in general. Combine "the medium is the message" with the basic, irresolvable distinctions between the spoken and written word and one faces a dilemma: the rhetorical critic is attempting to evaluate a dynamic medium with set standards and to compound the difficulty he is attempting to evaluate the impact of an extraordinarily "cool" medium (speech) with the almost antithetical, linear techniques of a very "hot" medium (print). At worst this dilemma leads one to conclude that written criticism of the oral mode is illogical and impossible. At best it lends support to those who say that current rhetorical criticism is characterized by a slavish cataloging of rules and techniques, and needs a more flexible, organic approach.[22]

Perhaps the most optimistic conclusion one can derive here is the influence of McLuhan himself. Using the medium of print, he has been able to stir up the thinking of communications experts throughout the country and even to capture the fancy of the lay public.

CONCLUSION

The views of Marshall McLuhan have been extraordinarily influential in recent years, especially in the area of mass media impact. For these views alone, McLuhan should be studied by anyone interested in communication or speech. In addition there are several more specific implications of McLuhan's thinking for the teacher of speech and the rhetorical critic. We have seen that McLuhan's views suggest possible new perspectives on the nature of oral discourse, the teaching of oral structure and style, the analysis of audiences, and the criticism of speechmaking. Although the list is by no means exhaustive or complete, perhaps it will serve to encourage further study by scholars in speech of ". . . the most provocative and controversial writer of this generation."[23]

[21] Nichols, p. 11.

[22] A strong exponent of this view is Edwin Black. See his *Rhetorical Criticism: A Study in Method* (New York: Macmillan Co., 1965), esp. pp. 36–90.

[23] Cited in Culkin, p. 51.

PART VIII THEORETICAL PROBES

20 DIMENSIONS OF THE CONCEPT OF RHETORIC

WAYNE E. BROCKRIEDE

Brockriede describes the components of a theoretical framework that he feels could be used to examine any rhetorical instance regardless of its cultural, ethical, or philosophical context. Thus he is following the orientation of his earlier article, "Toward a Contemporary Aristotelian Theory of Rhetoric." He strives toward a monistic theory of rhetoric.

Early in the present essay he outlines five controlling assumptions. To what degree do you agree with their validity? Can the rhetorical dimensions that he proposes be applied both in historical-critical research on rhetoric and in laboratory experimentation on persuasion? How does Brockriede's viewpoint relate to a philosophy of rhetoric and a theory of rhetoric?

Note also that his framework applies not just to public address but to a diversity of rhetorical acts, including interpersonal communication. And observe the varied sources, particularly Kenneth Burke, upon which he draws.

For an example of three of Brockriede's dimensions utilized by a rhetorical critic, see D. Ray Heisey, "The Rhetoric of the Arab-Israeli Conflict," *Quarterly Journal of Speech*, LVI (February 1970), 12–19.

Source: Quarterly Journal of Speech, LIV (February 1968), 1–12. Reprinted with permission of the author and the publisher.

During recent years a state of cold war has existed in the field of speech. Humanists who seek to understand rhetoric primarily through the use of historical scholarship and behavioral scientists who seek to develop a communication theory primarily through empirical description and experimental research have tended to see one another as threatening enemies. Yet members of these factions have the common objective of studying similar phenomena. The student of communication who conceives his study as focusing on pragmatic interaction of people and ideas is concerned with the rhetorical impulse within communication events.[1]

The purpose of this essay is to sketch the beginning and to encourage the further development of a system of dimensions for the study of rhetorical communication. Five assumptions implicit in this attempt should be stated explicitly from the outset.

First, the conception of rhetoric broadly as the study of how interpersonal relationships and attitudes are influenced within a situational context assumes the presence of the rhetorical impulse in such diverse acts as a speaker addressing an audience face to face or through mass media, a group of people conferring or conversing, a writer creating a drama or a letter to an editor, or a government or some other institution projecting an image.

Second, the concept of rhetoric must grow empirically from an observation and analysis of contemporary, as well as past, events.[2] The dimensions should be selected, developed, structured, and continuously revised to help explain and evaluate particular rhetorical acts.

Third, although the theorist, critic, or practitioner may focus his attention on a rhetorical act, such an act must be viewed as occurring within a matrix of interrelated contexts, campaigns, and processes.

Fourth, the rubrics of a rhetorical act are best viewed as dimensional, each reflecting a wide range of possible descriptions and not as expressing dichotomies.

Fifth, the dimensions of rhetoric are interrelational: each dimension bears a relationship to every other dimension.

This essay, therefore, represents an attempt to sketch a contemporary concept of interrelated interpersonal, attitudinal, and situational dimensions of a broadly conceived rhetorical act.

1

Traditional rhetoric places much less emphasis on interpersonal relationships than does the model presented in this paper. Even the concept of *ethos* frequently has been conceived as personal proof functioning rationalistically as a message variable.[3]

What are here developed as interpersonal dimensions may indeed

---

[1] Although my treatment differs from Dean C. Barnlund's excellent analysis in his "Toward a Meaning-Centered Philosophy of Communication," *Journal of Communication,* XII (December 1962), 197-211, the scope of my conception of rhetoric seems similar to the scope of his conception of communication. Gerald R. Miller in his *Speech Communication: A Behavioral Approach* (Indianapolis, Ind., 1966), makes explicit (p. 12) his synonymous usage of the terms rhetoric and speech communication.

[2] An argument which supports this claim is developed in my essay "Toward a Contemporary Aristotelian Theory of Rhetoric," *QJS,* LII (February 1966), 35-37.

[3] For example, in Lester Thonssen and A. Craig Baird's *Speech Criticism* (New York, 1948), the chapter on *ethos* (pp. 383-391) is subtitled "ethical proof in discourse."

function in an instrumental way, having some influence on a rhetorical act which aims primarily at attitudinal influence or situational appropriateness. But interpersonal dimensions themselves often represent the principal goals; and the establishment, change, or reinforcement of such interpersonal relationships as liking, power, and distance may exercise a controlling influence on the other dimensions.

Liking

This interpersonal dimension poses the question: how attracted to one another are the people who participate in a rhetorical act? Liking differs qualitatively and may refer to such continua as spiritual adoration—hate, sexual attraction—repulsion, friendship—enmity, and compatibility—incompatibility. In a dyadic act the feelings may or may not be mutual. When many people are involved—as in hearing a public address, participating in a discussion, or reading a best-seller, a single relationship may be characteristic—as when an audience becomes polarized, or relationships may vary—as when some discussants feel affection for a leader whereas others are repelled. Liking also differs in degree of intensity and in degree of susceptibility to change.

The change or reinforcement of the liking dimension may function as the primary purpose of a rhetorical act; courtship, for example, aims principally at affecting this relationship. Or increasing, maintaining, or decreasing the degree people like one another may be a by-product of a situation which has other chief aims. Or the liking relationship, though it remains essentially unchanged during a rhetorical act, may have a profound influence on whether other dimensions vary, as well as on how they vary.[4]

Power

Power may be defined as the capacity to exert interpersonal influence. Power may be the ultimate purpose or function, as in a power struggle, or it may be a by-product of or an influence on the controlling dimensions. The power dimension includes two primary variables.

First, what are the kinds of power? One is the influence a person has because others like him. The word *charisma* denotes this kind of power when it reaches a great magnitude. But personal magnetism exists also

---

[4] Hugh D. Duncan stresses this dimension in his *Communication and Social Order* (New York, 1962) when he says (p. 170) that "the study of *how men court each other* . . . will tell us much about the function of rhetoric in society." See also Kenneth Burke, *Rhetoric of Motives* in *A Grammar of Motives and a Rhetoric of Motives* (Cleveland, 1962), pp. 732–736. I make no attempt in this essay to catalogue the status of knowledge or to supply bibliographies concerning each of the dimensions discussed. I shall suggest, however, a source or two which will develop further each of the dimensions considered in this essay.

in lesser degrees. The power of personal attractiveness represents a kind of intersection of liking and power. A second type of power stems from a position or role in the social system. By having control over the assignment of sanctions, the allocation of rewards and punishments in a social system, a man merely by virtue of his office or role may be powerful. A third type is the control over the communication channels and other elements of the rhetorical situation. This situational power corresponds to what some people call the gatekeeper function. A fourth kind of power is an influence over the sources of information, the norms and attitudes, and the ideology. Such an influence seems to depend on the extent to which other people trust one's ideational competence generally and his special expertise on matters relevant to the rhetorical act, on their perceptions of his general willingness to express himself honestly and accurately and of his special candor on the particular relevant topics, and on their feelings of confidence in their abilities to predict accurately the meaning and significance attached to his statements and actions.[5] Finally, one exercises indirectly a degree of power by having access to and influence on other people who can exercise the other kinds of power more directly. So a first general variable of the power dimension is the degree with which people participating in a rhetorical act can manifest these kinds of power.

A second variable is power structure. Knowing how much power of what kind each rhetorical participant has may be less immediately relevant than knowing the relationship among the power statuses of the people involved. That is, power is relative rather than absolute. The significance of the power of a writer, for example, regardless of the amount or kind he may possess, depends on how much power he has relative to that of his readers. Two questions especially are important in an analysis of the power structure. How disparate are the power positions of the various participants of an act, and does the act function to increase, maintain, or decrease the disparity? How rigid or flexible is the structure, and does the rhetorical act function to increase, maintain, or decrease the stability?[6]

---

[5] Kenneth Andersen and Theodore Clevenger, Jr., provide an excellent synthesis of information on this kind of power in "A Summary of Experimental Research in Ethos," *Speech Monographs,* XXX (June 1963), 59–78.

[6] This dimension seems to have been ignored in the study of many rhetorical situations. It is only implied, partially, for example, in the public address doctrine of *ethos.* During recent years, however, under the headings of leadership and power structure, many small group specialists have emphasized it. See, for example, Dorwin Cartwright and Alvin Zander, *Group Dynamics: Research and Theory,* 2nd ed. (Evanston, Ill., 1960), pp. 487–809. Among a number of useful works in the field of political sociology which are relevant to an understanding of the function of power in rhetorical acts, see *Class, Status, and Power,* ed. Reinhard Bendix and Seymour Martin Lipset, 2nd ed. (New York, 1966), pp. 201–352.

Distance

The concept of distance is related to the other interpersonal dimensions. One generally feels "closer" to those persons he likes and "farther" from those he dislikes, but the greater the power disparity the greater the distance. Like all other dimensions, the establishment of an appropriate distance (whether decreasing, maintaining, or increasing it) may be a rhetorical act's primary function, an incidental outcome, or an influencing factor.

Two kinds of distance make up this dimension. One is an interpersonal distance between each two participants in a rhetorical act. The other is a social distance which exists within the structure of the group or groups within or related to the rhetorical act—such groups as audiences, committees, organizations, societies, and cultures. Although interpersonal and group distance are related closely and tend generally to covary, they are discrete variables in that two persons in a discussion group, for example, may move more closely together while the group structure is in the process of disintegrating.[7]

Several questions about the role of interpersonal and group distance in rhetorical situations seem important. How much distance (of each type) is optimal in achieving certain kinds of interpersonal, attitudinal, and situational rhetorical functions? What conditions of the other dimensions are most likely to increase, maintain, or decrease the distance (of each type)?

2

Controversial ideas which involve a choice among competing judgments, attitudes, and actions form a necessary part of any rhetorical act. Very often, although not always, such a choice is the primary operation, and the various interpersonal and situational dimensions merely create the environment in which the choice is made and influence how the choice is made. Traditionally, rhetoric seems rather consistently to have made this sort of assumption. The principal function of some rhetorical acts is interpersonal interaction or situational appropriateness, however, and the influence on attitudes in the making

[7] One of the shortcomings of the concept of interpersonal distance is that the term is not readily operationalized into specifiable behaviors. Consciously or unconsciously, however, people seem to have a sense of closeness or distance from others; such a feeling can influence rhetorical interaction. The philosophical basis for Kenneth Burke's rhetoric is the view that men are fundamentally divided. His concepts of identification and consubstantiality suggest that one of rhetoric's functions is to reduce man's interpersonal distance from man. See, for example, Burke, pp. 543–51. Edward T. Hall treats distance literally as a variable in communication situations in his *Silent Language* (Garden City, N. Y., 1959), pp. 187–209. The concept of social distance is implied in such terms in small group research as group cohesiveness, primary groups, and reference groups.

of choices is secondary. Attitude may be defined as the predisposition for preferential response to a situation. Two kinds of attitudes have rhetorical significance: attitudes toward the central idea in a choice-making situation and the ideological structure of other related attitudes and beliefs.

Central Idea

Several features of attitudes toward the central idea of a rhetorical situation require study.

First, although attitudes customarily have been considered as a point on a scale, this view is inadequate. As Carolyn Sherif, Muzafer Sherif, and Roger E. Nebergall have pointed out, a person's attitude may be described more accurately by placing various alternative positions on a controversy within three latitudes—of acceptance, of rejection, and of non-commitment.[8] On the policy of the United States toward Vietnam, for example, a person may have one favored position but place other positions within his latitude of acceptance; such additional positions are tolerable. He may have one position that he rejects more strongly than any other but place other positions within his latitude of rejection. Finally, because he lacks information, interest, or decisiveness, he may place other positions within his latitude of non-commitment. To understand or predict the attitudinal interaction in a rhetorical situation one must know whether its central idea falls within the participants' latitude of acceptance, rejection, or non-commitment.

Second, the degree of interest and the intensity of feeling with which the central idea confronted in a rhetorical act occupies a place in whatever latitude will influence potentially all other dimensions of that act.

Third, the way the various latitudes are structured is an influential variable. Sherif, Sherif, and Nebergall identify one such structure which they term ego-involvement. A person who is ego-involved in a given attitude tends to perceive relatively few discrete alternative positions, to have a narrow latitude of acceptance—sometimes accepting only one position, to have a broad latitude of rejection—lumping most positions as similarly intolerable, and to have little or no latitude of non-commitment.[9] The ego-involved hawk, for example, may accept only a strong determination to achieve a military victory, assimilating all positions close to that one; and he may reject all other stands, seeing little difference between unilateral withdrawal and attempts to negotiate that necessitate any genuine concessions to the adversary, and labeling anything less than total victory as appeasement.

[8] *Attitude and Attitude Change: The Social Judgment-Ego Involvement Approach* (Philadelphia, 1965), pp. 18–26.
[9] *Ibid.*, p. 233.

Fourth, a person's persuasibility on the central idea of a rhetorical act is a relevant variable. How likely is a person to respond positively to attempts to change his attitude? This question suggests the superiority of the Sherif, Sherif, and Nebergall analysis. The question is not the simple one of how likely is a person to move from "yes" to "no" or from favoring a negotiated settlement in Vietnam which does not involve the possibility of a coalition government in South Vietnam to one which does. It is the far more complex question of whether positions which are now assigned to one latitude can be moved to another one. This concept recognizes, for example, that to move a person from a position of rejection to one of non-commitment is significant persuasion. A person's persuasibility is related, of course, to the nature, intensity, and structure of his attitude.[10] An ego-involved person who feels strongly about an idea is less likely to change his attitude than one who is less ego-involved or less intense.

What the preceding discussion suggests is that the nature, intensity, structure, or persuasibility of the attitude of any participant toward the central idea in a rhetorical transaction will influence the other dimensions and be influenced by them. In addition, the relationship of the attitudes of each participant to those of others in the situation will influence their interaction together. The issue here can be focused in a single question: how similar are the people in a rhetorical act with respect to the nature, intensity, structure, and changeability of their attitudes toward the idea under focus in the rhetorical act? Or, to put the question in a slightly different way: to what extent can people identify with the attitudes of one another?[11]

Ideology

An attitude does not exist in a vacuum. One idea does not occur by itself. Rather, attitudes have homes in ideologies. The ideologies evoked in a rhetorical act influence, and may sometimes dominate, the other dimensions.

Several ideological structures may be identified. Attitudes may relate to other attitudes, to systems of values and norms, to ethical codes, and to philosophic presuppositions about the nature of man, the nature of reality, the nature of language, and the nature of knowledge. About each of these contexts two questions may be raised: What is the nature of the ideological structures of each participant in the act? How similar or different are the ideologies of the various participants?

[10] In addition, an individual's personality may be one of the determinants of his persuasibility on controversial propositions. See Irving L. Janis, Carl I. Hovland, et al., *Personality and Persuasibility* (New Haven, Conn., 1959), and Milton Rokeach, *The Open and Closed Mind* (New York, 1960).

[11] Kenneth Burke's concept of identification seems to relate to the attitude dimension as well as to the dimension of interpersonal distance.

The central idea of any rhetorical transaction evokes not only attitudes toward that idea but attitudes toward related ideas. In recent years several theories and approaches have developed: balance theory, the theory of cognitive dissonance, the congruity hypothesis, and the social judgment approach.[12] Although these formulations differ and the differences are argued heatedly, one principle seems accepted by most attitude theorists: man has an urge to think himself consistent, to try to achieve homeostasis within his system of attitudes.

Although relatively few persons work out a careful formulation of an ideology which consciously monitors various attitudes, each person very likely has an implicit ideology which unconsciously affects the development of any attitude in the system. Anyone attempting to change one attitude of a person, therefore, will profit from the admittedly difficult task of identifying that person's other attitudes and of considering how they may facilitate or retard such an attempt and how the target-attitude will, if changed, affect other attitudes. In addition, to understand the rhetorical interaction on some central idea one must also consider how similar or different one person's attitudes toward related ideas are to those of other people in the rhetorical act.

A second ideological variable is the system of values and norms subscribed to by the people in a rhetorical act. Just as a person's attitudes relate to his other attitudes, they relate also to more fundamental principles which he values. Whereas the first relationship may be viewed as a sort of part-to-part analogical inference, the second is a part-to-whole (or whole-to-part) inference. General values both evolve from many particular attitudes, and they also structure new experience in the development of new attitudes toward new situations.[13]

One of the most important sources of each person's fundamental values is his membership in small groups, organizations, societies, and cultures. The argument can be made that all values can be traced generally to a social origin, but some values especially can be associated closely with membership in a particular reference group—whether small group, organization, society, or culture. Such shared values are termed norms. When a rhetorical situation involves the actual or im-

[12] See Fritz Heider, "Attitudes and Cognitive Organizations," *Journal of Psychology,* XVL (April 1946), 107–114; Leon Festinger, *A Theory of Cognitive Dissonance* (Evanston, III., 1958); Charles E. Osgood, Percy Tannenbaum, and George Suci, *The Measurement of Meaning* (Urbana, III., 1957); and Sherif, Sherif, and Nebergall.

[13] In their essay "The American Value System: Premises for Persuasion," *Western Speech,* XXVI (Spring 1962), 83–91, Edward D. Steele and W. Charles Redding state, "Values, as they exist psychologically in the mind of the audience, have been generalized from the total experience of the culture and 'internalized' into the individual personalities of the listeners as guides to the right way to believe or act" (p. 84). Karl R. Wallace argues that general value premises function as the *substance* of rhetoric—as good reasons which support propositions or value judgments. See "The Substance of Rhetoric: Good Reasons," *QJS,* XLIX (October 1963), 239–249.

plied presence of such groups, the norms of those groups predictably are going to function as an ideology which will tend to set limits for attitudes of group members.[14]

A third kind of ideology is the ethical variable which raises two questions: What personal morality or public ethic guides the interaction of attitudes? Is the code of conduct acceptable to others who participate in the rhetorical act? A transaction of ideas viewed as unethical by someone with whom a person tries to interact will have adverse effects on many of the other dimensions.[15]

A fourth ideological variable consists of a person's philosophic presuppositions about the nature of man, the nature of reality, the nature of language, and the nature of knowledge. This variable probably functions relatively rarely as the primary goal of a rhetorical act, perhaps only when philosophers engage in dialogue, but it establishes a frame of reference within which attitudes interact. Is a man an object to be manipulated or a decision-maker in the process of making radical choices? To what extent does he behave rationally? To what extent is his rhetorical behavior determined for him and to what extent does he exercise free will? Does one take an Aristotelian, a Platonic, or a phenomenalistic stance on the question of the nature of reality? How does man acquire knowledge? To what extent does he come to know through a *priori* intellection, through revelation, through intuition, through memory, through empirical observation, through existential experience, or through scientific analysis?[16] How each person in a rhetorical act answers these questions, and the degree to which the various answers are similar, will influence how attitude interact.

3

A rhetorical act occurs only within a situation, and the nature of that act is influenced profoundly by the nature of the encompassing situation. Furthermore, on certain ceremonial occasions situational dimensions dominate the act. A speaker's function in a funeral oration, for example, may be merely to meet the expectations of the occasion. Six situational dimensions form a part of the conceptual framework advanced in this essay: format, channels, people, functions, method, and contexts.

---

[14] See A. Paul Hare, *Handbook for Small Research* (New York, 1962), pp. 23-61.

[15] Edward Rogge, in his "Evaluating the Ethics of a Speaker in a Democracy," *QJS,* XLV (December 1959), 419–425, suggests that the standards used to evaluate a speaker's ethics be those established by the audience and the society of which it is a part.

[16] The importance of the philosophic dimension of rhetoric is well argued by Otis M. Walter in "On Views of Rhetoric, Whether Conservative or Progressive," *QJS,* XLIX (December 1963), 367–382.

Format

The essential concern of this dimension is how procedures, norms, and conventions operate to determine who speaks and who listens.

Formats fall into two general types which anchor the ends of the dimension. At one extreme is a polarized situation in which one person functions as speaker or writer and others function as listeners or readers. At the other extreme is a type of conference situation in which the functions of the various participants rotate freely between speaking and listening.

Formats vary with respect to the degree of flexibility permitted rhetorical participants. In some situations, for example in written and electronic discourse, a rhetorician has little opportunity to revise his original plans within the act, although he may utilize feedback to designing subsequent acts in a campaign. In other situations a rhetorician has maximum opportunity to observe the reactions of others and to make appropriate decisions accordingly.[17]

Channels

The role of channels in a rhetorical act is manifested in three variables. First, is the communication conveyed verbally, nonverbally, or through a mixture of the two modes? Radio speaking and written messages are instances of the verbal channel; a silent vigil and pictures employ the nonverbal channel; and face-to-face speaking, television, and books which feature graphic materials illustrate the mixed mode.[18]

Second, if language is employed, is it in oral or written form? Although the distinction between these two channels needs no clarification,[19] their modes of transmission require analysis. Traditional rhetoric has long studied delivery as one of the canons. Although students of written composition have paid far less attention to the study of transmitting messages, such features as the selection of paper, binding, cryptology, and the like may influence the interaction between writer and reader more than the persons playing either role recognize. Delivery, whether in an oral or written channel, illustrates well the primary idea of this essay: that each dimension relates to every other dimension. Delivery will influence and be influenced by the interpersonal dimensions of liking, power, and distance; by the attitudes toward the

---

[17] See David K. Berlo, *The Process of Communication* (New York, 1960), pp. 111–116. Ironically, in public address, a format which offers considerable opportunity for communicative flexibility, the role of feedback has been analyzed very little.

[18] Marshall McLuhan's *The Medium is the Massage* (New York, 1967) is a notable attempt to make the nonverbal code as important in a book as the verbal.

[19] Joseph A. DeVito's study of "Comprehension Factors in Oral and Written Discourse of Skilled Communicators," *Speech Monographs*, XXXII (June 1965), 124–128, concluded that written discourse involved a more difficult vocabulary, simpler sentences, and a greater density of ideas than did oral discourse.

central idea and toward those related to it; and by the other situational dimensions of format, people, functions, method, and contexts.

Third, is the rhetoric transmitted directly or indirectly? A direct channel is a system of communication in which one person relates to someone else without the interference or aid of a third person or a mechanical device. The oral interpretation act, the speaker who reaches the newspaper reader via a reporter, the tape recording, television, and the two-step flow of communication all illustrate the indirect channel.[20] But indirectness admits of degrees. Messages may be transmitted through only one intermediary person or agency, or they may follow a circuitous track, as in a typical rumor, between its originator and its ultimate, and perhaps indefinite, destination.[21]

People

How rhetorical situations are populated forms six variables. One concerns the number of interacting people. Are they few or many?[22]

A second variable is the number of groups which function in the situation, whether as audiences or conferences. The range is from one to many. A speaker may address one particular audience or many audiences, either simultaneously or consecutively. A person may participate in a conference which operates virtually as a self-contained unit or in a conference involving multiple groups.

A third variable has to do with the degree to which the people are organized. The range is from a virtual absence of organization to the status of a highly structured and cohesive reference group.

A fourth variable, closely related to the third, involves the degree of homogeneity among the participating people. They may exhibit a high degree of homogeneity, they may be similar on some and different on other properties, or they may differ so much as to constitute essentially different groups even though they participate in the same situation.[23]

Fifth, participants in a rhetorical situation may vary widely in their

[20] The two-step flow of communication and the concept of opinion leadership has considerable applicability to rhetoric. See Elihu Katz and Paul F. Lazarsfeld, *Personal Influence* (Glencoe, Ill., 1955) and Elihu Katz, "The Two-Step Flow of Communication: An Up-to-Date Report on an Hypothesis," *Public Opinion Quarterly*, XXI (Spring 1957), 61–78.

[21] The classic study of rumor is Gordon W. Allport and Leo Postman, *Psychology of Rumor* (New York, 1917).

[22] I am inclined to include the intrapersonal communication of self-address within the scope of rhetoric. An individual's roles may interact intrapersonally and attitudinally in a variety of situational contexts in ways closely analogous to the interpersonal and attitudinal interaction of two or more persons. For support of this position, see Barnlund, 199–201, and Burke, pp. 561–563.

[23] The effect of a group's homogeneity and receptivity on the integration and polarization of an audience is admirably discussed in Charles H. Woolbert's pioneer monograph "The Audience," *Psychological Monographs*, XXI, No. 92 (June 1916), 37–54.

degree of awareness of their roles and in their degree of involvement in the situation.

Sixth, those who people a rhetorical situation engage in a range of relationships to that situation. One, some, many, or all of the participants may regard themselves or be regarded by others as depersonalized stimulus objects; as members or agents of a culture, institution, or group; as performing a role; as projecting an image; as manifesting a set of properties; or as selves with radical choices to make or commitments to uphold.

Functions

The functions of a rhetorical situation may be viewed from a general perspective or along interpersonal and attitudinal dimensions.

Some questions of situational function seem to apply both to the interpersonal and to the attitudinal aspects of a rhetorical act. To what extent are interpersonal relationships and/or attitudes to be reinforced or changed? What degrees of intensity of reinforcement or change does the situation call for? If change is to function, in what direction?

Other questions relate directly to the interpersonal dimension. Are people trying primarily to relate, identify, disengage, or in other ways to interact with others in the situation, or are they trying to express their "selves" conjointly? Are they trying to court, please, satisfy, tolerate, dissatisfy, or derogate one another? Are they trying to change or reinforce the power disparity or power structure of the situation? Are they trying to increase, maintain, or decrease social or interpersonal distance? Is group maintenance or group cohesiveness a relevant situational function?

Still other questions relate directly to three kinds of attitude influence. First, a person may present a message with a designative function —to present information, describe, define, amplify, clarify, make ambiguous, obfuscate, review, or synthesize ideas. Second, someone may present a message with an evaluative function—to praise, make commentary, hedge, criticize, or blame some person, object, situation, judgment, or policy. Third, someone may present a message with an advocative function—to solve a problem, create indecision, reinforce a present choice, foster delay, choose a change alternative, resolve a conflict, propose a compromise, or stimulate action.

The functions of rhetorical situations appear far more complex than implied by the traditional categories of inform, entertain, and persuade.

Method

Any situational function is manifested instrumentally through a number of message variables. These constitute the methodological dimension of the rhetorical act. Method is less often than other dimensions the ultimate function of the act; typically it plays the instrumental role of facilitating whatever dimension is primary.

Method includes the materials presented, the form in which they are structured, and the style in which materials and form are communicated.

Three questions about the material to be presented seem important. How much data should be presented? What kinds of data should be employed? From what sources should they be derived? These questions, of course, have no simple answers universally applicable.

The form variable may be analyzed in two ways. A distinction can be made between a sort of form-in-the-large which permeates the rhetorical method and a more microscopic set of structures which develop. The rhetorical act may be transacted through some conventional medium like an essay, a play, or a speech. A rhetorician may fulfill expectations by using identifiable forms in typical ways, or he may create new forms or employ old forms in new ways. Whether forms are appropriately new or old and whether their development is appropriately conventional or eccentric, of course, depends on the experience and expectations of the other people in the rhetorical act. The method may represent a straightforward management of materials to develop a central idea directly, or reflect an indirect ordering—for example, through the use of irony.[24] How prominent the form-in-the-large is to be is an important issue. Should the form become clearly evident in the discourse, or should it fulfill its function unobtrusively and not call any special attention to itself?

The form variable may also be viewed microscopically. This level of analysis includes a consideration of the logical connection between the material presented and the ideas advanced—which calls for the student of rhetoric to understand the logic of rhetorical interaction and the modes of reasoning appropriate to such interaction.[25] It includes a recognition of the structure which joins the ideas advanced into a pattern which amplifies or supports the central idea—which calls for an understanding of the patterns of expository and argumentative dis-

[24] For an excellent analysis of rhetorical irony, see Allan B. Karstetter, "Toward a Theory of Rhetorical Irony," *Speech Monographs,* XXXI (June 1964), 162–178.

[25] If one accepts the central idea of this essay that rhetoric is a system of interrelated dimensions, he must conclude that a rhetorical logic must accommodate the function of dimensions other than the one concerned with formal relationships among propositions. Irrelevant to rhetorical analysis is any logical system which assumes that man is only rational and that men do not vary, that ideas can be divorced from their affective content and from their ideological contexts, and that the only situation is that of the logician talking to the logician.

course, the analysis of a controversy into its issues, and the methods of problem-solving and negotiation.[26]

Specific formal structures may be recognizable immediately to others in the act and utilized in predictable ways, or they may be new and less obvious. Furthermore, the two levels of form in a discourse, the macroscopic and the microscopic, may function harmoniously toward the same end or constitute incongruity. Form, whether large or small, may be designed to facilitate information transfer or to disrupt it; to create a relatively narrow range of meanings and attitudinal responses or to maximize ambiguity; to present an optimal amount of material efficiently or to aim at redundancy; to achieve identification or alienation; to reinforce meanings and attitudes or to change them; and to increase or decrease the intensity of feelings toward the ideas.

Style, like form, may be viewed macroscopically or microscopically. Rhetorical style may be looked at from the point of view of broad symbolic strategy, a style-in-the-large. I take this concern to be behind much of the writing of Kenneth Burke.[27] Or it may be analyzed by looking at smaller units of analysis—at the level of the phoneme, word, sentence, or paragraph. Perhaps the writing of modern linguists may provide better ways of analyzing style microscopically than rhetoricians have followed traditionally.[28]

Many of the questions raised about form appear to apply also to style. Whether looked at large or small, style, too, provokes such issues as efficiency of information transfer, clarity *vs.* ambiguity, conciseness *vs.* redundancy, confidence *vs.* uncertainty, and identification *vs.* alienation. The issues can be resolved only by studying the particular interaction of the other dimensions in each unique rhetorical act.

Contexts

The contexts of time and place may alter in various ways how other dimensions function in the act. In this regard context is typical of situational dimensions. The substance of a rhetorical act is rarely located in the situation: it more characteristically focuses on the interpersonal and attitudinal categories. Aspects of the situation, including context, although not fundamental or ultimate, however, can alter decisively the other categories and hence change the substance of the act.

---

[26] Rhetoricians have tended to treat these various organizational patterns, like logic, as invariant structures, without due regard for the totality of the rhetorical situation—its people, its functions, and its contexts.

[27] Burke, for example, says (p. 567) that rhetoric "is rooted in an essential function of language itself, . . . the use of language as a symbolic means of inducing cooperation in beings that by nature respond to symbols." For Burke, rhetorical analysis is an attempt to unearth the essential linguistic strategies of the rhetorical agent.

[28] In "A Linguistic Analysis of Oral and Written Style," *QJS*, XLVIII (December, 1962), 419–422, Jane Blankenship applied the system of analysis which Charles C. Fries described in his book *The Structure of English* (New York, 1952).

In addition, time functions in another way. Each rhetorical act has some larger setting and fits into one or more ongoing processes.[29] For example, a novel may be a part of a movement or of several movements, a representation of an ideology or several ideologies, a moment in the career of the writer, a specimen of some formal or stylistic tendency, a phase in some long-term interpersonal relationship with a set of readers, et cetera. Several questions may suggest some of the ways a rhetorical act may relate to its contexts. Does an act occur relatively early or relatively late in one or more processes? To what extent is the act congruous with its larger framework? Does the act play one role in one context and a different, and perhaps conflicting, role in another?

4

Important to the student of rhetoric is the question of points of view. A rhetorical act will be perceived quite differently by each person who participates in it, and still differently by each person who observes and criticizes it from "the outside." Here, as elsewhere, "meanings are in people," not in discourses. Students of rhetoric must try to determine how the various participants and observers have perceived the dimensions of the act and to discover the extent to which such perceptions differ. The points of view of the relevant people become part of an important dimension of the act.

The consideration of point of view may have different implications for theorists, as compared with participants and critics. The theorist tends to be interested in generalizations at the highest level of abstraction he can achieve, whereas participants and critics tend to be interested in making decisions or judgments about one very particular and unique act.

Perhaps the most important single characteristic of rhetoric is that it is a matrix of complex and interrelated variables of the kind discussed in this paper. The theorist cannot meaningfully pluck from the system any single variable and hope to understand it apart from the others. How can one understand style, for example, without knowing how it interrelates with power structure, with distance, with attitudes and ideologies, with the demands of format and context—in short, with every other dimension of the act? Gross generalizations about stylistic characteristics which ignore the assumption that style functions very differently when placed in different combinations with the other variables simply will not do. Unfortunately for the prognosis of theo-

---

[29] Two recent books which display a contextual orientation to rhetoric are Wallace Fotheringham, *Perspectives on Persuasion* (Boston, 1966) and Huber W. Ellingsworth and Theodore Clevenger, Jr., *Speech and Social Action* (Englewood Cliffs, N. J., 1967).

retical advances in rhetoric, the combinations and permutations of the alternatives afforded by the various dimensions are so many as to approach infinity. But methods will have to be developed to pursue the sort of interrelational kind of analysis which an adequate theory of rhetoric requires.[30]

The practitioner may use such an interrelational analysis before, during, and after a transaction as a guide to the decisions he must make to give himself the best chance of interacting with others as he wishes.

The critic may profitably identify the single most compelling dimension of a rhetorical act under consideration and then investigate how that dimension interrelates with others which appear to be relevant. For example, a critic studying Nikita Khrushchev's interaction with the American public during his 1959 visit to this country might focus primary attention on Khrushchev's reduction of interpersonal distance between himself and his hosts in order to see how his distance-reducing rhetoric related to new American images of Khrushchev personally along liking and power dimensions; to his attempts to make attitudes and ideologies consubstantial; and to his use of various rhetorical situations for these functions. If a critic accepts the fundamental premise that each rhetorical act or process is unique, that dimensions interrelate in a way to create a unity never achieved in the past or in the future, then he commits himself to a search for a new way to select, structure, and weigh dimensions for each new act he criticizes.

My hope is that the dimensions described in this essay may provide a framework for theoretical development, practical decision-making, and critical analysis.

---

[30] Warren Weaver has argued that science must "make a third great advance which must be even greater than the nineteenth-century conquest of problems of simplicity or the twentieth-century victory over problems of disorganized complexity. Science must, over the next fifty years, learn to deal with these problems of organized complexity." See "Science and Complexity," in *The Scientist Speaks,* ed. Warren Weaver (New York, 1945), p. 7. Implicit in my essay is the belief that rhetoric represents a problem of "organized complexity."

21 ON SYSTEMS OF RHETORIC

DOUGLAS EHNINGER

Along with Otis Walter, Ehninger is urging pluralism in the study of
rhetoric. We should speak of rhetorics, plural, rather than rhetoric,
singular, when discussing theoretical systems that attempt to explain
practical discourse. The distinctive culture, philosophy, or psychology
of an era or nation may foster a distinctive rhetorical theory. (See
also Robert T. Oliver, *Culture and Communication,* chaps. 7 and 12.)
Consider in what ways Ehninger's analysis both strengthens and
undermines Wayne Brockriede's search for a monistic rhetorical
theory. Note, for example, Ehninger's comments on form and content
in a theory of rhetoric.

Ehninger contends that "a rhetoric which conceives of truth as a
transcendent entity . . . automatically rules itself out as an instrument
for doing the practical work of the world." To some degree, Richard
M. Weaver's view of rhetoric presents such a stance of Platonic
idealism. Would you agree with Ehninger's criticism?

Ehninger also argues that a concern for the ethics of communication is a mark of any sound rhetoric. Do you agree? The following
essays by Eubanks and Baker and by Wallace focus on such an issue:
To what extent must an ethic of rhetoric be an integral part of any
theory or philosophy of rhetoric?

Source: Philosophy and Rhetoric, 1 (Summer 1968), 131–144. Reprinted with
permission of the author and the publisher.

I

In this paper I shall be concerned with rhetorical systems as systems.
A rhetoric I define as an organized, consistent, coherent way of
talking about practical discourse in any of its forms or modes. By practical discourse I mean discourse, written or oral, that seeks to inform,
evaluate, or persuade, and therefore is to be distinguished from discourse that seeks to please, elevate, or depict. An organized, consistent,
coherent way of talking about something, in line with my present pur-

Parts of this paper constitute a modified and expanded version of ideas first forward in "On Rhetoric and Rhetorics," *Western Speech,* Vol. XXXI, 1967, pp. 242–249.

pose, I call a system. In this sense, not only the rhetoric embodied in a single treatise, but also the rhetoric embodied collectively in the treatises of a given place or period constitutes a system, and may be spoken of as such.

In the remarks that follow I shall be concerned with the second of these possibilities. Specifically, I shall attempt to describe the rhetorics of three historical periods in terms broad enough to exhibit their essential characteristics as systems, and then to suggest certain practical uses of an analysis conducted at this level.

It would be naive to suppose that in the characterizations I offer it will be easy to walk a line between the obvious on the one side and the disputable or false on the other. Nor do I expect that the formulations I advance or the inferences I draw will escape criticism. Because not all of the rhetorical treatises of a period fall into a mold, an attempt to treat that period as a system means that one must select from diverse possibilities the trends and emphases that are dominant. Because any one treatise, insofar as it pretends to completeness, is a complex construct, involving a delicate balance among ethical, aesthetic, semantic, and pragmatic elements, attempts to fit it into a pattern inevitably invite refutation by the citation of isolated passages.

But while the hazards are sizable the rewards beckon. Unlike microscopic sightings, which atomize and divide, a macroscopic view extending over an entire genus of treatises submerges differences and details so as to call forth the common characteristics of rhetorical systems as organized wholes—the parts of which they are composed, the joints at which they are articulated, and the weaknesses to which they are prone.

Of these advantages, however, I shall speak further in the final section of this paper. Initially, I turn to the task of characterizing the rhetorics of three historical periods in terms broad enough to display their common nature as systems. I chose as case studies for my investigation what I regard as the three crucial eras in the development of Western rhetorical thought—the classical period, the late eighteenth century, and the period extending from the early 1930's to the present time.

II

The rhetoric of the classical period arose out of a two-fold problem or need.

First, with the development of democratic institutions in the city states of Sicily and Greece, speechmaking as an activity found new avenues of expression and gained in importance until it came to be regarded as an art form as well as a social instrument. What was this phenomenon upon which men depended for the making of laws, the administration of justice, and the honoring of heroes? What was the essential nature of the speech act? Of what parts did this act consist? Upon what faculties or arts did it depend? How could it systematically be described and talked about? And, second, how could proficiency in the important business of performing this speech act be taught in a society where every man must act as his own lawyer and his own legislator? How might instruction in speechmaking be methodized and imparted to the masses?

These two needs, as limited and shaped by the social and intellectual milieu in which the new activity of speechmaking found itself, were the decisive factors in determining the nature of the classical rhetoric. Because this rhetoric operated in an aural world it became the art or science of oral rather than of written discourse. Because its principal functions were to argue the relative merits of laws and policies and to attack or defend from attack in the courtroom, it became primarily the art of persuasion. Because skill in speaking had to be imparted to the masses rhetoric was written with an eye to easy prescription and stressed the development of mechanical or "artificial" procedures and routines. Because speaking was regarded as a fine art as well as a practical tool, rhetoric was given both aesthetic and pragmatic dimensions.

But while all of these properties and others must be recognized in a full description of the classical rhetoric, the one characteristic which perhaps most adequately distinguishes it as a system is its basically grammatical nature. For, without denying other achievements, it still must be said that the central concern and principal contribution of the classical rhetoric were the development of the syntax of the speech act—the delineating and naming of the parts of that act and the tracing of the permutations and combinations of which these parts permit. And this emphasis is entirely understandable. Before the classical writers could consider the pragmatic or aesthetic aspects of speechmaking, they first had to determine what the act of speaking entailed and to devise a grammar for talking about its parts and their relationships.

The work of the classical rhetoricians in devising such a grammar was admirable. So well, indeed, did they perform this task that even today any system of rhetoric which fails to encompass the basic terms and relationships which they isolated is properly regarded as incomplete. They defined or located the speech act itself in two important ways: first, methodologically, by distinguishing rhetoric from grammar, logic, and poetic; and second, substantively, by exploring the relations rhetoric bears to politics and ethics. They divided the speech act into its functional parts of speaker, speech, and audience-occasion, and speculated upon the relative importance of each of these parts in determining the success of the whole. They distinguished among the kinds or types of speeches which they found in the world about them —the legislative, judicial, and epideictic—and described the characteristic uses of each. They recognized the various arts or "offices" upon which oral communication depends—invention, disposition, style, memory, and delivery—and they assigned a specific function to each. As sub-classifications within the various *officia,* they devised vocabularies for discussing types of proofs, characters of style, and the parts of a speech. And, finally, they arranged this grammar into a pattern which permitted its easy acquisition by the aspiring student.

But while as a grammatically centered and pedagogically oriented system the classical rhetoric had strengths, its focus on grammar and pedagogy also made for weaknesses.

First, in their desire to draw lines between phenomena which by nature blend into another—to divide, compartmentalize, and name— the ancients gave if not a false, at least a painfully oversimplified picture of the relationships between invention and disposition and invention and style. Indeed, save perhaps in the case of delivery—and even here modern studies in paralanguage give grounds for doubt—the divisions among all the *officia* tend to be artificial rather than real.

Second, in their desire to render the art of speaking teachable, and teachable to the average man, the classical writers were led to depend too much on preprocessed materials and modes of expression; to reduce to formula or routine, matters inherently incapable of such reduction; to provide, as in the *status* and the topics, purely "artificial" substitutes for knowledge and cogitation—substitutes which by converting *noesis* to rote might equalize individual differences in industry and ability.

Third, and most important, in their emphasis upon the speech act as such and hampered by the primitive psychology and epistemology with which they worked, as a group the classical writers tended either to scant or to present a patently naive account of the relation between the speech act and the mind of the listener.

III

Whereas the rhetoric of the classical period was basically "grammatical" in nature, the rhetoric of the period we now are to examine is best described as "psychological." For it was the major contribution of the "new British rhetoric" of the later eighteenth century, as embodied principally in such works as Lord Kames' *Elements of Criticism* (1761), John Ogilvie's *Philosophical and Critical Observations* (1774), George Campbell's *Philosophy of Rhetoric* (1776), and Joseph Priestley's *Lec-*

tures on Oratory and Criticism (1777), that it corrected the major deficiency of the classical system by working out a series of detailed statements concerning the relation between the communicative act and the mind of the listener-reader.

And here, too, the new emphasis or interest arose in response to a felt need and was shaped by the environment in which that need emerged. For as Locke and his successors among the British empiricists began to develop more sophisticated systems of psychology and epistemology, not only did the ancients' lack of attention to the message-mind relationship seem a more glaring deficiency, but many of the traditional assumptions concerning how men know or are persuaded no longer were acceptable.

So far as the student of rhetorical systems is concerned, it is immaterial that most of the doctrines which the new rhetoricians chose as groundings for their work—the faculty and associational psychologies, the common sense philosophy, and the like—no longer are fashionable. What is important is that, taking these doctrines as premises, the British rhetoricians of the period worked out a more sophisticated statement of the message-mind relationship than had hitherto been possible, and that here again the statement was shaped by the environment in which the need arose.

In their effort to carry rhetoric beyond the grammar of the speech act, with its attendant pedagogical rules and cautions—to bring it, as Campbell said, to a "new country" where rules might be validated by checking them against those principles of the human understanding from whence they sprang[1]—the architects of the new system gave rhetoric an epistemological rather than a grammatical or a logical starting point. Instead of approaching rhetoric through an analysis of what might be said on behalf of a cause, as had the ancients, they approached it through an analysis of the mind of the listener-reader, premising their doctrine upon assumptions concerning the ways in which men come to know what they know, believe what they believe, and feel what they feel. From such an analysis, they assumed, the radical principles of rhetoric could be inferred and, as Campbell said, validated. In short, whereas the ancients had built a subject- or substance-centered rhetoric, the eighteenth-century theorists built an audience-centered one. They classified speeches in terms of the effect the speaker sought to produce upon his listener—"to enlighten the understanding, to please the imagination, to move the passions, or to influence the will."[2] They categorized proofs according to the ways in which listeners come to believe—by experience, analogy, testimony,

[1] George Campbell, *The Philosophy of Rhetoric*, ed. Lloyd Bitzer (Carbondale, Ill., 1963), p. li.
[2] *Ibid.*, p. 1.

and the calculation of chances.[3] They fused the traditional areas of invention and arrangement into the broader concept of the conduct or "management" of a discourse and included in this rubric all of the grosser resources, both substantive and methodological, by which the listener could be persuaded.[4] They rejected the view that rhetoric is a "counterpart" of dialectic or logic, and declared it to be an "off-shoot" of logical studies. Then, with rhetoric dependent upon logic for its routines of analysis and proof, they took the bold step of ruling the tasks of search and discovery entirely out of the art, and of substituting in their stead a new doctrine of invention conceived of as the framing and use of proofs that had previously been derived.[5]

How shall we evaluate this "new" rhetoric? Although now largely dated, there can be little question, I think, but that on the whole it was a remarkable achievement and represented a level of sophistication not envisioned by the ancients. At the same time, however, it is equally clear that this new system, as had the classical rhetoric, suffered from too intense a preoccupation with one aspect of the communication spectrum. While the ancients had focused on the grammar of the speech act at the expense of exploring how that act is related to the listener, so the eighteenth-century writers focused on the speaker-listener relationship at cost of developing an improved grammar of the act itself. Consequently, as in the case of Priestley,[6] they gave the traditional concepts new tortured meanings, or like Campbell they accepted the ancient grammar and buried it in their works—de-emphasized it until the parts of the speech act and the arts or offices upon which the act depends tended to lose identity as discrete units.

Even more important, however, in their preoccupation with the message-mind relationship the architects of the "new" rhetoric gave insufficient attention to another vital dimension of a complete and rounded theory of communication. And this is the role that practical discourse plays in society—the function it performs and should perform in promoting social cohesion and exercising social control.

In two different senses the "new" rhetoric of the eighteenth century was almost entirely an armchair construct—a product of the study rather than of the forum. First, it was largely unrelated to and uninterested in speaking and writing as they existed in the world about it. It was a hypothetical or "if, then" rhetoric—a self-contained theoretical

[3] Ibid., pp. 50–58. Cf. Richard Whately, Elements of Rhetoric, ed. Douglas Ehninger (Carbondale, Ill., 1963), pp. 46–108.
[4] Hugh Blair, Lectures on Rhetoric and Belles Lettres, ed. Harold Harding, 2 vols. (Carbondale, Ill., 1965), II, 127–155, etc.
[5] Whately, pp. 4, 35–167 passim.
[6] Joseph Priestley, Lectures on Oratory and Criticism, ed. Vincent M. Bevilacqua and Richard Murphy (Carbondale, Ill., 1965), Lectures, II–IV, VI–VII, etc.

study which might equally well exist if actual discourses never were or never had been composed. Campbell, who in the *Philosophy* defends the study of "eloquence" on the ground that it furnishes the quickest, surest, and pleasantest way to knowledge of the human mind, reserves most of his practical advice on speaking for the strangely unphilosophical *Lectures on Systematic Theology and Pulpit Eloquence* (1807). Joseph Priestley regards his *Lectures on Oratory* as a practical illustration of the associational psychology of David Hartley.[7] And Hugh Blair, by allying rhetoric with *belles lettres,* places that discipline at the service of the critic as well as of the speaker or writer.[8]

Finally, and more briefly, as one might imagine of a system that largely predates the development of experimental techniques of investigation and verification, the "new" rhetoric was armchair in the sense that for the most part it consisted of inferences drawn from premises based upon intuition or common sense.

IV

The third and last of the period systems we are to examine extends from the early 1930's to the present time, and encompasses developments which, for the most part, have occurred here in the United States.

If the classical rhetoric may be characterized as "grammatical" and the "new" rhetoric of the eighteenth century as "psychological," the rhetoric of our third period may best be described as "social" or "sociological." For while as a system contemporary rhetoric is unusually complex and embraces many specialized strands of interest, all of these strands find unity in the fact that at bottom they view rhetoric as an instrument for understanding and improving human relations.

Like systems of the past, the contemporary system arises out of a felt need and is shaped by the intellectual and social milieu in which rhetoric today finds itself. And here the need is simple but compelling. From the personal to the national and international levels tensions and breakdowns in human relations now, as never before, may result not only in maladjusted personalities or in misunderstanding among individuals, but in depressions, wars, and the suicide of the race itself.

Under such circumstances it is natural that rhetoric as a form of verbal interaction among persons and groups should be concerned with the part it can play in promoting human understanding and in improving the processes by which man communicates with man.

This motive is reflected in the thinking of Kenneth Burke who argues

[7] *Ibid.,* Preface, p. i.
[8] See Blair, *Lectures* XX–XXIV, XXXV–XLVII *passim.*

that because language is symbolic action rhetorical analysis can throw light upon human relations and motives generally, while rhetoric as a social force arising out of an atmosphere of divisiveness can promote consubstantiality and peace through the process of identification.[9] Similarly, it underlies I. A. Richard's definition of rhetoric as a study of the causes and remedies of misunderstanding and accounts for his interest in metaphor and in "comprehending."[10]

Proponents of group discussion, under the influence of Dewey's instrumentalism and the explorations of the group dynamists, seek to implement the ideal of improved human relations by developing a specialized rhetoric of reflective problem solving. Students of communication theory, influenced by the terminology and insights of the electronics engineers, believe that an understanding of transmission systems will help to eliminate many of the blockages that occur when man speaks to man. The General Semanticists profess to find in a neuter or feckless mode of communication a cure for many of the world's social ills. Writers on argument, aware that traditional proof patterns are inapplicable to disputes on moral issues, seek a logic of "ought propositions," drawn with a particular eye to the problems of "conflict resolution."

But these workers and others throughout the broad field of contemporary rhetoric do not find unity only in their concern with the social aspects of improved communication. They are bound still more closely together by their common belief that at the root of many of the misunderstandings which impair or block communications are man's language and his habits of using and abusing it—a conviction bolstered by the growing realization that language is not a pliable medium which through struggle may be molded to one's will, but rather is itself a shaping force which goes far toward determining how man will conceive of himself and of his world.

Therefore, while the ancients centered principally upon methods for analyzing the substance or subject matter of a "cause" and while the eighteenth-century framers of the "new" rhetoric emphasized the message-mind relationship, contemporary writers find a locus of interest in language as the vehicle by which the message is transmitted. Beyond this, however, they recognize that while language is the central instrument of human communication, other symbol systems, some of which lie beneath the sender's or receiver's threshold of awareness, also may carry messages which influence thought or behavior.

This new focus, no less than the ones which preceded it, has had both desirable and undesirable results. The encompassment within

[9] Kenneth Burke, A Rhetoric of Motives (New York, 1950), pp. xiv–xv.
[10] I. A. Richards, The Philosophy of Rhetoric (New York, 1936), pp. 3, 89–138; Speculative Instruments (Chicago, 1955), pp. 17–38.

rhetoric of appeals which are at least partially "unconscious"[11] has extended the traditional range of that science, and in so doing has provided a more comprehensive picture of the role which rhetorical forces play in promoting social cohesion and effecting social control. On the other hand, since this extension carried to its fullest would render any stimulus-response situation rhetorical, rhetoric is in danger of losing its identity as a discrete discipline. Indeed, even today it is moot to dispute whether one may with profit talk of a rhetoric of clothes, or of social status, or, for that matter, of a rhetoric of the spotlight.[12]

And, second, the current interest in vehicles of message transmission, coupled with the premium which quantitative studies in communication research place upon ever more effective transmission, threatens the concern which a sound rhetoric should have for message content and for the ethical and aesthetic dimensions of communication. If a rhetoric is to pretend to completeness, it must be concerned not only with means, but with ends. Besides asking what does communicate and persuade, it must ask what should persuade and what that which persuades should persuade to. Moreover, because at bottom ethical and pragmatic considerations are inseparable from the problem of form, a complete rhetoric also must have an aesthetic dimension.

If, then, as there is reason to suspect, the present emphasis on the vehicle of transmission may threaten the integrity of rhetoric as a bounded discipline or impair those relations which guarantee its character as a humane subject, it may be well in the future to watch this development with more than ordinary care.

V

As I remarked at the outset, this paper has two purposes: (1) to attempt to describe the rhetorics of three periods in terms broad enough to exhibit their essential characteristics as systems, and (2) to suggest some of the uses of an analysis conducted at this level. Having described the three rhetorics, I now inquire into the uses which such analysis may have.

First, I would argue that attempts to characterize the rhetorics of various places or periods at the systems level are useful because they

[11] See Kenneth Burke, "Rhetoric—Old and New," *Journal of General Education,* V (April 1951), 203. "If I had to sum up in one word the difference between the 'old' rhetoric and a 'new' (a rhetoric reinvigorated by fresh insights which the 'new' sciences contributed to the subject), I would reduce it to this: The key term for the old rhetoric was 'persuasion' and its stress was upon deliberate design. The key term for the new rhetoric would be 'identification,' which can include a partially 'unconscious' factor in appeal."

[12] See Donald C. Bryant, "Rhetoric: Its Function and Scope," *Quarterly Journal of Speech,* XXXIX (December 1953), 405.

introduce a healthy and much needed relativism into studies still too much dominated by the notion of the classical rhetoric as a preferred archetype from which all departures are greater or lesser aberrations.

As our survey has suggested, the collective rhetorics of a period, as well as the rhetoric embodied in a single treatise, are time- and culture-bound. Systems of rhetoric arise out of a felt need and are shaped in part by the intellectual and social environment in which the need exists. No matter how sound internally or how imposing architecturally a given system may be—no matter how much its ethical or aesthetic groundings may arouse our admiration—to regard it as a universally applicable paradigm is to overlook a fundamental fact concerning the very nature of rhetoric.

From this it follows that the continuing dialogue on the question, What is rhetoric? except as an academic exercise, is largely profitless. If there is no one generic rhetoric which, like a Platonic Idea, is lurking in the shadows awaiting him who shall have the acuteness to discern it, the search for a defining quality can only end in error or frustration. It would serve the cause of rhetorical studies in general, I think, if instead of continuing this dialogue we openly adopted the plural of the noun and spoke of the history or theory of "rhetorics."

But more important than any reform in notation which might be effected by the laying of the one-rhetoric myth is the fact that a view which allows for many rhetorics rather than a single preferred one pointedly reminds us that in the final analysis the worth of a rhetorical system cannot be divorced from pragmatic considerations. It cannot be merely good or bad; it must be good or bad for something. Abstractly considered, a system geared to the Platonic ideal of communicating truth in order to make men better is to be ranked above one devoted to the ornamenting of language or the tricks of persuasion, and without doubt every "good" rhetoric has as its ultimate purpose the communication of "truth." But, at the same time, a rhetoric which conceives of truth as a transcendent entity and requires a perfect knowledge of the soul as a condition for its successful transmittal automatically rules itself out as an instrument for doing the practical work of the world, and for this reason is less preferable than a system geared to the communication of contingent truths as estalished by probable rather than apodeictic proofs. In short, the problem of evaluating a rhetoric is a complex one, calling for a delicate balancing of the ideal with the utilitarian and for a precarious adjustment of ends to means. A study of rhetorical systems as systems, I believe, may contribute to our understanding of this fact.

Second, I would contend that analysis of the sort here attempted is useful because it helps to clarify the roles which form and substance play in the creation of a rhetoric. Our discussion appears to show that while the form a rhetoric assumes is a joint product of need and environment, its content or subject matter in each case is supplied by all or some of the constituents of the communication process. Indeed, if a system of rhetoric did not have these constituents as its subject matter, it would not be a system of rhetoric but a system of another sort.

Because systems of rhetoric share in part or in whole the same content or substance, no matter how much they vary in form or purpose they have inescapable elements of commonality. Therefore, looked at from one point of view they are different rather than alike, while from another they are alike rather than different. It is, I suggest a failure on the part of the disputants to make clear how they are viewing a rhetoric which lies at the basis of the wearisome controversy concerning the classical or non-classical orientation of the rhetorics of George Campbell or Kenneth Burke.[13] In any event, by making their respective points of view clear, the parties to this argument almost certainly could narrow the area of dispute.

Third, analysis of rhetorics at the systems level, I believe, is useful because it directs attention to the dangers and difficulties involved in constructing a rhetoric. And surely this information in helpful both in evaluating systems of the past and in building systems to meet the changing needs of the future.

Because even by the loose definition adopted here a system is an organized and coherent way of looking at something, unless an account of the communication process has a distinctive emphasis or focus—is ordered in terms of a hierarchy of ends and is marked by a distinguishing method—it is not a system but a random collection of observations and precepts. And yet it would appear from our discussion that emphasis in one direction may lead to unwarranted deemphasis in another. For if the classical rhetoric focused on the grammar of the speech act at the expense of exploring the message-minded relationship, and if the "new" rhetoric of the eighteenth century emphasized this relationship at the cost of advancing the grammar of the act, so the concern of contemporary theorists with the vehicle of transmission and its more efficient use threatens to detract interest from the crucial problem of message content.

In a different vein, our analysis underscores the fact that he who would construct a rhetoric of any sort must draw lines and erect boundaries where in fact none exist, and hence to this extent always must give an unreliable account of the territory and processes he attempts to map. On at least two counts practical discourse resists

---

[13] See, for example, Douglas McDermott, "George Campbell and the Classical Tradition," *Quarterly Journal of Speech*, XLIX (December 1963), 403–409.

systematizing. First, human communication itself is a process—a fluid, on-going, circular movement without a definite beginning, middle, or end. In order to talk about communication at all not only must one arbitrarily slice off a segment of the whole, but he must momentarily stop or freeze motion within this segment, thus imposing a false stasis upon a kinetic phenomenon. And, second, discourse resists systematizing for the quite different reason that the several arts or skills upon which writing or speaking depend cannot be compartmentalized. Style glides imperceptibly into invention on the one hand and disposition on the other, while memory, as Ramus suggested,[14] is dependent on both, and invention and disposition, as the formulary rhetoric recognized, may perform interchangeable functions.[15] It is, I think, no exaggeration to say that a system of rhetoric never has and that very probably none ever will satisfactorily solve the foregoing problems.

And finally under this head, an analysis on the systems level confirms that while a distinctive grammar must lie at the basis of every rhetorical system a narrow focus upon grammar is the least healthy and productive way of regarding rhetoric. Because rhetorical concepts may profitably be divided into only a limited number of parts and usefully combined or arranged in only a limited number of ways, after these possibilities have been exhausted innovation must consist of pointless elaborations and refinements. Hence, with the passage of time the distinctions drawn by a grammatically oriented rhetoric tend to become needlessly minute, its rules are multiplied beyond warrant, and ever growing areas of doctrine are reduced to formula and routine.[16] If rhetoric is to have status as a humane discipline, clearly it must develop its psychological and social dimensions. In proportion as it does so, however, our analysis also indicates that rhetoric may become a challenging and illuminating field for study—one worthy of attention by the best minds of an age. The great rhetorical systems of the past and present stand as testimony to this fact.

Fourth and last, I would argue the usefulness of examining rhetorics as systems for what such study may suggest concerning a possible metasystem of rhetorics and the promise which this metasystem holds for the future. For as our analysis suggests—and I believe an examina-

---

[14] See *P. Rami Scholarum Dialecticarum, seu Animadversionum in Organum Aristotelis, libri XX*, Recens emendati per Joan. Piscatorem Argentinensem (Frankfurt, 1581), p. 593.
[15] See Wilbur Samuel Howell, *Logic and Rhetoric in England, 1500–1700* (Princeton, N. J., 1956), pp. 138–145.
[16] Besides the excessive refinements worked by the classical rhetoricians in the areas of invention and disposition, the sixteenth-century rhetoric of style may be taken as an example of this tendency; for this rhetoric, in its concern to distinguish and name all possible deviations from the normal and usual patterns of expression, was no less grammatical in nature than was the routinized rhetoric of the ancients.

tion of additional systems would confirm—while in one sense the major rhetorics of the Western world may properly be described as revolutionary, in another sense they may perhaps be regarded as evolutionary. Although each of the systems we have examined overthrew the premise or starting point of its predecessor for a premise that was radically different and distinctively its own, it also appears that in each case the new starting point not only corrected a deficiency in the preceding system but encompassed that system to pass beyond it. Just as the "new" rhetoric of the eighteenth century, though it accepted much of the classical grammar, raised its sights above the grammatical to develop an account of the message-mind relationship, so contemporary theorists accept the crucial position which this relationship must occupy in a fruitful rhetoric, and entertain the still broader purpose of exploring the social significance of the communication act in all its forms and uses.

Whether in the long view all major systems of rhetoric tend to correct deficiencies in their predecessors and to pass beyond them is a complex question, and one which cannot be divorced from a careful consideration of the social and intellectual environment in which each system arises. It would seem, however, that through the ages, and despite occasional setbacks, rhetorics have constantly become both richer in content and more embracing in scope. Perhaps the central lesson to be learned from an analysis of the rhetorics of various periods considered as systems is that while the final word on rhetorics never has and probably never will be said, there is reason for optimism concerning the future of rhetoric as a discipline—reason to believe that as man's knowledge grows and his attempts to talk about practical discourse in a coherent and consistent fashion improve, rhetorics ever will become more penetrating and more fruitful.

22 TOWARD AN AXIOLOGY OF RHETORIC

RALPH T. EUBANKS
VIRGIL BAKER

One view of rhetoric sees its central function in a message source advising an audience by demonstrating good reasons for a specific choice among probable alternatives. Rhetoric aims at influencing human conduct. Choices among rhetorical means and ends necessitate standards of values and ethics. Eubanks and Baker advocate such a view. "The central function of rhetoric," for them, "is to crystallize and transmit human values, the 'what-fors' of a culture." They argue that "rhetoric must become boldly axiological, seeking out and committing itself to a sound system of civilizing values." Such a conception of rhetoric could easily apply to any rhetorical theory in any culture; whatever the nature of a specific culture, a rhetorical theory within that culture should be axiological.

But from their general position they move to urging that a contemporary theory of rhetoric be committed to a specific value system, namely the eight goal-values classified by Lasswell and Kaplan. Hence Eubanks and Baker are prescriptive in their view; they urge adoption of a designated value system as the axiological content of rhetoric. See Baker and Eubanks, *Speech in Personal and Public Affairs*, chaps. 6 and 7; Eubanks, "Nihilism and the Problem of a Worthy Rhetoric," *Southern Speech Journal*, XXXIII (Spring 1968), 187–199. For a different axiological view of rhetoric, see Parke Burgess, "The Rhetoric of Moral Conflict: Two Critical Dimensions," *Quarterly Journal of Speech*, LVI (April 1970), 120–130.

Consider the nature of your own viewpoint. Should teachers of rhetoric specify the value content of rhetorical theory or should they simply urge that a rhetorical theory must reflect value assumptions and that rhetorical practice must utilize value premises?

Source: Quarterly Journal of Speech, XLVII (April 1962), 157–168. Reprinted with permission of the authors and the publisher.

"What I relate," Nietzsche wrote near the close of the nineteenth century, "is the history of the next two centuries. I describe what is coming, what can no longer come differently: the advent of nihilism."[1]

[1] Friedrich Nietzsche, *The Will to Power*, Preface.

This passage is prescient when considered in the light of the deepening moral crisis of modern man, who finds it increasingly hard to accept his world as one of history and action and to distinguish and choose between better and worse. One of the most poignant truths of the present human situation is its axiological impotence. Introducing a recent symposium on human values, Abraham Maslow wrote: "The ultimate disease of our time is valuelessness."[2] More than a decade ago in a study of the moral decay of the West, Richard M. Weaver warned: "We approach a condition in which we shall be amoral without the capacity to perceive it and degraded without means to measure our descent."[3] Modern man's present state of anhedonia is, without question, "more crucially dangerous than ever before in history."[4] It may be his finest fortune not to have lost completely his power to perceive the extent of his moral affliction.

Multiplying signs show his deepening concern. New lines of research have been recently opened in the field of value theory; hopeful minds from diverse academic disciplines are searching for ways of helping twentieth-century man regain his axiological health.[5] We are inspired to believe that modern man may yet make—to use Arnold J. Toynbee's terms of cultural rise and fall—a corporate "response" to the "challenge" that faces him.

This epochal challenge holds special pertinence to liberal education in general and to rhetorical education in particular. Each derives its *raison d'etre* from its potential for helping man with the related questions of whether he shall be free of the forces that work to brutalize him and, if so, how he shall use his "burden of freedom." Both are thus centrally and persistently concerned with human values, here taken to mean universal concepts basic to civil decision and action. Human values are therefore the ultimate ground of human action; they are also a concomitant of human freedom. Since man can "transcend" through consciousness an objective situation of which he is a part, he can have a hand in shaping his destiny by the "exercise of choice based on values."[6] In a nutshell, man can have freedom only because he has

[2] Abraham Maslow (ed.), *New Knowledge in Human Values* (New York, 1959), p. vii.

[3] Richard M. Weaver, *Ideas Have Consequences* (Chicago, 1948), p. 10.

[4] Maslow, p. vii.

[5] In addition to Maslow, the following studies illustrate some of the new lines of investigation in value theory: Clyde Kluckhohn, et al., "Values and Value-Orientations in the Theory of Action," in *Toward a General Theory of Action*, ed. Talcott Parsons and Edward A. Shils (Cambridge, Mass., 1951), pp. 388–433; Charles Morris, *Varieties of Human Value* (Chicago, 1956); Dewitt H. Parker, *The Philosophy of Value* (Ann Arbor, 1957); Otto von Mering, *A Grammar of Human Values* (Pittsburgh, 1961); and P. Sorokin (ed.), *Symposium: Forms and Techniques of Altruistic and Spiritual Growth* (Boston, 1954).

[6] Walter A. Weisskopf, "Existence and Values," in Maslow, pp. 108–109.

a scheme of values; he is—as Joseph Wood Krutch called him—"The Animal Which Can Prefer."[7]

The tradition of liberal education has been one of deep involvement with the issue of how man may best use his freedom. Historically its mission has been to develop the whole man, to prepare men, in Milton's words, "to perform justly, skilfully, and magnanimously, all the offices, both private and public, of peace and war."[8] Yet ironically, when the "great society" most needs the help of liberal education in solving its problems of value, the liberal arts colleges are found to be in disintegration. They are boldly charged with having forsaken their mission. Writes one critic: "They have to a large extent abandoned their ancient and honorable task of training young people to live informed, intelligent, and integrated lives. They seem to have forgotten the admonition of Montaigne that 'the object of education is to make, not a scholar, but a man.' "[9] Ironically too, the ideal teacher of the times appears to be one whose work is animated by the spirit of determinism and amorality. "For a half century," observes the president of Boston College, Michael Walsh, "educators have been avoiding the problems of teaching values and *teachers have been priding themselves in their ability to employ a rhetoric of non-commitment.*"[10] American liberal education has thus neglected its crucial responsibility for transmitting knowledge about and faith in abiding human values—for helping man with the problem of what he will do with his freedom. "At this moment," declares Walsh, "when civilization seems faced with a choice between survival and suicide, [the] responsibility to choose and to declare the values upon which choice is to be based has never been more terrifying or more immediate."[11]

Rhetoric has a vital relevance to the value illnesses of twentieth-century man. Rhetoric is a dynamic force in the nurture of human values; it must therefore find a central place in any plan which claims concern for man's quest for values, and that looks toward the amelioration of man's present state of anhedonia. The basic meaning of rhetoric in the Western tradition, as Duhamel notes, is "the discovery of and persuasion to right action."[12] And "right action" is central in man's value-world, for it places before him the crucial question of how he

[7] Joseph Wood Krutch, *The Measure of Man* (New York, 1954), p. 172.

[8] John Milton, "Of Education."

[9] Earl J. McGrath, *The Graduate School and the Decline of Liberal Education* (New York, 1959), p. vi.

[10] Michael P. Walsh, S.J., "Values in Education," *Vital Speeches*, XXVI (June 15, 1960), 529. Italics supplied. Cf. discussion of the "modern abdication of direct, responsible judgment" in Jacques Barzun, *The House of Intellect* (New York, 1959), pp. 245ff.

[11] Walsh, p. 529.

[12] P. Albert Duhamel, "The Function of Rhetoric as Effective Expression," *Journal of the History of Ideas*, X (June 1949), 356.

shall use his freedom. Behind the proposals and theses of public utterance are value propositions. In a sense, human values are fundamental
in rhetoric. "It is impossible," observes Richard M. Weaver in his
analysis of Plato's *Phaedrus*, "to talk about rhetoric as effective expression without having as a term giving intelligibility to the whole discourse, the Good. . . ."[13] Rhetoric's essential preoccupation, then, is
with abiding human values. Richard Murphy declares pointedly: "The
art of rhetoric is used to express and activate principles we believe in,
the substance of things for which we live."[14] In a word, the central
function of rhetoric is to crystalize and transmit human values, the
"what-fors" of a culture. Put another way, rhetoric is purposive speech
about the human condition.

Yet contemporary rhetorical education, like liberal education, cannot
be said to be discharging fully its responsibility in the realm of human
values. We are painfully aware that teachers of public address do not
always practice a rhetoric commitment. Indeed, as Murphy suggests,
some of them maintain the amorality of rhetoric, taking the ground
that to discriminate among values may lead to their being labeled
"propagandizers."[15] Similarly, rhetorical critics occasionally run out on
their duty to examine and to pass judgment on a speaker's dialectical
and axiological bearings. Barnet Baskerville, noting this slackness, has
pointed out that such a critic offers "the excuse that truth is relative,
that everyone is entitled to his own opinion, and that the rhetorical
critic's task is to describe and evaluate the orator's skill in his craft and
not to become entangled in complex ethical considerations."[16] What
Baskerville describes is pseudo-criticism, which not only contributes
to the dehumanization of rhetoric but also aggravates mankind's
present condition of "valuelessness."

To make rhetoric a more potent power in generating "right action"
it must be related *directly* to important human values. Rhetoric must
become boldly axiological, seeking out and committing itself to a
sound system of civilizing values. Only then can it move out of the
world of "dis-value" and become a positive force for the amelioration
of man's present condition of anhedonia. Only then can it become, in
the fullest meaning of the term, a "rhetoric of commitment." Such a
rhetoric will attain the humanizing function assigned to it in Bacon's
analysis, of "applying reason to the imagination for the better moving
of the will."[17]

[13] Richard M. Weaver, *The Ethics of Rhetoric* (Chicago, 1953), p. 25.
[14] Richard Murphy, "Preface to an Ethic of Rhetoric," *The Rhetorical Idiom,* ed.
Donald C. Bryant (Ithaca, New York, 1958), p. 141.
[15] *Ibid.,* p. 129.
[16] Barnet Baskerville, "Emerson as a Critic of Oratory," *The Southern Speech Journal,*
XVIII (December 1953), 404.
[17] *The Advancement of Learning,* Bk. 2, Sec. XVIII.

Let us try to sketch the broad outlines for an axiological approach to rhetoric. First are presented the critical determinants, the rationale, for such an approach. Second is described a value analysis which may serve as a guide for the planning and conduct of rhetorical discourse. Finally, a set of empirical guides for the teaching of a rhetoric of values is described. Five terms are crucial and therefore need definition. The term *axiology* (from the Greek *axios,* meaning valuable) is used in its usual sense as the study of value phenomena. *Values,* generically defined, are conceptions of the desirable which shape human "action commitments."[18] *Rhetoric* means, comprehensively, "the rationale of informative and suasory discourse."[19] Abstracted from its functional phase, rhetoric also means tendentious speech having to do with man's symbolic universe of value. The term *Justice* is used to mean a social condition of equity fashioned from the commitment of individual persons to the classic ideals of liberty, equality, and fraternity under "a rule of law." *Democracy* refers to any social order which creates and fosters the values and institutions necessary for the fullest development of the individual human being.[20] Democracy is interpreted to mean the common instrumentality of Justice.

1

What, let us first ask, are to be our rational guides in maintaining the essential validity of a rhetoric of values? No attempt is made here to offer an exhaustive analysis; rather, only those propositions which appear most obvious and cogent are presented.

The conception of the central function of rhetoric as enhancement of human values bears the sanction of classical tradition. Analysis of the theory and practice of rhetoric in the ancient Western civilizations clearly shows the basically axiological mission of rhetoric. In Plato's ideal system of rhetoric, the speaker was to have "such a high moral purpose in all his work that he will ever be concerned about saying that which is 'acceptable to God.'"[21] Quite to the point here is Plato's use of the twin themes of love (*eros*) and beauty (*kalos*) in the *Phaedrus* to illuminate the rhetorical motif. In this dialogue, as Richard M.

[18] The definition is based upon the discussions of the meaning of values found in Kluckhohn, pp. 394–396, and Parker, pp. 3–29.

[19] Donald C. Bryant, "Rhetoric: Its Functions and Its Scope," *QJS,* XXXIX (December 1953), 404.

[20] Conceived as polity, *democracy* refers to "a form of government by which the ultimate control of the machinery of government is committed to a numerical majority of the community." John Morley, *Oracles on Man and Government* (London, 1923), p. 29.

[21] Everett Lee Hunt, "Plato and Aristotle on Rhetoric and Rhetoricians," *Studies in Rhetoric and Public Speaking in Honor of James A. Winans* (Ithaca, New York, 1925), p. 38.

Weaver observes, the "noble rhetorician" is "aware of axiological systems that have ontic status."[22]

Aristotle was also sensitive to the connections between the art of rhetoric and men's conceptions of the preferable. His efforts to locate rhetoric in man's universe of knowledge show, for example, his awareness of the axiological character of his topic. In the early pages of *The Rhetoric,* he affirms that "Rhetoric is a kind of offshoot, on the one hand, of Dialectic, and, on the other, of that study of Ethics which may properly be called 'political.' "[23] From this generalization and the exposition immediately following, Aristotle's meaning emerges: rhetoric conjoins argumentative method with ethical theory. Insofar as the popular and probable axioms employed by rhetoric constitute the bases of wise civil decision and action, rhetoric is first, last and always, an axiological pursuit.[24] Aristotle also expresses the aims of each kind of rhetoric in value terms. The ends of deliberative speaking are *expediency* and *inexpediency,* of forensic speaking, *justice* and *injustice,* of epideictic speaking, *honor* and *dishonor.*[25] Still more impressive evidence of Aristotle's realization of the axiological nature of his topic is his preoccupation with the desired and the desirable in his lengthy analysis of the premises from which a speaker must argue in the various kinds of rhetoric.[26]

Especially relevant to our thesis is the pedagogy of Isocrates, who postulated the highest cultural function for the "art of discourse." In the Isocratic system of general education (*paideia*), the axiological motif is evident. Not only must the rhetor concern himself with those causes which are "great and honorable, devoted to the welfare of man and the common good," he should choose from "all the actions of men which bear upon his subject those examples which are most illustrious and most edifying."[27] The Isocratic orator was to be, above all, a student of moral values and duties, of the estimable in human conduct.

Under the strong influence of his Greek predecessors, Cicero kept

[22] Weaver, *Ethics of Rhetoric,* p. 17.

[23] *The Rhetoric of Aristotle,* trans. Lane Cooper (New York, 1932), p. 5. Cooper's interpolation is worthy of note: "With Aristotle, Ethics, the science dealing with individual conduct, shades off into Politics (a broader subject), which deals with the conduct and activities of men in groups—the State."

[24] In this connection it might be noted that while Aristotle insists that as a "faculty" (distinguished from a "science") rhetoric has no subject matter of its own, yet he does devote the bulk of Book I to an analysis of "Goods" as related to public affairs.

[25] Cooper (trans.), pp. 16–18.

[26] Positing *happiness* as the "end which determines what [men] choose and what they avoid," he analyzes the "internal" and "external" Goods (conceptions of the preferable) which lead to happiness. See *Rhetoric 1360ᵇ et passim.*

[27] Isocrates, *Nicocles* 10–13. Cf. Prodicus in Bromley Smith, "Prodicus of Ceos: The Sire of Synonymy," *QJS,* VI (April 1920), 51.

rhetoric in the established tradition. To him the study of rhetoric was the pursuit of humane wisdom. Rhetoric had led men from the brutish to the civilized state.[28] His ideal speaker, the *doctus orator,* was dedicated to the nurture of moral ideals.[29] The "eloquent wisdom" of which Cicero speaks rests upon a study of "virtues" (character values). Advising his son in *De Officiis,* he asserts that a study of the cardinal virtues is essential so that "the relations of man to man in human society may be conserved, and . . . largeness and nobility of soul may be revealed."[30]

The view of rhetoric as a force of social cohesion whose ultimate business is the nurture of moral and political values was continued in Quintilian with his elaboration of a system of rhetorical education for the "good man." In attempting a synthesis of the Classical view, Tacitus wrote: "For them [the ancients] the one thing needful [to the practice of the rhetoric] was to stock the mind with those accomplishments which deal with good and evil, virtue and vice, justice and injustice."[31] In the Classical analysis, then, rhetoric and *axios* were intimately associated. On this point perhaps the final word should go to J. H. Randall, who, in appraising the influence of Aristotle's *Rhetoric,* has written: "It is hardly too much to trace back through Cicero to Aristotle the central conviction running through the whole tradition of literary humanism in medieval and modern times . . . that the study of good writing and good speaking must be indissolubly wedded to the study of good living."[32]

The very logic of rhetorical discourse suggests another determinant for developing an axiological approach to the teaching and practice of rhetoric. The logical function of rhetoric in man's sociocultural universe is the realization of the highest goals of human life, expressible through the concepts of Justice and Order. The concept of Justice synthesizes the classic trinity of democratic ideals, liberty, equality, and fraternity, whose central premise is the essential worthfulness and profound potentialities of the individual human being. Rhetoric, as the method of compulsive address about the human situation, thus joins the instrumentality of democracy toward the realization of a Society of Justice and Order. The broader logic of rhetoric, then, is the maintenance of the conditions necessary to a Society of Justice. But the democratic approach to Justice is the ideal of liberty which opens the door to the realization of latent human possibilities. In a less comprehensive sense, the basic and sweaty burden of rhetoric is the main-

---

[28] *De Inventione* i. 2–3; *De Oratore* i. 33.
[29] *De Oratore* i. 32; ii. 35; iii. 142–143.
[30] *De Officiis* i. 5.
[31] Tacitus, *Dialogue on Oratory* 31.
[32] John H. Randall, Jr., *Aristotle* (New York, 1960), pp. 286–287.

tenance of freedom. The ultimate sanction of freedom, as T. V. Smith has observed, lies in "the very constitutionality of all living forms."[33] Thonssen and Baird have written: "The inviolable logic of [rhetorical] discourse is to secure, safeguard, and preserve liberty."[34] But rhetoric can only achieve its logical end insofar as it is joined effectively to *axios*. Similarly, from the theory of preferential conduct rhetoric draws its potential for helping man decide wisely how he will use the freedom he owns.

We are now in position to affirm our second premise: *The conception of the logical end of rhetoric as the realization of Justice suggests the wisdom of making more direct the association between rhetorical method and axiology.* From such a union a genuinely effective "rhetoric of commitment" can be wrought. For its part, rhetoric supplies the methodology by which man may both discover sound alternatives and urge their adoption. It operates *in* freedom and *for* freedom. "Persuasion involves choice, will," explains Kenneth Burke; "it is directed to man only insofar as he is *free*."[35] If rhetoric has any sort of *special* subject matter province, that substance is constituted in the popular and probable value axioms related to the civil decision making of a free society. Rhetoric and the study of "choice" behavior share a common rootage in the essential nature of being; their common fruit, ideally termed, is the *summum bonum*. "Axiology," observes R. S. Hartman, "puts the spine into democratic ideology. It shows with crystal clarity the infinite and unique value of the human person."[36] Rhetoric, as the great energizer of judgment decisions in public affairs, draws its potency from axiology. Together, axiology and rhetoric may offer some genuine hope for restoration of vitality to man's moral life. Perhaps these are the twin levers with which man, once again, can move his world.

2

With these determinants for a rhetoric of values in mind, let us now (a) consider an instance of a sound, usable value typology, and (b) offer some suggestions for translating the theory into classroom practice.

Since the establishment of a rhetoric of values rests ultimately upon an understanding of values as one of the "available means of persuasion," an accounting of the role of values in human conduct should

[33] T. V. Smith and Eduard C. Lindeman, *The Democratic Way of Life* (New York, 1955), p. 46.
[34] Lester Thonssen and A. Craig Baird, *Speech Criticism* (New York, 1948), p. 472.
[35] Kenneth Burke, *A Rhetoric of Motives* (New York, 1950), p. 50.
[36] R. S. Hartman, "The Science of Value," in Maslow, p. 32.

first be given. Values were earlier defined as "conceptions of the desirable" which shape human "action commitments." In the rhetorical sense, *human values* have been described as logical constructs of the good which provide the bases of civil decision and action. Both definitions will help provide access to a rhetoric of values.

The literature of axiology contains a wealth of knowledge useful to the rhetorician. First of all, values are generally perceived as concepts by which "preferential" conduct is governed. Most discussions of values, regardless of the special field of interest, rest upon a view of the good as not that which is merely desired but rather as that which "ought" to be desired (i.e., the "desirable"). Distinguishing sharply between morally justifiable preference and preference determined by impulse or expediency, Kluckhohn and associates write: "Value is more than mere preference; it is limited to those types of preferential behavior based upon conceptions of the desirable."[37] Again, these conceptions are described generally as sociocultural creations. Human values are indeed—to borrow L. von Bertalanffy's phrase—"symbolic universes" of speech and thought that have been shaped and verified in human history.[38] The concept "culture" is therefore roughly equivalent to the concept "human values." Yet these logical constructs of the preferable are presumed to have a physiological origin. Man's unique symbol-making power enables him to convert the "ergs" of psychobiological "drive" into conceptions of the desirable. Leslie White, the anthropologist, has characterized symbolism itself as "that modification of the human organism which allows it to transform physiological drive into cultural values."[39] Further, man's conceptions of the culturally preferable are normative ("ought") conceptions which come to have great suasive power and regulative strength. In ontological terms, "value is Man's essential being, put as an imperative against him."[40] In whatever verbal form they may be expressed, value statements are hortative in character: they function as "commands." In rhetoric, as Marie Hochmuth Nichols has observed, cultural values are presented as "symbols of authority designed to evoke response."[41] For example, when an American president-elect implores the nation in his Inaugural Address to "ask not what your country can do for you—ask what you

---

[37] Kluckhohn, p. 422. John Dewey, one of the most influential American exponents of the "right" theory of values, perceived genuine good as the resolution of conflict among "incompatible impulses and habits," leading to "an orderly release of actions." See his *Human Nature and Conduct* (New York, 1922), p. 211.

[38] Ludwig von Bertalanffy, "Human Values in A Changing World," in Maslow, p. 68.

[39] Cited in Kluckhohn, p. 401.

[40] Paul Tillich, "Is a Science of Human Values Possible?" in Maslow, p. 195.

[41] Marie K. Hochmuth, "The Criticism of Rhetoric," in Marie K. Hochmuth (ed.), *A History and Criticism of American Public Address* (New York, 1955), III, 17.

can do for your country,"[42] he is exhorting them to honor their *commitment* to the traditional American values, "self-reliance" and "patriotism"—cultural values that are subsumed in still higher goods, *power* and *rectitude*.

Insofar as human values represent in part desirable states to be striven for, some of their suasive force may be accounted for through the highest, or more human, order of motivation. This level of motivation, called by Allport "propriate striving," refers to the goal-seeking, tension-producing level of human behavior as opposed to the lower, or *homeostatic* level, which is characterized by drive-reduction, "opportunistic adjustment," and the maintaining of "steady states" within the organism.[43] Just as ideals contribute immeasurably to the "go" of adult human life, so also do human values. The realm of ideals and the realm of values are, in fact, almost co-extensive. Values are also regulative, functioning to dissuade as well as to persuade. Any culture abounds in symbols of command which serve to "restrain or canalize impulses in terms of wider and more perduring goals."[44]

The suasive potential of human values has not been extensively investigated. One recent study in the field of public address is suggestive, however. Russel Windes, in a rhetorical analysis of Adlai E. Stevenson's 1956 campaign speaking, sought to isolate the rhetorical factors associated with Stevenson's "effective" and "ineffective" efforts. One of the characteristics of the typical "effective" speech—as opposed to the typical "ineffective" speech—was emphasis on "appeals to values rather than needs."[45] To sum up: Human values are doubly important in the highest order of human motivation. Not only do they supply the *criteria* for choosing among alternative courses of conduct, they may also serve as desirable (and possible) *goals* or states that are critical in human transactions beyond the homeostatic level of drive-reduction.

One of the most promising value analyses for making rhetorical education more directly a function of democratic ideology is that formulated by Lasswell. Fashioned around the concept of "power relationships in the social process," this analysis is in the ethico-political tradition. "In the social process," explains Lasswell, *"Man pursues Values through Institutions on Resources."*[46] Lasswell's analysis embraces eight "representative" goal-values which he relates as follows to the "institutions usually specialized to each in our civilization":

[42] John F. Kennedy, "Inaugural Address," *The New York Times,* January 20, 1961.
[43] See Gordon F. Allport, *Becoming: Basic Considerations for a Psychology of Personality* (Yale Paperbound, 1960), pp. 65–68.
[44] Kluckhohn, p. 399.
[45] Russel R. Windes, Jr., "A Study of Effective and Ineffective Presidential Campaign Speaking," *SM,* XXVIII (March 1961), 48.
[46] Harold D. Lasswell, *Power and Personality* (New York, 1948), p. 17.

Value	Institution
Power	Government
Respect	Social class distinction
Affection	Family, friendship
Rectitude	Church, home
Well-being	Hospital, clinic
Wealth	Business
Enlightenment	Research, education
Skill	Occupations[47]

Lasswell and Kaplan have classified these values into two groups: "welfare" values (*well-being, wealth, skill,* and *enlightenment*), and "deference" values (*power, respect, rectitude,* and *affection*). Welfare values are described as "those whose possession to a certain degree is a necessary condition for the maintenance of the physical activity of the person." Deference values, on the other hand, are those that "consist in being taken into consideration in the acts of others and of the self."[48]

Both "welfare" and "deference" values are manifestly important in the life of democratic man. *Well-being* refers to "physical and psychic integrity"; *wealth* means "services of goods and persons accruing to the individual in any way whatever"; *skill* means "proficiency in any practice whatever, whether in arts or crafts, trade or profession"; and *enlightenment* refers to "knowledge, insight, and information concerning personal and cultural relations."[49] Profoundly critical to the good health of a democratic commonwealth are the "deference" values. *Power,* or "participation in the making of decisions," is one of the so-called "democratic variables." Of this goal-value, Lasswell and Kaplan have written: "The concept of power is perhaps the most fundamental in political science: the political process is the shaping, distribution, and exercise of power (in a wider sense, of all the deference values, or of influence in general)."[50] *Affection,* or love, which includes both a reproductive and a productive aspect is the great leavening value of the human enterprise. Writes Maslow: "Love is union with somebody, or something, outside oneself, *under the condition of retaining the separateness and integrity of one's own self.*"[51] The centrality of human love in the life of democratic man is self-evident. Another cardinal democratic goal-value is *rectitude,* or uprightness, which makes possible a just commonwealth built upon a "rule of law." A human—as

---

[47] *Ibid.*
[48] Harold D. Lasswell and Abraham Kaplan, *Power and Society: A Framework for Political Inquiry* (New Haven, Conn., 1950), pp. 55–56.
[49] *Ibid.;* Lasswell, pp. 16–17.
[50] Lasswell and Kaplan, p. 75
[51] Maslow, "Values, Psychology, and Human Existence," p. 153.

distinguished from an inhuman—society is only possible insofar as its members give allegiance to morality. Another important "deference" value in Lasswell's analysis is *respect,* or "the value of status, of honor, recognition."[52]

Lasswell's value typology consists of human values deemed fundamental for a rhetoric of values keyed to the concept of human dignity and to the power relations of a democratic polity. From these eight "master" conceptions of the desirable should flow most of the volitional statements of popular discourse: "We must educate our youth" (*enlightenment*); "Let us seek full employment" (*wealth*), et cetera. The Lasswell typology may thus be viewed as a framework of "demand" symbols from which are drawn the innumerable value-axioms rhetoricians invoke in the shaping and promulgation of policy. This value typology, or a close approximation of it, would seem inevitable for a rhetoric of democratic commitment. It can supply rhetoric with a sound axiology, and also furnishes a motivational analysis, adequate to the planning and conduct of rhetorical discourse.

The Lasswall typology—consisting as it does of those large conceptions of the desirable in a democratic commonwealth—may indeed serve as a substitute for existing motives typologies in a thoroughgoing rhetoric of commitment. Inevitably, the Lasswell formulation would replace those "wants" typologies based on a homeostatic drive-reduction view of human behavior. As demonstrated earlier, values themselves are suasive, functioning as compelling "demand" symbols. But their compulsive quality must also be ultimately associated with a psychobiological origin. As a "needs" typology for a rhetoric of values the Lasswell list combines the "desired" and the "desirable," conjoins "wish" and "ought." Thus, it provides rhetorical motivation with both a cognitive and an affective dimension. And, finally, it offers a motivational formula for rhetorical practice and instruction that combines homeostasis and "propriate striving," tension-reduction and tension-creating.

Adoption of a rhetoric of values alters in a limited, though significant way, the motivational data of contemporary rhetoric. An axiology furnishes another major "means of persuasion," analyzable and usable, to enrich the already abundant literature on attitudes, sentiments, opinion, stereotypes, and attention. It may be made even more effective if wedded to Walter's typology of "motivational situations." Based upon a view of the rhetorical situation as a "problem" situation, the Walter analysis includes five basic motivational situations labeled as the *"Difficulty Situation,"* the *"Goal-Oriented Situation,"* the *"Barrier Situation,"* the *"Threat Situation,"* and the *"Identification Situation."*

---

[52] Lasswell and Kaplan, p. 56.

For each of these "situations" are offered typical "lines of argument" a speaker may use with his audience. The *"topoi"* of Walter's analysis are related to *pathos.*[53] Since these *topoi* concern the choice of alternative paths of conduct, their effectiveness might be enhanced by relating them also to a set of master conceptions of the good.

Manifestly, a rhetoric wedded to axiology must become a more potent force of cultural cohesion. Aberle and associates define a society as "a group of human beings sharing a self-sufficient system of action which is capable of existing longer than the life-span of an individual, the group being recruited at least in part by the sexual reproduction of its members."[54] Preservation of a "self-sufficient system of action" rests in large measure on a society's ability to keep alive those master symbols of demand which inform its decision-making and shape its power relations. Such a rhetoric, preoccupied with humane substance, would bear little resemblance to the hedonistic rhetoric of Plato's *Gorgias,* described by Socrates as a "knack" for "procuring a certain gratification and pleasure."[55] Nor would it resemble the rhetoric of conditioned reflex and cultural regression practiced by the "hidden persuaders" of mid-twentieth-century America.

3

No attempt is made here to draft a full set of empirical guides to the teaching of a rhetoric of democratic values; rather some key suggestions are given for translating the theory into classroom practice.

The teacher of public address must seek first, of course, to reflect in his own classroom conduct the human values for which he contends. Quite obviously, to do so would be to abandon forever the nerveless contention that to become a critic of ideas and values (content) in the classroom is to become a "propagandizer." Other implications are also quite clear. The teacher of a rhetoric of values will find himself immersed in humanistic studies, from which he may learn that the world of human experience must be examined, interpreted, and communicated in terms of some coherent system of human values. In his private life as well as in his public life, he will become vigorously involved in the great Moral Discussion which for three millennia has been carried on continuously in Western civilization. No longer shall he permit himself to be deceived by the facile doctrine of "cultural relativism" which claims that "what is" must be the valid measure of "what ought

[53] Otis M. Walter, "Toward an Analysis of Motivation," *QJS,* XLI (October 1955), 271–278.

[54] D. F. Aberle, *et al.,* "The Functional Prerequisites of a Society," *Ethics,* LX (January 1950), 101.

[55] *Gorgias* 462.

to be." In fine, he shall find himself practicing wisely and proudly—in the grand Western tradition—a "rhetoric of commitment."

In the management of the units of instruction in public address courses, the most obvious opportunities for refashioning lie in the realm of subject and purpose. As a first step, the relationship between the basic general ends of rhetoric and the values of the axiology can be developed. Thus, for example, in the axiology outlined here, the values of *well-being, affection,* and *rectitude* are typically nurtured by the speech *to inspire;* those of *respect and power* by the speech *to convince;* those of *wealth* and *skill* by the speech *to activate;* and the value of *enlightenment* by the speech to inform. The public address teacher may also sensitize his students to the axiological implications of topic and thesis selection, providing them with an abundance of topics and issues which involve them in questions of value. Such topics and issues may be found ready at hand, of course, in the traditional disciplines of art, literature, political science, ethics, religion, and history, and in the realm of contemporary public affairs. If the general aim is to put rhetorical education into the business of helping students make wise choices in the realm of human values with the ultimate goal that of creating human excellence, both public and private, students of rhetoric may also be required to make speeches on the Great Ideas of Western Man. In this connection, we can draw upon the 102 recurring themes of the "Great Conversation," making accessible to our students at least the well-known two-volume *Syntopicon,* if not the whole set, *Great Books of the Western World.* We can also deepen the axiological color of our public address courses by including speaking assignments which may be called "Studies in Greatness." In such assignments, students would be asked to prepare and deliver speeches on great persons in various areas of human endeavor of both the past and the present. In these assignments lies a bright opportunity to teach a genuinely humane rhetoric. As Gerald W. Johnson has written: "We are equal to all that we can understand; and to the extent that we can understand true greatness as it appears in men, and how and why it appears, we have the radiant hope of employing that force to carry us forward, not into a new world, but a new universe of power, beauty, and truth."[56]

If the public address teacher aspires to the development of expositors and persuaders who can speak sanely to the so-called "unsolvable problems" of their own generation, he will miss no opportunity to acquaint them with the substance of the past. He shall remember that rhetorical truth is probable truth which becomes the more trustworthy as it is informed by and developed from the accumulated wisdom of

[56] Gerald W. Johnson, "Emerson's Scholar: A New Chapter in His Biography," *The Key Reporter,* XXIII (July 1958), 3.

mankind. To help the student know and appreciate the wisdom of Western culture is to go a long way toward the establishment of a thoroughly axiological rhetoric. But no headway can be made until the student perceives that "The human being must live in a present that is enriched and sustained by a past; it is his experience stored up in the form of memory which enables him to be something more than an automaton responding to sensory impingements."[57] In a word, the student must come to realize that the men of each new generation are —as Bernard of Chartes put it—like dwarfs seated upon the shoulders of a giant: they can judge more discerningly between better and worse if they have the eyes of human history to help them see.[58]

Two procedures may be suggested for linking rhetorical education more closely with the substance of the past. First of all, the public address teacher can insist that his students know the *background* as well as the foreground of any public issue they undertake to examine, whether in an extemporaneous speech, a debate, or a discussion. He can demand, unapologetically, the quality of research that Lincoln extracted of himself in the building of his famous "Cooper Union Address." And he shall discover in this procedure the best antidote to the ill-devised proposal, the surest means of infusing soberness into his students' counsels on public questions.

The road to a "rhetoric of commitment" should perhaps prove shorter were we also to revive in our classrooms one of the older customs of the great universities—the custom of requiring the pro-pounding of a philosophical thesis which, as Cotton Mather phrased it, the student had to "defend manfully."[59] In this manner we could bring our students face to face with grave philosophical questions calculated both to tax their mentality and to deepen the humanity that lies within them.[60] Yet to do this would first require on our part the conviction that such universal issues as man's destiny are neither too profound nor too disturbing to take up. Beyond this would be wholehearted acceptance of the view that rhetoric is tendentious utterance about the human condition, and that rhetorical education is justifiable, not as it merely advances a student's career, but as it helps to make of him a fully civilized human being.

Relevant also to the problem of making rhetorical education more richly axiological is the question of language instruction. If the teacher

[57] Richard M. Weaver, "Individuality and Modernity," *Essays on Individuality,* ed. Felix Morley (Philadelphia, 1958), p. 67.

[58] Cited by Walter Lippmann, "Education vs. Western Civilization," *The American Scholar,* X (Winter 1940–1941), 184.

[59] *Ibid.,* p. 192.

[60] For an example of a recent effort to link American rhetorical education to "persistent and unresolved questions," see Lester Thonssen and William L. Finkel, *Ideas That Matter: A Sourcebook for Speakers* (New York, 1961).

of public address is serious in his democratic and humane allegiances, then he cannot in good conscience propagate any theory of language which seeks to undermine the symbolistic operations of language. Rather, he shall stoutly uphold what Richard M. Weaver has termed "the philosophical quality of language." He shall perceive that he who seeks for "some neutral [linguistic] means which will be a nonconductor of the current called 'emotion' and its concomitant of evaluation," is not only worshipping a false idol but is also contributing to mankind's present state of amorality and emptiness.[61] He shall seek to prevent the isolation of language from the noumenal world, upholding the integrity not only of the process of *definition* but also of rhetorical *figuration*. If indeed he genuinely wishes to put axiological virility into his language instruction, he must begin with a conception of language which affirms the constitutive powers of the human mind and recognizes the reality of man's subjective universe of emotion and value. Such a conception would see rhetoric as being "rooted in an essential function of language itself . . . the use of language as a symbolic means of inducing cooperation in beings that by nature respond to symbols."[62] With such a conception of language he would also understand the scope of word reference to be "determined by forces within the psychic constitution and not outside it."[63] The teaching practices that should emanate from this view of language, or style, are at once obvious and far-reaching. As students of language, teachers of rhetoric will go for guidance not to Korzybski, but to Plato and Longinus and Emerson; not to S. I. Hayakawa or Benjamin Lee Whorf, but to Richard M. Weaver and Donald C. Bryant. And if the teacher should need heart, he might recall Barzun's wise dictum: "The state of the mother tongue is the index of our control over destiny."[64]

4

In this essay an attempt has been made to develop a rationale for rhetorical education which offers some promise of helping twentieth-century man in the solution of the cataclysmic problems of value which beset him. The rhetoric described has been called an axiological rhetoric, or a "rhetoric of commitment." Keyed to master conceptions of the "desirable" in a democratic commonwealth rather than to the merely "desired," this rhetoric would stress the axiological more than the purely psychological, the cultural more than the merely personal,

---

[61] Weaver, *Ideas Have Consequences*, p. 152.
[62] Kenneth Burke, p. 43.
[63] Richard M. Weaver, "Relativism and the Use of Language" (Paper read at Emory University, 1959), p. 6.
[64] Barzun, p. 27.

the moral more than the manipulative. Such a rhetoric, the authors believe, would vitally involve both its teachers and its students in the pursuit of humane wisdom without which modern man may hardly hope to stay the engines of nihilism. And under the aegis of such a rhetoric, the ancient art itself can be brought closer to the Platonic ideal echoed in one of Socrates' replies to Gorgias—the ideal of a rhetoric whose "propositions are always about justice."[65]

[65] *Gorgias* 460.

23 THE SUBSTANCE OF RHETORIC: GOOD REASONS

KARL R. WALLACE

Ethical and moral values, and relevant information about them, comprise the basic substance of rhetoric. Wallace offers this "hypothesis" for examination and testing by contemporary rhetorical scholars. Several points in this essay are particularly noteworthy. Along with Eubanks and Baker, Wallace sees values as forming the necessary foundation of rhetorical theory and practice. But unlike them, he does not prescribe a specific set of values as the only valid content. Instead he contends that a comprehensive rhetorical theory must offer viewpoints on three essential value categories: the desirable, the obligatory, and the praiseworthy.

In addition, Wallace offers the concept of "good reasons" as a useful one to describe fundamental rhetorical substance. He explains, "A good reason is a statement offered in support of an *ought* proposition or of a value judgment." The concept of good reasons would encompass the traditional classical notions of ethos, logos, and pathos while avoiding sharp demarcations between them.

Consider this question about the nature of good reasons as described by Wallace: Are good reasons in a specific rhetorical situation to be determined by the specific audience addressed, by societal groups, or by some independent objective standards of evidence and reasoning? See also Wallace, "Rhetoric and Advising," *Southern Speech Journal,* XXIX (Summer 1964), 279–287.

Source: Quarterly Journal of Speech, XLIX (October 1963), 239–249. Reprinted with permission of the author and the publisher.

Rhetorical theorists have always recognized that speeches have content and substance, and that the content of a particular speech is derived from the setting and occasion. Yet unlike classical rhetoricians who presented systems of invention, modern writers who offer theories of rhetoric are unclear and uncertain what to say about the materials of discourse. They will include in their theories statements about methods, principles, techniques, and styles of discourse; that is, they talk of the forms and the handling of ideas and are mostly silent about the substance of utterance. Perhaps they are silent for three main reasons. Under the influence of structural linguistics, rhetoricians may uncritically believe that language is like the symbols of music and mathematics—empty and devoid of substantial meanings. Or they may overlook the full implication of Donald Bryant's reference to rhetoric as an art of adjusting ideas to people and people to ideas.[1] The notion of adjustment—and for that matter, adaptation—directs attention chiefly to acts of manipulation and treatment. It is easily to forget that one cannot engage in manipulation without manipulating something, and that speakers and audiences stand on common ground only through commonalities of meaning and partial identities of experience. If this simple fact is acknowledged, there always bobs up that old, bothersome question: With what ideas, with what materials do speakers adjust and adapt to their hearers? Finally, for the last century or so students of rhetoric seem to have been trapped into accepting a sort of scientific realism, or perhaps I might better say, a naive realism. The argument runs something like this: Since man derives his substantial information and knowledge through his sensory apparatus and since the natural sciences have successfully claimed for themselves both the acquisition and interpretation of sensory materials, discourse is left with nothing to say about the real world that does not properly belong to the sciences. Furthermore, since the behavioral sciences and the disciplines of philosophy and ethics have asserted property rights over the study of human experience and conduct, rhetoric has nothing to say about the behavior of speakers and listeners that these sciences cannot say with greater reliability and authority. Ergo, the substance of discourse comes from finding the right scientific and historical facts and of consulting the right authority. To me this is very much like saying that rhetoric is nothing more than the art of framing information and of translating it into intelligible terms for the popular audience.

1

My position is this. First, rhetorical theory must deal with the substance of discourse as well as with structure and style. Second, the basic materials of discourse are (1) ethical and moral values and (2) information relevant to these. Third, ethics deals with the theory of goods and values, and from ethics rhetoric can make adaptations that will result in a modern system of topics.

In developing these ideas we must try at the outset to indicate what we mean by *substance*. The concept has carried many meanings, but

---

[1] The point of view is fully expressed in Donald C. Bryant, "Rhetoric: Its Functions and Its Scope," *QJS*, XXXIX (December 1953), 401–424.

the ones that are relevant here may be suggested by calling attention to certain words as correlatives. On one side are *substance, matter, material, content,* and *subject matter.* On the other are *form, structure, order, arrangement, organization, shape,* and *figure.* The words on each side reveal overlapping meanings. This fact must be recognized, of course. But what is important is that the terms on one side are not fully intelligible in the absence of the terms on the other. The notion of form is useless without the notions of matter and material; the notions of order and arrangement are senseless without the notions of matter and substance—of something to be ordered and arranged. In every case we recognize the relationship of figure and shape to that which is figured and shaped, the relationship of form to that which is formed—to that which is material and substantial. In the same sets of words there is also lurking the idea of substratum—of that which stands under, of support. In this sense, form is inconceivable without something as its basis. One does not arrange and order bricks, or think of arranging or ordering them, without having bricks or the idea thereof. One does not build a house without a foundation, nor an oration without spoken or written words and the meanings they carry.

In what sense, then, do we understand substance? An attempt to meet this question requires us to regard an utterance, a linguistic event, a speech, as an object. There are natural objects. These exist, or come into being, without the agency of man. They are the things of land and sea, vegetable and mineral. We say, depending upon our point of view, that natural objects are made by God, by Nature, or by some mysterious force. There are artificial objects, and these are said, in our language, to be man-made. Among these are language itself and whatever one makes with language—novels, poems, commands, instructions, laws, speeches, et cetera. If speeches are objects, rhetoric is related to speeches as theory is related to behavior. Since a theorist tries to explain the particular group of objects, events, and behaviors in which he is interested, a rhetorician endeavors to explain what speeches are, and this task involves his setting forth what speeches are about and how they come about. If speeches exhibit substance and materials—and it is nonsense to say that they do not—the rhetorician must, among other things, characterize the substance of speeches, the materials of which they are made. Theories of rhetoric in the classical tradition, as we know, almost always said a good deal about the substance and materials of speeches. Under the heads Invention and Topics, they described the general materials of speeches and their chief kinds, together with lines of argument that often recurred. Except for Kenneth Burke, the principal writers on modern rhetorical theory—e.g., I. A. Richards—neglect substance and concentrate on processes, methods, techniques, and effects. Most of our textbooks pay little attention to what speeches are about; rather, their point of view is pedagogical. They concentrate on how to make a speech and deliver it. I do not think this condition of affairs could long endure if rhetoric were to rediscover and reassert its concern with subject matter.

Rhetoric, then, ought to deal with the substance, the substratum or foundations of speeches. What is this stuff? In answer to this question, I shall offer three propositions. First, the underlying materials of speeches, and indeed of most human talk and discussion, are assertions and statements that concern human behavior and conduct. They are prompted by situations and contexts that present us with choices and that require us to respond with appropriate decisions and actions. Second, such statements are usually called judgments and appraisals. They reflect human interests and values, and the nature of value-judgments and the way of justifying them are the special, technical, and expert concern of ethics. Third, the appearance and use of value-judgments in practical discourse are the proper, although not the sole, concern of the theory and practice of rhetoric.

Probably most thoughtful persons will at once agree that the foundation materials of speeches are statements that are evoked by the need to make choices in order that we may act or get ready to act or to appraise our acts after their doing. Furthermore, choosing itself is a substantive act and the statement of a choice is a substantive statement. Rhetoricians will recall that the time-honored classifications of speeches are based upon the typical choice-situations that audiences confront. The deliberative or political kind of speech helps an audience decide what it *ought* to do, and the materials most often appearing are those that bear on the particular audience's ends and purposes and the means to those ends. More specifically, so Aristotle thought, these things give rise to considerations of what is good and evil and what is useful, and these again with respect to the problems of war and peace, of national defense, of taxation (or support of the state in relation to the citizen's purse), of the standard of living (or the welfare of the citizen), and of the making of laws and the good that laws can do. The forensic or legal speech helps a jury to decide upon the manner of treating a person who is accused of breaking the moral codes enshrined in law. What is justice in the case at hand? Is the man guilty or innocent? And if guilty, how should he be treated? The epideictic speech helps an audience to assess the ethics and morality of a person's actions. Whether the decision is to praise or blame him will depend upon whether his acts are judged virtuous, noble, right, and good. Evidently, then, large numbers of speeches employ statements whose content is ethical or moral, or they use language in a setting and in ways that logically imply ethical and moral ideas.

Still it may be asked whether there are not speeches in situations that have nothing to do with ethics and morality? What about discourse that is called informative, expository, or scientific?

We consider this question by pointing out that we often label a speech informative when in its proper context it is persuasive. Thomas Huxley's famous lecture, "On a Piece of Chalk," consists predominantly of factual sentences, yet to its English audiences in the 1870's it functioned as a plea for evolution. Much discourse and discussion that is thought of as didactic is probably persuasive in effect if not in intent. The character and bias of the state and nation function to select what is taught in the public schools. The teacher-learner relationship is accordingly less neutral and colorless than we think. Moreover, many teachers employ a method of learning that encourages students to think for themselves, to weigh and consider, to be intelligently appreciative and critical, to select and reject ideas and information that function indirectly, if not directly, to build attitudes and determine preferences. Furthermore, much newspaper discourse is in response to the widespread belief that knowledge is a good thing, and that certain kinds of materials and events are interesting, useful, and satisfying to readers, and other kinds are not. In brief, it would appear that expository speaking and writing recognizes choices and values that differ from those of persuasive discourse principally in that they are more remote and less apparent. So in saying that the materials and the substrata of speeches come about in response to contexts that present alternative possibilities, I want to include what is ordinarily thought of as informative utterance. First, much exposition is functionally persuasive, whether in intent or effect. This fact we have just remarked upon. Second, scientific discourse in itself cannot be utterly devoid of value. It owes its being to two assumptions: (1) knowledge in itself is a good thing, and (2) the information transmitted is accurate, reliable, valid, and true. Furthermore, scientific reporting of observations and experiments—and the criticism thereof—involves *what* a scientist did and did not do, *how* he did it and did not do it, and *why* he did it in one way rather than another. The scientist cannot escape choices, whether he is addressing other scientists or a popular audience. His decisions are anchored in contexts governed by rules, conventions, and practices, whether they be those of the scientist or those of the non-scientist public.

2

Although the basic substance of speeches comprises statements that are made when human beings must make choices, the consideration of such statements in their special and technical character is the proper concern of ethics. To support this assertion I must indicate what students of ethics today seem to be focusing on.[2] Despite differences in their special points of view and in the treatment of their material, they see the human being as he uses his reason in practical situations that involve choice and decision. Practical reason is revealed in judgments that guide man's conduct, i.e., judgments are statements having to do with action, motives, feelings, emotions, attitudes, and values. They are responses to one of two fundamental kinds of questions: What shall I do or believe? What ought I to do?[3] Both Toulmin and Baier talk in terms that are familiar to every historian and theorist of rhetoric.[4] Practical reason, for example, appears in three types of behavior: deliberation, justification, and explanation. Deliberation uses reason prior to the act. Justification and explanation use reason after the act. When we justify, we praise or blame; we use terms like right and wrong, good and bad; in general we *appraise*. When we explain, we show what moved the agent and use terms untinctured by praise or censure. Because these three types of rational behavior are carried on almost exclusively in symbolic and linguistic terms, some writers tend to treat ethics as consisting of statements, of kinds of statements, and of the content of statements. Of proper concern are statements in whose predicates are the words, *is a desirable thing, is morally obligatory, is morally admirable or reprehensible, is a good thing, is praiseworthy,* and the like.[5] Included, furthermore, are all statements that imply, though they do not specify, such evaluative words. Edwards achieves considerable simplicity when, following Broad and Findlay, as he says, he presents his theory in terms of two classes of judgments.[6] The first is the value-judgment or moral judgment in which key predicate words are *good, desirable, worthwhile,* and their equivalents. The second is the *judgment of obligation,* as signalled by words like *ought, oblige,* and *duty.* We may say, then, that students of ethics are concerned with choice situations that are always signalled by the question, "What ought I to do?" They are concerned, also, with the rational and reasonable responses that human beings make to the question, i.e., with the judgments that we use in making choices and in justifying them.

    [2] My chief informants have been Richard B. Brandt, *Ethical Theory: The Problems of Normative and Critical Ethics* (Englewood Cliffs, N.J., 1959); Kurt Baier, *The Moral Point of View: A Rational Basis of Ethics* (Ithaca, N.Y., 1958); Paul Edwards, *The Logic of Moral Discourse* (Glencoe, Ill., 1955); P. H. Nowell-Smith, *Ethics* (Baltimore, Md., 1954 [Penguin Books]); Philip Blair Rice, *On the Knowledge of Good and Evil* (New York, 1955); Charles L. Stevenson, *Ethics and Language* (New Haven, 1944); and Stephen Edelston Toulmin, *An Examination of the Place of Reason in Ethics* (Cambridge, Eng., 1961).
    [3] Baier, p. 46.
    [4] For example, see Baier, pp. 148–156.
    [5] See Brandt, pp. 2–4.
    [6] Edwards, p. 141.

Since judgments either state values directly or imply them indirectly, ethics as a study examines all values that influence action and are imbedded in judgments. It attempts to explain value-terms and how they are used, to classify them, and to find values that apply widely to our actions. Those of greatest generality are called standards or criteria of conduct. Some of them are compressed in concepts with which all of us are familiar: good and evil, pleasant-unpleasant, duty, obligation, self-interest, altruism, truth-telling, promise-keeping, honesty, fairness, courage, law-observance, utility, right and wrong, and the like. They appear typically in general statements called rules of conduct, regulations, laws, codes, principles, and moral maxims. With such values in mind, ethics also asks and tries to answer questions like these: Why these values rather than some other ones? And are the methods employed to identify them valid and trustworthy? In a word, modern ethics undertakes to present a theory of values which includes an account of how value-judgments are justified.

It would seem apparent, accordingly, that ethics as a study derives its materials in large measure from men's linguistic behavior when they must choose among alternatives. Their behavior constitutes judgments, and these appear in their reasonings when they deliberate, explain, and justify their choices. It is possible to observe such behavior systematically, to analyze it and theorize about it, and this ethics does. It is also possible to observe such behavior, to note what judgments all men, or most men, or wise men, or the wisest of men in practice accept or reject, and to perceive which of these recur in the materials and premises of men's reasonings. This is what classical rhetorical theory did, and this is what modern rhetorical theory should do. If the modern rhetorical theorist feels that he cannot in his textbook present a workable account of the material basis of speeches, perhaps much as Aristotle did in the *Rhetoric,* at least he can assert that rhetoric is related to ethics as theory is to practice. He can point out that the science of ethics deals with moral principles and standards of conduct as they are abstracted from practice, and that the art of rhetoric encounters moral principles in particular situations, in specific cases in which man in his social and political roles must make up his mind and act in concert, or be ready to act in concert.

If the materials of rhetorical discourse are fundamentally the same as the materials of ethics, it should be possible to derive a scheme of rhetorical topics from the study of ethics. Indeed, this can be done. I shall present now a brief outline of *topoi.* In doing so I am not suggesting that it is a perfect product and ready for incorporation into a textbook on public speaking. I am only to point the way to a practical instrument.

First I shall sketch the general categories of values that help us to decide whether our decisions and actions are good or bad, right or wrong. There appear to be three, all-embracing classes—the desirable, the obligatory, and the admirable or praiseworthy, and their opposites.[7]

Whether or not something is desirable depends upon one's motives, goals, or ends—upon that for the sake of which we act. We act to reduce certain painful or unpleasant tensions. We rid ourselves of disease and illness to restore health; we banish hunger by seeking and eating food. On the other hand, some tensions produce pleasure, the chief among these being activity associated with sexual behavior, competitive activity in both work and play, and aesthetic excitement. Pleasurable tensions are involved, too, in activity that is venturesome and that involves learning and knowing. We desire things, also, that are in our own interests. Among interests, some are primarily self-centered, such as property and security (although both of these directly depend on social institutions and practices). Some interests are directly social—those for the sake of the general welfare. Other interests are professional, vocational, and recreational in nature. Desirable, furthermore, is personal and group achievement and its attendant pleasure and exhilaration. We derive satisfaction in making and creating something. We take pleasure and pride in achieving the "right" self-image. With this image is associated status—the respect and deference of others to us, and the power and ability to do what we wish. Desirable, moreover, is freedom of choice and action; undesirable are arbitrary restraints. A much-prized good is being loved and liked by others. Finally, there is an overriding, hedonistic desire, that of seeking anything that gives us pleasure and of avoiding acts and states of being that are painful or unpleasant. These, then, are things generally regarded as desirable and good. They are reflected directly or indirectly in the statements through which we make choices and explain or defend them.

Things that are morally obligatory and acts that are praiseworthy seem to acquire their meaning and force in the sort of regard that others have for us. The self-image is built up through the approvals and disapprovals of others, and thus we learn what is "right" and "wrong." Our integrity, our respect for ourselves, is a function of social rewards and sanctions. On the other hand, acts that are desirable and conduct that is goal-directed and that is said to be motivated, all seem to be built around, and come to focus on, the individual organism. The distinction between the desirable and the obligatory appears to be imbedded in our language. It is acceptable to say that playing golf is a good thing to do, but it is odd to say that playing golf is a right thing to do, or that golf playing is a matter of duty.

---

[7] In developing general categories of values, I have been most helped by Brandt.

Within the class of things obligatory are duties. These are acts specified by one's position or role in a group or in a social institution. With
respect to the family, a father has duties. With respect to his profession, a physician, a lawyer, a teacher has duties. With respect to the
state, a governor has duties, and so does the citizen. There are obligatory actions so deeply woven into the social fabric that, once learned,
they are rarely examined. They are truth-telling, promise-keeping, the
paying of debts, and obeying the law. Finally, there are the *mores* of
the group, as revealed in codes, customs, commandments, and moral
maxims, and enforced by unwritten, social sanctions.

The last class of goods and values is that of the praiseworthy-blame-
worthy, the admirable-reprehensible. These value-terms are meant to
refer to character traits, to behavior classes that have become stable,
to what in the older literature of ethics were usually called *virtues*.
Among these is conscientiousness, a term that refers not to some
mystical, innate sense of the good, but to a concern for living up to
one's own self-image and for fulfilling one's obligations. There are,
too, the familiar virtue names—kindliness, fairness, courage, veracity,
honesty, prudence, persistence, tolerance, reliability, and good will
(i.e., concern for the welfare of others). Although space does not permit the elaboration of these behavior traits, two or three observations
should be made. Some writers call these traits *extrinsic* goods, or instrumental goods, because possession of them leads to the acquisition
of other goods and ends. Honesty, for example, leads more often to
desirable ends and less often to punishments than stealing and cheating. Although these terms may enter into all kinds of value-judgments,
their long usage and genetic development suggest that they typically
apply to behavior that is completed and past. Hence, to some writers
they are technical terms of appraisal, and we use them most appropriately when we size up conduct that has become history. Yet terms of
appraisal often appear in deliberative or policy contexts with persuasive intent. As Aristotle once observed, to praise a man is to hold
him up for the imitation of others.

3

This sketch of value categories has been presented entirely from
the point of view of ethics. The categories represent a sort of *topoi*
of values. Doubtless it is evident that rhetorical topics can be derived
from them. One has only to recall the ordinary ways of analyzing a
problem—the Dewey steps in problem-solving, for example, and the
surveys for a proposition of fact and a proposition of policy—to perceive that they refer to situations in the present and the past and point
to the possible future in terms that are ethical and moral. Such schemata of analytical thought originally had their basis in the logic of

choice, decision, and conduct. Their long use and ready application have turned them into formulae whose derivation has been forgotten.

In presenting *topoi* of ethical values, I am not forgetting that the system must also include political values. Although this is not the place to spell out the significant differences between politics and ethics, we do well to remember that politics can be properly included within the scope of ethics, for the art of government is the art of adjusting the desires and values of the individual to the desires and values of others. Accordingly, rhetorical topics derived from ethics will point to political topics in the ways that genus relates to species, in those ways that the general idea suggests the specific idea. So some ethical premises will in use be indistinguishable from political premises. Take, for example, Kant's famous categorical imperative: Do only that thing which you would will all others to do. It appears to apply to political conduct as well as to individual conduct.

Nevertheless, some rhetorical topics will be characteristically political. We all know where to look for them. Government may be viewed as the formal instrument whereby individuals accept a system of law for the benefits of themselves and of each other. Hence from the point of view of politics there is always a triadic relationship of parties: the individual, the political group in which the individual plays the role and goes under the name of *citizen,* and the governor or ruler. With this relationship in mind, one can at once locate the foci of political explanations and arguments. These will center on such concepts as the powers, obligations, and duties of both the ruler and the citizen. These in turn derive much of their meaning from the concepts of liberty, freedom, and justice, and from our ideas about rights, both individual rights and civil rights. From these spring the standards, rules, and maxims of political conduct. Some political theorists, for example, believe that Roman law settled our custom of defining "private affairs in terms of rights, and public affairs in terms of power and responsibilities."[8] Political rules become the substantial bases and premises of appraisals and judgments. They also dictate the method and tone of rational criticism. These, perhaps, are our special heritage from the Greek.[9] Possibly the deep-rooted, long-unquestioned habit of waiving aside the "constitutionality" of debate propositions has led debaters to ignore the real sources of arguments that are simultaneously material, moving, and interesting.

To see that a *topoi* of values would indeed be possible we need only to glance swiftly at the debater's issues and sources of argument. The debater refers to "evils" and "difficulties" that give rise to "prob-

[8] D. G. Hitchner and W. H. Harbold, *Modern Government: A Survey of Political Science* (New York, 1962), p. 175.

[9] *Ibid.,* p. 174.

lems." These terms, I suggest, can refer only to situations, persons, groups, or institutions that have experienced unpleasant tensions of one kind or another. They are frustrated because they haven't secured their desires, their goals, their pleasures, and their interests. Somebody is threatening their freedoms, their status, or their power. Somebody is accused of breaking the law, and his character and that of witnesses and of the trial system itself are put to the test. Self-interest, vested interest, or the entrenched power of some group or institution is interfering with the general welfare.

Once the debater has located the evils of the situation, he defines the problem. His explanation of it cannot avoid value-judgments and even his facts that support explanation function in a context of values. If the question be medical care for the aged, the description of the present state of medical care may well support different interpretations of the problem and point to different decisions.

Such, then, are the kinds of materials which, assembled and analyzed, provide the basis of decision. The decision itself—the solution of the problem—emerges either as a proposition in which the words *should* or *ought* appear, or as a proposition in which value-terms are expressed or clearly implied—e.g., the party is innocent (or guilty), the state has an obligation to provide employment opportunities for everyone, this person or this institution is responsible for doing so-and-so. It is well to remark that the *ought* in a proposition of policy means more than a vague pointing to the future. It is a decision in response to the question, What ought we to believe or do? And this question is always, so Baier asserts, an ethical or moral one.[10] Moreover, an *ought* proposition carries a meaning of obligation about it, such that if one accepts the proposition one feels bound to do what is specified or implied.[11] With either individuals or institutions in mind, one can ask sensible questions: Are obligations to be found in the context of the problem? Who is obligated to whom? What is the nature of the obligation? Furthermore; an *ought* seems always to imply that the decision is the best thing to do; it suggests that the speaker has compared all relevant alternatives.[12]

Perhaps enough has been said to show that many rhetorical *topoi* may be readily derived from ethical and moral materials. Indeed, I believe that topics and lines of argument *inevitably*, in the nature of things, lead the investigator to ethical and moral considerations, guide him to decisions and propositions that are ethical and moral, and furnish him with most of the explanations and arguments that support his decision and in whose terms he will recommend it to the con-

[10] Baier, p. 86.
[11] Brandt, esp. pp. 353–354.
[12] *Ibid.*

sideration of an audience. If modern rhetoricians will face the fact that language symbols are not empty symbols, like those of symbolic logic and mathematics, that the language of practical discourse bears meanings that testify to man's attempt to identify and solve problems of action and conduct, modern rhetoric will formulate a theory of invention and will present a plan of *topoi* in the language of ethics and morals.

4

If rhetoricians would see the materials of speeches in this light, they would do well, I believe, to take a special term from the field of ethics and employ it, perhaps with minor adjustments. The term is *good reason,* or in the plural form, *good reasons.* What are these? A good reason is a statement offered in support of an *ought* proposition or of a value-judgment. Good reasons are a number of statements, consistent with each other, in support of an *ought* proposition or of a value-judgment. Some examples may prove illuminating.

The Federal government ought to provide for the medical care of the aged. (Or, more technically: It is desirable that the Federal government . . . .)

It will contribute to the security of the aged.
It will be in the welfare of everybody.
It is in the interest of equity.
The aged spend a disproportionate amount of their income on medical care.
Their bill for drugs is twice that of persons in age brackets below 60.
The government has an obligation to finance medical care for the aged.

X should not have copied from Y's paper.
It was an act of cheating.
Cheating is wrong.

Jones made a good speech.
It conformed to most of the principles and rules of speechmaking.
Its consequences will be good.

This man ought not be elected sheriff.
He is not qualified to hold the office.
He cannot be depended on.

These illustrations serve to point out what good reasons are and what they support. If the rhetorician were to adopt the term, good reasons, he would have a technical label that refers to all the materials of argument and explanation.

There are advantages to the use of the term, good reasons. Both rhetorician and teacher would be ever reminding the speaker, as well as themselves, that the substance of rhetorical proof has to do with values and value-judgments, i.e., with what is held to be good. One can scarcely declare that something is desirable without showing its relevance to values. It may be desirable, for example, to adjust the balance of power between management and labor, on the ground that justice has become too partisan, that basic rights are not being respected, and the like. Moreover, the word *reason* indicates that the process of proof is a rational one and can be used to cover such traditional forms of reasoning as deduction and induction, the syllogism, generalization, analogy, causation, and correlation. Furthermore, the term *good reason* implies the indissoluble relationship between content and form, and keeps attention on what form is saying. If we could become accustomed to the concept, good reasons, we might cease worrying over our failure to find perfect syllogisms in the arguments of everyday life; rather, we would recognize, as the examination of practical reason seems to indicate, that reasons which govern practice are quite different from the syllogism as usually presented. I think that most ethicists would agree that the measurement of validity in practical discourse quite commonly resides in the general principle and its applicability. Brandt has this to say on the point: "Any particular ethical statement that is valid *can be supported by a valid general principle. . . .*"[13] X should not have copied from Y's paper, for in doing so he cheated, and cheating is wrong. In this case, clearly there are facts that could or could not be established. Clearly, the general principle, "cheating is wrong," is relevant and functions as a warrant. The principle is applicable, or is applicable as qualified, if particular circumstances call for qualification. The principle itself is valid to the extent that it corresponds with the beliefs and conduct of the group which gives it sanction. Such statements, Edwards observes, are objective in the sense that they are independent of the speaker's subjective attitudes. It is true, of course, that the speaker's attitude may prompt his giving a general principle as a reason; nevertheless, the general principle can be tested for its truth-value quite apart from his attitude.[14] What a good reason is is to some extent fixed by human nature and to a very large extent by generally accepted principles and practices which make social life, as we understand it, possible. In a word, the concept of good reasons embraces both the substance and the processes of practical reason. One could do worse than characterize rhetoric as the art of finding and effectively presenting good reasons.

If rhetoricians could accept good reasons as the substance of discourse, we would immediately secure additional advantages. Any distinctions that modern rhetoric may be trying to maintain between logical, ethical, and emotional modes of proof would immediately

[13] *Ibid.,* p. 20.
[14] Edwards, pp. 148, 157.

become unreal and useless, except for purposes of historical criticism. For the practitioner, both communicator and respondent, the correct questions would always be: What is my choice? What are the supporting and explanatory statements? What information is trustworthy? It would be absurd to ask: Is my choice a logical one? Shall I support my position by logical, ethical, or emotional means? For the theorist, analyst, and critic of discourse, the disappearance of those weasel concepts, logical proof and emotional proof, would permit a description of the materials of practical discourse in terms of two broad categories: materials deriving from the specific occasion, and materials consisting of general value-judgments. Furthermore, perhaps practitioners would get into the habit of applying first and foremost to any instance of communication, the searching queries: Who or what is the responsible agent? What person or agent is taking the responsibility, or should take it? If the proposition be supported by reasons that immediately or ultimately relate to value-statements whose content reflects the desirable, the obligatory, and the admirable, then for whom is the message desirable and admirable? Upon whom do the obligations and duties rest? Discourse to which such questions are habitually applied cannot long remain abstract, distant, colorless, and unreal. Rather, it could well become personal and direct. The speechmaking of the Greeks, who understood ethos, was eminently personal.

5

It seems probable that if students of rhetoric looked to the substance as well as to the forms of practical discourse they would discover a set of statements or value-axioms that would constitute a modern system of invention. The axioms would consist of those political and ethical values that apply to public discussion. Derived in theory from politics and ethics and in practice from the rules and conventions that speakers appeal to explicitly and implicitly when they explain, advocate, deliberate upon, and justify their choices, the axioms would serve as a base for finding good reasons and thus for providing fundamental materials in any given case of rhetorical discourse. Eubanks and Baker have recently reminded rhetoricians of Aristotle's position that "If rhetoric has any sort of *special* subject matter province, that substance is constituted in the popular and probable value axioms related to the civil decision making of a free society."[15] The hypothesis should be put to the test.

[15] Ralph T. Eubanks and Virgil L. Baker, "Toward an Axiology of Rhetoric," *QJS*, XLVIII (April 1962), 162.

24 THE LIMITS OF RHETORIC

MAURICE NATANSON

This essay is of interest for at least four reasons. First, the author attempts to describe the boundaries and relationships of dialectic and rhetoric. He explores the meaning of Aristotle's contention that rhetoric is the counterpart of dialectic. Second, some of Richard M. Weaver's insights concerning rhetoric and dialectic are basic to Natanson's analysis. Third, this explication by Natanson, who is a professor of philosophy, illustrates the growing rapprochement between the disciplines of philosophy and rhetoric.

Finally, at the end of the essay, the author proposes a hierarchy of aspects of rhetoric for purposes of rhetorical study. He urges a distinction, for example, between a philosophy (dialectic) of rhetoric and a general rationale (theory) of rhetoric. To what extent does this distinction seem valid and useful? After you have completed reading this essay, try to formulate clear definitions of such terms as *dialectic, rhetoric,* and *philosophy.*

Source: Quarterly Journal of Speech, XLI (April 1955), 133–139. Reprinted with permission of the author and the publisher.

There are signs of a new excitement in the discipline of contemporary rhetoric; but there are also indications of basic difficulties in the discussions going on to determine the proper province of rhetoric and the possible meaning of a "philosophy of rhetoric." As a philosopher, I think that an effort to show the relationship between rhetoric and philosophy might lead to some clarification of the underlying issues. If the philosopher cannot give the answers, he can perhaps clarify the questions.

But first, what do these "difficulties" in the discussions about rhetoric consist in? Undoubtedly one vast difficulty is generated by the very term "rhetoric." As Bryant points out, rhetoric may mean ". . . bombast; high-sounding words without content; oratorical falsification to hide meanings; sophistry, ornamentation and the study of figures of speech . . . and finally, least commonly of all, the whole art of spoken discourse, especially persuasive discourse."[1] The classical Aristotelian definition of rhetoric is no longer adequate to dispel all these variant connotations, but the inadequacy of defining rhetoric as "the faculty of observing in any given case the available means of persuasion" is to be explained at a different, far deeper level. It will be here that we come to the nucleus of the difficulties regarding rhetoric.

It would appear that what characterizes the Aristotelian as well as recent definitions of rhetoric is a stress on its functional and dynamic character. As Bryant writes:

> Rhetoric is primarily concerned with the relations of ideas to the thoughts, feelings, motives, and behavior of men. Rhetoric as distinct from the learnings which it uses is dynamic; it is concerned with movement. It *does* rather than *is*. It is method rather than matter. It is chiefly involved with bringing about a condition, rather than discovering or testing a condition.[2]

Now the emphasis on the directional and pragmatic aspect of rhetoric leads immediately to the question, *Is* rhetoric truly to be characterized as functional, and is the rhetorical function that of "adjusting ideas to people and . . . people to ideas"?[3] The fundamental difficulty, it seems to me, that has confused the discussion is a failure on the part of the analyst to distinguish between the theory of rhetoric and the practice of rhetoric: the former involves ultimately a philosophy of rhetoric; the latter presupposes that philosophy and directs its attention to the structure of rhetorical technique and methodology. But before proceeding to the analysis of these elements, I think it necessary to examine more carefully what is meant by the functional aspect of rhetoric, since my claim is that much confusion is created by assuming this interpretation of the nature of rhetoric.

It is well known that Aristotle begins his *Rhetoric* by asserting that "Rhetoric is the counterpart of Dialectic." If dialectic is the art of logical discussion, then rhetoric is the art of public speaking; but the distinction between rhetoric and dialectic is a more profound one. Dialectic, for Aristotle, has as its object the achievement of knowledge; rhetoric, persuasion. Dialectic strives for and may achieve *epistēmē;* rhetoric, *doxa.* Thus rhetoric is subordinate in the hierarchy of knowledge to dialectic as belief is subordinate to knowledge. Now if we consider the relationship between the Aristotelian rhetoric and the Platonic critique of rhetoric, it becomes evident that Aristotle has articulated a division between rhetoric and dialectic for definite reasons:

---

[1] Donald C. Bryant, "Rhetoric: Its Functions and Its Scope," *QJS*, XXXIX (December 1953), 402.

[2] *Ibid.*, p. 412; cf. Hoyt H. Hudson, "The Field of Rhetoric," *QJSE*, IX (April 1923), 180, where the essence of rhetoric is held to be "adaptation to the end of influencing hearers."

[3] Bryant, *op. cit.*, p. 413.

essentially, for the rescue of "good" rhetoric from "bad," i.e., from sophistic rhetoric. Good rhetoric, as Plato pointed out in *Phaedrus,* presupposes dialectic: persuasion presupposes truth. The division of rhetoric and dialectic warns us against confounding truth with its artful presentation and at the same time shows that they are separate facets of a single universe of discourse: the intelligible world.[4] But what really separates knowledge from belief, dialectic from rhetoric? It is here that we come to the problem of function.

It is certainly the case that Aristotle, after distinguishing between rhetoric and dialectic, proceeds to analyze the applicative uses of rhetoric. His discussions of the modes of persuasion stress the functional character of rhetorical method. Thus the subject matter of rhetoric becomes evidenced in the problems of speaker and audience, political oratory and its devices, etc. And it is precisely here that the subsequent tradition of rhetoric takes its point of departure and so abandons the awareness of the intimate nexus between rhetoric and dialectic; and it is here that confusions begin to germinate.

For Plato, rhetoric—good rhetoric, that is—aspired to be (but was not) *technē,* i.e., art involving knowledge.[5] While dialectic alone could achieve the status of *theōria,* rhetoric nevertheless had a powerful bond which tied it to knowledge. Though Aristotle's division of rhetoric and dialectic preserves the original intention of that bond, his stress on the subject matter of rhetoric (the modes of persuasion) lends itself to a misleading emphasis on rhetorical technique and to a lack of emphasis on the theoretical aspects of rhetoric. In other words, instead of a philosophy of rhetoric, we have drawn from Aristotle a manual of oratorical technique and a debater's guide. The ultimate import of this attitude towards rhetoric is an interpretation of the nature of rhetoric which holds it to be functional in character, directed toward practical problems of convincing and persuading, and so aimed at a pragmatic, instigative goal: rhetoric is conceived of in terms of men in action.

Now it is the thesis of this paper that this stress on the functional, pragmatic character of rhetoric is the origin of the confusion regarding the role and province of rhetoric today, and further that the confusion consists precisely in the fact that the Platonic and Aristotelian emphasis on the link between dialectic and rhetoric has been ignored in favor of the pragmatic subject matter with the result that the theoretical nature of rhetoric is obscured. It is my contention that a reapproach to the nature of rhetoric is possible through a philosophical examination of its foundations in dialectic.

---

[4] Cf. E. M. Cope, *An Introduction to Aristotle's Rhetoric* (London and Cambridge: Macmillan & Co., 1867), p. 6.

[5] See Werner Jaeger, *Paideia* (New York: Oxford University Press, 1944), Vol. III, Ch. 8.

The need for re-examination of the nature and scope of rhetoric is voiced in many and diverse quarters today, but the stress on the relationship of philosophy to rhetoric is not a recent development. As a matter of fact, it is Bishop Whately who makes the point in connection with a criticism of Cicero as rhetorician:

Cicero is hardly to be reckoned among the number [of rhetoricians]; for he delighted so much more in the practice than in the theory of his art, that he is perpetually drawn off from the rigid philosophical analysis of its principles, into discursive declamations, always eloquent indeed, and often interesting, but adverse to regularity of system, and frequently as unsatisfactory to the practical student as to the philosopher.[6]

The rhetorician, then, according to Whately, must attend seriously to the philosophical problems which are at the root of his discipline. With regard to logic, Whately writes: "Rhetoric being in truth an offshoot of Logic, that Rhetorician must labor under great disadvantages who is not only ill acquainted with that system, but also utterly unconscious of his deficiency."[7] Unfortunately, as I. A. Richards points out,[8] Whately does not follow his own advice, with the result that instead of taking "a broad philosophical view of the principles of the Art," Whately gives us "a very ably arranged and discussed collection of prudential Rules about the best sorts of things to say in various argumentative situations, the order in which to bring out your propositions and proofs and examples. . . ."[9] Just as Richards correctly points out Whately's failure to carry out his own directive, so we must also add that Richards fails to carry out a sustained inquiry into the philosophy of rhetoric, though he does develop one subsidiary line of approach, that of the analysis of linguistic structure and meaning. The philosophy of rhetoric remains then an unexamined realm; and it is especially interesting that a volume published in 1953 takes as its theme the relationship between philosophy and rhetoric and seeks a radical reapproach to the ancient dualism of rhetoric and dialectic. We shall take Richard Weaver's *Ethics and Rhetoric*[10] as a point of departure in analyzing the problem before us.

Weaver begins his study of rhetoric by calling us back to the original Aristotelian distinction between rhetoric and dialectic. As we indicated before, rhetoric is concerned with persuasion, dialectic with truth. However, it is necessary to remember that for Aristotle, *both* rhetoric and dialectic are concerned with the world of probability, both begin with the commonsense reality of contingency, not with the realm of

---

[6] Richard Whately, *Elements of Rhetoric* (New York: Sheldon & Co., 1867), p. 24.
[7] *Ibid.*, p. 26.
[8] I. A. Richards, *The Philosophy of Rhetoric* (New York and London: Oxford University Press, 1936), p. 7.
[9] *Ibid.*, p. 7.
[10] (Chicago: Henry Regnery Co., 1953).

apodeictic logic. Aristotle's distinction between scientific knowledge (which includes the organon of deductive logic) and argumentative inquiry (which includes both rhetoric and dialectic) makes clear the difference between the formal deductive syllogism which begins with stipulated premises and arrives then at necessary conclusions and, on the other hand, rhetoric and dialectic, which inquire into the empirical grounds of propositions in an effort to establish the truth and then make clear the available means of its artful presentation.[11] For Aristotle, deductive logic cannot provide any proof of its ultimate premises: such proof is the task of dialectic.[12] The ultimate foundations of science and formal logic, then, rest on dialectic: logic is concerned with validity, dialectic with truth. Thus Weaver writes: "Dialectic is a method of investigation whose object is the establishment of truth about doubtful propositions."[13]

Now it would appear that there are different fields of study dialectic may pursue: the scientific method of induction in the field of botany is quite different from the endeavor to establish the truth in matters of politics or ethics. Which field of dialectic will rhetoric concern itself with? Weaver holds:

There is a branch of dialectic which contributes to "choice or avoidance" and it is with this that rhetoric is regularly found joined. Generally speaking, this is a rhetoric involving questions of policy, and the dialectic which precedes it will determine not the application of positive terms but that of terms which are subject to the contingency of evaluation.[14]

The dialectic which seeks to establish terms having to do with policy is in an intimate relationship with rhetoric, for rhetoric is meaningful only if dialectic is presupposed. As Weaver says, "there is . . . no true rhetoric without dialectic, for the dialectic provides that basis of 'high speculation about nature' without which rhetoric in the narrower sense has nothing to work upon."[15] It is this internal connection, rooted in the very nature of rhetoric, that provides Weaver with his *rapprochement* between rhetoric and philosophy.

Weaver's original contribution to the problem is expressed in a particular characterization of dialectic. Turning to a more nearly Platonic than Aristotelian conception of dialectic (though the Neo-Aristotelian overtones are obvious), Weaver interprets dialectic as a distinguishable stage in argumentation: "Dialectic is that stage which defines the sub-

[11] Cf. James H. McBurney, "The Place of the Enthymeme in Rhetorical Theory," *SM*, III (1936), 52.

[12] Cf. W. Windelband, *A History of Philosophy* (New York: The Macmillan Company, 1901), p. 137; also P. Albert Duhamel, "The Function of Rhetoric as Effective Expression," *Journal of the History of Ideas*, X (June 1949), 345.

[13] *Op. cit.*, p. 15.

[14] *Ibid.*, p. 16.

[15] *Ibid.*, p. 17.

ject satisfactorily with regard to the *logos,* or the set of propositions making up some coherent universe of discourse; and we can therefore say that a dialectical position is established when its relation to an opposite has been made clear and it is thus rationally rather than empirically sustained."[16] This view of dialectic as purely conceptual leads to a notion of rhetoric as applicative or practical. Thus for Weaver "the urgency of facts is never a dialectical concern";[17] "what a successful dialectic secures . . . is not actuality but possibility; and what rhetoric thereafter accomplishes is to take any dialectically secured position . . . and show its relationship to the world of prudential conduct."[18] The relationship between dialectic and rhetoric may now be stated as Weaver understands it.

Rhetoric in the wider sense includes dialectic,[19] in so far as dialectic has already functioned in providing the rhetorician with the truth, or in so far as the application of a dialectically secured position is made to the real world. The action that rhetoric professes presupposes in this sense the understanding that good action always involves. This being so, Weaver's point emerges: the duty of rhetoric in the widest sense is "to bring together action and understanding into a whole that is greater than scientific perception."[20] By itself, then, rhetoric is blind, for it has not truth; concomitantly, an isolated dialectic is empty, for it never engages the issues of the empirical world. Combined, dialectic and rhetoric constitute an instrument for reapproaching the multiple problems of politics, ethics, linguistics, and literary criticism. But in what sense does this union of rhetoric and dialectic provide us with a *rapprochement* between rhetoric and philosophy? At this point we must return to the original problem and see where the argument has led us.

We began, it may be recalled, with the functional stress which is placed on rhetoric today and suggested that much of the confusion regarding the nature and province of rhetoric is due to the divorce between rhetoric and dialectic. Our thesis here converges with that of Weaver, for it is precisely Weaver's point, as we have just seen, that rhetoric must go with dialectic if it is to be meaningful. Now the union of rhetoric with dialectic means, in Weaver's terms, a return of rhetoric to a dialectic understood not as the "art of logical discussion" but in the much broader sense of the conceptual ordering of propositions into coherent structures of an a priori nature. Dialectic in this sense is no longer "argumentative inquiry" but rather, I submit, philosophical

16 *Ibid.,* p. 27.
17 *Ibid.,* p. 27.
18 *Ibid.,* pp. 27–28.
19 *Ibid.,* p. 15.
20 *Ibid.,* p. 24.

inquiry. The unification of rhetoric and dialectic is really the *rapprochement* between philosophy and rhetoric because dialectic is given a unique interpretation: dialectic constitutes the true philosophy of rhetoric.

Understood in this way, the original Platonic and Aristotelian notions of rhetoric and dialectic become clarified: the philosophy of rhetoric achieves the Platonic idea of *technē,* and the Aristotelian idea of dialectic is seen in its most challenging aspect. Rhetoric ceases to be the *technique* of persuasion and truly becomes the *art* it was originally held to be, an art, however, which sustains itself only in and through its involvement with dialectic.

If all this is true, the question naturally arises, What, after all, is the subject matter of the philosophy of rhetoric? Granted the meaningfulness of interpreting rhetoric in this way, what is to be done with the interpretation? Have we invoked Whately's criticism of Cicero, Richards' criticism of Whately, and added our criticism of Richards, only to fall into the same trap ourselves? The unavoidable question is, What problems constitute the subject matter of the philosophy of rhetoric, and how may such a philosophy be articulated? Obviously, we can offer only a fragmentary indication here of the way in which we would approach these problems.

Let us return once again to Aristotle's concept of dialectic. As we noted, dialectic is understood by Aristotle as operating in the realm of probability, not necessity. Dialectic seeks the truth but conducts the search in the midst of the real world of contingency and doubt.[21] Now the new enriched conception of dialectic that we are offering here—dialectic understood as the philosophy of rhetoric—concerns itself not with fact but with the theoretical structure that is logically prior to fact. How is such an a priori system related to the contingent world? The question then is, What is the relationship of dialectical theory to rhetorical fact? Stated in still another way, the question is, What is the relationship of theory to practice? All of these questions are transpositions of our fundamental problem: the true province of rhetoric. The answer to these questions and the exploration of the fundamental problem lead necessarily to the nature of philosophy itself. To answer the question, What is the subject matter of the philosophy of rhetoric, we must investigate the foundational discipline of philosophy, which is the bedrock, the ultimate and absolute ground of all inquiry.

I propose to understand by philosophy the critique of presuppositions. Philosophy in its synthetic aspect seeks to comprehend the nature

---

[21] The tremendous philosophical problem of the meaning of "probability" in common-sense reality is necessarily beyond the scope of this paper.

of reality by inquiring critically into the categories of reality: quantity, quality, relation, and modality, to refer to the Kantian categories. In its analytic aspect philosophy attempts to bring to clarity the meaning of terms which are basic and crucial to the conceptual structure of all special disciplines. So in history, for example, analytic philosophy investigates the meaning of such terms as "fact," "event," "cause," "effect," "consequence," etc. These are the basic terms out of which history constructs its subject matter and builds its schemata. Both the synthetic and analytic aspects of philosophy turn upon a single, though complex, focal point: the systematic and persistent exploration of elements and themes which are taken for granted in both common-sense reality and in the special disciplines. Thus, philosophy is the critique of such presuppositions as the belief in the existence of an external world, of other fellow men in that world, of communication between those fellow men, etc. Philosophy does not deny the existence of these things; rather it seeks to express their meaningful structure, to bring to complete clarity the conditions which make common-sense experience possible and comprehensible. As a critique of presuppositions, philosophy is a reflexive discipline, i.e., it not only takes for investigation objects and problems external to it, but it also seeks to understand itself. Philosophy is self-problematic: it is the only discipline that begins by inquiring into its own nature and goes on to examine its own instruments of inquiry. The subject matter of philosophy, then, consists of the categories of reality and the basic terms of all particular disciplines; the ultimate goal of the critique of these elements is the reconstruction of the real in perfect self-clarity and illumination.

If this may be taken as the nature of philosophy generally, what is the province of the philosophy of rhetoric? I would suggest that the philosophy of rhetoric directs itself toward the following problems: the relationship between language and what language denotes; the relationship between mind and what mind is aware of; the relationship between knowledge and what knowledge is "of"; the relationship between consciousness and its various contents; etc. Now what differentiates these problems from their generalized setting in the theory of knowledge is the particular kind of context in which these problems arise in rhetoric. Instead of the general problem of meaning, the philosopher of rhetoric is interested in how this problem arises with regard to speaker and listener, poet and reader, playwright and audience. Instead of the epistemology of consciousness, the philosopher of rhetoric directs his attention to those states of consciousness manifest in persuasion. Instead of the generalized problem of knowledge, the philosopher of rhetoric attends to the status of that knowledge which the persuader seeks to persuade us of.

The philosophy of rhetoric, then, has as its subject matter the application of the critique of presuppositions to those presuppositions which characterize the fundamental scope of rhetoric: presuppositions in the relationship of speaker and listener, the persuader and the one persuaded, judger and the thing judged. *The specific object of inquiry here is not the technique of speaking or persuading or judging but the very meaning of these activities.* Thus rhetoric stands in relation to philosophy as science stands in relation to philosophy. In both cases, philosophy investigates what both disciplines presuppose: knowledge, existence, communication, and value. Just as the philosophy of science analyzes the meaning of such elements as "fact," "causation," and "law," so the philosophy of rhetoric studies the elements of "language," "meaning," and "persuasion." This brings us to the question of the relationship of the philosophy of rhetoric to rhetoric in the narrower sense.

The conclusion of our analysis may be expressed in a typology or hierarchical ordering of the different aspects of rhetoric. This will help to make clear precisely what is meant by rhetoric in the broader and narower sense of the term. Going from the narrower meaning down to the broadest meaning, we have the following aspects of rhetoric: rhetorical intention in speech or writing, the technique of persuasion, the general rationale of persuasion, and finally the philosophy of rhetoric. Rhetoric in the narrower aspect involves rhetorical intention in the sense that a speaker or writer may devote his effort to persuade for some cause or object. Since much of what is commonly called "bad" rhetoric frequently is found in such efforts, the field of rhetoric understood as the technique of persuasion is systematically studied and taught. Here the teacher of rhetoric investigates the devices and modes of argument, the outline for which is to be found in Aristotle's *Rhetoric* or other classical rhetorics. Reflection of a critical order on the significance and nature of the technique of persuasion brings us to rhetoric understood as the general rationale of persuasion. This is what might be termed the "theory" of rhetoric in so far as the central principles of rhetoric are examined and ordered. The emphasis is on the general principles of rhetoric as rhetoric is intimately related to functional, pragmatically directed contexts. Finally, we come to the critique of the rationale of rhetoric which inquires into the underlying assumptions, the philosophical grounds of all the elements of rhetoric.[22] It

[22] It is interesting to note that Donald C. Bryant approaches a similar typology, though he stops short of the philosophy of rhetoric as we understand it. Speaking of the rhetorician, Bryant writes, *op. cit.,* p. 408: "the term *rhetorician* will sometimes mean the formulator and philosopher of rhetorical theory; sometimes the teacher of the technique of discourse; sometimes the speaker with rhetorical intention; and finally the student or scholar whose concern is the literary or social or behavioral study of rhetoric. I have been tempted to invent terms to avoid certain of these ambiguities

is here that a philosophy of rhetoric finds its placement. If rhetoric is bound to and founded on dialectic, and dialectic on philosophy, then the limits of rhetoric find their expression in the matrix of philosophical inquiry.

---

such as *logology*, or even *rhetoristic* (parallel with *sophistic*), but the game would probably not be worth the candle." Our point in this paper has been to show that not only is the game worth the candle, but that in a sense without the game no ultimate rhetoric is possible.

25 THE RHETORICAL SITUATION

LLOYD BITZER

Kenneth Burke contends that an accurate analysis of a rhetorical situation reveals the motivations that give rise to the discourse. Burke further believes that rhetorical works are strategic, stylized answers to questions posed by the situation in which they arise. In the following illuminating essay, Bitzer identifies the characteristics of a rhetorical situation, the "nature of those contexts in which speakers and writers create rhetorical discourse."

The essay is a detailed explanation of the basic elements in the following definition: "Rhetorical situation may be defined as a complex of persons, events, objects, and relations presenting an actual or potential exigence which can be completely or partially removed if discourse, introduced into the situation, can so constrain human decision or action as to bring about the significant modification of the exigence." Standing alone this definition seems abstruse and jargon-laden; but Bitzer's analysis affords a meaningful elaboration of it. He seeks to augment past scholarly efforts that have focused on the speaker's methods and the speech itself at the expense of studying the situation that stimulated the discourse. For a critical analysis of Bitzer's view and an alternative behavioral framework to it see K. E. Wilkerson, "On Evaluating Theories of Rhetoric," *Philosophy and Rhetoric*, 3 (Spring 1970), 82–96.

Note that Bitzer's conception of rhetorical situation easily encompasses the stress on audience analysis common to much recent rhetorical theorizing. For different conceptions of rhetorical situations, see Otis Walter, "Toward an Analysis of Motivation," *Quarterly Journal of Speech*, XLI (October 1955), 271–278; Walter R. Fisher, "A Motive View of Communication," *Quarterly Journal of Speech*, LVI (April 1970), 131–139.

Source: Philosophy and Rhetoric, 1 (January 1968), 1–14. Reprinted with permission of the author and the publisher.

If someone says, That is a dangerous situation, his words suggest the presence of events, persons, or objects which threaten him, someone else, or something of value. If someone remarks, I find myself in an embarrassing situation, again the statement implies certain situational characteristics. If someone remarks that he found himself in an ethical situation, we understand that he probably either contemplated or made some choice of action from a sense of duty or obligation or with a view to the Good. In other words, there are circumstances of this or that kind of structure which are recognized as ethical, dangerous, or embarrassing. What characteristics, then, are implied when one refers to "the rhetorical situation"—the context in which speakers or writers create rhetorical discourse? Perhaps this question is puzzling because "situation" is not a standard term in the vocabulary of rhetorical theory. "Audience" is standard; so also are "speaker," "subject," occasion," and "speech." If I were to ask, "What is a rhetorical audience?" or "What is a rhetorical subject?"—the reader would catch the meaning of my question.

When I ask, What is a rhetorical situation?, I want to know the nature of those contexts in which speakers or writers create rhetorical discourse: How should they be described? What are their characteristics? Why and how do they result in the creation of rhetoric? By analogy, a theorist of science might well ask, What are the characteristics of situations which inspire scientific thought? A philosopher might ask, What is the nature of the situation in which a philosopher "does philosophy"? And a theorist of poetry might ask, How shall we describe the context in which poetry comes into existence?

The presence of rhetorical discourse obviously indicates the presence of a rhetorical situation. The Declaration of Independence, Lincoln's Gettysburg Address, Churchill's Address on Dunkirk, John F. Kennedy's Inaugural Address—each is a clear instance of rhetoric and each indicates the presence of a situation. While the existence of a rhetorical address is a reliable sign of the existence of situation, it does not follow that a situation exists only when the discourse exists. Each reader probably can recall a specific time and place when there was opportunity to speak on some urgent matter, and after the opportunity was gone he created in private thought the speech he should have uttered earlier in the situation. It is clear that situations are not always accompanied by discourse. Nor should we assume that a rhetorical address gives existence to the situation; on the contrary, it is the situation which calls the discourse into existence. Clement Attlee once said that Winston Churchill went around looking for "finest hours." The point to observe is that Churchill found them—the crisis situations—and spoke in response to them.

No major theorist has treated rhetorical situation thoroughly as a distinct subject in rhetorical theory; many ignore it. Those rhetoricians who discuss situation do so indirectly—as does Aristotle, for example, who is led to consider situation when he treats types of discourse. None, to my knowledge, has asked the nature of rhetorical situation. Instead rhetoricians have asked: What is the process by which the orator creates and presents discourse? What is the nature of rhetorical discourse? What sorts of interaction occur between speaker, audience, subject, and occasion? Typically the questions which trigger theories of rhetoric focus upon the orator's method or upon the discourse itself, rather than upon the situation which invites the orator's application of his method and the creation of discourse. Thus rhetoricians distinguish among and characterize the types of speeches (forensic, deliberative, epideictic); they treat issues, types of proof, lines of argument, strategies of ethical and emotional persuasion, the parts of a discourse and the functions of these parts, qualities of styles, figures of speech. They cover approximately the same materials, the formal aspects of rhetorical method and discourse, whether focusing upon method, product or process; while conceptions of situation are implicit in some theories of rhetoric, none explicitly treat the formal aspects of situation.

I hope that enough has been said to show that the question—What is a rhetorical situation?—is not an idle one. I propose in what follows to set forth part of a theory of situation. This essay, therefore, should be understood as an attempt to revive the notion of rhetorical situation, to provide at least the outline of an adequate conception of it, and to establish it as a controlling and fundamental concern of rhetorical theory.

I

It seems clear that rhetoric is situational. In saying this, I do not mean merely that understanding a speech hinges upon understanding the context of meaning in which the speech is located. Virtually no utterance is fully intelligible unless meaning-context and utterance are understood; this is true of rhetorical and non-rhetorical discourse. Meaning-context is a general condition of human communication and is not synonymous with rhetorical situation. Nor do I mean merely that rhetoric occurs in a setting which involves interaction of speaker, audience, subject, and communicative purpose. This is too general, since many types of utterances—philosophical, scientific, poetic, and rhetorical—occur in such settings. Nor would I equate rhetorical situation with persuasive situation, which exists whenever an audience can be changed in belief or action by means of speech. Every audience at any moment is capable of being changed in some way by speech; persuasive situation is altogether general.

Finally, I do not mean that a rhetorical discourse must be embedded in historic context in the sense that a living tree must be rooted in soil. A tree does not obtain its character-as-tree from the soil, but rhetorical discourse, I shall argue, does obtain its character-as-rhetorical from the situation which generates it. Rhetorical works belong to the class of things which obtain their character from the circumstances of the historic context in which they occur. A rhetorical work is analogous to a moral action rather than to a tree. An act is moral because it is an act performed in a situation of a certain kind; similarly, a work is rhetorical because it is a response to a situation of a certain kind.

In order to clarify rhetoric-as-essentially-related-to-situation, we should acknowledge a viewpoint that is commonplace but fundamental: a work of rhetoric is pragmatic; it comes into existence for the sake of something beyond itself; it functions ultimately to produce action or change in the world; it performs some task. In short, rhetoric is a mode of altering reality, not by the direct application of energy to objects, but by the creation of discourse which changes reality through the mediation of thought and action. The rhetor alters reality by bringing into existence a discourse of such a character that the audience, in thought and action, is so engaged that it becomes mediator of change. In this rhetoric is always persuasive.

To say that rhetorical discourse comes into being in order to effect change is altogether general. We need to understand that a particular discourse comes into existence because of some specific condition or situation which invites utterance. Bronislaw Malinowski refers to just this sort of situation in his discussion of primitive language, which he finds to be essentially pragmatic and "embedded in situation." He describes a party of fishermen in the Trobriand Islands whose functional speech occurs in a "context of situation."

The canoes glide slowly and noiselessly, punted by men especially good at this task and always used for it. Other experts who know the bottom of the lagoon . . . are on the look-out for fish. . . . Customary signs, or sounds or words are uttered. Sometimes a sentence full of technical references to the channels or patches on the lagoon has to be spoken; sometimes . . . a conventional cry is uttered. . . . Again, a word of command is passed here and there, a technical expression or explanation which serves to harmonize their behavior towards other men. . . . An animated scene, full of movement, follows, and now that the fish are in their power the fishermen speak loudly, and give vent to their feelings. Short, telling exclamations fly about, which might be rendered by such words as: "Pull in," "Let go," "Shift further," "Lift the net."

In this whole scene, "each utterance is essentially bound up with the context of situation and with the aim of the pursuit. . . . The structure of all this linguistic material is inextricably mixed up with, and dependent upon, the course of the activity in which the utterances are embedded." Later the observer remarks: "In its primitive uses, language functions as a link in concerted human activity, as a piece of human behaviour. It is a mode of action and not an instrument of reflection."[1]

These statements about primitive language and the "context of situation" provide for us a preliminary model of rhetorical situation. Let us regard rhetorical situation as a natural context of persons, events, objects, relations, and an exigence which strongly invites utterance; this invited utterance participates naturally in the situation, is in many instances necessary to the completion of situational activity, and by means of its participation with situation obtains its meaning and its rhetorical character. In Malinowski's example, the situation is the fishing expedition—consisting of objects, persons, events, and relations—and the ruling exigence, the success of the hunt. The situation dictates the sorts of observations to be made; it dictates the significant physical and verbal responses; and, we must admit, it constrains the words which are uttered in the same sense that it constrains the physical acts of paddling the canoes and throwing the nets. The verbal responses to the demands imposed by this situation are clearly as functional and necessary as the physical responses.

Traditional theories of rhetoric have dealt, of course, not with the sorts of primitive utterances described by Malinowski—"stop here," "throw the nets," "move closer"—but with larger units of speech which come more readily under the guidance of artistic principle and method. The difference between oratory and primitive utterance, however, is not a difference in function; the clear instances of rhetorical discourse and the fishermen's utterances are similarly functional and similarly situational. Observing both the traditions of the expedition and the facts before him, the leader of the fishermen finds himself *obliged* to speak at a given moment—to command, to supply information, to praise or blame—to respond appropriately to the situation. Clear instances of artistic rhetoric exhibit the same character: Cicero's speeches against Cataline were called forth by a specific union of persons, events, objects, and relations, and by an exigence which amounted to an imperative stimulus; the speeches in the Senate rotunda three days after the assassination of the President of the United States were actually required by the situation. So controlling is situation that we should consider it the very ground of rhetorical activity, whether that activity is primitive and productive of a simple utterance or artistic and productive of the Gettysburg Address.

Hence, to say that rhetoric is situational means: (1) rhetorical discourse comes into existence as a response to situation, in the same sense that an answer comes into existence in response to a question,

---

[1] "The Problem of Meaning in Primitive Languages," sections III and IV. This essay appears as a supplement in Ogden and Richards' *The Meaning of Meaning*.

or a solution in response to a problem; (2) a speech is given *rhetorical* significance by the situation, just as a unit of discourse is given significance *as* answer or *as* solution by the question or problem; (3) a rhetorical situation must exist as a necessary condition of rhetorical discourse, just as a question must exist as a necessary condition of an answer; (4) many questions go unanswered and many problems remain unsolved; similarly, many rhetorical situations mature and decay without giving birth to rhetorical utterance; (5) a situation is rhetorical insofar as it needs and invites discourse capable of participating with situation and thereby altering its reality; (6) discourse is rhetorical insofar as it functions, (or seeks to function) as a fitting response to a situation which needs and invites it. (7) Finally, the situation controls the rhetorical response in the same sense that the question controls the answer and the problem controls the solution. Not the rhetor and not persuasive intent, but the situation is the source and ground of rhetorical activity—and, I should add, of rhetorical criticism.

II

Let us now amplify the nature of situation by providing a formal definition and examining constituents. Rhetorical situation may be defined as a complex of persons, events, objects, and relations presenting an actual or potential exigence which can be completely or partially removed if discourse, introduced into the situation, can so constrain human decision or action as to bring about the significant modification of the exigence. Prior to the creation and presentation of discourse, there are three constituents of any rhetorical situation: the first is the *exigence;* the second and third are elements of the complex, namely the *audience* to be constrained in decision and action, and the *constraints* which influence the rhetor and can be brought to bear upon the audience.

Any *exigence* is an imperfection marked by urgency; it is a defect, an obstacle, something waiting to be done, a thing which is other than it should be. In almost any sort of context, there will be numerous exigences, but not all are elements of a rhetorical situation—not all are rhetorical exigences. An exigence which cannot be modified is not rhetorical; thus, whatever comes about of necessity and cannot be changed—death, winter, and some natural disasters, for instance— are exigences to be sure, but they are not rhetorical. Further, an exigence which can be modified only by means other than discourse is not rhetorical; thus, an exigence is not rhetorical when its modification requires merely one's own action or the application of a tool, but neither requires nor invites the assistance of discourse. An exigence is rhetorical when it is capable of positive modification and when positive modification requires discourse or can be assisted by discourse. For example, suppose that a man's acts are injurious to others and that the quality of his acts can be changed only if discourse is addressed to him; the exigence—his injurious acts—is then unmistakably rhetorical. The pollution of our air is also a rhetorical exigence because its positive modification—reduction of pollution—strongly invites the assistance of discourse producing public awareness, indignation, and action of the right kind. Frequently rhetors encounter exigences which defy easy classification because of the absence of information enabling precise analysis and certain judgment—they may or may not be rhetorical. An attorney whose client has been convicted may strongly believe that a higher court would reject his appeal to have the verdict overturned, but because the matter is uncertain—because the exigence *might* be rhetorical—he elects to appeal. In this and similar instances of indeterminate exigences the rhetor's decision to speak is based mainly upon the urgency of the exigence and the probability that the exigence is rhetorical.

In any rhetorical situation there will be at least one controlling exigence which functions as the organizing principle: it specifies the audience to be addressed and the change to be effected. The exigence may or may not be perceived clearly by the rhetor or other persons in the situation; it may be strong or weak depending upon the clarity of their perception and the degree of their interest in it; it may be real or unreal depending on the facts of the case; it may be important or trivial; it may be such that discourse can completely remove it, or it may persist in spite of repeated modifications; it may be completely familiar—one of a type of exigences occurring frequently in our experience—or it may be totally new, unique. When it is perceived and when it is strong and important, then it constrains the thought and action of the perceiver who may respond rhetorically if he is in a position to do so.

The second constituent is the *audience*. Since rhetorical discourse produces change by influencing the decision and action of persons who function as mediators of change, it follows that rhetoric always requires an audience—even in those cases when a person engages himself or ideal mind as audience. It is clear also that a rhetorical audience must be distinguished from a body of mere hearers or readers: properly speaking, a rhetorical audience consists only of those persons who are capable of being influenced by discourse and of being mediators of change.

Neither scientific nor poetic discourse requires an audience in the same sense. Indeed, neither requires an audience in order to produce its end; the scientist can produce a discourse expressive or generative of knowledge without engaging another mind, and the poet's creative purpose is accomplished when the work is composed. It is true, of course, that scientists and poets present their works to audiences, but their audiences are not necessarily rhetorical. The scientific audience consists of persons capable of receiving knowledge, and the poetic audience, of persons capable of participating in aesthetic experiences induced by the poetry. But the rhetorical audience must be capable of serving as mediator of the change which the discourse functions to produce.

Besides exigence and audience, every rhetorical situation contains a set of *constraints* made up of persons, events, objects, and relations which are parts of the situation because they have the power to constrain decision and action needed to modify the exigence. Standard sources of constraint include beliefs, attitudes, documents, facts, traditions, images, interests, motives and the like; and when the orator enters the situation, his discourse not only harnesses constraints given by situation but provides additional important constraints—for example, his personal character, his logical proofs, and his style. There are two main classes of contraints: (1) those originated or managed by the rhetor and his method (Aristotle called these "artistic proofs"), and (2) those other constraints, in the situation, which may be operative (Aristotle's "inartistic proofs"). Both classes must be divided so as to separate those constraints that are proper from those that are improper.

These three constituents—exigence, audience, constraints—comprise everything relevant in a rhetorical situation. When the orator, invited by situation, enters it and creates and presents discourse, then both he and his speech are additional constituents.

III

I have broadly sketched a conception of rhetorical situation and discussed constituents. The following are general characteristics or features.

1. Rhetorical discourse is called into existence by situation; the situation which the rhetor perceives amounts to an invitation to create and present discourse. The clearest instances of rhetorical speaking and writing are strongly invited—often required. The situation generated by the assassination of President Kennedy was so highly structured and compelling that one could predict with near certainty the types and themes of forthcoming discourse. With the first reports of the assassination, there immediately developed a most urgent need for information; in response, reporters created hundreds of messages. Later as the situation altered, other exigences arose: the fantastic events in Dallas had to be explained; it was necessary to eulogize the dead President; the public needed to be assured that the transfer of government to

new hands would be orderly. These messages were not idle performances. This historic situation was so compelling and clear that the responses were created almost out of necessity. The responses—news reports, explanations, eulogies—participated with the situation and positively modified the several exigences. Surely the power of situation is evident when one can predict that such discourse will be uttered. How else explain the phenomenon? One cannot say that the situation is the function of the speaker's intention, for in this case the speakers' intentions were determined by the situation. One cannot say that the rhetorical transaction is simply a response of the speaker to the demands or expectations of an audience, for the expectations of the audience were themselves keyed to a tragic historic fact. Also, we must recognize that there came into existence countless eulogies to John F. Kennedy that never reached a public; they were filed, entered in diaries, or created in thought.

In contrast, imagine a person spending his time writing eulogies of men and women who never existed: his speeches meet no rhetorical situations; they are summoned into existence not by real events, but by his own imagination. They may exhibit formal features which we consider rhetorical—such ethical and emotional appeals, and stylistic patterns; conceivably one of these fictive eulogies is even persuasive to someone; yet all remain unrhetorical unless, through the oddest of circumstances, one of them by chance should fit a situation. Neither the presence of formal features in the discourse nor persuasive effect in a reader or hearer can be regarded as reliable marks of rhetorical discourse: A speech will be rhetorical when it is a response to the kind of situation which is rhetorical.

2. Although rhetorical situation invites response, it obviously does not invite just any response. Thus the second characteristic of rhetorical situation is that it invites a *fitting* response, a response that fits the situation. Lincoln's Gettysburg Address was a most fitting response to the relevant features of the historic context which invited its existence and gave it rhetorical significance. Imagine for a moment the Gettysburg Address entirely separated from its situation and existing for us independent of any rhetorical context: as a discourse which does not "fit" any rhetorical situation, it becomes either poetry or declamation, without rhetorical significance. In reality, however, the address continues to have profound rhetorical value precisely because some features of the Gettysburg situation persist; and the Gettysburg Address continues to participate with situation and to alter it.

Consider another instance. During one week of the 1964 presidential campaign, three events of national and international significance all but obscured the campaign: Khrushchev was suddenly deposed, China exploded an atomic bomb, and in England the Conservative Party was defeated by Labour. Any student of rhetoric could have given odds that President Johnson, in a major address, would speak to the significance of these events, and he did; his response to the situation generated by the events was fitting. Suppose that the President had treated not these events and their significance but the national budget, or imagine that he had reminisced about his childhood on a Texas farm. The critic of rhetoric would have said rightly, "He missed the mark; his speech did not fit; he did not speak to the pressing issues—the rhetorical situation shaped by the three crucial events of the week demanded a response, and he failed to provide the proper one."

3. If it makes sense to say that situation invites a "fitting" response, then situation must somehow prescribe the response which fits. To say that a rhetorical response fits a situation is to say that it meets the requirements established by the situation. A situation which is strong and clear dictates the purpose, theme, matter, and style of the response. Normally, the inauguration of a President of the United States demands an address which speaks to the nation's purposes, the central national and international problems, the unity of contesting parties; it demands speech style marked by dignity. What is evidenced on this occasion is the power of situation to constrain a fitting response. One might say metaphorically that every situation prescribes its fitting response; the rhetor may or may not read the prescription accurately.

4. The exigence and the complex of persons, objects, events and relations which generate rhetorical discourse are located in reality, are objective and publicly observable historic facts in the world we experience, are therefore available for scrutiny by an observer or critic who attends to them. To say the situation is objective, publicly observable, and historic means that it is real or genuine—that our critical examination will certify its existence. Real situations are to be distinguished from sophistic ones in which, for example, a contrived exigence is asserted to be real; from spurious situations in which the existence or alleged existence of constituents is the result of error or ignorance; and from fantasy in which exigence, audience, and constraints may all be the imaginary objects of a mind at play.

The rhetorical situation as real is to be distinguished also from a fictive rhetorical situation. The speech of a character in a novel or play may be clearly required by a fictive rhetorical situation—a situation established by the story itself; but the speech is not genuinely rhetorical, even though, considered in itself, it looks exactly like a courtroom address or a senate speech. It is realistic, made so by fictive context. But the situation is not real, not grounded in history; neither the fictive situation nor the discourse generated by it is rhetorical. We should note, however, that the fictive rhetorical discourse within a play or novel may become genuinely rhetorical outside fictive context—if there is a real situation for which the discourse is a rhetorical response. Also, of course, the play or novel itself may be understood as a rhetorical response having poetic form.

5. Rhetorical situations exhibit structures which are simple or complex, and more or less organized. A situation's structure is simple when there are relatively few elements which must be made to interact; the fishing expedition is a case in point—there is a clear and easy relationship among utterances, the audiences, constraints, and exigence. Franklin D. Roosevelt's brief Declaration of War speech is another example: the message exists as a response to one clear exigence easily perceived by one major audience, and the one overpowering constraint is the necessity of war. On the other hand, the structure of a situation is complex when many elements must be made to interact: practically any presidential political campaign provides numerous complex rhetorical situations.

A situation, whether simple or complex, will be highly structured or loosely structured. It is highly structured when all of its elements are located and readied for the task to be performed. Malinowski's example, the fishing expedition, is a situation which is relatively simple and highly structured; everything is ordered to the task to be performed. The usual courtroom case is a good example of a situation which is complex and highly structured. The jury is not a random and scattered audience but a selected and concentrated one; it knows its relation to judge, law, defendant, counsels; it is instructed in what to observe and what to disregard. The judge is located and prepared; he knows exactly his relation to jury, law, counsels, defendant. The counsels know the ultimate object of their case; they know what they must prove; they know the audience and can easily reach it. This situation will be even more highly structured if the issue of the case is sharp, the evidence decisive, and the law clear. On the other hand, consider a complex but loosely structured situation, William Lloyd Garrison preaching abolition from town to town. He is actually looking for an audience and for constraints; even when he finds an audience, he does not know that it is a genuinely rhetorical audience—one able to be mediator of change. Or consider the plight of many contemporary civil rights advocates who, failing to locate compelling constraints and rhetorical audiences, abandon rhetorical discourse in favor of physical action.

Situations may become weakened in structure due to complexity or disconnectedness. A list of causes includes these: (a) a single situation may involve numerous exigences; (b) exigences in the same situation may be incompatible; (c) two or more simultaneous rhetorical situations may compete for our attention, as in some parliamentary debates; (d) at a given moment, persons comprising the audience of situation

A may also be the audience of situations B, C, and D; (e) the rhetorical audience may be scattered, uneducated, regarding its duties and powers, or it may dissipate; (f) constraints may be limited in number and force, and they may be incompatible. This is enough to suggest the sorts of things which weaken the structure of situations.

6. Finally, rhetorical situations come into existence, then either mature or decay or mature and persist—conceivably some persist indefinitely. In any case, situations grow and come to maturity; they evolve to just the time when a rhetorical discourse would be most fitting. In Malinowski's example, there comes a time in the situation when the leader of the fishermen should say, "Throw the nets." In the situation generated by the assassination of the President, there was a time for giving descriptive accounts of the scene in Dallas, later a time for giving eulogies. In a political campaign, there is a time for generating an issue and a time for answering a charge. Every rhetorical situation in principle evolves to a propitious moment for the fitting rhetorical response. After this moment, most situations decay; we all have the experience of creating a rhetorical response when it is too late to make it public.

Some situations, on the other hand, persist; this is why it is possible to have a body of truly *rhetorical* literature. The Gettysburg Address, Burke's Speech to the Electors of Bristol, Socrates' Apology—these are more than historical documents, more than specimens for stylistic or logical analysis. They exist as rhetorical responses *for us* precisely because they speak to situations which persist—which are in some measure universal.

Due to either the nature of things or convention, or both, some situations recur. The courtroom is the focus for several kinds of situations generating the speech of accusation, the speech of defense, the charge to the jury. From day to day, year to year, comparable situations occur, prompting comparable responses; hence rhetorical forms are born and a special vocabulary, grammar, and style are established. This is true also of the situation which invites the inaugural address of a President. The situation recurs and, because we experience situations and the rhetorical responses to them, a form of discourse is not only established but comes to have a power of its own—the tradition itself tends to function as a constraint upon any new response in the form.

IV

In the best of all possible worlds, there would be communication perhaps, but no rhetoric—since exigences would not arise. In our real world, however, rhetorical exigences abound; the world really invites change—change conceived and effected by human agents who quite properly address a mediating audience. The practical justification of rhetoric is analogous to that of scientific inquiry: the world presents objects to be known, puzzles to be resolved, complexities to be understood—hence the practical need for scientific inquiry and discourse; similarly, the world presents imperfections to be modified by means of discourse—hence the practical need for rhetorical investigation and discourse. As a discipline, scientific method is justified philosophically insofar as it provides principles, concepts, and procedures by which we come to know reality; similarly, rhetoric as a discipline is justified philosophically insofar as it provides principles, concepts, and procedures by which we effect valuable changes in reality. Thus rhetoric is distinguished from the mere craft of persuasion which, although it is a legitimate object of scientific investigation, lacks philosophical warrant as a practical discipline.

BIBLIOGRAPHY
OF SOURCES FOR FURTHER READING

ISSUES IN THEORY CONSTRUCTION

Barnlund, Dean. "Toward a Meaning-Centered Philosophy of Communication." *Journal of Communication,* XII (December 1962), pp. 197–211.

Bitzer, Lloyd, and Edwin Black, eds. *The Prospect of Rhetoric: Report of the National Developmental Project.* New York: Prentice-Hall, 1971.

Bormann, Ernest. *Theory and Research in the Communicative Arts.* New York: Holt, Rinehart, and Winston, 1966, Chaps. 3–6.

Bowers, John W. *Designing the Communication Experiment.* New York: Random House, 1970, espec. pp. 111–119.

———. "The Pre-Scientific Function of Rhetorical Criticism," in Thomas Nilsen, ed., *Essays on Rhetorical Criticism.* New York: Random House, 1968, pp. 126–145.

Campbell, Karlyn Kohrs. "The Ontological Foundations of Rhetorical Theory." *Philosophy and Rhetoric,* 3 (Spring 1970), pp. 97–108.

Clevenger, Theodore. "The Interaction of Descriptive and Experimental Research in the Development of Rhetorical Theory." *Central States Speech Journal,* XVI (February 1965), pp. 7–12.

Driessel, A. Berkley. "Communications Theory and Research Strategy: A Metatheoretical Analysis." *Journal of Communication,* XVII (June 1967), pp. 92–107.

Emmert, Philip, and William D. Brooks, eds. *Methods of Research in Communication.* Boston: Houghton Mifflin, 1970.

Kaplan, Abraham. *The Conduct of Inquiry.* San Francisco: Chandler, 1964, Chaps. 3, 4, and 8.

Miller, Gerald R. *Speech Communication: A Behavioral Approach.* Indianapolis: Bobbs-Merrill, 1966, Chaps. 2, 3, and 4.

Oliver, Robert T. *Culture and Communication.* Springfield, Ill.: Charles C Thomas, 1962, Chaps. 7 and 12.

Smith, Dennis R. "The Fallacy of 'Communication Breakdown.'" *Quarterly Journal of Speech,* LVI (December 1970), pp. 343–346.

Steinmann, Martin. "Rhetorical Research." *College English,* XXVII (January 1966), pp. 278–285.

Thayer, Lee. "On Theory-Building in Communication: Some Conceptual Problems." *Journal of Communication,* 13 (December 1963), pp. 217–235.

Thompson, Wayne N. *Quantitative Research in Public Address and Communication.* New York: Random House, 1967, Chaps. 1 and 7.

———. "An Assessment of Quantitative Research in Speech." *Quarterly Journal of Speech,* LV (February 1969), pp. 61–68.

Wilkerson, K. E. "On Evaluating Theories of Rhetoric." *Philosophy and Rhetoric,* 3 (Spring 1970), pp. 82–96.

Williams, Kenneth R. "Speech Communication Research: One World or Two?" *Central States Speech Journal,* XXI (Fall 1970), pp. 175–180.

KENNETH BURKE

Burke, Kenneth. *Attitudes Toward History,* rev. 2nd ed. Los Altos, Cal.: Hermes, 1959; Beacon Press paperback, 1961.

————. *Counter-Statement,* 2nd ed. Los Altos, Cal.: Hermes, 1953.

————. *A Grammar of Motives.* New York: Prentice-Hall, 1945; reissued University of California Press, 1969.

————. *Language as Symbolic Action.* Berkeley: University of California Press, 1966.

————. *Permanence and Change: An Anatomy of Purpose,* 2nd rev. ed. Los Altos, Cal.: Hermes, 1954; Bobbs-Merrill paperback ed. with intro. by Hugh D. Duncan, 1965.

————. *The Philosophy of Literary Form.* Baton Rouge: Louisiana State University Press, 1941; reissued L.S.U. Press, 1969; abridged Vintage paperback edition, 1957.

————. *A Rhetoric of Motives.* New York: Prentice-Hall, 1950; reissued University of California Press, 1969.

————. *The Rhetoric of Religion.* Boston: Beacon Press, 1961.

Duncan, Hugh D. *Communication and Social Order.* New York: Bedminster Press, 1962.

————. *Symbols in Society.* New York: Oxford University Press, 1968.

Fogarty, Daniel. *Roots for a New Rhetoric.* New York: Teachers College of Columbia University, 1959; reprinted Russell and Russell, 1968, Chap. 3.

Holland, L. Virginia. *Counterpoint: Kenneth Burke and Aristotle's Theories of Rhetoric.* New York: Philosophical Library, 1959.

Hyman, Stanley Edgar. *The Armed Vision,* rev. ed. New York: Vintage Books, 1955. Chap. 10.

Macksoud, S. John. "Kenneth Burke on Perspective and Rhetoric." *Western Speech,* XXXIII (Summer 1969), pp. 169–174.

Marlin, Charles L. *"Ad Bellum Purificandum:* The Rhetorical Uses of Kenneth Burke." Ph. D. dissertation, Indiana University, 1967.

Rosenfeld, Lawrence B. "Set Theory: Key to the Understanding of Kenneth Burke's Use of the Term 'Identification.'" *Western Speech,* XXXIII (Summer 1969), pp. 175–183.

Rueckert, William. *Kenneth Burke and the Drama of Human Relations.* Minneapolis: University of Minnesota Press, 1963.

Rueckert, William, ed. *Critical Responses to Kenneth Burke, 1924-1966.* Minneapolis: University of Minnesota Press, 1969.

Schwartz, Joseph. "Kenneth Burke, Aristotle, and the Future of Rhetoric." *College Composition and Communication,* 17 (December 1966), pp. 210–216.

Starosta, William. "United Nations: Burkeian Construct." M.A. thesis, Indiana University, 1970.

IVOR A. RICHARDS

Corts, Paul R. "I. A. Richards on Rhetoric and Criticism." *Southern Speech Journal,* XXXVI (Winter 1970), pp. 115–126.

Fogarty, Daniel. *Roots for a New Rhetoric.* New York: Teachers College of Columbia University, 1959; reprinted Russell and Russell, 1968, Chap. 2.

Hotopf, W. H. N. *Language, Thought and Comprehension: A Case Study of the Writing of I. A. Richards.* Bloomington: Indiana University Press, 1965.

Hyman, Stanley Edgar. *The Armed Vision,* rev. ed. New York: Vintage Books, 1955, Chap. 9.

Maham, Marilyn M. "I. A. Richards' Contributions to Rhetorical Theory." M. A. thesis, Stanford University, 1964.

Ogden, C. K., and I. A. Richards. *The Meaning of Meaning.* 1923; reprinted as Harvest Book paperback.

Richards, I. A. *Design for Escape: World Education Through Modern Media*. New York: Harcourt Brace Jovanovich, 1968.

————. *How to Read a Page*. New York: Norton, 1942.

————. *Interpretation in Teaching*. New York: Harcourt Brace Jovanovich, 1938.

————. *The Philosophy of Rhetoric*. New York: Oxford University Press, 1936; Galaxy Book paperback, 1965.

————. *Practical Criticism*. 1929; reprinted as Harvest Book paperback, 1956.

————. *Principles of Literary Criticism*. 1925; reprinted as Harvest Book paperback, n.d.

————. *So Much Nearer*. New York: Harcourt Brace Jovanovich, 1968.

————. *Speculative Instruments*. Chicago: University of Chicago Press, 1955; reprinted as Harvest Book paperback, n.d.

Schiller, Jerome P. *I. A. Richards' Theory of Literature*. New Haven: Yale University Press, 1969.

Sondel, Bess. *The Humanity of Words*. Cleveland: World, 1958, Part Two.

Van Graber, Marilyn. "I. A. Richards: A Rhetorical Construct." Ph.D. dissertation, University of Iowa, 1968.

RICHARD M. WEAVER

Bilsky, Manuel, Richard M. Weaver *et al.* "Looking for an Argument." *College English,* 14 (January 1953), pp. 210–216.

Clark, Thomas D. "The Philosophical Bases of Richard M. Weaver's View of Rhetoric." M.A. thesis, Indiana University, 1969.

Davidson, Donald. "Grammar and Rhetoric: The Teacher's Problem." *Quarterly Journal of Speech,* XXXIX (December 1953), pp. 424–436.

Hamlin, J. Robert. "The Rhetorical Mind of Richard Weaver: An Expository Critique of his Ideas on Rhetoric." Ph.D. dissertation, University of Oklahoma, 1971.

Hayakawa, S. I. *Symbol, Status, and Personality*. New York: Harcourt Brace Jovanovich, 1963, pp. 154–170, 182–185.

Johannesen, Richard L. "Richard Weaver's View of Rhetoric and Criticism." *Southern Speech Journal,* XXXII (Winter 1966), pp. 133–145.

————, Rennard Strickland, and Ralph T. Eubanks, eds. *Language Is Sermonic: Richard M. Weaver on the Nature of Rhetoric*. Baton Rouge: Louisiana State University Press, 1970.

Kendall, Willmoore. "How to Read Richard Weaver." *Intercollegiate Review,* 2 (September 1965), pp. 77–86.

Montgomery, Marion. "Richard Weaver Against the Establishment." *The Georgia Review,* XXIII (Winter 1969), pp. 433–459.

Natanson, Maurice. "The Limits of Rhetoric." *Quarterly Journal of Speech,* XLI (April 1955), pp. 133–139.

Smith, William R. *History as Argument*. The Hague: Mouton, 1966, espec. pp. 7–**8**, 171–204.

————. *The Rhetoric of American Politics*. Westport, Conn.: Greenwood Pub. Co., 1969, espec. pp. 14–37, 432, 438.

Weaver, Richard M. *Composition: A Course in Rhetoric and Writing*. New York: Holt, Rinehart, and Winston, 1957; rev. ed., 1967, with Richard S. Beal, as *Rhetoric and Composition: A Course in Writing and Reading*.

————. *The Ethics of Rhetoric*. Chicago: Regnery, 1953; Gateway paperback ed., **1965**.

————. *Ideas Have Consequences*. Chicago: University of Chicago Press, 1948; Phoenix Books paperback, 1959.

————. *Life Without Prejudice and Other Essays*. Chicago: Regnery, 1965.

————. *The Southern Tradition at Bay*. New Rochelle, N.Y.: Arlington House, 1968.

————. "Two Orators." *Modern Age,* 14 (Summer-Fall 1970), pp. 226–242.

————. "Up From Liberalism." *Modern Age,* 3 (Winter 1958–1959), pp. 21–32.

————. *Visions of Order.* Baton Rouge: Louisiana State University Press, 1964.

CHAIM PERELMAN

Arnold, Carroll C. "Perelman's New Rhetoric." *Quarterly Journal of Speech,* LVI (February 1970), pp. 87–92.

Dearin, Ray D. "Chaim Perelman's Theory of Rhetoric." Ph.D. dissertation, University of Illinois, 1970.

Florescu, Vasile. "Rhetoric and Its Rehabilitation in Contemporary Philosophy." *Philosophy and Rhetoric,* 3 (Fall 1970), pp. 193–224, espec. 210–221.

Kozy, John. Essay review of Perelman and Olbrechts-Tyteca, *The New Rhetoric. Philosophy and Rhetoric,* 3 (Fall 1970), pp. 249–254.

Loreau, Max. "Rhetoric as the Logic of the Behavioral Sciences." *Quarterly Journal of Speech,* LI (December 1965), pp. 455–463

Natanson, Maurice, and Henry W. Johnstone, Jr., eds. *Philosophy, Rhetoric, and Argumentation.* University Park, Pa.: Pennsylvania State University Press, 1965, Chaps. 6–10.

Perelman, Chaim. *An Historical Introduction to Philosophical Thinking,* trans. Kenneth Brown. New York: Random House, 1965.

————. "How Do We Apply Reason to Values?" *Journal of Philosophy,* (December 22, 1955), pp. 797–802.

————. *The Idea of Justice and the Problem of Argument.* New York: Humanities Press, 1963.

————. "Rhetoric and Philosophy." *Philosophy and Rhetoric,* 1 (January 1968), pp. 15–24.

————. "Value Judgments, Justifications, and Argumentation." *Philosophy Today,* 6 (1961), pp. 45–51.

———— and L. Olbrechts-Tyteca. *The New Rhetoric,* trans. John Wilkinson and Purcell Weaver. South Bend: University of Notre Dame Press, 1969; originally published in French in 1958.

———— and L. Olbrechts-Tyteca. *Rhétorique et Philosophie.* Paris: Presses Universitaires de France, 1952.

Stone, Julius. *Legal System and Lawyers' Reasonings.* Stanford, Cal.: Stanford University Press, 1964, pp. 325–337.

STEPHEN TOULMIN

Anderson, Ray, and C. David Mortensen. "Logic and Marketplace Argumentation." *Quarterly Journal of Speech,* LIII (April 1967), pp. 143–151.

Cooley, J. C. "On Mr. Toulmin's Revolution in Logic." *Journal of Philosophy,* 56 (1959), pp. 297–319.

Cowan, J. L. "The Uses of Argument—An Apology for Logic." *Mind,* 73 (January 1964), pp. 27–45.

Ehninger, Douglas, and Wayne Brockriede. *Decision by Debate.* New York: Dodd, Mead, 1963, Chaps. 8, 10, 11, and 15.

Marsh, Patrick. "A Model for Arguing Directive Propositions." *Journal of the American Forensic Association,* VI (Winter 1969), pp. 1–11.

McCroskey, James. "Toulmin and the Basic Course." *Speech Teacher,* 14 (March 1965), pp. 91–100.

Toulmin, Stephen. *The Uses of Argument.* New York: Cambridge University Press, 1958; paperback, 1964.

Trent, Jimmie. "Toulmin Model of Argument: An Examination and Extension." *Quarterly Journal of Speech,* LIV (October 1968), pp. 252–259.

Windes, Russell, and Arthur Hastings. *Argumentation and Advocacy.* New York: Random House, 1965, Chap. 5.

MARSHALL McLUHAN

Bridwell, James H. "Marshall McLuhan: An Experience." *Central States Speech Journal,* XXI (Fall 1970), pp. 154–159.

Carey, James W. "Harold Adams Innis and Marshall McLuhan." *Antioch Review,* XXVII (Spring 1967), pp. 5–39. Reprinted in Rosenthal, *McLuhan: Pro and Con,* pp. 270–308.

Carpenter, Edmund, and Marshall McLuhan, eds. *Explorations in Communication.* Boston: Beacon Press, 1960; paperback, 1966.

Costigan, James I. "Communication Theory in the Works of Marshall McLuhan." Ph.D. dissertation, Southern Illinois University, 1970.

Crosby, Harry, and George Bond, eds. *The McLuhan Explosion: A Casebook on Marshall McLuhan and Understanding Media.* New York: American Book Co., 1968.

Finkelstein, Sidney. *Sense and Nonsense of McLuhan.* New York: International Publishers, 1968.

Mahony, Patrick. "McLuhan in the Light of Classical Rhetorical Theory." *College Composition and Comunication,* XX (February 1969), pp. 12–17.

McLuhan, Marshall. "Ancient Quarrel in Modern America." *Classical Journal,* XLI (January 1946), pp. 156–162.

————. *Culture is Our Business.* New York: McGraw-Hill, 1970.

————. *The Gutenberg Galaxy.* Toronto: University of Toronto Press, 1962.

————. *The Mechanical Bride.* New York: Vanguard Press, 1951.

————. Interview in *Playboy* magazine, March 1969, pp. 53–74, 158.

————. "Poetic and Rhetorical Exegesis." *Sewanee Review,* 52 (April 1944), pp. 266–276.

————. *Understanding Media.* New York: McGraw-Hill, 1965.

————. *The Interior Landscape: The Literary Criticism of Marshall McLuhan, 1943–1962,* ed. Eugene McNamara. New York: McGraw-Hill, 1969.

———— with Wilfred Watson. *From Cliché to Archetype.* New York: Viking, 1970.

———— and Quentin Fiore. *The Medium is the Massage.* New York: Bantam paperback, 1967.

———— and Quentin Fiore. *War and Peace in the Global Village.* New York: McGraw-Hill, 1968.

————and Harley Parker. *Counterblast.* New York: Harcourt Brace Jovanovich, 1969.

McNulty, Thomas M. "Marshalling McLuhan: Contributions of Marshall McLuhan to Contemporary Rhetorical Theory." M.A. thesis, Indiana University, 1968.

Miller, Jonathan. *Marshall McLuhan.* New York: Viking Press, 1971.

Ong, Walter J. *The Presence of the Word.* New Haven: Yale University Press, 1967, pp. 17–110.

Rosenthal, Raymond, ed. *McLuhan: Pro and Con.* New York: Funk and Wagnalls, 1968.

Stearn, Gerald, ed. *McLuhan: Hot and Cool.* New York: Dial Press, 1967.

Theall, Donald F. *The Medium is the Rear View Mirror: Understanding McLuhan.* Montreal: McGill-Queen's University Press, 1971.

THEORETICAL PROBES

Batty, Paul W. "Eric Hoffer's Theory of Mass Persuasion." Ph.D. dissertation, University of Illinois, 1970.

Black, Edwin. *Rhetorical Criticism: A Study in Method.* New York: Macmillan, 1965, Chaps. 4–6.

————. "The Second Persona." *Quarterly Journal of Speech,* LVI (April 1970), pp. 109–119.

Booth, Wayne. "The Rhetorical Stance." *College Composition and Communication,* 14 (October 1963), pp. 139–145.

Bosmajian, Haig. "Obscenity and Protest." *Today's Speech,* 18 (Winter 1970), pp. 9–14.

Bowers, John W. and Donovan J. Ochs. *The Rhetoric of Agitation and Control.* Reading, Mass.: Addison-Wesley, 1971.

Bryant, Donald. "Rhetoric: Its Functions and Its Scope." *Quarterly Journal of Speech,* XXXIX (December 1953), pp. 401–424.

Corbett, Edward P. J. "The Rhetoric of the Open Hand and the Closed Fist." *College Composition and Communication,* XX (December 1969), pp. 288–296.

Corder, Jim W. *Uses of Rhetoric.* Philadelphia: Lippincott, 1971.

Cronkite, Gary L. "Logic, Emotion, and the Paradigm of Persuasion." *Quarterly Journal of Speech,* L (February 1964), pp. 13–18.

Delia, Jesse G. "The Logic Fallacy, Cognitive Theory, and the Enthymeme: A Search for the Foundations of Reasoned Discourse." *Quarterly Journal of Speech,* LVI (April 1970), pp. 140–148.

Douglass, Rodney B., and Carroll C. Arnold. "On Analysis of *Logos:* A Methodological Inquiry." *Quarterly Journal of Speech,* LVI (February 1970), pp. 22–32.

Ehninger, Douglas. "Argument as Method: Its Nature, Its Limitations, and Its Uses." *Speech Monographs,* XXXVII (June 1970), pp. 101–110.

Eubanks, Ralph T. "Nihilism and the Problem of a Worthy Rhetoric." *Southern Speech Journal,* XXXIII (Spring 1968), pp. 187–199.

Fisher, Walter R. "A Motive View of Communication." *Quarterly Journal of Speech,* LVI (April 1970), pp. 131–139.

Fogarty, Daniel. *Roots for a New Rhetoric.* New York: Teachers College of Columbia University, 1959; reprinted Russell and Russell, 1968, pp. 1–7, 116–140.

Friedman, Maurice S. *Martin Buber: The Life of Dialogue.* New York: Harper Torchbook, 1960, pp. 57–97, 123–126, 176–183.

Golden, James, and Richard Rieke. *The Rhetoric of Black Americans.* Columbus, Ohio: Charles Merrill, 1971.

Gorrell, Robert M., ed. *Rhetoric: Theories for Application.* Champaign, Ill.: National Council of Teachers of English, 1967.

Gregg, Richard B. "The Ego-Function of the Rhetoric of Protest," *Philosophy and Rhetoric,* 4 (Spring 1971), pp. 71–91.

Haiman, Franklyn S. "The Rhetoric of 1968: A Farewell to Rational Discourse," in Wil Linkugel, R. R. Allen, and Richard L. Johannesen, eds., *Contemporary American Speeches,* 2nd ed. Belmont, Cal.: Wadsworth, 1969, pp. 153–167.

Hastings, Arthur. "Metaphor in Rhetoric." *Western Speech,* XXXIV (Summer 1970), pp. 181–193.

Johannesen, Richard L., ed. *Ethics and Persuasion: Selected Readings.* New York: Random House, 1967.

Johannesen, Richard L. "Ethics of Persuasion: Some Perspectives," in Robert King, ed., *Marketing and the New Science of Planning.* Chicago: American Marketing Association, 1969, pp. 541–546.

Kinneavy, James E. "The Basic Aims of Discourse." *College Composition and Communication,* XX (December 1969), pp. 297–313.

McNally, James R. "Toward a Definition of Rhetoric." *Philosophy and Rhetoric,* 3 (Spring 1970), pp. 71–81.

Maccoby, Nathan. "The New 'Scientific' Rhetoric," in Wilbur Schramm, ed., *The Science of Human Communication.* New York: Basic Books, 1963, pp. 41–53.

Natanson, Maurice, and Henry W. Johnstone, Jr., eds. *Philosophy, Rhetoric, and Argumentation.* University Park: Pennsylvania State University Press, 1965.

Nilsen, Thomas R. *Ethics of Speech Communication.* Indianapolis: Bobbs-Merrill, 1966.

Osborn, Michael, and Douglas Ehninger. "The Metaphor in Public Address." *Speech Monographs,* XXIX (August 1962), pp. 223–234.

Petrie, Hugh G. "Practical Reasoning: Some Examples." *Philosophy and Rhetoric,* 4 (Winter 1971), pp. 29–41.

Preston, Ivan L. "Communication: Is It Always Persuasion?" *Quarterly Journal of Speech,* LV (October 1969), pp. 312–315.

Ried, Paul. "A Spectrum of Persuasive Design." *Speech Teacher,* XIII (March 1964), pp. 87–95.

Rosenthal, Paul. "The Concept of Ethos and the Structure of Persuasion." *Speech Monographs,* XXXIII (June 1966), pp. 114–126.

Scott, Robert. "On Viewing Rhetoric as Epistemic." *Central States Speech Journal,* XVIII (February 1967), pp. 9–17.

—— and Wayne Brockriede. *The Rhetoric of Black Power.* New York: Harper and Row, 1969.

—— and Donald Smith. "The Rhetoric of Confrontation." *Quarterly Journal of Speech,* LV (February 1969), pp. 1–8.

Sillars, Malcolm. "Rhetoric as Act." *Quarterly Journal of Speech,* L (October 1964), pp. 277–284.

Simons, Herbert W. "Confrontation as a Pattern of Persuasion in University Settings." *Central States Speech Journal,* XX (Fall 1969), pp. 163–170.

Smith, Arthur L. *Rhetoric of Black Revolution.* Boston: Allyn and Bacon, 1969.

Smith, David H., ed. *What Rhetoric (Communication Theory) Is Appropriate for Contemporary Speech Communication?* 1969, available from the Speech Communication Association, Statler Hilton Hotel, N.Y., 10001, $1.50.

Smith III, Nelson J. "Logic for the New Rhetoric." *College Composition and Communication,* XX (December 1969), pp. 305–314.

Smith, Raymond G. *Speech Communication: Theory and Models.* New York: Harper and Row, 1970.

Steele, Edward, and W. Charles Redding. "The American Value System: Premises for Persuasion." *Western Speech,* XXVI (Spring 1962), pp. 83–91.

Steinmann, Martin, ed. *New Rhetorics.* New York: Scribners, 1967.

Wallace, Karl. "Rhetoric and Advising." *Southern Speech Journal,* XXIX (Summer 1964), pp. 279–287.

——. *Understanding Discourse: The Speech Act and Rhetorical Action.* Baton Rouge: Louisiana State University Press, 1970.

Winterowd, W. Ross. *Rhetoric: A Synthesis.* New York: Holt, Rinehart, and Winston, 1968.

INDEX OF SELECTED CONCEPTS

71 72 73 74   7 6 5 4 3 2 1